Occupational Safety, Health & Environment and Sustainable Economic Development

Editorial Board

About the Editor

Pradeep Chaturvedi, Chairman of the Institution of Engineers (India), Delhi State Centre, is a Mechanical Engineer and an energy and environment expert. He has been involved with sustainable development issues, mainly the energy policy and planning and implementation of environment friendly sustainable energy projects for over three decades in India and other Asian and Pacific countries. As a Member of the Perspective Planning Group of Planning Commission, preparing Development Vision 2020, he contributed 'India's Energy Vision 2020'. He has been actively involved with the formulation of Energy Conservation Act 2001 and the Electricity Bill 2001.

Mr. Chaturvedi has been involved with the Studies Programme of the World Energy Council since 1983. His understanding of energy issues of the South Asia Region, in the global context, has been widely appreciated.

Mr. Chaturvedi was deeply involved with the preparatory phase of the World Summit of Sustainable Development. He is also involved in the follow-up phase.

Mr. Chaturvedi is Vice-Chairman of the UNESCO sponsored World Renewable Energy Network; and Vice Chairman of the World Environment Foundation, both based in UK; and President of the Bio Energy Society of India. He is also a Visiting Faculty at IIT, Delhi.

Mr. Chaturvedi has authored six and edited 25 books on Energy Management and Sustainable Development. These books are widely referred to understand the situation in the country.

Occupational Safety, Health & Environment and Sustainable Economic Development

Proceedings of the Safety Convention – 2006

Edited by

Pradeep Chaturvedi

Organisers

Safety and Quality Forum | **Quality Council of India**

in collobration with

Bureau of Indian Standards
Export Inspection Council of India

CONCEPT PUBLISHING COMPANY, NEW DELHI-110 059

Cataloging in Publication Data—DK
Courtesy: D.K. Agencies (P) Ltd. <docinfo@dkagencies.com>

Occupational safety, health & environment and sustainable economic development : proceedings of the Safety Convention-2006 / edited by Pradeep Chaturvedi ; organisers, Safety and Quality Forum, Quality Council of India ; in collaboration with Bureau of Indian Standards, Export Inspection Council of India.

p. cm.
In Indian context.
Includes bibliographical references.
Includes index.
ISBN 8180694135

1. Industrial safety—India—Congresses. 2. Industrial hygiene—India—Congresses. I. Chaturvedi, Pradeep, 1946- II. Institution of Engineers (India). Safety and Quality Forum. III. Quality Council of India.

DDC 363.110 954 22

ISBN 81-8069-413-5

First Published 2007

Published and Printed by
Ashok Kumar Mittal
Concept Publishing Company
A/15-16, Commercial Block, Mohan Garden
New Delhi-110059 (India)
Phones: 25351460, 25351794
Fax: 091-11-25357103
E-mail: publishing@conceptpub.com

Preface

Safety Convention 2006 was an excellent opportunity to discuss critical and important issues relating to Occupational Safety, Health and Environment and Sustainable Economic Development. Larger number of participants turned out for this event and interact on emerging issues and experiences of different agencies.

The Convention emphasised on dealing with new issues of terrorism, infrastructure development and social development and related safety issues. These areas were identified as critical and solutions needed inputs from engineering faculties. None of the issues can find a permanent solution; but experts were encouraged to suggest contextual solutions. These needed to be studied on a long term and continuous basis. Extensive perspective studies and modelling for scenaries were considered necessary to create 'risk assessment' analysis and project 'risk management' strategies. A multi-disciplinary cross-sectoral approach was considered necessary, with the government agencies taking the lead. Thus, broader issues of safety were considered in the public domain and needed specific control of government agencies.

The areas relatable to infrastructure and industry were considered as a part of sustainable economic development strategy. Role of public and private sectors were considered equally important. Whereas safety focus was considered equally important for all players, but the public sector was asked to take extra precaution as they are dealing with large public (or government) investments. The private sector operators are crucial in promoting safety environment as they have flexibility in operation and decision-making and can acquire and adopt safety measures more appropriately and in shortest possible time.

Manpower development and skills building for safety measure has been identified as a major area of concern. It is necessary to introduce safety engineering as a subject at all undergraduate engineering courses. A thorough benchmark study may be conducted on identifing the safety manpower and engineering. ITI diploma and degree level courses may be introduced.

The general public and workers are important stakeholders in ensuring safety environment. Awareness programmes for audience from school level to post graduate level should be developed and disseminated.

Public-Private partnership, with advice and assistance from professional institutions like IEI, has to be established, into the government support. CSR funds can be utilized to develop safety measures.

The Institution of Engineers (I) has established a benchmark and would like other professional organisations to also launch similar steps.

September 30, 2006
New Delhi-110 002

Pradeep Chaturvedi
Chairman
Safety and Quality Forum
The Institution of Engineers (India)

Introduction

Three years is considered a small time for laying foundation for any major movement that has impact on social and economic development of the country. The two safety conventions organized by the Forum created an extraordinary impact and identified need for such an activity being undertaken on a regular basis. In response, the third Safety Convention took shape with the theme "Occupational Safety, Health and Environment and Sustainable Economic Development". Decision to organize Safety Convention 2006 was taken a year back and ever since continuous efforts were made to assess the impact of our Safety Movement and to develop new benchmarks for safety.

In these turbulent times the awareness in modern society of the daily hazards has reached a significant level. This awareness occurred as a result of some major accidents in various parts of the world, the consequence of which had a powerful impact on the public mind. The present day business jargon include 'risk management' and 'risk assessment' as phrases that are used in diverse industries and companies. In the commercial world, a structured approach to risk management is emphasised for success in increasingly volatile and difficult external environment. Even the very survival of the companies is a risk to be taken seriously. It has, therefore, become an important aspect in the 21st century to develop a business model that really works.

Realising that India has complex business growth pattern where public sector undertakings have a dominant role in the growth of the economy, capital investment in these units can really be converted into ensuring the higher productivity and thereby enhancing the net value of the assets. There are examples when the public sector organizations have not removed any worker but adopted a 'business model' where the productivity per person employee has increased four-times and thereby their trained manpower has been fully and appropriately utilized. Appropriate training measures under a visionary approach indicate that the economic reforms process is not necessarily reducing the number of jobs but can also be increasing the productivity to the levels where everyone is gainfully employed. In the longer term it provides safety for the employees and a safety network for the employers. Realising the importance of environmentally sound and safe development the theme for the year was carefully chosen. Whereas the 'Occupational Safety, Health and Environment' aspects are amply covered in invited papers and voluntary papers, the 'Sustainable Economic Development' part is reflected in various Case Studies received from Award winning companies and organizations. The Convention is therefore organized in the following sessions to comprehensively cover all aspects.

(i) Overview Session
(ii) Environment, Occupational Safety and Health
(iii) Food Safety
(iv) Safety - Some Innovative Experiences
(v) Safety in Energy Sector
(vi) Disaster Management & Safety
(vii) Industry Safety
(viii) OSH Certification
(ix) Safety - Some Innovative Experiences

Since we started the journey three years back it has been possible for us to convince a number of other stakeholders to join us and be partners in the safety movement. It gives me pleasure to write that the Safety Convention 2006 have partners such as Quality Council of India, Export Inspection Council of India, Bureau of Indian Standards, National Safety Council and Vellore Institute of Technology. In addition, the Convention also has the sponsorship support of ONGC, Indian Oil, NTPC, HUDCO, Indian Railways, VST Industries, Mfar Construction, Jindal Steels Ltd and others. The continuous networking and support indicates that we have reached a stage of safety movement where all stakeholders are willing to work jointly and as equal partners. This Convention also has support of various professional engineering societies and the government departments.

The plan for Safety Convention 2006 was given shape in the Advisory Committee under the Chairmanship of Shri S.P. Sharma, Director General, Bureau of Indian Standards with active participation of Lt. Gen. B.S. Dhaliwal, E-in-C, Corps of Engineers, Indian Army; Shri Girdhar J. Gyani, Secretary General, Quality Council of India; and Shri K.C. Gupta, Secretary General, National Safety Council; Shri K.K. Gupta, Executive Director, IOC; Dr. S.K. Agrawal, General Manager, Powergrid Corporation Ltd.; and Dr. U.S. Hazra, Executive Director, ONGC provided important support for organizing this Convention.

The Technical Committee, under the Chairmanship of Prof. G.S. Yadava, has worked untiringly to prepare this volume. Shri Anil Jouhri, Adviser, QCI was extremely helpful in identifying and coordinating technical support to streamline the technical programme. Smt. Shashi Sareen, Director, EICI strengthened the food safety part of the programme. Shri R.N. Rajpoot, Shri Devendra Gill and Shri Subhash Chander also provided support for the Technical Programme.

Shri R.K. Bagrodia, Chairman, IEI-DSC; and Shri R.K. Gupta, Hony Secretary, IEI-DSC coordinated the whole organizational arrangements. Shri Praveen Singh, Officer Admn. ensured that the preparation for the Convention were carefully executed.

Shri Ashok Mittal and Shri Nitin Mittal of Concept Publishing Company appropriately edited the papers and presented in the best quality.

These papers are also being made available in the CD Rom format for quick retrieval and for use by the individuals. I hope the readers will find it as a valuable document.

September 6, 2006
New Delhi

Pradeep Chaturvedi
Chairman
Safety and Quality Forum
The Institution of Engineers (India)

Contents

Section–IV
Safety in Energy Sector

Section–V
Disaster Management & Safety

Section–VI
Industrial Safety

Section–I

Environment, Occupational Safety and Health

1

LEGAL FRAMEWORK FOR OCCUPATIONAL SAFETY AND HEALTH IN INDIA

Lt. Col. Harsha Lakshmi Narayana*

ABSTRACT

Even though the responsibility of protecting the safety and health of the workers at the work place from occupational hazards and risks rests exclusively with the employee, the onus of ensuring that the systems that are placed satisfy the expectations of all parties concerned, by designing and putting in place a legal framework in the form of Acts, Rules and Regulations and guidelines rests with the Government. Also, these legal frameworks must be in conformation with the International treaties, covenants, and conventions. In the absence of these legal frameworks economic progress of a society will be hampered due to reduced productivity, labour unrest and redundancy of the workforce. In India, with a plethora of legislations to ensure Safety and Health of the workers at the work place, it is very essential that they are constantly revised to meet the challenges of a rapidly changing work environment. Legislation alone cannot ensure occupational safety and health. Active and earnest participation of all parties involved, i.e. government, employers and employees is essential to make enforcement of OSH measures a success.

Introduction

With the advancement of technology, globalization and free markets there is immense pressure on the industrial sector to enhance production for survival in a highly competitive and economically fluctuating market. For their survival, organizations have been undergoing transformations in the form of mergers, acquisitions, and reorganizations, changes in working conditions and work processes at a rate unheard of hitherto. The importance of enforcing systems to ensure occupational health and safety at the work place to increase productivity and reduce redundancy of workers has been acknowledged by all agencies involved in the formulation of policies, its implementation, and effective monitoring, i.e., Government, employers and employees. This has brought in a necessity for the older legislations to be replaced with newer legislations, to cater to the changing environment, so as to ensure the health and safety of the workers which may arise out of occupational hazards are addressed in a more holistic manner.

---

*BE, MIE, FIV, MBA, PGDHRL, Deputy Project Manager, Married Accommodation Project, Delhi.

The factors which pose a risk or hazard to the health and safety of workers at the work place are physical agents like noise, vibrations and radiation, chemical agents, biological agents, physical hazards like falling, work place transport, dangerous machinery and electricity and work related stress. Therefore, for any OSH measure to be effectively implemented it is of paramount importance that the risks and hazards are identified correctly and the potential damage that they can cause assessed realistically and then corrective measures implemented to reduce the hazard. Advancing technolgy, discovery and inventions of new materials, new processes and techniques of manufacturing have all added on to the requirement of constantly reviewing the occupational safety and health standards.

Importance of Occupational Safety and Health (OSH)

Occupational safety and health is that discipline of management that is concerned with protecting the safety, health and welfare of employees, organisations, and others affected by the work they undertake.[1] Occupational safety and health standards are broadly classified into four groups or categories.[2]

- Standards which aim at guiding policies for action, such as the Occupational Safety and Health Convention, the Occupational Health Services Convention and their accompanying Recommendations.
- Protection in given branches of economic activity including mining, the building industry, commerce and offices and dock work.
- Measures of protection, e.g. guarding of machinery, medical examination of young workers, maximum weight of loads to be transported by a single worker.
- Protection against specific risks, e.g. ionizing radiation, benzene, asbestos, prevention of occupational cancer, prevention of air pollution, noise and vibration in the working environment and safety in the use of chemicals including the prevention of major industrial accidents.

There are both direct and indirect costs of accidents that occur at work place which is due to lack of OSH in organisations. While direct costs are those costs that are attributed to the medical treatment of the employee, cost of finding and training a replacement for the period of sickness of the employee and damage to the equipment in case of accidents. Indirect costs constitute under utilization of capacity of production, reduced life span of equipment that have been repaired after the damage and reduction in sales due to adverse publicity of poor OSH standards.

Keeping in view the above costs invovled OSH management systems are avocated are for the following reasons:

- Ensure that there is a safe and healthy working environment
- Identify and control actual and perceived hazards
- Encourage safety and health management
- Comply with legal and organizational obligations to avoid costly litigations
- Constantly evaluate the environment to improve existing safety and health standards

- Ensure correct recording and reporting of adherence or violations of safety and health norms
- Identify needs and provide training on safety and health
- To avoid economic losses due to loss of productive manhours, reduction in efficiency, human resource turnover and negative reputation in the market.

In a joint press release issued by WHO and ILO in Geneva on 25 April, 2005, it has been estimated that while job related accidents and illness claim more than two million lives annually, there are almost 268 million non-fatal work place accidents in which the victims miss at least three days of work as a result, as well as 160 million new cases of work related illness.[3] In a later press release of the ILO during the 95th ILO conference held at Geneva from 31 May to 16 June, 2006 the ILO estimates that nearly 6,000 workers die everyday due to work related accidents or illness the worldover.[4] This huge deficit in manpower will definitely have a negative impact on the scales of econmics. Therefore, the importance of good OSH management systems in organizations cannot be undermined and neglected.

Legal Framework for OSH in India

India being a Socialist country and great importance being placed on the welfare and well being of the citizens, the basic statutory requirements of OSH have been embedded in the Constitution of India, which every organization is legally bound to follow. Apart from this there are also a plethora of statutory Acts, Rules and Regulations which spell out the mandatory requirements to maintain a minimum level of OSH standards. In addition, by virtue of being a member of the WTO and ILO, India has ratified and signed various International treaties and covenants which endure to promote occupational safety and health. Therefore, it is essential that the OSH management systems at the bottom level, i.e., organizational level should encompass all these statutory requirements for them to be effective. A model that can be adopted for designing OSH standards in an organization is given below in Figure 1:

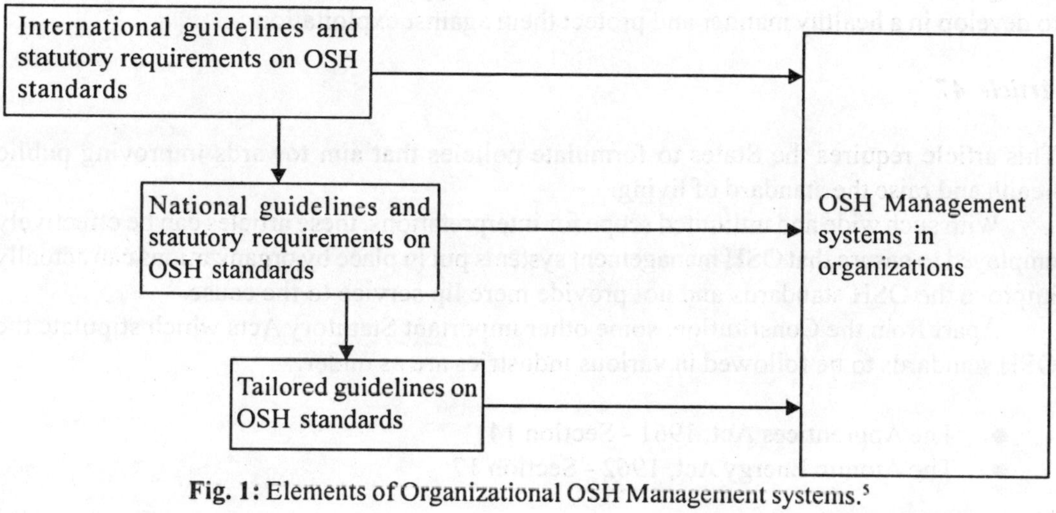

Fig. 1: Elements of Organizational OSH Management systems.[5]

The primary objective of having these standards specified by law are to :

- Ensure minimum and uniform standards of OSH throughout the country and dispense the differences in its administration by various agencies, and
- Provide yardsticks for measurements and evaluation of OSH standards.

The provisions for OSH provided in the various statutory frameworks in India are as under:

Constitution of India

Article 21

Under the ambit of Article 21 of the Contitution that provides for protection of life and personal liberty. The Courts in India have been liberal in its interpretations and have encompassed various issues in their judgments which highlights that OSH is necessary for protection of life. In one case the Supreme Court has ruled that public health and ecology have priority over loss of revenue, therefore, organisations cannot ignore and refuse to implement OSH measures on the plea that it is non-profitable.[6] The Apex Court has also ruled that checks and safeguards should be adopted to guard against the ill effects of radiation of X-rays,[7] necessity of pollution free air and water for full enjoyment of life.[8]

Article 24

This article restricts the employment of children below the age of fourteen years in any factory or mine or in any other hazardous employment.

Article 39(e) & (f)

These articles requires the States to direct its policies towards ensuring that the health and strength of workers are not abused and provide for opportunities and facilities for children to develop in a healthy manner and protect them against exploitation.

Article 47

This article requires the States to formulate policies that aim towards improving public health and raise the standard of living.

With such wide and unlimited scope for interpretations, these articles can be effectively employed to ensure that OSH management systems put in place by organizations can actually improve the OSH standards and not provide mere lip service to the cause.

Apart from the Constitution, some other important Statutory Acts which stipulate the OSH standards to be followed in various industries are as under:

- The Apprentices Act, 1961 - Section 14
- The Atomic Energy Act, 1962 - Section 17

- The Beedi and Cigar Workers (Condition of Employment) Act, 1966 - Sections 8 to 17
- The Building and other Construction Workers (Regulation of Employment and Conditions of Service) Act, 1996 - Sections 28 to 38
- The Child Labour (Prohibition and Regulation) Act, 1986 - Section 13
- The Contract Labour (Regulation and Abolition) Act, 1970 - Section 16 to 19
- The Factories Act, 1948 - Sections 11 to 49
- The Inter State Migrant Workmen (Regulation of Employment and Consitions of Service) Act, 1979 - Section 16
- The Mines Act, 1952 - Sections 19 to 21
- The Plantations Labour Act, 1951 - Sections 8 to 18

The Bureau of Indian Standards (BIS) has also published IS 15001: 2000 Indian Standard on Occupational Health and Safety Management Systems - Specification and Guidance for Use, which is based on OHSAS-18000 and adapted to the Indian needs. In IS 15001 the process of improving OSH has been broadly classified under the following heads - planning, implementation and operation, measurement and evaluation, and management review. Similarly, The National Building Code, 2005 published by the BIS specifies the safety measures that have to be adopted in the construction industry,[9] which is the second largest occupation provider after agriculture and provides livelihood to almost 10 per cent of the country's population.

The objectives of all these Acts and standards is to ensure that employers take all practicable steps to ensure the health and safety of the employees at work by:

- providing a safe working environment, and maintaining facilities for staff members' safety and health,
- ensuring plant and equipment on the premises are safe,
- ensuring staff members are not exposed to hazards,
- developing emergency procedures,
- ensuring that no action or inaction by any employee is likely to cause harm to themselves or any other person, and
- create a safety organisation within the organisation to evaluate and monitor the OSH aspects.

Unfortunately, none of these Acts stipulate any minimum threshold levels of OSH standards that have to be adopted. This has lead to complication in its interpretation, implementation and monitoring.

Problems Facing Implementation of OSH Measures in India

In spite of the labyrinth of laws there have been many hurdles in effectively implmenting OSH measures across the country. According to the data for the year 2001available with the ILO for India there have been 3,02,000 work related deaths amongst an econmically active population of 444 million.[10] Some of the reasons which have been identified as the culprits for the ineffective implementation of OSH measures are:

Incorrect Assessment of Risks

The basic requirement before formulation of any Act pertaining to OSH is to assess the potential risks and hazards accurately and thereafter evolve measures to prevent them or reduce their probability of occurrence. However, in India there are no laws governing OSH in the major occupations, i.e., agriculture and construction industry. Agriculture being the major occupation in the country, there are no laws or standards of OSH to be followed in the agricultural industry. These workers are exposed to water borne diseases, fumes of pesticides and other air pollutants which not only cause deaths but also long-term non-fatal illness. Being in the unorganised sector of the industry, like the construction industry, there are no laws governing their functioning, monitoring and reporting of accidents mechanisms. Accidents due to mechanized farming, some of which are fatal take place regularly all over the country but are not reported. The incidents in Mangalore, Karnataka, where in large number of villagers took ill and also children with deformities were born was traced to the use of pesticides for the cashewnut crop which is grown in the area, or in Kerala where children born with deformities were traced to consumption of fishes which were infected with chemicals in the fertilizers used for agriculture are all examples of the neglect of OSH aspect in the largest industry in the country. Even according to ILO reports the use of pesticides causes some 70,000 poisoning deaths each year, and at least seven million cases of acute and long-term non-fatal illnesses.[11]

The NBC 2005 has addressed the OSH aspects in the construction industry and comprehensive guidelines have been issued. Part 7 of the Code lays down the aspects of safety that have to be adhered to during construction activities. Unfortunately, all these involve finances and the investments does not reap any returns to the contractors. Hence, the effectiveness of these guidelines needs to be assessed in a realistic manner.

Government Policies

- The creation of Special Economic Zones (SEZ) in the country to encourgae development of backward areas by providing subsidies is another stumbling block in the implementation of OSH measures. Since these industries are established in backward areas the main objective is to generate employment. Efforts to implement stringent OSH measures may be counter productive and lead to closure of the industries. A case in example is Mahindra Industries who had to shut down their plant in Mysore in the mid-80s due to the death of a few workers during construction and negligence due to inadequate OSH measures. So in this Catch 22 situation enforcing implementation of OSH measures may not be a easy task. Realistic review of the situation and redrafting of statutory laws of OSH measures will have to be done to strike a balance between the economic policies and functional requirements.
- The tendency of industries to grow around existing and developed communcation hubs puts tremendous pressure on the scarce resources and increases their prices exhorbitantly. In their endevour to maximise profits the first vicitm of cost reduction will be OSH aspects. For example, the cost of land, electricity and water, which are the basic essentials for the establishment of an industry, are high in and around

the developed cities and are inescapable expenditures. However, the fourth essential commodity, human resource is available in surplus and cheaply, thanks to the unemployment and poverty in the country, that the management does not even have to blink an eyelid in exploiting them. This calls for realistic Environmental Impact Assessments, which has to address the issues of OSH along with the other issues and cater for the costs of implementation of OSH measures in the initial project proposals.

Composition of the Workforce

With a major chunk of the economically active workforce being uneducated, migratory in nature and from the unorganised sector, it is very difficult to make them realise the importance of OSH practices and standards. Also, the employers play truant in implementing OSH measures and exploit the helpless conditions of the employees and resort to OSH measures as an eyewash for the inspecting staff of the various Government agencies. The precarious conditions of the employees due to poverty and unemployment problems in the country, restricts them against raising their voice over OSH issues. Exhorbitant costs of litigation, time delays in deciding cases relating to labour issues and reluctance of employers to implement awards by judgments deters employees from engaging in legal battles over these issues. Any attempts to implement OSH measures without the active and sincere participation of all stakeholders is futile. Legislations to prevent harassment of employees who champion the cause of OSH will go a long way in improving OSH standards in the country.

Inadequate Enforcing Authorities

According to a study carried out, the number of Health and Factory Inspectors in India are far too small. For example, for the NCT of Delhi, there are only three Factory Inspectors. They were in-charge of 6496 factories covered by the Factories Act at the end of 1999. That is not even one Inspector per 2000 factories, whereas a reasonable ratio would be one per 250, i.e. 24 Inspectors in all. Due to this scarcity of staff, regular visits to companies are virtually impossible, and inspectors react only when complaints are lodged or accidents are reported.[12] Therefore, enforcement is more of reactive nature rather than proactive which is preferred for successful implementation of OSH measures.

Minuscule Penalties

The economical gains obtained by violation of the OSH provisions listed out in the Act outweighs the penalties specified by leaps and bounds and hence, there is no fear or hesitation to violate them. For example, the Factories Act, which is the leading Act with regard to OSH standards, specifies a fine of Rs. 500 for the violation and Rs. 75 everyday thereafter for the contravention is continued.

Lack of Collective Consensus on OSH Issues

The associations of employees do not take any initiative in insisting on implementation of OSH measures. There is always a trade off for the economic incentives in the form of bonus and other perks against the insistance of OSH measures in the industry. Issues related to accidents are addressed after occurrence and settled with compensation without any preventive measures being contemplated. OSH is the last thing on any trade unions agenda. Till date there has been no record of any trade union championing the OSH issues during negotiations.

Lack of Data

Revision of legislation to keep pace with the changing environmental demands can be undertaken based on realistic data which has to be collected, compiled and analysed. Even though India has ratified the C 160 Labour Statistics Convention, 1985, on 1 April, 1992, and is required to collect, compile and publish basic labour statistics, this has not been done. In the absence of realistic data, revision of exisitng laws to encompass the changed environmental conditions into its realm cannot be undertaken.

Recommendations to Improve Occupational Safety and Health

Having examined the present status of the legal framework existing in India for OSH and the shortcomings in its implementation, some recommendations propounded for improving the same are:

- Since prevention is important in reducing these hazards, attempts to enhance the awareness of the employers and employees to the OSH norms should be made by:
  - Including it as a subject in all job oriented courses to make the employees sensitive to the importance of OSH practices.
  - Conducting workshops and seminars to constantly remind all concerned about the importance and necessity of following occupational safety and health norms.
  - Making it mandatory to evaluate and file reports of the state of occupational safety and health practices and standards in all establishment.
- Keeping in mind the environment in which the industry operates, design legislation and policies for ensuring OSH and device mechanism to monitor and ensure that they are followed.
- Involve the Unions and Associations of the employees and employers, probably by linking their existence /registrations based on the level of adherence of OSH norms in their organizations.
- Increasing penalties to an extent that it negates the economical gains obtained by violating the safety and health norms stipulated by law.
- Constitute industry specific bodies to revaluate the applicablity of guidelines, rules and regulations and legislations regularly, keeping in mind the changing enivronment in which the industry operates.
- Speedy disposal of cases pertaining to OSH violations by various statutory bodies constituted to monitor the adherence of the statutory requirements of OSH.
- Financial incentives like tax rebates, discounting etc. for industries who have a proven record of OSH to mitigate their financial burden and encourage others to follow suit.

- Include the financial cost of OSH measures into the cost analysis of the project at the inception stage and then continue to calcuate the pay back period, so that they are part of the planning parameters.

Conclusion

Occupational safety and health is an important aspect for the progress of the country and to improve the economic condition of the nation and its citizens. New technologies and developments at the work place, the work environment and work organizations and the growing mechanization and industrialization in the country which is the result of globalization has given rise to new thresholds of occupational and work related diseases and injuries. In addition, demographic changes in working populations call for new strategies and programme to counter occupational safety and health hazards in the country. International treaties mandate that local laws must be in conformation with certain obligations stipulated by them. Legislations must cater for these changing demands of the industry.

Safety and health at work are important matters and should be given due consideration in policies at all levels, i.e. national and organizational levels. Safety and health at work are preventable and the endeavour should be to prevent them at the very onset by using legislative, technical, research, training and education, information and economic instruments. Safe designs of the work place and processes are of prime importance to prevent and reduce the risks and hazards which threaten occupational safety and health. Practical experiences have illustrated that preventive measures are economically beneficial in the long run and also increases employee morale, reduces employee turnover and improves market credibility. In a country like India where there are vast cultural, educational and ethical values differences, legislations can only act as guidelines. The employers must realize their moral responsibility towards the country and their employees and sincerely attempt to enforce OSH measures without comparing the economic returns for their investments.

NOTES

1. Occupational Safety and Health - http://en.wikipedia.org/wiki/Occupational safety and health.
2. Catalogue of ILO publications on Occupational Safety and Health - An International Occupational Safety and Health Information Centre, ILO, publication, http://turva.me.tut.fi/cis/home.
3. Number of work-related accidents and illnesses continues to increase - http://www.who.int/occupational_health.
4. ILO Press release No. ILO/06/34 dated 15 June 2006. http://www.ilo.org.
5. Modified and adopted from Guidelines for Occupational Safety and Health Management Systems - ILO OSH 2001, ILO, Geneva, 2001, page 4.
6. M.C. Mehta *vs.* Union of India (1987) Supp. SCC 131: AIR 1987 SC 1086.
7. M.K. Sharma *vs.* Bharat Electronics Ltd. (1987) 3 SCC 231 : AIR 1987 SC 1972: (1987) Cr LJ 1908.
8. Subash Kumar *vs.* State of Bihar, AIR 1991 SC 420/1991(1) SCC 598.

9. Strategy to Enhance the Standing of India's Construction Industry : Review of Strengths and Weaknesses of Existing Systems and Technology by Prof. H.S. Mejie and others, *Civil Engineering and Construction Review*, Feb. 2005.

10. World Day for Safety and Health at Work-2005: A Background paper - An ILO. Publication, http://www.ilo.org.

11. WHO and ILO Joint news release dated 28 Apr. 2005 - http://www.who.int/occupational_health/en.

12. *Regulations on Occupational Safety & Health* by Carsten Joerges - http://www.ccsindia.org/RP01.

2

INSURANCE RESPONSE FOR OCCUPATIONAL SAFETY AND HEALTH IN THE WAKE OF NEW RISKS

Deepak Godbole*

ABSTRACT

Human activities are exposed to different risks that arise from internal or external factors. However, in order to sustain growth, one must try to control, eliminate or minimise the harmful impact of unforeseen risks. Risk, by definition, has a degree of uncertainty associated with it. A mechanism, therefore, needs to be evolved to perceive the emerging risks, understand the impact and to tackle risks successfully through a well-defined strategy. An effective risk management structure involves understanding the risks in any initiative and taking informed decisions on whether and how to manage risks.

The risk cycle never stops. Some forms of risks seem to come under control. While traditional risks like fire, flood are relatively containable in physical world, digital risk, cyber risks, atomic risk, chemical risk exposures seem uncontainable. But, once some experience is gained, with the use of statistical analysis, probability and the law of large numbers, risk management techniques and insurance covers get developed.

Of late, a new risk in the form of Bird Flu has emerged. It has multiple effects and is capable of creating a large scale epidemic. There is widespread concern among policy-makers and public health experts about the possibility of a worldwide epidemic of avian influenza. The scope of the outbreaks is historically unprecedented, not been known before to spread so widely and so rapidly.

Pandemic like SARS is likely to have an impact of about 2 per cent of GDP on demand side and 5 per cent of GDP on the supply side. A report by Lee and McKibbin estimate the effect of SARS as 2.6 per cent of GDP impact in Hong Kong, 1.1 per cent of GDP in China and about 0.5 per cent of GDP in Taiwan and Singapore.

On the one hand, there is a school of thought who believes that loss potential of things such as bird flu are fundamentally uninsurable and that the State should serve as the ultimate risk manager in such instances. On the other hand, there are some others who believe that the private sector and the free-markets are in the best position to adjudicate and manage these risks for those who choose to insure privately.

Cleanliness, hygiene, sanitation, education/awareness, early warnings, vaccination, destruction of affected birds, quarantine, etc. are some efforts/techniques to avoid potential losses. However,

*Chief Manager, GIC of India, Mumbai.

there is no guarantee that losses may not occur. Insurance essentially steps in as a post disaster financing technique. Life insurance industry has been threatened by the possibility of bird flu impact on human beings. While there is no new cover required to be devised, the industry's assumptions of business based on probability and statistics may be at risk. However, insurers in some part of the world have seen it as an opportunity to develop new products and offer insurance coverages to potential exposures/losses arising out of bird flu.

Key Words: risk, insurance, pandemic, loss, economic impact.

Risk

The word "risk" means and conveys meanings such as "peril, danger, hazard or chance of bad consequences". Nothing in life is certain - be it no matter what, from business to medicine to the weather. Human activities are exposed to different risks that arise from internal or external factors. However, in order to sustain growth, one must try to control, eliminate or minimise the harmful impact of unforeseen risks.

Peril is the cause of loss. Hazard is a condition that may create or increase the chance of a loss arising from a given peril or under a given condition. Identification of the future challenges and the nature of risks/threats is essential for efficient management and taking precautionary measures. Risk, by definition, has a degree of uncertainty associated with it. A mechanism, therefore, needs to be evolved to perceive the emerging risks, understand the impact and to tackle risks successfully through a well-defined strategy.

Risk Management

"Risk Management" is a process of directing and controlling the resources and activities in order to minimise adverse effects of accidental losses. It is a highly technical job, which calls for a thorough professional approach and commitment of the management. Risk management is a technique involving different steps, namely:-

Risk identification,
Risk evaluation and measurement,
Risk control through reduction/elimination,
Risk retention, and
Risk transfer.

Whenever there is uncertainty, there is involvement of risk. The instinct for security is one of the basic motivating factors determining human attitudes. As a sequel to this quest for security, insurance technique must have evolved. The urge to provide protection against loss of life and property prompts people to make some sacrifice willingly in order to achieve security through collective co-operation. An effective risk management structure involves understanding the risks in any initiative and taking informed decisions on whether and how to manage risks.

New Risks

Risk denotes potential downside of an action or happening. The risk cycle never stops. Some forms of risks seem to come under control. Talking of health risks, cholera, plague were considered fatal diseases at one time but have been largely under control now. However, newer risks such as AIDS, SARS, etc. unheard of a few years back have emerged.

While traditional risks like fire, flood are relatively containable in physical world, digital risk, cyber risks, atomic risk, chemical risk exposures seem uncontainable. But as data is fundamental component of any risk process and models are the tools to supplement the risk process, once some experience is gained, with the use of statistical analysis, probability and the law of large numbers, risk management techniques and insurance covers get developed because human beings develop the abilities to master risks by minimizing threats and maximizing opportunities.

Bird Flu Potential Exposures

Scientists believe that all bird species are susceptible to infection but that some are more resistant than others. Wild waterfowl, especially ducks, are a so-called natural reservoir of influenza viruses, including the bird flu. The birds carry the virus without displaying any symptoms of the disease and can spread the virus over great distances while remaining healthy. Of late, a new risk in the form of Bird Flu has emerged. It has multiple effects and is capable of creating a large scale epidemic. There is widespread concern among policy-makers and public health experts about the possibility of a worldwide epidemic of avian influenza. Such pandemics though appear new, are not totally new if one takes a look at about last 100 years. Records show three similar incidents in the 20th century, of which one, the 1918-1919 Spanish flu outbreak, is estimated to have killed over 500,000 people in the U.S. and up to 50 million worldwide.

Although proved deadly for poultry, avian influenza viruses in the past have rarely caused severe disease in humans. However, in 1997, a highly pathogenic strain of bird flu known as H5N1 jumped from birds to humans during an outbreak among poultry in Hong Kong. The 1997 event was notable for two reasons. First, molecular studies indicated that the genetic make up of the human and avian viruses were virtually identical, indicating direct transmission from birds to humans. Second, the H5N1 virus caused severe illness with extreme mortality among humans. Of the 18 persons known to be infected, six died. The outbreak ended after authorities slaughtered Hong Kong's entire stock of poultry (about 1.5 million birds). The Hong Kong episode put world health officials on alert because the H5N1 strain had fulfilled two of the three prerequisites for a pandemic. First, the strain was a new virus subtype to which the population would have little or no immunity and second, the virus had the ability to replicate in humans and cause serious illness. However, the virus still has not developed the ability to be transmitted efficiently from human to human. Since the 1997 episode in Hong Kong, there have been several outbreaks of the H5N1 influenza around the world leading to infections among poultry and suspected cases among humans. The first human infection occurred in Hong Kong in February 2003, when a nine-year-old boy and his father became sick after a trip to southern China. The man, who was 33, died, but his son recovered.

Then, in 2004, the H5N1 virus spread among poultry populations in South-east Asia, with outbreaks of influenza reported in two separate waves. The first wave, in January and February, affected Vietnam, Japan, Korea, Thailand, Laos, Cambodia, Indonesia and China. The second wave, which began in July and continued into 2005, included outbreaks in the same countries including India as well. More recently, the virus has shown up in Russia, Kazakhstan, Turkey and Romania. The scope of the outbreaks is historically unprecedented, not been known before to spread so widely and so rapidly.

To date, close contact with infected poultry is thought to be required for human infection, but the danger exists that the virus will evolve in a way that allows for efficient human-to-human transmission. If the virus does acquire that capability, a worldwide epidemic, or pandemic, could occur. Such an outbreak could have substantial consequences for people and economic activity around the world.

Probability of a Pandemic Outbreak

There is no scientific basis to calculate the probability of an influenza pandemic in near future. However, history provides a gauge to judge those chances at least roughly. Since 1700, there have been between 10 and 13 influenza pandemics (or probable pandemics) in the world, including the three that have occurred since the beginning of the 20th century. Those pandemics have taken place at irregular intervals, with as little as two years separating some outbreaks and as many as 55 years separating others. Hence, one could assume that there is a roughly 3 per cent to 4 per cent probability of a pandemic occurring in any given year. Gauging the severity of a potential pandemic is more difficult. Of the three pandemics that have occurred since the beginning of the 20th century, two were mild and one was severe, suggesting a fairly high probability of a severe event. However, given the evidence of an existing epidemic of H5N1 in birds and the possibility that it might mutate to circulate efficiently in humans, the probability of a severe pandemic may exceed the historical frequency.

Potential Losses and Economic Effects

Based on past influenza pandemics and the SARS outbreak, the most important effects would be a sharp decline in demand as people avoid community places such as shops, cinema halls, rail/road/air transport, restaurants, etc. During a severe pandemic, hospitals, clinics and doctors' offices would probably be overburdened and servicing of clients would be difficult. Health care workers might also be exposed to the disease, resulting in further strains on the health care system's capacity. As the pandemic progressed, interregional and international travel would dramatically decline. Activities that required social contact would be sharply cut, which would lead to significant declines in retail trade, meetings, exhibitions, trade fairs, seminars and conferences. People would avoid public places, such as community centers and public transport. Attendance at theaters, sporting events, museums and restaurants would decline.

The general slowdown in economic activity would reduce gross domestic product (GDP). Business confidence would be dented, the supply of labour would be restricted (owing to illness, mortality, and absenteeism spurred by fear of contracting the disease), supply chains would be strained as transportation systems would be disrupted and arrears and default rates on consumer and business debt would probably rise somewhat. As per Meltzer, Cox and Fukuda, (the economic impact of pandemic influenza) pandemic like SARS is likely to have an impact of about 2 per cent of GDP on demand side and 5 per cent of GDP on the supply side. A report by Lee and McKibbin estimate the effect of SARS as 2.6 per cent of GDP impact in Hong Kong, 1.1 per cent of GDP in China and about 0.5 per cent of GDP in Taiwan and Singapore.

A study undertaken by Theodre Schultz in 1964, titled 'Transforming Traditional Agriculture' says that due to pandemic in 1960 in India, some 8 per cent of agricultural workforce succumbed to illness and agricultural output declined by over 3 per cent.

Approaches to New Risks for Occupational Safety and Health from the Angle of Insurability

On the one hand, there is a school of thought who believes that loss potential of things such as bird flu are fundamentally uninsurable and that the State should serve as the ultimate risk manager in such instances. On the other hand, there are some others who believe that the private sector and the free-markets are in the best position to adjudicate and manage these risks for those who choose to insure privately.

Working on a worse case scenario on account of 'bird flu' scenario, potential losses may not be limited to risk to human lives but might go far beyond that. e.g. poultry farms could be forced to destroy all birds causing financial distress, products already in market may be recalled, workers involved in the handling of poultry could be at risk, business might have difficulty operating in normal patterns because a large percentage of employees might be unable or unwilling to come to work for the duration of the outbreak and/or quarantine, business interruption to not only poultries but also to processing units, transporters, stockists, hotels and restaurants, loss of income due to fall in number of tourists, extra expenses for advertising on how to combat disease. And, there could be litigation leading to payments to third parties affected due to infected birds. Thus, even a fear of bird flu epidemic would bring in far reaching ramifications on account of economic losses.

Insurance for Occupational Safety and Health

Cleanliness, hygiene, sanitation, education/awareness, early warnings, vaccination, destruction of affected birds, quarantine, etc. are some efforts/techniques to avoid potential losses. However, there is no guarantee that losses may not occur. Insurance essentially steps in as a post disaster financing technique.

A group of scientific community believes that a global pandemic of human influenza is overdue and inevitable. World Health Organisation (WHO), identifies 6 stages of alerts and states that world is currently at stage 3 where virus is not spreading to humans. Stage 4 will be bird-to-human transmission, stage 5 will be human-to-human transmission and stage 6 being efficient and sustained human-to-human transmission. WHO, however, feels that predictions of mortality cannot be made before a pandemic virus emerges and begins to spread. WHO has given a three point plan on the basis of 6 stage alert. First, take care of hygiene, reduce opportunities of infection and strengthen early warning systems. Second, contain/delay the spread at source and third, reduce morbidity, mortality and social disruption.

Bird flu threat has not remained localized in some parts of the world. Life insurance industry has been threatened by the possibility of bird flu impact on human beings. Experts at Fitch rating agency say that there could be 600,000 deaths and claims across Europe and US could be as high as $ 50 bn. While there is no new cover required to be devised, the industry's assumptions of business based on probability and statistics may be at risk.

However, insurers in some part of the world have seen it as an opportunity to develop new products and offer insurance coverages to potential exposures/losses arising out of bird flu. Some Chinese insurers have launched a policy that would pay the insured if they are infected by the H5N1 virus. The cover valid for a year for anyone aged 3 to 70, would cost 100 Yuan for each 200,000 Yuan of compensation. Beneficiaries of the 200-Yuan (US $ 24.7) policy are eligible for a payout of up to 100,000 Yuan (US $ 12,400) if the holder dies of bird flu. Progressive poultry owners in Vietnam have bought insurance policies on one million chickens raised on farms, attaching a certificate for 100 million dong ($ 6, 372) to each bird sold. There is also a scope for insurance to take care of other losses resulting into business disruption etc. Covers such as business interruption insurance are available to ensure business continuity.

REFERENCES

World Health Organisation (WHO): Various publications.

International Monetary Fund: The global economic and financial impact of an avian flu pandemic and the role of IMF.

3

OCCUPATIONAL HEALTH AND SAFETY (OH&S) MANAGEMENT SYSTEM AND RELATED STANDARDS

N.K. Pal*

Introduction

In the era of globalization and competitive market survival becomes the foremost issue to an organization and according to Peter Druker in such situation the guiding principle of business economics should not be maximization of profit but avoidance of loss. According to International Labour Organization (ILO) every year about 1.2 million workforce died through accidents and occupational diseases, over 2 million work place accidents take place every year, and over 160 million workers suffer from occupational related diseases. Certain amount of risk, however small it may be is always associated with each and every activity and organization should continuously strive to reduce the number and severity of those risks to protect its people from unintentional injury & death and also to minimize the loss of property. The rapid technological changes, extensive use of hazardous chemicals/processes are posing a serious threat to the workers and put a challenge to the mankind on occupational health and safety issue. Most organizations are facing ever increasing challenges due to high incidence of injury & illness, lost working days, increasing OH&S regulations, rising compensation costs, etc. Traditional safety programs that consider safety as a separate function than a part of all functions, and focuses on injuries, illness and other end-of-pipeline measures to comply with the regulations are not effective and in fact no longer valid to manage OH&S issues. All over the world it has now been realized that legislation alone can not guaranty an accident free environment and their enforcement will not help in achieving the desired objectives of safe working condition. Adoption of a structured approach for the identification of hazards, their risk evaluation and control of risks through comprehensive framework of OH&S management system are felt essential to ensure an accident free industrial environment.

*Director (Chemical), Bureau of Indian Standards, New Delhi

Standards on OH&S Management System

Considering the above facts and an urgent demand from the industries attempts were made all over the world both at national and international level to develop standards on OH&SMS.

At National Level

BSI, UK has brought out BS 8800-1996 Guide to OH&S management system which is perhaps the first formalized OH&S-MS that provides a template for the development of any national/international standard on OH&SMS. In the next year Australia/New Zealand has brought AS/NZS 4804:1997 OH&S management systems - General guidelines and principles, assessment and supporting techniques.

Bureau of Indian Standards, National Standards body of India through its Occupational safety & health and chemical hazards sectional Committee, CHD 8 has brought out the following three Indian standards relevant to OH&S management system and its auditing:

(i) IS 18001:2000 Occupational Health and Safety Management System - Specification with guidance for use.
(ii) IS 15656:2006 Hazard Identification and Risk Analysis - Code of Practice
(iii) IS 14489:1998 Code of Practice on Occupational Safety and Health Audit

IS 18001:2000

To meet the urgent demand from the industry for a recognizable OH&SMS specification for the assessment and certification of OH&SMS, BIS has developed IS 18001. This standard provides the industry a systematic, structured and documented framework to address OH&S issues effectively and in an auditable manner. This standard intends to assist the organization to develop a systematic approach to management of OH&S in such a way as to protect their employees and others whose health & safety may be affected by the organization's activity. The standard specifies the requirement of OH&S Management System for assessment and certification purpose. The identification of hazard, risk assessment and control is the most important part of this standard which varies greatly across industries, ranging from simple assessments to complex quantitative analysis with extensive documentation. The standard emphasis the use of widely accepted frameworks of managing OH&S through:

(i) Identification of hazards, assessment & control, and
(ii) the hierarchy of control methods
    (a) Elimination/Substitution
    (b) Engineering control
    (c) Administrative control
    (d) PPE

This standard has been developed to be compatible with ISO 9001 (Quality) and ISO 14001 (Environmental) management system standards in order to facilitate the integration of Quality, Environment and OH&S Management Systems by organizations if they wish to do so. A comparative study is given in Annex A to show the commonality amongst OH&S elements and ISO 14001/ISO 9001 elements.

The introduction of Occupational Health and Safety (OH&S) management system into the existing overall management system should be considered within a general management system model.

Principle 1	-	Commitment & Policy - should define its OH&S Policy and ensure commitment to OH&S-MS
Principle 2	-	Planning - should plan to fulfil its OH&S Policy, objective & targets
Principle 3	-	Implementation & operation - for effective implementation, an organization should develop the capabilities and support mechanism necessary to achieve its OH&S policy, objective and targets
Principle 4	-	Measurement & Evaluation - should measure, monitor and evaluate its OH&S performance and take preventive & corrective action
Principle 5	-	Management Review - should regularly review and continually improve its OH&S - MS with the objective of improving its OH&S performance.

Keeping the above principles in mind, the management system is best viewed as an organizing framework that should be continually monitored and periodically reviewed to provide effective direction for an organization's OH&S activities in response to changing internal and external factors.

This standard is applicable to any organization that wishes to:

(a) implement, maintain and improve on OH&S-MS
(b) Assure itself of conformance with its stated OH&S policy
(c) Demonstrate such conformance to others
(d) Seek certification of its OH&S-MS by an external agency
(e) Make a self-declaration of conformance with the standard.

All the requirements of this standard are intended to be incorporated into any OH&S-MS. The extent of application will depend on such factors as the OH&S policy, the nature of its activities and the conditions in which is operates.

The benefits of implementing a systematic and effective OH&S-MS as per IS 18001 include the following:

— reducing the number of personnel injuries through preventive and control of work place hazard.
— reducing the risk of major accident.
— reducing the material loss caused by accident and in production interruptions.

— ensuring that appropriate legislation is addressed.
— meeting increasing importance of OH&S for public image.
— Servicing the possibility for an integrated management system including Quality, Environment and OH&S.

IS 15656:2006

Hazard identification, risk assessment and risk control are the essential elements of any OH&S management system. IS 15656: 2006 Indian standard on Hazard Identification and Risk Analysis - Code of Practice is intended for safety professionals and engineers in the areas of chemical plant safety to upgrade safety performance of the plants and covers the methods of identifying, assessing and reducing hazards including evaluation and selection of methods for particular application. The Code describes the essential nature of each of the above sequence of steps and describes a variety of techniques for identifying hazards and the quantification of accident consequence and the frequency towards the final risk estimation at each stage. The overall methodology presented in this code allows systematic identification of hazards as well as quantification of the risks associated with the operation of process plants. Applied with due expertise and rigor the prescribed methodology can help the user to understand the relative levels of hazards and risk potential in an installation. This aids the selection and prioritization of necessary strategies for accident prevention and limiting their consequences. Therefore, the code can be used for improving plant safety performance as well as to reduce human and property losses. This standard will thus be an essential adjunct to IS 18001.

IS 14489:1998

Assessment of company's OH&SMS for its conformity to the specified requirement of the standards, implementation and maintenance level by third party (certifying agency) is very much essential for its acceptance internationally and also a tool for improving the performance of its OH&SMS. BIS has formulated IS 14489:1998 code of practice on OH&S audit. This standard provides guidelines for establishing, planning, conductive and documenting audits on OH&SMS at work place. Details guidelines on audit safety aspects i.e. Audit goals, Audit objectives, Roles and Responsibilities of auditors and auditee, Audit scope, Frequency of audit, planning, execution and documentation of audit have been provided in this standard.

At International level

After the successful implementation of ISO 9001 & ISO 14001, there was an attempt to develop similar standard to manage occupational health & safety through ISO. However it was not successful no consensus could be reached on this issue at ISO. Moreover considering the mandates of ILO, it was felt that to develop any standard on management of OH&S at international level, ILO is the right forum. Accordingly ILO took initiative and published *ILO-OSH 2001 Guidelines on occupational safety and health management system.* These guidelines are voluntary and have designed as practical tool for assisting organizations and competent institutions at national level as a means of achieving continual improvement in OHS performance.

At national level ILO-OSH guidelines should be used to:

(i) establish a national framework for OSH management system, preferably supported by national laws and regulations.
(ii) provide guidance for the development of both national and tailored guidelines on OHS management systems to respond appropriately to the real needs of the organizations.

At the level of organization, the guidelines are intended to:

(i) provide guidance regarding the integration of OHS management system elements in the organization as a component of policy and management arrangements.
(ii) motivate all members of the organization in applying OHS management principles and methods to continually improve OHS performance.

Conclusion

Implementation of OH&S Management System will not only help to improve safety and health of workers but also help the organizations to improve quality of their product and services and the environment conditions prevailing in the working place. BIS is operating its OH&S management system certification scheme as per IS 18001. The details about the certification procedure is available in BIS website (ww.bis.org.in). Though a number of Indian industries are taking certification against OHSAS 18001 it is to be noted that OHSAS 18001 is not a British Standard, it is formulated by a consortium of certifying agencies in collaboration with BSI,UK. Moreover, India being a member body of ISO, will try to ensure that ISO should adopt IS 18001 as ISO standard in case in future it decides to take up formulation of OH&S management system standard. In view of the above it is desirable that Indian industries should come forward for getting their units certified as per IS 18001:2000.

Section–II
Food Safety

4

FOOD SAFETY AND THE COMMON MAN

K.S. Premavalli*

ABSTRACT

Food safety is a significant and growing issue in the food industry. A common man, known as the consumer, is a multifaceted group because of their difference in age, life experiences, health, knowledge, culture, sex, nutritional needs, family status, purchasing power, occupation and literary level. These human factors make the vision of food safety as a complex factor in satisfying the consumer needs of safe foods requirement. The food safety generally refers not only to the food prepared in clean, hygienic way and devoid of undesirable microorganisms, but also encompass the important issues of contaminants, food additives, food packaging, agricultural practices, presence of toxins, food borne pathogens, etc. Besides these, the effect of food processing methods on the safety concerns, the chemicals used for imparting functional properties and how far the foods are natural and covers traditional touch of preparation and taste of foods are also very important factors which address the food safety.

The implementation and control of food safety require an application of potential common sense practices, following regulatory measures, defining the risk goals and overcoming those with safety solutions, statistical process control, etc. The quality measures in terms of GMP, HACCP, GRAS status of additives, etc., are of major concern for the safety of the food product. In a nutshell, the food traceability "from farm to fork" and from "stable to table" is an important principle to be thought off in the field of food safety for the consumer.

Introduction

Food Safety is the present issue attached to the wholesome, nutritious functional foods which has greatest attachment to the consumer, bringing awareness in consumer and covers the major quality aspects of the product. Food safety is an inherent characteristics expected by the people, viewed by the people, made known to people through media. However, the measurements covers the sensory characteristics, microbial profile, contaminants, presence of toxins etc. The preventive measures for achieving food safety encompass the better raw material selection, better processing method, quality checks, use of safe additives etc.

*Scientist 'F', Head, Food Preservation, Defence Food Research Laboratory, Siddarthanagar, Mysore-570 011

However, the present day common man expects that the food looks well, smells well, packed well, labelled with nutritional facts and storage conditions to be mentioned on the pack. The amalgamation of safety concerns by the industry with the requirements of the consumer leads to quality product with common man's confidence.

Details on Safety of Food

The food safety to a common man refers to the food preparation in clean and presentable manner and not creating any health hazard, while scientists refers to the important issues starting from agricultural practices, quality of raw material, processing method, packaging, storage and distribution of the products, quality checks at various steps of processing and the final product. The agricultural practices and the resultant produce refers to the usage of pest control compounds, biologicals used in animal agriculture and industrial chemicals as environmental pollutants for which the safety measures called for are usage of pesticides below the limits specified by PFA, reduction of contamination through biological and safe environment, away from harmful product industries and elimination of harmful odorous compounds in the industry. Quality raw material refers to the absoluteness of quality, satisfying the requirements of quality as per the specifications laid down by the statutory bodies, such as PFA, BIS, AGMARK. The processing of the product with reference to safety is dependent on the requirements of the product, partial processed product, the shelf-life thereby the methods of dehydration, freezing, hurdle processing, minimal processing, fermentation, tetra pack processing etc., can be followed. Secondly, the adequacy of packaging at par with the shelf-life of the product needs an emphasis considering the permeability characteristics of the packaging material, printability, and mechanical strengths of packaging materials. Besides these, the automation of the whole process makes the product more safe for which food engineering section assembling the linkages for equipments for on line process will be the main strength. Food scientist gives the priority for storage stability of the processed product which is one of the main criteria for marketing and distribution.

The consumer health safety is of major concern in the present scenario where the outbreaks due to the staple pin in the food, cockroaches in soft drink bottles, death due to illicit liquor, food poisoning due to bacterial contamination etc., are occurring frequently. The real issues of food safety has been reported well by US Department of Agriculture. Food contamination and spoilage leads to food hazards moving to infectious diseases. The order of importance as per USDA is mycotoxins, bacterial toxins, food borne bacterial infections, chemical residues, natural toxicants, process induced toxicants, viral infections, food additives, toxicants formed in the body and parasitic infections. Over the ages, it is established that groundnuts, and other nuts are the source of aflatoxins which leads to ergotism, alimentary toxic aleukia. Agricultural practices are being improved to minimize mold contamination. The neurotoxins through *C. botulinum* and the enterotoxins of other species are the causative factors of food poisoning. Bacterial infections leading to gastro-intestinal disturbances, fever, diarrhea etc., though pointed towards the Salmonellosis, the actual disease mechanisms are yet to be understood. About 25 per cent of outbreaks of food borne infections is because of viral attacks where the detection itself is a major constraint.

The naturally occurring toxicants may be in milk, nuts, vegetables etc., are to be explored for overcoming the problems. On one hand, the elimination of soy trypsin inhibitors, phytic acid which reduces the absorption in the human system and their fate in processing of foods needs to be addressed. On the other hand, how to identify and eliminate the poisonous mushrooms, toxic alkaloids of potatoes, sulphur compounds of onion etc., which are not safe to humans. The holistic health of humans both mental as well as physiological satisfaction is a realistic approach which needs to be addressed. The chemical residues in the form of pesticides, the residue limits of chemical additives used during processing also causes a cumulative effect leading to diseased conditions and fatal diseases such as cancer. The present day thinking of organic foods development though reduces the problem of chemical residues, the soil quality, over constant use of pesticides contributes for the problems. Secondly, the increased awareness and production of organic foods may be better solution.

Besides, understanding the problems of food safety, the implementation of control measures is of prime importance. The applications of regulatory measures, defining of risk goals and overcoming those with safety solutions, statistical process control etc., will automatically bring the safety to the product. Safety measures include the quality measures in terms of GMP, HACCP, GRAS status of additives with the certification of ISO:9001:2000 and the salient features of these are:

GMP

- Permises
- Facilities
- MSD operations
- Hygiene and food safety
- Management responsibility

HACCP

- Characterize the product
- Process-flow diagram
- Identify the hazards
- Quantify the hazards and reccurence
- Identify control requirements
- Identify CCP's
- Corrective action
- Verification requirements
- Implementation
- Audit and Improve

ISO:9001:2000

Basic requirements

- Leadership
- Commitment
- Participation

- Documentation
- Standardization
- Formalization
- Verification
- Certification

Conclusion

Food safety is a major concern to the common man and it can be achieved by multi-dimensional approach by way of creating awareness, identifying the causative factors and overcoming with the solutions of food safety measures. In the present situation, the implementation of safety measures with a clear cut protocol of food manufacture with the inclusion of quality control measures is the requirement to get the safety food.

REFERENCES

Manfred Kroger, 2005, www.nutriwatch.org.

Capacity building for Food Safety, CBP newsletter, Vol.1, Issue 4, April 2006.

UPTAKE OF BENOMYL FUNGICIDE FROM POST HARVEST TREATMENT AND ITS PERSISTENCE IN MODIFIED ATMOSPHERE STORED BANANA FRUITS

K.P. Sudheer*, Pitam Chandra**, V.T. Gajbhiye*** and Rajesh Kumar****

ABSTRACT

Freshly harvested banana fruits were dipped in 500 ppm benomyl solution for 2 minutes to sterilise the field carry-over fungal infection. These fruits were air dried before being subjected to modified atmosphere (MA) storage studies. A controlled ventilation system, called the silicone membrane system, was developed to obtain the desired MA condition at a low control and energy cost. The benomyl treated fruits were stored at ambient and cold storage (at 13°C) conditions. The bananas could store for more than 30 days and 120 days at ambient and 13°C temperature, respectively. This increased shelf life due to the combined effect of fungicide treatment and MA storage condition.

The stored bananas were analysed for the residual benomyl content at different duration (days) of storage at both ambient and 13°C. This exercise was carried out for both banana pulp and peel. The method proposed allows the determination of carbendazim, derivative of benomyl in both banana pulp and peel. The conversion of benomyl into carbendazim takes place entirely during extraction (ethyl acetate and ammonia solution). A successive acid-base treatment provides the clean-up and the converted carbendazim is determined by HPLC [Water's HPLC equipped with Waters 501 pump, Waters 484 tuneable absorbence detector, Rheodyne (20 µl loop) injector and a Lechrosorb RP-8 column of 250 × 3.9 mm (10µm)]. The total procedure involves three steps, viz. extraction, clean-up and estimation. The results showed that the banana pulp did not have any residual benomyl in it after a storage period of 80 days at 13°C and 25 days at ambient temperature. But the analysis after 40 days at cold conditions (13°C) showed a residue of 0.083 ppm of benomyl in banana pulp. However, this is within the Maximum Residue Limit (MRL) of benomyl, which is 1 ppm, as recommended by FAO.

Residue analysis of banana peel showed a positive result in all the samples. Banana peel contained a residual benomyl of 1.619 and 0.986 ppm after a storage period of 40 and 80 days, respectively,

*Department of Post Harvest Technology, RARS, Ambalavayal, Kerala Agricultural University, Tavanur-673 593, *e-mail*: drkpsudheer@rediffmail.com

**Assistant Director General (Agricultural Engineering), Krishi Anusandhan Bhavan, ICAR, New Delhi-110 012.

***Division of Agricultural Chemicals, IARI, Pusa, New Delhi-110 012.

****Division of Agricultural Chemicals, IARI, Pusa, New Delhi-110 012.

at 13°C. The residual benomyl for banana peel at ambient temperature was 0.744 ppm after 30 days of storage. This reduction in residual benomyl is due to its decomposition during storage period. More over the rate of decomposition is faster, when the produce is stored above 25°C (ambient condition). This results shows that 500 ppm benomyl treatment could be effectively used to control the pathological diseases without affecting the quality and safety of MA stored banana fruits.

Introduction

Banana is one of the most nutritious and oldest cultivated tropical fruit crop of India. Due to non-availability of efficient post harvest techniques the estimated loss of bananas varies from 12 to19 per cent. Modified Atmosphere Storage (MAS) is an effective way to increase the shelf life of bananas without compromising its quality. The available Modified Atmosphere (MA)/Controlled Atmosphere (CA) storage systems commonly used for the conservation of perishable agricultural products usually involves high capital expenditure both in construction and maintenance. So, a cost effective and environmentally safe technique to create a required MA system using the silicone membrane by controlled ventilation in the storage unit was developed and evaluated for banana fruits.

Among the major post harvest diseases of banana, stem end rot and anthracnose are predominant. Highly effective control of these diseases is possible by post harvest dip treatment of fruits in benomyl solution. The combined effects of benomyl fungicide and modified atmosphere storage on post harvest storage life and quality aspects are major objectives of the present study.

Review of Literature

Banana fruit rots were found to be effectively controlled by thiabendazole and benomyl (Satyan *et al.*, 1992). It is reported that the banana fruits when treated high concentrations of benomyl (1000 ppm) and thiobendazole had an excellent control of stem end rot without causing skin blemishes but affecting the taste of ripened fruit. Benomyl at 50 to 400 ppm gave best results for control of stem end rot disease of banana fruits.

Dipping of fruits in 500 ppm of benomyl delayed ripening, increased firmness, increased shelf life (Nair and Tung, 1992) and reduced rotting (Satyan *et al.*, 1992) considerably compared to control. Jones (1991) observed that benomyl at 500 ppm controlled the crown rot by *Fusarium pallidoroseum* but failed to control *Verticillium* sp. Benomyl as well as prochlorag at 500 ppm dip treatment effectively controlled stem end rot and anthracnose caused by *Colletotrichum musae, Fusarium moniliforme* and *Fusarium pallidoroseum* during post harvest decay of banana (Wade *et al.*, 1993).

The effectiveness of the fungicidal treatment may be enhanced by heating the water into which the fruit are dipped. The optimum recommendations varied between different research workers, but 500 ppm benomyl in water at 55°C for 5 minutes appeared generally effective without damaging the fruit.

Material and Methods

The experimental material, banana fruit (cv. Dwarf Cavendish), was obtained from fruit and vegetable market, Azadpur, New Delhi. The graded banana fruits were first washed and then surface sterilised by dipping in 500 ppm. benomyl solution for 2 min. These fruits were air-dried and molten wax, which contained 80 : 20 paraffin wax and coconut oil, with a benomyl concentration of 500 ppm, was applied at the stem end to prevent moisture loss as well as stem end rotting. The surface sterilised fruits in 500 ppm benomyl were stored at ambient temperature and 13°C for MAS treatments of 4 levels of CO_2 (2, 4, 6 and 8 per cent), and Regular Atmosphere (RA) as control. Ethylene absorbent @ 8 g./kg. was used in all treatments.

Design of MA Storage Unit

MAS units of 2 kg. capacity were developed and its performance was evaluated. The main design criteria for a stable gas concentration during storage are proper selection of membrane and its window area. Procedure to calculate the membrane area required are based on the level of CO_2 and O_2 desired in the storage chamber. The basic equation for calculation of membrane area is described in Sudheer *et al.* (2001) and can be summarised by the following equations :

$$\text{Membrane area at ambient condition (cm}^2) = e^{(-0.2191\,x + 0.3794\,y)} \quad \text{.........(1)}$$

$$\text{Membrane area at 13°C (cm}^2) = e^{(-0.4219\,x + 0.4524\,y)} \quad \text{........................ (2)}$$

Where 'x' and 'y' are required levels of CO_2 and O_2 to be maintained in MAS units in percentage.

Polyethylene Tetra Phthalate (PET) containers of 7000 ml capacity were used for the storage studies. The lids of the bottles were cut open to different areas to place the silicone membrane of different surface areas to maintain the desired CO_2 and O_2 concentrations as described by equations (1) and (2).

Evaluation of Modified Atmosphere Storage System for Banana

Storage of Banana at Ambient Condition

Two kg. of banana fruits of same size at mature green stage were selected at random for each treatment. The temperature and RH data were recorded for the ambient storage during the period of experiment. During the storage period, the temperature varied from 28.5°C to 30°C and the relative humidity varied from a minimum of 72 per cent to a maximum of 90 per cent. The MA units with silicon membranes were developed as per the equations. Pre-treated banana fruits weighing approximately 2 kg. were stored in the MA units along with ethylene absorbent sachets (16 g.). After securing the lid tightly, the lid joint was covered with a gum tape. The storage experiments were terminated either by 10 per cent moisture loss or spoilage or by the complete development of yellow colour. Three replications of each treatment (2, 4, 6 and 8 per cent CO_2) were taken out for the residual analysis.

Storage of Banana in Cold Storage at 13°C

The pre-treated bananas were stored in cold storage in the same way as in the case of ambient storage. The storage temperature was maintained at a rage of 13 ±0.5°C and 85-90 per cent RH. The treatments were laid out in a similar way as that of ambient storage. The stored products were evaluated for their residue content.

Residual Analysis for Benomyl Fungicide

As benomyl was used in the pre-treatment of banana fruits, residual analysis was done to check the level of the same compound after storage. Samples of both fresh and stored were obtained from both conditions (ambient and cold storage at 13°C) to find out the presence of any traces of compounds such as benomyl or its derivatives carberndazim. The procedure followed is given below :

Principle: The method proposed allows the determination of carbendazim derivative of benomyl in both banana pulp and peel. The conversion of benomyl into carbendazim takes place entirely during extraction (ethyl acetate and ammonia solution). A successive acid-base treatment provides the clean-up and the converted carbendazim is determined by HPLC. The total procedure involves three steps mainly Extraction, Clean-up and Estimation. These are discussed in the same order.

Extraction: Fifty gram of chopped or blended banana pulp or peel was transferred into a blender jar and 5 g. celite, 5 ml of 30 per cent ammonia solution, 150 ml of ethyl acetate, and 25 g. of anhydrous sodium sulphate were added and the contents were blended at moderate speed in a mixer or equivalent apparatus for 3 minutes. Filter the content through buckner funnel and collect it in a 300 ml flask. Repeat the extraction of solid residues with two additional 50 ml portions of ethyl acetate (Saroni *et al.*, 1996).

Clean-up: The combine extracts was evaporated to a small volume using a water bath. Add 2 ml of concentrated HCl to the residue and quantitatively transfer the aqueous acid solution into a 125 ml seperatory funnel. Cool to room temperature, add 50 ml of n-hexane to the separatory funnel, shake for 2 minutes, and allow the phases to separate. Discard the hexane layer. Repeat the hexane wash two more times, using additional 50 ml portions of solvent for each wash. Discard the hexane washes.

Quantitatively transfer the aqueous phase to 150 ml beaker, small volumes of distilled water as rinse. Add 6.5 N NaOH solution to set the pH 8 to 9 of the residue solution. The pesticide is then extracted with three 50 ml portions of ethyl acetate. Each extraction consists of 1 to 2 minute shaking period. Allow the phases to separate and discard the aqueous wash. Concentrate the ethyl acetate extract to dryness and immediately dissolve the residue in HPLC grade methanol and make-up the volume to 10 ml. The dissolved residue was filtered before HPLC analysis.

Estimation: Estimation was carried out by a Water's HPLC equipped with Waters 501 pump, Waters 484 tuneable absorbence detector, Rheodyne (20 μl loop) injector and a Lechrosorb RP-8 column of 250 × 3.9 mm (10 μm). The solvent system used was methanol: water (70 : 30) with a flow rate of 0.6 ml/min. The max used for estimation was 221 nm. The peak area was calculated by using the computer software - base 810. Prepare standard solution of 10 ppm and read its relative peak area and retention time. Compare the reading with the peak data of pulp and peel samples at the similar conditions of HPLC. The amount of benomyl in parts per million is as follows :

$$\text{ppm Benomyl} = \frac{\text{Peak area of sample} \times \text{conc. of standard} \times \text{volume make-up of sample}}{\text{Peak area of standard} \times \text{weight of sample taken}} \quad \text{.....................} \quad (3)$$

Results

Storage Studies of Banana Fruit

The aim of storage in modified atmosphere is to increase the shelf life and thereby extend the period of availability of freshly harvested produce in their most useable form by altering the relative proportion of atmospheric gases that surround the product (Day, 1992). The shelf life of banana under various MA storage conditions at two different temperatures has been assessed by different quality parameters. At both temperatures, banana stored in silicon membrane showed a significant increase in shelf life compared to regular atmosphere storage. At ambient conditions, the control fruits (i.e. regular atmosphere - RA) could store only up to 10 days. The MA stored fruits exhibited a shelf life of 30 days with a low physiological loss in weight and decay.

The MA advantage increased many folds at 13°C storage temperature. The control fruits at regular atmosphere could stored for 40 days. The MA stored fruits could store up to 120 days with low PLW and high organoleptic quality. This increase in shelf life is due to the effect of modified storage condition and benomyl pre-treatment.

Residual Analysis for Benomyl Fungicide

The stored bananas were analysed for the residual benomyl content at different duration (days) of storage at both ambient and 13°C. This exercise was carried out for both banana pulp and peel. The results showed that the banana pulp did not have any residual benomyl in it after a storage period of 80 days at 13°C and 25 days at ambient temperature. But the analysis after 40 days at cold conditions (13°C) showed a residue of 0.083 ppm of benomyl in banana pulp. However, this is within the Maximum Residue Limit (MRL) of benomyl, which is 1 ppm, as recommended by FAO (FAO, 1993).

Residue analysis of banana peel showed a positive result in all the samples. Banana peel contained a residual benomyl of 1.619 and 0.986 ppm after a storage period of 40 and 80 days, respectively, at 13°C. The residual benomyl for banana peel at ambient temperature was 0.744 ppm after 25 days of storage. This reduction in residual benomyl may be due to its decomposition during storage period as reported by Please, *et al.* (1973). The rate of decomposition is faster, when the produce is stored above 25°C (Calmon and Sayag, 1976). This may be the reason for low residual benomyl of both banana pulp and peel stored at ambient temperature.

Conclusion

The present investigation was undertaken to increase the shelf life of banana and thereby extend the period of availability of harvested produce as fresh as possible. A controlled ventilation system, called the silicon membrane system, was developed to obtain the desired MA condition at a low control and energy cost. The MA stored banana fruits could store for more than 30 days and 120 days at ambient and 13°C temperatures, respectively. This multi-fold increase in shelf life is due to the effect of benomyl treatment and modified atmosphere storage. The results showed that the banana pulp did not have any residual benomyl in it after a storage period of 80 days at 13°C and 25 days at ambient temperature. This results revealed that 500 ppm benomyl treatment could be an effective pre-treatment to control the pathological diseases without affecting the quality and safety of banana fruits. The added advantage of this technique is environmental safety and energy efficiency.

It was observed that the fluctuation of price in case of banana is for a period of 90 days. Therefore, if a technology is made available to preserve the bananas for a period of 90 days, it should help the farmers, venders and others to ensure steady availability of bananas in the market as well as for banana processing plants. The results indicate that the green bananas could be stored and transported at temperatures substantially higher than 13°C with the use of silicone membrane based MA system for up to 30 days after harvesting. Consequently, the refrigeration costs would be reduced to a great extent. The proposal to use this system of storage and handling for exporting green bananas which generally requires more than 30 days by sea transport, appears promising in reducing the export costs and there by improving its share in the world market.

REFERENCES

Calmon, J.P. and Sayag, D.R. (1976). *J. Agric. Fd.Chem.*, 24: 311-426.

Day, B.P.F. (1992). *Guidelines for the Manufacture and Handling of Modified Atmosphere Packed Food Products*, Technical mannual No. 84, Campden Food and Prink Research Association, Chipping Campden, Glos, U.K.

FAO (1993). *Pesticide residues in food*, Vol. 2, Codex Alimentarian Commission.

Jones, D.R. (1991). Chemical control of crown rot in Queensland bananas. *Austr. J. Exp. Agric.*, 31 (5): 693-698.

Nair, H. and Tung, H.F. (1992). Low oxygen effect and storage of modified atmosphere storage bananas (Musa, AA group). *Acta Hort.* 292: 209-215.

Please, H.L., Gardiner, J.A. and Holt, R.F. (1973). 'Benomyl', In: *Analytical methods for pesticides and plant growth regulators*, Vol. VII, (ed. Gunter Zweing), Academic Press, New York.

Satyan, S.H., Scott, K.J.; Best, D.J. (1992). Effects of storage temperature and MAs on cooking bananas grown in New South Wales. *Tropical Agric*., 69(3): 263-267.

Scaroni, I., Previati, M.P., and Bovolenta, A. (1996) Fungicide residues in foods. In: *Handbook of Food Analysis*, Vol. 2, Residues and other food component analysis. (ed. L.M.L.Nollet).: 1487-1488.

Sudheer, K.P., P. Chandra and R.K., Pal. 2001. Design of Controlled Ventilation System for Banana Storage, Paper presented in XXXV ISAE Annual Convention & National Symposium at OUAT, Bhubaneswar, January, 22-24, 2001.

Wade, N.L., Campbell, L.C. and Bishop, D.G. (1980). Tissue permeability and membrane lipid composition of ripening banana fruits. *J. Experimental Bot.*, 31: 123, 975-982.

Section–III

Safety in Construction Sector

6

SAFETY IN CONSTRUCTION WORKSITES: SAIL Experience

Shashi Kant*

ABSTRACT

Steel industry no doubt, poses one of the most difficult challenges in the area of safety, health and environment when compared to many other industries. Steel industry is generally based on the cascading effect of various unit operations. These construction activities need to be carried out in close proximity of operational units. Therefore safety in construction job assumes immense importance and its requirements become more complex and demanding. Prevention of accidents on construction sites is the responsibility of each concerned employee in respective areas of work. SAIL has adopted and promulgated an "Occupational Safety & Health Policy" as an instrument for creating awareness about safe and healthy work practices and for maintaining safety and health consciousness amongst the employees at all levels of the company.

This paper attempts to highlight the major concerns and measures taken to ensure safe working conditions in SAIL. The safety culture we want to shape in construction worksites, is characterized by behaviours that focus on safe, health, timely completion of projects and ensuring safety for everyone.

Many recommendations would come after the accident but how are we going to follow the same is the big question. Generally for a few days they would be adhered to but after some time people would come to their old behaviour and all recommendations vanish away. Safety is an emotive word having different connotations for different people in different circumstances, at different times and at different places. In common parlance, safety means "Being safe, freedom from risks and dangers", when put in industrial practice, it means removal/reduction of different types of accidents. To a conceptualist, it means loss prevention in totality.

Introduction

Many steel plants in our country are going to augment the production facilities through increased capacity expansion and modernization. These construction activities need to be carried out in close proximity of operational units. Therefore safety in construction job

*Executive Director (Safety), SAIL Safety Organisation, Doranda (PO), Ranchi- 834002.
E-mail : edsafety@sail-rdcis.com

assumes immense importance and its requirements become more complex and demanding. Prevention of accidents on construction sites is the responsibility of each concerned employee in respective areas of work. The philosophy of safety should reach the grassroots level so that safe working procedure becomes an integral part of our work culture. Protocol system, safety clearances and monitoring systems are therefore required to achieve incidence of zero accident.

Business Plan

To take off from the platform of turnaround effected during 2003-2004, Steel Authority of India Limited [SAIL] formulated Corporate Plan 2012 as a part of its growth strategy. Achievement of the envisaged levels of production will enable SAIL to maintain its dominant position in the Indian steel industry in the years to come. The CP 2012 envisages an investment of Rs. 25000 crore for upgrading existing facilities and expanding some of the units to ensure a competitive edge and sustained viability of the organization in future. Success of the plan would be influenced greatly by the safety assurance for the workers involved in implementing it. While mobilizing and equipping the large workforce necessary for these projects, concerted efforts will be made to train and educate them so that these activities are carried out without any accidents. Everyday new workers by the dozens would be participating in the projects in new, unfamiliar surroundings.

SAIL strongly believes in maintaining ethical and social standards while serving its corporate social responsibility - an approach that recognizes a multiple bottom line, including among other things, creating a safe and healthy environment and nurturing an active, resilient community along with its more traditional focus on profits. Naturally, SAIL gives adequate emphasis on safety of human resources and assets of the company along with production and productivity, cost reduction and quality.

Occupational Safety and Health Policy of SAIL

SAIL has adopted and promulgated an "Occupational Safety & Health Policy" as an instrument for creating awareness about safe and healthy work practices and for maintaining safety and health consciousness amongst the employees at all levels of the company. This shows that safety and health of its employees are a major concern of SAIL. The Safety Organisation is designed to comprise of a multi-disciplinary team of relevant specialists for technical guidance, advice and direction to the plants and units.

The Policy includes commitment to :

(a) Safety of its employees and those living in neighbourhood
(b) Demand accountability and provide resources
(c) Place Safety as a responsibility of all employees
(d) Incorporate Safety in all work procedures
(e) Impart training to create Safety consciousness
(f) Enhance Safety through participative fora
(g) Comply to relevant legal requirements

(h) Conduct Audits of Safety performance
(i) Recognize that Safety performance is necessary for our success.

Support from Company, Plant Management and Trade Unions

At the company level we have a corporate SAIL Safety Organisation based at Ranchi to guide, monitor, co-ordinate and help SAIL Plants/Units in complex activity and that the company has a moral, economic, social and legal obligations to prevent hazards, provide healthy environment and guard against all possible hazards and risks.

At Steel Industry level the steel majors viz. SAIL, TISCO, RINL and Ispat Steel, other member organizations from the area of steel making, construction and designs; National Trade Unions like INTUC, AITUC, HMS, CITU; Specialist Agencies like NSC have established Joint Committee on Safety, Health and Environment of the Steel Industry (JCSSI). JCSSI considers the issues relating to safety and gives guidelines to the member industrial units including SAIL as to how to take care of the safety of the workmen. JCSSI has published materials on Safety Education and Training, Safety practices and procedures, statutory safety provisions and safety rules, Safety codes for contractors, Safety Manual, etc. JCSSI holds seminars on safety related issues. JCSSI holds competitions in the areas of safety poster, safety essay, safety calendar design, etc. JCSSI awards *Suraksha Purashkar* to the Steel Plants for maintaining higher safety standards and also associates with SAIL Safety Awards. All these help promote safety activities.

a. Corporate Level
1. Safety Advisory Board
2. SAIL Safety Organisation

b. Industry Level
3. JCSSI, NJCS

c. Plant Level
4. Central Safety Committee
5. Safety Appliances Committee
6. Road Safety Committee
7. House Keeping Committee

d. Department Level
8. Departmental Safety Committees

At Plant level Safety Engineering Departments have been set up to co-ordinate the safety activities of the Plant. There are joint committees consisting of representatives of Management and Trade Unions for each Plant named as Central Safety Committee and the Apex Committee. The Safety Engineering Departments are headed by senior executives of the Plant. At the Department level also each department has departmental safety committees consisting of the representatives of the Management and the Union to review the safety activities and to help management in promoting safety.

Accident Analysis

Among the major concerns that had from analysis of the safety is the increasing problem of contractor safety. From the analysis, it is found that the contractor employees' fatalities accounted for 93 per cent during last 13 years in project works. Modernization of Durgapur and Rourkela steel plants had more number of fatalities i.e. 34 per cent and 61 per cent respectively. The cause-wise analysis of these fatal accidents is shown in the pie chart.

Cause-wise analysis of fatal accidents
in SAIL during Project Works

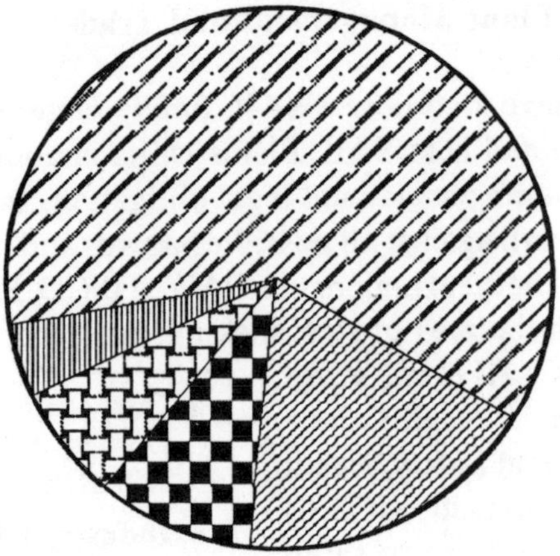

Fall from height	:	61%
Caught/crush/pressed/hit by objects	:	18%
Rail and Road	:	09%
Electrocution	:	07%
Suffocation/buried	:	05%

Measures taken to Ensure Safe Working Conditions

SAIL is presently drawing out special guidelines on the following areas in the matter of construction safety. Contractors' employees are carrying out mostly the construction activity inside the work premises.

(a) Implementing Inter-Plant Standards - steel industry (IPSS)

- Safety in contract works (IPSS:1-11-011-01)
- Safety in contract works in mines (IPSS:1-11-010-01)
- Safety Procedure for Working at Height by Contractor's Workers

(b) Special instructions issued by corporate safety to plants/units like

- Banning of bamboo scaffolding;
- Encourage use of steel scaffolding;
- Use of full body harness instead of safety belt;
- Use of safety net, fall arrestors while working at height;
- Creation of Project safety department, as like in Bhilai Steel Plant;
- Adhering to BIS/IS standards available in Construction activities;

(c) Contractor Safety Audit
(d) Penal action

For regular employees also, the above standards/safety measures being formulated separately and are liable to follow the same.

IPSS on Safety in Contract Works

This standard was adopted in May 2001 by SAIL, TISCO and RINL, which provides guidance to all concerned in accident prevention during construction activities. This standard demands the contractors' workmen to participate in the safety awareness, health care and safety training programs that are being organized by the Employer or the Contractor. The unique point in this standard is that there will a Memorandum of Understanding (MoU), shall be signed between the Contractor and representative of the Contracts Department (on behalf of the Plant) before the award of the contract.

The contractor shall provide/nominate at least one full time safety supervisor. On request, Employer through SED will arrange general safety training to contract workmen. Job safety training/induction will be a compulsory thing for every job to start with. Regarding PPEs, the Contractor will provide all the PPEs and safety appliances required to carry out the job to all the workmen deployed by the contractor and also ensure that his workmen use those PPE and safety appliances while on the job. The contractor shall not pay any cash in lieu of PPE to the workers.

The following aspects are covered in the 'General Term & Conditions' of the standard.

- Safety Induction
- System of safety clearance
- Ensuring use of user-friendly PPEs
- Use of height pass after proper medical check up
- Inclusion of safety violation penalty clause
- Ensuring proper supervision during execution of contract works.

The terms and conditions also demand the contractor to maintain register and documents and submit periodic reports and returns, furnish information/report relating to accident occurring in the area of work to competent authority in time. The contractor shall abide by the provisions of all statutory acts and rules as applicable.

The contractor shall obtain specific permission in accordance with IPSS: 1-11-007-01 "Procedure for Permit to Work" and IPSS:1-11-005-98 "Procedure for working at heights by contractor's workers" from the Plant's Safety Engineering Department before commencing the following:

(a) Working in operating plant/equipment
(b) Working at height
(c) Working in areas expected to have toxic/poisonous gases
(d) Major activity irrespective of the clearance already obtained
(e) Wherever there are hazards of electricity, moving machinery, etc.

The contractor will ensure that the shut down/clearance is taken before sending workers to such locations particularly in the area where there are hazards of gases, electricity, moving machinery, etc. The executing department will take necessary shutdown before commencement of job in that area.

Safety Measures Taken

Learning is the process by which a relatively lasting change in behaviour occurs as a result of past experience and knowledge is created through its transformation. Learning can also be defined as increasing one's capacity to take effective action. It has been SAIL's endeavour to institutionalize organizational learning in all operational areas, including safety. Learning derived after investigating the cause and measures taken to prevent recurrence of such incidents are being put into the existing system for system up gradation. Presented are here brief description of few accidents occurred during project stage.

- While the contractor worker positioning a bunker plate at 45m level, he fell down from the platform; as the rope of his safety belt came out of the anchor;
- While the contractor worker opening a bolt at 33m level, he slipped from the structure. The lifeline of the safety belt got snapped;
- While the contractor employee was engaged in welding of roof truss, he fell from 27m level along with his safety belt;
- In the process of making a scaffold he fell down from a height pf 10 m;
- While shifting an electrical weighing about one tonne, panel board slipped and fell on him;
- The contractor injured due to fall of a fabricated plate (2 × 3 m size) on the same level;
- While a regular employee was giving signal to crane operator, a roof truss fell on him;
- While excavation for installation of a new machine, the sidewall collapsed;
- The contractor crushed due to parapet wall collapse while digging a trench near the wall.

If we analyse fatal accidents occurred during project and modernization in SAIL plants and units, a large number of fatal accidents occurred due to fall from height. It accounts nearly 61 per cent. The following measures had been taken to arrest fatal accidents due to fall from height.

- Banning of bamboo scaffolding in work premises and encouraging to use of steel scaffolding;
- Use of full body harness instead of safety belt;
- Use of safety net, fall arrestors while working at height;
- Compulsory medical fitness and height pass for jobs at heights;
- Safety induction training for working at heights;
- Only 24 volts hand lamps to be used.

Another major reason for fatal accidents are due to hit/caught between moving machinery/objects. Existence of numerous rotating equipments in the construction worksites is a constant risk to the workers. Special campaign is being organized for 'not to wear loose garments' while working near moving machines, especially in winter session. To control the risk, the following activities are being strengthened:

- Insisting on use appropriate and tested lifting tools and tackles and equipments
- Display of safe working loads in the lifting equipments
- Regular inspection for machine guarding
- Insisting on to wear appropriate safety appliances
- Campaign against wearing loose garments.

One more area of concern is road accidents at worksites. Following measures were emphasized:

- Proper loading of material and securing of the same
- Controlling speed of vehicle
- Compulsory use of crash helmets
- Examining fitness of vehicles and drivers, etc.

The different types of accidents including fatal occurred during project and modernization period were investigated and analyzed. Various committees have recommended the following safety measures and the same would be monitored during any construction activities inside the work premises. The contractor is mainly responsible for all and the executing department would be demanding the same.

- Safe means of access to working place
- Precautions in demolition under competent supervisor
- Safe handling or use of explosive under the control of competent person
- Erection, installation, use and maintenance of transporting equipment and lifting equipment and appointment of competent person
- Adequate and suitable lighting
- Precautions to prevent inhalation of dust, fumes, gases, or vapours, secure and maintain ventilation
- Limits of weights to be lifted or moved by workers
- Safe transport of workers
- Steps to be taken to prevent danger to workers from live electric wires or apparatus
- Safe handling and use of tools operated by compressed air
- Special protocol to work in confined space (IPSS for confined space working).

In SAIL plants, fatal accidents had occurred during Excavation work. It has to be properly planned, managed, supervised and carried out to prevent any untoward incidents. Special attention is being paid in the area.

- Providing side supports with timber, sheet, etc.
- Fencing of all sides and placing of sign boards/red flag
- Keeping workers away from excavators and/or any moving parts

- Insisting to store spoil or other materials away from sides of excavations
- Supervision of installation, alteration or removal of excavation support.

Role of Near Miss Cases

Analysis of number of accidents reveals that a large proportion of accidents, incidents and near miss occurrences follow from unsafe acts that are a result of underlying deficiencies in safety management. Some of the accidents happen due to result of both failures at an individual level (e.g. attitudes towards safety) and at a company level (policies and practices relating to safety). Now focus on the organizational values that might enhance risk management and safe performance in complex and hazardous conditions.

The safety culture we want to shape in construction worksites, is characterized by behaviours that focus on safe, health, timely completion of projects and ensuring safety for everyone. This culture, called the "want-to" safety culture, is the outcome of a collaborative effort between management and contractor and their workers. The pyramid illustrates the conceptual framework for helping an organization evolve towards a want to safety culture. The base of the pyramid is regulatory/statutory compliance. At a minimum, basic compliance with regulations demonstrate to employees that the company is committed to safety. This is going to give a massage to workers that the company's commitment to safety.

The next step is to minimize the occurrence of near misses. A near miss is any event that could have resulted in injury, but didn't, because of some behaviour the individual did to keep safe. So, minimizing near misses will minimize first aid injuries, serious cases and fatalities. Investigation of near miss occurrences is a very useful measure of health and safety performance as well as enabling organizations to learn from such errors. The process involves the analysis of events, which may have led to accidents with a view to preventing more serious outcomes in the future. Within the industry generally and particularly in construction worksites, monitoring of near miss occurrences makes a positive contribution to organizational learning and ultimately leads to safety improvements.

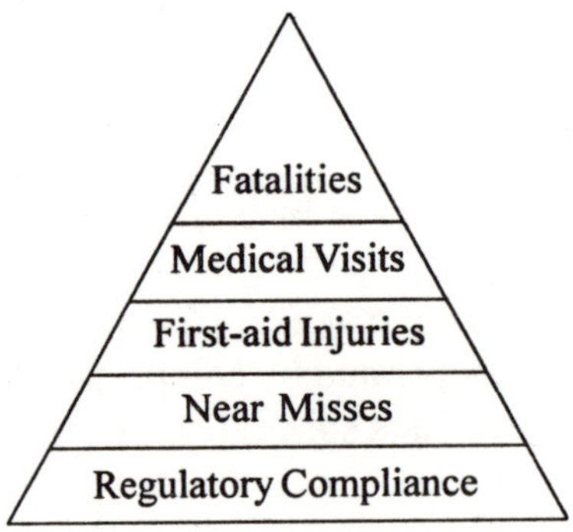

Contractor Safety Audit

Bhilai Steel Plant/SAIL had developed a system of auditing the Contractor Work area. The format is shown below:

सुरक्षा अभियांत्रिकी विभाग - भिलाई इस्पात संयंत्र

.... विभाग में ठेका श्रमिक सुरक्षा अंकेक्षण।

सहयोगी : ....अंकेक्षण दिनांक : .... पिछले अंकेक्षण की तिथि ....

पिछले अंकेक्षण के बाद पूरे होने वाले ठेके .... उसके बाद दिये गये ठेके ....वर्ष भर चलने वाले ठेके ....ठेकेदारों का सुरक्षा अंकेक्षण किया गया

क्रमांक	विवरण	1	2	3
1.0	**वि.स. अधिकारी के रजिस्टर से :**			
1.1	क्या वि.स.अ. का रजिस्टर निर्धारित प्रारूप में है			
1.2	ठेकेदार का नाम			
1.3	ठेका क्र. वर्क आर्डर क्र.			
1.4	कार्यस्थल			
1.5	कार्य–विवरण			
1.6	आपरेटिंग अथॉरिटी			
1.7	सुपरवाइजर की संख्या एवं नाम			
1.8	कार्य अवधि .... से .... तक			
1.9	गेट पास जारी किये गये .... सी.पी.एफ./नान-सी.पी.एफ.			
2.0	**प्रशिक्षण :**			
2.1	सुरक्षा प्रशिक्षण प्रथम चरण में			
2.2	सुरक्षा प्रशिक्षण दूसरे चरण में .... कार्य संबंधी - दिनांक व द्वारा			
2.3	हाइट पास हेतु प्रशिक्षण .... दिनांक एवं संख्या			

Contd. ....

क्रमांक	विवरण	1	2	3
3.0	**अंकेक्षण दिवस पर :**			
3.1	दैनिक उपस्थिति पंजी .... कौन भरता है/कहाँ रहता है।			
3.2	कुल उपस्थिति			
3.3	कार्यस्थल पर उपस्थिति			
3.4	कार्यस्थल पर अनुपस्थिति व कारण			
4.0	**कार्यस्थल पर :**			
4.1	सुरक्षा उपकरणों की वस्तुस्थिति .... बी.एस.पी. हेलमेट का उपयोग			
4.2	सुरक्षा बेल्ट–आई.एस.आई. नान-आई.एस.आई.			
4.3	सुरक्षा बेल्ट–BSP द्वारा प्रदत्त			
4.4	औजारों की स्थिति			
4.5	असुरक्षित कार्य या परिस्थिति (यदि हो)			
4.6	वर्क परमिट/शट डाउन दिया गया			
4.7	सुपरवाइजर की उपस्थिति			
5.0	**ठेके का आंकलन :**			
5.1	स.अभि.विभाग द्वारा चेतावनी पत्र			
5.2	वि.स.अ. द्वारा चेतावनी पत्र			
5.3	क्या आपरेटिंग अथॉरिटी वि.स.अ. में कार्य .... संबंधी सुरक्षा की जानकारी लेता है।			
5.4	चेतावनी पत्रों पर की गई कार्यवाही			
5.5	अन्य बिन्दु			

विभाग : .... विभागीय सुरक्षा अधिकारी प्रतिनिधि–सुरक्षा अभियांत्रिकी विभाग

प्रतिलिपि : 1. सहायक महा प्रबंधक (सुरक्षा)

2. महा प्रबंधक

The same system is being adopted in other steel plants. A team consisting a Safety Officer and Departmental Safety Officer of concerned department is inspecting the work area. The violations are being taken up with the contractor to rectify it as early as possible; otherwisc possible of getting warning memos from Head of Safety of the plant. If the violation persists or continues, the work will be stopped till it rectifies.

Penal Action

SAIL is having the system of taking penal action against the contractor. The violations with respect to safety, non-use of safety appliances, etc. are being dealt with by issuing warning letters/memos, counselling, debarring and fine.

Conclusion

According to a safety benchmarking pilot study conducted by the Working Group on Safety and Occupational Health of the International Iron and Steel Institute (IISI), the major concerns that had arisen from the study, is the increasing problem of contractor safety.

Accordingly, SAIL has laid a special thrust on the area of safety of contractor workers. Preventing accidents and ill health, and meeting standards and guidance is the objective. The only way to check on all these things is to look at what is actually happening. Therefore, the worksites itself must be checked and monitored. Inspections and audits are a vary important part of this process. Executing department must make arrangements to inspect their control measures and investigate potential hazards in the worksites. By all this, we would be able to inculcate a radical change in the outlook towards safety in the construction worksites.

In the end, the Challenges Ahead before us is for developing a sense of safety for self and colleagues and others are:

(a) Use of proper tools and rejection of unsafe tools and slings, etc.;
(b) Proper upkeep and maintenance of cranes;
(c) Use of personal protective equipments like shoes;
(d) Fluorescent dresses to be made compulsory;
(e) Special attention of female workforce like loose garments, safety sandals, helmets, etc.;
(f) Use of cutting tools with flash back arrestors;
(g) Transport through fit and healthy vehicles;
(h) Proper house keeping at construction sites;
(i) Coordination between the various contracting firms as regards safety;
(j) Technology: painting of structures and columns etc. continues to be primitive by hanging on bamboo scaffolds.

REFERENCES

SAIL Safety Policy.
Various Safety manuals of SAIL Plants/Units.
Accident Prevention Manual, NSC, USA.
IPSS Standards/Manuals of JCSSI.

7

CONSTRAINTS AND SOLUTIONS IN ENFORCING SAFETY IN CONSTRUCTION WORKS

T.V. Sudhikumaran*

ABSTRACT

The Construction Industry is said to be as old as the human civilization itself and was a prominent area of concern right from time immemorial. We know in general the way some of these are constructed using slaves with no consideration to safety. To mention a few monumental constructions; we have the Pyramids of Egypt, the Great Wall of China, etc. In the present context of industrialization and economical development through construction, the structure, method and configuration has assumed great proportion not only in terms of the construction machinery and equipments, but also in terms of the increased potential of construction accidents. We use the manpower coupled with machinery and equipments along with the unfriendly ambience in today's construction. Construction is a lobour intensive activity and that too mostly unorganized, unskilled and mostly illiterate workmen. Further for major projects, parallel activities are carried out.

Industrial accidents especially in the construction sites are considered to be a social issue and a major concern and a greater challenge. Indian construction industry is the second largest employer and economic activity next only to agriculture. It is a fact; the industrial accidental injuries and deaths from construction industry are next only to the road accidents in India. This presentation attempts to bring out the various practical issues, challenges and constraints faced in enforcing Safety at construction sites and its possible solutions based on the achievements at our Construction units at NPCIL projects.

Introduction

Let us broadly speak about the accident scenario, its causes and precautions in general terms. The various accident causation models will out line the importance of a various scientific preventive methods. Right from the Heinrichs Model of Accident Causation to the present Behaviour Based Accident models, the one common concern is the Man in Control. Accident is as a result of a failure on any of the links in the chain connecting from unsafe conditions/practices to the Accident itself. I will try to refresh your informations on this by

*Addl. Chief Engineer (IS & F), Kaiga Generating Station and Kaiga Project 3&4, Nuclear Power Corporation of India Ltd.

just narrating it. Further, we see that the unsafe conditions can be removed by Engineering methods. Unsafe practice deals with the knowledge, skill and alertness of the person and is responsible for majority of the accidental injuries or deaths. Proper training and supervision coupled with Personal Protective Equipments can help remove this aspect. It is the Engineer/ Supervisor on the job and who is present throughout at site; who can control the accident. We have to integrate Safety with the other aspects of the job to get a proper result.

Detailed Descriptions

(a) Accident Causation (Constraints and Solutions for Prevention)

(i) Accident is caused by a combination of a series of factors and gives sufficient warning signals before one actually occurs. We should be sensitive to these signals and symptoms to take corrective measures before it actually occurs. Ultimately, the accident philosophy is not yet different from the one predicted by the Safety Scientist/philosopher Heinrich. Let us analyze how best it is for us to use to get an accident free work place.

(ii) The Heinrich's Domino of accident causation gives the sequences as

Constraints	*Solutions*
An injury is preceded by an accident.	Stop accidents by scientific means
An accident is preceded by unsafe act (U/A) /unsafe condition (U/C)	Detect and correct (U/A)/(U/C) prior to accident through planned Safety surveys.
Unsafe act (U/A)/unsafe condition (U/C)- is the potential for the accident.	Select proper personnel/train for U/A and provide Engineering corrections for U/C.
Faults of persons are responsible for unsafe act/practices.	Proper selection/training and provide better Supervision.
The faults of persons are inherited from social environment/ancestry. In the Birds domino, it is replaced with Lack of Management control.	The unsafe working methods of seniors/ colleagues and the assumption that accident is a matter of luck gives wrong inheritance should change.

We can use this for accident prevention practically. Very specifically the cause of a construction accident is almost solely based on unsafe act and unsafe practices. The Bird's theory of Accident causation model explains the "Faults of Management"- replacing the Accured from Ancestry-philosophy.

(iii) *Heinrich's Triangle of Accident:* Another classic method for accident prevention is the "The Heinrich's triangle of accident" which gives us insight into the cause of an accident. The triangle brings out:

1 Fatality/Serious Accident is preceded by
29 Minor Accidents
300 First-aid Injuries

As per this, we have 329 occasions to prevent one serious or fatal injury. In the advanced concept of accident prevention, the chances of prevention are made broader with the modified triangle of accident causation. It brings out that

One serious/fatal injury
10 Reportable injuries
100 First-aid injuries
10000 Near misses
100000 Behaviour based safety problems

(b) Type of Accidents

Now let us see some important type of accidents in construction sites.

(i)Fall of Persons : One of the most common types of accident in a construction site is due to fall of persons. The constraints leading to this cause are many as indicated below:

(ii) Fall of Material : Now comes next prominent causation factor of construction accident in the form of fall of material. The fall of material may start even from the time of excavation onwards. The different aspects are briefed below and the possible solutions of which are self-explanatory.

Constraints	*Solutions*
Access and Approach to place of Work: Absence of proper access/approach to a place of work at higher elevations.	Providing a proper approach/access to all places of work however elevated it is. This will encourage not only the workers to perform more efficiently but also for better Supervisory coverage leading to improved quality of work preventing accident.
Working Platform: Absence of working platform or improper working platform.	A proper working platform with approach and handrails will not only improve the safety aspects but also the quality and out put preventing an accident.
Floor openings: Floor openings/unguarded floor edges/loose planks/lack of railing/gaps between planks/temporary set up/improper scaffolding/lack of lateral stability and so on.	Unguarded floor opening is one of the main causes of fall from an elevated place to the ground level or form ground level to some basement area and has caused many fatalities. Guarding/covering such openings should be given immediate priority as soon as it is formed on desshuttering. Stair wells should be provided with a hand rail without leaving it as it is.

Contd. ......

Constraints	*Solutions*
Non-use of PPEs and Poor Work Practices: Non-use of/improper use of Safety belts, fall arrestor system, safety net, etc. The line managers/top manager unknowingly accepts the degradation in the use of PPEs as and when they visit the site and some site person talks to them without using the PPE. Also they fail to question in general when some one is found without PPEs at site. This practice should change drastically. Question the site Engineer for violation if any. Industrial safety in construction management deserves utmost attention; especially on work at height as well as welding and cutting job. Workers are yet to understand the concept that PPEs (Personal Protective Equipments) are part of their body when they are at construction site.	With all the Engineering corrections in place, the use of Safety belt in construction area is a must to stop a fall. It shall be used with proper anchoring of its lifeline. Any degradation in this practice shall not be accepted. For straight climbing and descending a fall arrestor system shall be used and wherever it is not practical, a double lifeline Safety Belt shall be used. Please do not accept any degradation. This is practically possible. The concept that use of PPEs retards the movement freedom need to be corrected. A batsman is able to make records in cricket match with all PPEs- we know. For example; Safety Helmet has saved many lives in the past and is an important construction Safety requirement.
Height Passes: Unsuitability for working at height like aerophobia and other medical unfitness can be eliminated by this.	A height pass system shall be insisted and practiced and the persons issued with height pass shall undergo a medical check-up.
PEP talk: Absence of PEP talks or pre-job briefing on accident potential and safety precautions. PEP talk helps in preventing accident to a great length.	A Safety PEP talk is a must in the beginning of each day for about 10 minutes concentrating on the day's activity with a particular crew and the potential areas and precautionary measures to be taken.
Non-availability of trained manpower: Mobilizing large number of workforce for a short period affects the HSE management at construction sites. It becomes imperative to employ more agricultural workers in construction sites due to non-availability of trained workforce and to accommodate the personnel form around. These workforces are unaware of the hazards and risk existing in the industry. Training such workers in short duration to meet the required level of HSE standards becomes a task of over whelming proportions.	Whenever a crew comes to the site, an induction training need to be provided specifically concentrating the work situation and activities and the procedure to be strictly followed in the project. Further, gate pass for entry should be issued only after ensuring this and re-issue of gate pass should be done only after retraining on Safety. Regular task based Safety training should also form a part of the Programme.

Contd. ......

Constraints	*Solutions*
Non-availability of training facility: If we look at Indian construction industry only, it employs 31 million persons - second only to Agriculture in terms of employment. Out of this 85 per cent of workforce is drawn from the rural background. They lack technical perspective and industry relevant commonsense. Other 15 per cent workers have their training through trial and error method. This should change.	There is a need to expand the training and skill programme both in terms of content as well as geographical reach. So an induction training before the person is put on the job at site should be done. Specific training on working at height and confined spaces should be given. It is practically possible, if we give some additional attention. We could succeed at NPCIL on this, very much.
Lack of enforcement by line managers: This is the real crux of the problem. Sincere intention of implementation of the Safety measures through line managers to be exhibited.	Top management should account line management to achieve an accident free status. The saying, "No one can be more Loyal than the King" applies here. It is possible.

- Collapse of earth from the sides of the pit due to improper slope, under cutting or caving in. Storing material at the edge of excavated pits within the restricted zone.
- Improper material handling, stacking, storing, loading, transporting, etc.
- Use of lifting tackles and tools and machineries without thorough inspection and load testing.
- Defective cranes without limit switches, overload relays and non-lubricated bearing parts or cheap hired cranes without any a history of major repair/modifications.
- Improper slinging and rigging practices including poor splicing, inadequate bulldog grips, etc.
- Keeping loose materials at elevated places and poor house keeping.
- Lack of toe boards on handrails.
- Collapse of temporary structure/scaffolding etc.
- Improper and inadequate supervision or poor quality Supervision.

(iii) Electric Shock : Electric shock is a matter of concern whether in construction work or elsewhere but the chances of electrical shock/fatality is quite high in a construction site due to the poor electrical safety practices of temporary nature:

- Use of single insulated wires in place of cables and that to with poor joints - Use Cables only.
- Lack of earthing and inserting bare wires in the sockets - Provide earthing and Plug tops.
- Exposed extension boards/domestic extension boards and lack of ON/OFF switch- Use Industrial type of extension boards and with ON-OFF switch.
- Non-use of ELCBs - Route all portable connections through ELCB.

- Poorly maintained and poorly insulated portable equipments - Practice Regular Preventive maintenance.
- Very long electrical cables from the place of supply to the place of use - The switch point should be easily accessible and nearby while connecting.
- Unqualified/Unskilled electricians: - engage only qualified and authorised electricians.
- Poor preventive maintenance of portable and pedestal electrical power driven tools- Regular preventive maintenance without waiting for break downs.

(c) Some more Typical Constraints other than the above

Based on Field experience, let me bring out some more constraints faced in an Indian scenario of construction as given below:

Some of the research finding related to construction industry by ILO showed that the fatality rates in construction industry were more than 4 times that of manufacturing industry. The possibility of labour accidents arising in the construction industry is more than 40 per cent in comparison with other industrial part together. The cross-section of workforce falling in the accident category is in the age group between 20 and 30. It is also a revealing fact that construction sites in developing countries are 10 times more dangerous than the industrialized nation. We are not an exception. What we require at this moment at any

Constraints	*Possible Solutions*
Lack of comprehensive plan: To reduce gestation period; presently projects are executed on a fast track with parallel activities. Currently projects are taking only 50 per cent of the times what similar projects used to take earlier in the 90's. Clients are highly eager to get the facility handed over to them for quick return.	As a result of squeezed completion schedules, the total and comprehensive advance plan to integrate safety in the project management by contractors is often taking a backseat. A Job hazard analysis for each hazardous job can be done breaking up the job into various activities and detecting hazards at each such activity with possible solutions to take care of this situation.
Poor Electrical cables/Wires and layout: Electrical cables with poor joints and passing across without any concern on cable dressings is stressed again to bring out the concern on this once more. Welding cables meeting electrical cables and lack of earthing, lack of return leads, lack of shielding and non-use of PPEs etc.	Electrical cables should be properly planned and laid to avoid passing on the floor and can be routed along the sides or hanged from the roof. Wherever joint is provided double insulation should be done. For welding; use of lugs, insulated joints and routing the cable separately from electrical cables can be done. Further, concern can be provided on welding return lead, welding permit, shielding of fluxes, PPEs, etc.

Contd. ......

Constraints	*Solutions*
Gas cutting/welding: Lack of valve caps, dragging and rolling, lack of supports, flash back arrestor, poor hoses, tieing with wires instead of clamps and unskilled personnel on the welding cutting job.	Please do not accept any gas cylinder without a valve cap during its transporting, storage and internal movement. Flash back arrestor either regulator mounted or torch mounted can be used. Hoses can be ensured with proper IS marking with proper colour code. Also fire proof sheets can be kept to prevent welding sparks/splatters falling below or so. A welding/cutting permit for construction will be of help.
Deficiencies tolerated in material handling like use of cranes and chain pulley blocks without regular inspection/testing, poor splicing, wrong use of bulldog grips, use of poor quality ropes and defective ropes, etc.	Enforce testing and inspection of cranes and lifting machineries in the beginning and regularly and ensure that no temporary splicing is permitted. Bulldog grips should be properly used and also riggers and signalmen are posted for the job.
The presence of illiterate workers and unskilled workers and the temporary nature of employment creates a challenge. It is generally observed that these workers are insensitive to unsafe conditions and unsafe acts. Further, the contractors - sub-contractors - piece worker - labour supply system compounds the issue. The contractor Resident Managers is often reluctant to incur expenditure necessary for ensuring safety at construction sites.	Make the employees/workers safety sensitive by PEP talks and provide and audit for financial provisions kept for enforcing safety like in other activities of the work.
Ownership for safety by Line management: Safety is a line management function. However line managers often forget their role to enforce Industrial safety at their work front and merely concentrate on achieving their physical progress. Moreover Senior Managers rarely instill and enforce the line managers with their responsibility on industrial safety nor they are made accountable for any safety lapse.	Every line managers have major responsibility to demonstrate the safety culture at work front. Senior Mangers should take account of this as well.

Contd. ......

Constraints	*Solutions*
Retention of Experienced workforce: Due to remoteness and lack of facilities in terms of entertainment, trained workforce leave the site for better prospects at the first opportunity. Especially most of the major construction sites will generally be in remote areas.	This aspect needs to be considered in the labour colony of the contractor by taking initiative by the client.

construction site is a good leader and motivation to strengthen the foundation of safety culture. It is necessary in this the era of globalization that the Indian Contracting companies must ensure that safety management function is integrated with overall project management system and safety culture is inculcated through occupational safety, health and environment management system.

How did we Address the Issues?

We should take a broad ranging approach in its continual efforts to improve safety. We have to establish the concept that Safety in line management function. We have to take stock of the injury details including first-aid cases and near misses while assessing a line managers' performance. We should conduct discussions and seminars specifically for line managers and make it integral part of their work. The system of safety should find a place in the contract document and the cost details should be worked out and checked for implementation. Each contractor's Safety records should form a part of the tender assessment and given a credit while awarding the work. Client should ensure that all Safety requirements are met and cross check with their own Safety assessment.

Safety should be made measurable in addition to its qualitative nature.

Wherever Safety Officers are posted by the contractor as required by the client, it should not be a point of meeting the legal requirement alone; it should be for effective implementation, monitoring and Auditing the safety functions of the contractor.

Conclusion

While concluding; this is to mention that, it is the managerial leadership in terms of their attitude, values, basic beliefs and behaviours and the quality of their interactions with the workforce that will bring the safety culture in to any project. This should be practiced. We need to change our school of thought from Policeman to Coach and a Guide from Safety Officers work point of view. Now mentor is the Buzzword. As we look into the future, it is the people who will make the safety a success. We can make a good progress in our plants and projects and need to continue to improve. Safety practices in the field at all levels should undergo a drastic change in the Indian scenario. What we should try to create is a sense of pride in what we do. Every Safety Officer shall be a human performance agent "by"

Jennifer-Huinink Arnott. He is the human performance communication specialist. This should be made in practice by all, including the line managers.

REFERENCES

Industrial Accident Prevention by H.W. Heinrich, Dan Petersen and Nestor Roos.

Accident Prevention Manual, National Safety Council, USA.

Constraints and solutions in Enforcing Industrial Safety - Paper by T.V. Sudhikumaran, in the 16th Heads of IS & F Meeting of NPCIL at NUB Mumbai, on 18.5.06.

Proceedings of 19th DAE Safety and Occupational Professionals Meet at Kaiga on November 2002.

8

SAFETY ASPECTS IN PLANNING AND CONSTRUCTION

K.M. Soni*

ABSTRACT

Safety in industrial set ups was given due recognition after the employer realized the cost of accidents in terms of compensation, loss of working days, loss of machinery and even labour unrest. In construction sector, importance of safety has not been realized due to workers being in unorganized* sector and poverty and unemployment problems in the country. But due to and enactment of statutory laws, awareness generation among workers for their rights and liberalization and globalization process, employers and contractors will have to follow the safety norms not only for the workers but also to achieve quality in construction and assurance of structural safety to the customers. Hence, safety is going to be of prime concern in near future in the construction. Issues related to safety requirements in construction have been discussed along with the importance of safety programmes.

Introduction

Safety in construction has not been given due recognition in the country due to absence of the safety culture. It was presumed that the safety aspects would enhance the cost and thus these need not to be incorporated in the construction to make construction economical and have a low value of cost benefit ratio. Also in general, safety was related to workers safety only. But due to poverty, unemployment and workers being in unorganized sector, workers always had a fear of losing job if they raised the issue of safety norms even if it was in the statuary or contractual requirement. In case of accidents, workers were left on the mercy of the contractors for compensation. Few might have paid a small amount as compensation but many of them even did not think to talk to them before shunting them out from the construction site. But with the government statutory provisions and increased awareness, appointment of labour welfare officers and establishment of labour courts, contractors and employers had to pay the compensation particularly in big cities. Since the amount of workmen

*Superintending Engineer, C.P.W.D., Indraprastha Bhawan, New Delhi.
email: krishna59soni@yahoo.co.in

compensation became more compared to implementation of safety provisions for the workers, many contractors particularly in the large projects and where accidents risk is high started making provision of safety requirements in their work sites. This has led to initiation of safety concept in construction for workers.

Safety in construction is not limited to workers safety only. If the structure is not safe during its execution and thereafter during its designed life, it can pose safety problems not only to the workers but also to many others. Therefore, a structure must be safe from its execution to its life period, which is possible only if it has been planned, designed and maintained as per codal requirements and quality standards. Thus safety is closely related to the quality. But quality was given a secondary preference over economy due to non-availability of adequate financial resources resulting to adoption of minimum possible standards for construction in general and also due to adopting policy of using labour intensive technologies. In such circumstances safety was further at lower preference. After liberalization and globalization, number of projects started in the country and a lot of financial investment started coming to the country, mechanization and quality came simultaneously so also the safety concept in the construction sector.

Safety Requirements

Safety in the construction includes:

(i) Safety of the structure during its construction and maintenance stage.
(ii) Safety of the workers.
(iii) Safety of the public in general.

Structural Safety

Structural safety is important during construction as well as maintenance stage. Thus a structural safety is to be considered for its lifecycle. Provisions for safety during construction may include the followings:

(a) Foundation safety.
(b) Structural safety during normal and critical conditions.
(c) Fire safety.
(d) Safety due to temporary structures erected for construction.

Foundation of the structure poses a problem of distress as well as failure. Many times, soil investigation is not carried out and foundation is designed on some assumption basis just to save a very small amount to be invested on geotechnical investigation. Also many a times soil investigation is inadequately done. A general concept may sometimes leads to distress of structures that on increasing width or depth of foundation bearing capacity of the soil will increase which may not be true in all conditions. In Salt lake area of Kolkata, upper soil layer is sand as Ganga sand was filled up in the area but below this layer a highly compressible layer is available. Some private constructions collapsed during Gujarat earthquake because the foundation was not adequate. Many small buildings in private construction fall down on vertical extensions. Also cracks and other type of distresses can be seen in many buildings and roads because of inadequate investigations. Liquefaction potential in loose fine-grained soils in earthquake prone regions is very important to be evaluated but the same is normally ignored in the geotechnical investigation, which may lead to foundation failure. In geotechnical investigation, there are number of agencies involved who are not expert but provide consultancy and charge a little less than the good agencies charge. There is no system for selection of good investigation agencies in the country.

Structural safety of a structure is important at execution stage and during post construction stage. Many structures collapse during execution stage. These failures are mostly due to some of the following reasons:

(i) Unsafe design.
(ii) Not following the correct design. The design might have been revised but old execution made based on old drawing. Old drawing is not destroyed, kept at site and even an entry is not made of its revision in the old drawing.
(iii) Collapse of temporary structures like failure of scaffolding, centering and shuttering.
(iv) Incorrect sequence of removal of props like removal of props from fixed side in a cantilever.
(v) Removal of centring and shuttering before specified and required stripping period.
(vi) Use of different grades and types of materials not considered in the design like use of PPC in place of OPC and removing centring and shuttering specified for OPC.
(vii) Poor quality of work.
(viii) Sudden change of conditions like partly constructed underground tank can float if water gets filled up around it due to sudden rains and there is huge uplift which is more than the load of the tank.
(ix) Poor detailing like no overlap of the reinforcement or even say no provision of weep holes in a retaining wall or in a boundary wall leading to water pressure on one side of wall not designed for.

Collapse of the structures at post construction period is also common. These failures may be under normal conditions as well as during critical conditions like earthquakes, cyclones and floods. Some of the reasons are numerated in the followings:

(i) Removal of load bearing structural members.
(ii) Additions and alterations.
(iii) Due to changed conditions because of construction of other structures like underground metro construction may create distress in adjoining structures.
(iv) Natural disasters like earthquakes etc. for which the structures are not designed.
(v) Aging of structures and residual strength not adequate to take loads.
(vi) Poor maintenance conditions leading to deterioration of strength of the structural members.
(vii) Changed use like a building designed for office building being used for library or a cinema hall.
(viii) Poor drainage conditions around the building or rise of ground water table leading to reduction in bearing capacity of the soil.

Safety during maintenance stage includes safety of the structural as well as non-structural members, their repair and maintenance and also safety due to temporary structures or arrangements made for carrying out maintenance. Some of the services are not compatible to the life of the structure like plumbing services. But plumbing and sanitary pipes are not changed after their useful life leading to seepage, which corrode the reinforcement and lead to distress in the structure.

Workers Safety

Workers safety is to be planned and implemented during construction as well during maintenance operations. Workers safety is not given due recognition due to the followings:

(i) Economic considerations.
(ii) Non-availability of safety gadgets.
(iii) Old and outlived machines and equipment.
(iv) No provisions of site and work specific safety measures.
(v) No provisions for health and welfare measures.
(vi) Poor knowledge of machines, equipment and the safety provisions.
(vii) Unawareness.
(viii) Due to bad workmanship.
(ix) Non-adoption of safety measures by workers.
(x) Workers not abiding to safety rules.

Short-term economic consideration is main reason of non-adoption of safety measures by the contractors because they appear to be economical however ultimately in long run they may prove to be costly. They may not make available even basic safety gadgets like helmets and safety belts and may feel that they have achieved economy but even small accidents in two years may lead to higher cost than the cost of safety gadgets. Safety gadgets should be adequate and as per site requirement. Therefore, these are to be planned according to site and work specific requirements.

But it is not always necessary that contractors do not make available safety gadgets or do not make safety provisions. Many times workers do not follow safety rules and even may not use the available safety gadgets regularly. Even workers sometimes meet accidents with their own bad workmanship like not providing correct joint in props or not taking out nails from earlier used props. Most of the labour in the country is illiterate and unskilled. The labour also works seasonally. During festival and harvesting seasons, they normally visit their hometowns. During harvesting they harvest the crops, make some stock of foodgrains for their use and take care of their habitats as this suits to them as well as to the season in the country. During festival season like Diwali, the season is also of social gatherings and marriages, which they utilize for their social obligations. Therefore, the labour do not give high attention to the awareness of the safety measures and also the contractors do not make them aware as they are not sure about the labour workforce whether the same workers are going to work for them.

Public Safety

Like structural and workers safety, public safety is also to be considered during construction as well as during maintenance stage. The provisions for public safety may be required due to the followings:

(i) Storage of construction materials on public roads or public places.
(ii) Fall of construction material due to no provision of barricading and curtains.
(iii) Direct access to site because of no barricading.
(iv) Deep excavations in close vicinity of existing structures without taking sufficient precautions to affect other property.
(v) Excavations in unprotected areas without protecting them with barricading and without display of warning signs.
(vi) Air, water or noise pollution like adopting driven piles for foundation in a habitat area.
(vii) No provisions of basic facilities to workers thereby encroachment by them to public facilities or their misuse.

In the country, though there are adequate laws, rules and regulations but they are seldom followed. Basic reason being that the cost of following such rules and laws works out to be high considering the economic status of an average person. An average person may not make use of ready mix concrete as it may prove him costly compared to cast *in situ* concrete. But during this process he will spread all the materials and cause inconveniences to others. Also a person who can afford may not really bother about public inconvenience due to his status in the society like an influential person may adopt driven piles for his building even if causes a lot of noise pollution for the residents in the area. Therefore, public safety is really not given due importance in the country but this may not last long particularly in cities as the people are now more informative to laws and their rights.

From the above discussion, it can be construed that a safety culture is required to be inculcated in the construction. Like any other activity, safety is also required to be planned, designed, implemented, controlled and reviewed for making changes in policy based on its appraisal. Thus a safety cycle is to be created by having a safety policy in the organizations.

Safety Policy

Safety policy also is to be framed by the top management as any other policy. Preparation of safety policy must include the participation of all stakeholders so that it is planned and designed in the manner that it is implementable. Safety policy should be based on the organization culture and should not just be copied from other organizations where it is being implemented for a long time. It should include the provisions, which are acceptable and implementable in a reasonable period and then should be promulgated and reviewed from time to time. Once the considerable progress is achieved, policy can be revised by adopting more elaborative and stringent safety norms. All the components of the policy like planning, designing, implementation, control and review/appraisal should be indicated clearly and well documented in the policy document.

Planning

Soni (2005, 2006) has described various stages of construction in which safety is to be considered. Safety is to be planned in construction activities right from the concept stage of the project. At present no provision is made in the estimates for safety provisions and as nothing is available free of cost, final result is before us. Even if the employer through contract provisions like in Central P.W.D. contracts makes the safety provisions mandatory, cost for safety provisions find no place in justification cost statements. Therefore, first step should be to include the cost of safety provisions and labour welfare measures in the preliminary estimates and also in the justification. Though it may depend upon the size of the project, beginning can be made from any amount say 0.5 per cent.

Next stage of planning for safety is basically engineering safety which include provision for adequate and reliable survey and investigation including testing of materials, structural safety provisions, fire safety provisions, electrical safety provisions, use of durability based and environment friendly materials and technologies, and strict quality control measures (Soni, 2006).

Idea has been generated that the items of safety requirements can be included in the bill of quantities (BOQ) (Soni, 2006, Patwardhan & Shah, 2006) and it sounds quite well that if the items were paid for, certainly they would be implemented. In case, items are to be included in BOQ, it is to be done in planning stage. It would be proper to examine this issue in detail. Suppose scaffolding or barricading is made part of the BOQ, it can be done and is being included in many contracts. What is required is the provision of designed centring/ scaffolding particularly in complex structures, which is normally made. Therefore, such provisions for structural safety can be made part of BOQ easily and only their implementation is required in execution stage. Particularly in maintenance contracts, these provisions should be made. Similarly provisions for public safety can be made part of the BOQ.

But provisions for workers safety have been suggested to be included in the BOQ. Suppose, helmets are to be provided and this is made part of the contract, it is very difficult to measure how many workers have actually used them or in case, one is not using, how much money is to be deducted from the contractor. Also how will they be accounted for once the work is complete as the helmets will become the property of the employer? However labour welfare measures like provisions of toilets, canteen facilities, jhuggies, crèche, etc. can be made part of BOQ. But major problem in the cities particularly in metropolitan cities is the availability of land and the objection of residents in the vicinity of the site for construction of such facilities. Even now many employers do not provide the place for construction of jhuggies/huts for labour what to talk about construction of other basic facilities. In such circumstances, whole concept of making them part of BOQ sound hollow. In the time to come, there will be a need of construction of multistoried dwelling units for labourers, which can be taken on rent by the contractors where all other facilities will be built in. In those circumstances, the provisions of the cost component will be required to be taken in the estimates. It is better that builders start thinking in this direction soon.

Therefore, it appears to be viable that cost component of safety gadgets required for workers are taken in the cost estimates and also in justification statements to start with so the contractor knows that he has been paid and this provision remains part of the special conditions.

Planning for safety is really a tough job for non-engineered structures where even structural safety measures are not adopted. This may be due to poor conditions of people, unawareness of safety norms, non-availability of designers and standard designs and greed (Soni, 2006). For a check on non-engineered unsafe structures, the role of local bodies, public, government, and engineers is important. The engineers should play a major role in dissemination of knowledge of structural safety norms to stop non-engineered unsafe construction. Soni (2006) has moved an idea of providing subsidy in earthquake prone regions to make their dwelling units earthquake resistant so that loss of lives and property during earthquakes could be minimized.

Designing

If safety is to be designed, it should consider all the provisions whether for the structure, workers or the public. If the structural safety is considered, design codes and National Building Code are available along with many guidelines, reference manuals, and computer programmes. Therefore, there should not be a safety problem if the structure is designed according to codal requirements. Design is to be carried out by a structural designer who has an expertise in it. At present there is no government or autonomous society/institute who certifies the designers. Therefore, it is the high time that some engineering body starts registration of designers for the benefit of the public and the society. It is essential that not only structure is designed but also the entire temporary and safety structures are designed. If a road is under widening or a culvert or a bridge is under construction, there should be no reason that diversion is not designed and commuters are left to high inconveniences. Similarly if a slab is being cast, its centring is not designed. If for fire safety, a corridor or staircase is to be designed, it should be done according to the codal requirements. Therefore, it is important that safety process is included in the design process whether it is earthquake safety, fire safety or workers safety requirements. Local bodies like fire authorities have made mandatory to get the drawings cleared by them before execution. Some banks that are financing the construction activities have also made mandatory requirements for providing loans only if the reputed institutions certify the structural designs. This is a good beginning in the field of structural safety. Local bodies can also enlist reputed and qualified structural designers and clear the drawings for construction only if they certify these. Probably this beginning has also been made in some places but to make the designers accountable, some society should also start registering them.

Implementation

Planning is extremely important process but its implementation is equally important. Many contract documents provides for safety provisions but are hardly implemented. For not implementing these provisions contractor as well as the employer are responsible. In case a contractor has not considered cost of safety provisions in his bid, he will avoid implementing them and if the employer has not implemented safety norms right from the beginning of the work, it would be difficult to implement at a later stage. Apart from this, inertia plays an important role and neither contractor nor employer will implement them so easily, hence, it is up to the top management to see that these provisions are implemented. Even the workers may feel that the safety gadgets are a burden initially due to inertia effect. But once it is implemented and everyone is used to it, safety will become part of the work culture. It is like wearing helmets while riding a bike. A person, who has used it, will not go out without it but it has not been implemented seriously in some city, everyone would like to avoid it.

Control

As already mentioned, inertia would not allow one to go for safety measures whether it is structural safety in engineered or non-engineered structures, workers safety or environmental safety. Therefore, it is to be controlled initially at a larger scale and more frequently and later may be occasionally. For controlling safety, organizations may require safety manuals, formation of safety implementation committees, and safety review committee, safety codes, and safety awareness generation programmes, institution of safety awards for various units and individuals, etc. Also if the safety measures are not implemented, penalties and punishment are to be defined in policy documents. It should also be understood that the controls are not only for penalties or the punishments. By imposing penalties and punishment, no policy can be implemented. If large number of people offends the rules, it indicates that the policy is not suitable for the organization and needs a considerable change. Therefore controls also include the appraisal system.

Appraisal is to be taken from all stakeholders to know the roadblocks in safety implementation programmes. In general top management sometimes feels that appraisal is only to be given by the top management only and changes are to make accordingly and the revised policy also becomes difficult to implement. Therefore 360° appraisal is better than the appraisal from top level only. Such appraisal is to be considered and policy reviewed and corrective measures incorporated in planning and designing of safety policy. Therefore safety policy needs to be flexible and re-planning is to be done according to review and appraisal.

Stakeholders

Stakeholders in the safety programme implementation in construction (including maintenance) include all who are responsible for taking up construction and are the beneficiaries. During planning stage, surveyors, consultants, architects, planning engineers, local bodies and structural engineers have a major role to play. During execution, site engineers, quality managers, contractors, and workers are the stakeholders. During maintenance stage, planners and maintenance engineers have to play their major role. In all the stages, employer who either is beneficiary or the financier has the greatest role to play in safety management. Therefore, all stakeholders are to understand concept and importance of the safety, introduce safety in their work culture then only the safety programme can be successful.

It becomes very difficult to make coordination if there are many stakeholders as each of them has his own limited goals and may ignore the basic organizational objective. Therefore, it is essential that the coordination is made at the senior level and monitoring is done else it would be very difficult to achieve the objective. For example, an architect can say that his duty is to design a structure, which is aesthetically good, and it is upto the designer to see that the structure is designed which is safe for earthquakes. A designer provides for such a heavy reinforcement that it becomes difficult to pour the concrete in a column or in a beam and pose a difficulty for a site engineer but he says that it is not his job to see how the concreting will be done. Similarly a planner says that he has put a condition in the bid documents that the contractor will make double scaffolding but he is not ready to make it a part of BOQ or load the justification. Therefore in such circumstances, no safety programme can be implemented. In actual conditions, such situations do arise. Therefore, coordination is a must right from the concept stage to completion stage between different stakeholders.

Training and Awareness

As already discussed, safety culture is not easy to be inculcate in the construction due to inertia factor. Therefore the inertia is to be removed. Training and awareness generation programmes among all the stakeholders can only do this. Awareness is generated through seminars and conferences for middle level and top level managers but organizations have to spread the awareness to lower level through manuals, workshops, meetings, lectures, and site demonstrations, etc. Particularly for workers level, such programmes can be included in various training centres now being opened for construction workers. Contractors play an important role in safety implementation programmes, therefore, contractor associations should be requested to arrange safety awareness programmes for the contractors and also for their workers.

Public safety is of prime importance as the accidents whether during normal time or during disasters not only kill people but affects nation's economy. Therefore, training and awareness programmes among general people particularly due to structural safety during earthquakes should be arranged at large scales through local bodies.

Cost Benefit Ratio of Safety Programme

In engineering profession, always cost benefit ratio is worked out before taking up any project or programme. There has been a tradition that only direct cost IS considered and indirect cost or indirect benefits are ignored due to the fact that indirect cost or benefits cannot be measured or even estimated easily. If one worker has died due to non-implementation of safety norms, direct cost is worked out based on the compensation paid to the family of the worker. But the cost of sufferings of his family is ignored which is really difficult to estimate or even think unless this incident has occurred to somebody. Think for the structural safety when number of people die due to non-provision of earthquake safety measures in the structures may be buildings or dams, cost saved may be five per cent but can the direct and indirect cost of loss be estimated? Every accident and probably most of the natural disasters can also truly be considered man made accidents if the structures have been built without incorporating safety measures for which technology and knowledge are available. They create a large impact on individuals, society and nation as a whole in terms of losses and progress. Probably accidents send the people many years back in their development, and also to the nation. Think yourself if somebody sends you at the stage when you started before twenty years, you will realize the benefit of the safety measures and probably will not look for its meagre cost. One added advantage is when one thinks for safety, quality gets built in automatically so the contribution to nation's economy also.

Conclusions

Construction poses safety problems to workers as well as to general public. Along with workers safety, structural safety is important which is required to be considered for the life period of the structure. Safety in construction is required to be considered from the concept stage to maintenance stage as it is very difficult to implement the safety norms if the same have not been considered in planning and design stage. This can be achieved by investing a small amount during construction and maintenance, which would reduce the accidents and prove to be economical in long run. Cost of safety provisions should be considered in the preliminary estimates and structural safety requirements should be made part of the bill of quantities. A safety policy should be made in the organizations and awareness should be generated for safety among all the stakeholders. Cost benefit analysis should not be made based on direct cost forming the base for not adopting the safety norms.

REFERENCES

Patwardhan, A.V. and Shah, M.H. (2006). Converting Human Dignity Issues into Contractual Obligations in Construction and Building Industry. *Journal of Indian Buildings Congress*, Vol. XIII, No. II, pp. 123-131.

Soni, K.M. (2005). *Safety in Infrastructure Development*. Proceedings of Challenges of Occupational Safety and Health. The Institution of Engineers (India). September, pp 324-328.

Soni, K.M. (2006). *Safety Management in Construction*. New Buildings Material & Construction World, Vol. 11, Issue 7.

SAFETY DURING CONSTRUCTION OF TRANSMISSION LINE

S.K. Agrawal,* Pankaj Kumar** and Ravi Bhushan***

ABSTRACT

Construction of transmission lines in POWERGRID is mostly being got done through leading transmission lines contractors, who in turn either construct transmission lines by themselves or they sublet construction work to subcontractors. Generally, it is seen that these subcontractors further sublet the construction work to the local contracting agencies with a view of more profitability, ease of management of local man power and easing all other local and industrial relation problems. Some contractors are over enthusiastic in name and fame for completion of transmission lines before schedule. POWERGRID has to construct the transmission lines under very tight schedule to keep pace with National requirements. By doing so contractors at times are bypassing/not adhering the essential safety norms, safety guidelines and safe work practices essentially required to be observed during the construction of transmission lines and substations with the result the workers met with Fatal/Non-Fatal injuries.

During the construction of transmission lines, safety precautions at all levels is essential but because of the tight schedule, meeting targets, unhealthy lifting tools and tackles, lack of Protective Gears and limitations of experienced manpower deployed for both supervision or execution of works. POWERGRID has experienced number of Fatal/Non-Fatal accidents during the construction of transmission lines.

Introduction

Power Grid Corporation of India Ltd. (POWERGRID) is one of the largest transmission utility of the world and being recognized as central transmission utility in India for wheeling of power at the central sector. POWERGRID is presently operating and maintaining 55,000 Ckt. Kms. of transmission lines at 765kV, 400 kV, 220 kV, 132: kV and ± 500kV HVDC system with 95 substations, criss-crossing the entire length and breadth of India. Prime

*GM (OS), Powergrid, New Delhi
**DGM (OS), Powergrid, New Delhi
***Ch. Mgr. (OS), Powergrid, New Delhi

Minister of India has set out the target for providing of quality power to every village by 2012. To meet the challenges thousands of CKT Kms. of transmission lines of different voltages are being added every year to form National Grid.

Keeping in mind the paramount importance of precious loss of human lives, loss of materials and nevertheless delay in execution of the project POWERGRID management constantly reviews its practices and procedures for safety and take appropriate actions accordingly. All laurels go waste, if, a single accident occurred in POWERGRID. In this paper thrust has been given and explained in detail how POWERGRID has made significant effort to develop safety as a culture rather than mere compliance to statutory requirements and adopt safe work practices and procedures during the construction of transmission lines so as to minimize the precious loss of human lives.

Safety During Excavation and Casting of Foundation

Transmission lines foundations are generally dig more three metres or more than that and there is always possibility of workers to trap in the pit if the soil starta is very loose and proper safety procedure are not being adopted by the workers. So before starting foundation work, soil investigation strata especially of loose soil should be known and in case of loose soil/black cotton soil or where the water table is 0.75 mtr. below the ground level in such cases contractor be advised to make perfect arrangement of dewatering by deploying numbers of dewatering pumps around the pit and shuttering be erected to avoid collapse of pit in such stretches. Mostly foundations work is being executed by the small subcontractor who cannot manage better quality of shuttering and requisite boring and dewatering arrangement in loose foundations in such cases where pit collapsing chances are more main contractor who have enough resources of experienced manpower, machinery and equipment to dig such foundations and cast such dangerous locations departmentally. It is advisable to use good quality wooden shuttering or support of shuttering with strong iron angle of requisite strength and planks to comply with the requirement of IS 3764 "Safety during excavation work". Steel shuttering arrangement is the best alternative but it is very expensive and hence normally contractors do not prefer to procure it for few locations.

Dewatering pumps to be installed in case of water table is near the ground level

Jacks for fixing of template placed very near to edge of pit

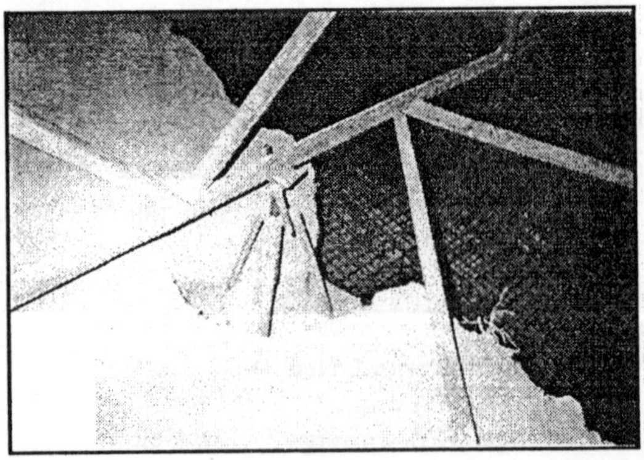

(i) All excavations should be inspected thoroughly by a competent person before start of work to assess the hazard during excavation and accordingly take remedial measures.

(ii) Where subsoil water level is very high and pit collapsing chances are more, good quality shuttering will be effective along with boring and dewatering arrangement with the help of adequate number of dewatering pumps.

(iii) Dewatering should be continued for 24 to 48 hours up to the opening time of form boxes to avoid accident during opening of form boxes.

(iv) Vertical excavation in foundation shall be avoided, generally 1:4 slope or step cutting is considered safe. For loose, soft or slushy soil inclination of slope shall be increased suitably.

(v) Excavated soil shall be stacking at least1.5 Mtrs. or half the depth of pit which ever is more, away from the edge of pit.

(vi) Generally, jacks are being used for erection of tower template required during casting of foundation it is advisable that these jacks are placed on wooden/steel base, so as to transmit the load of template uniformly on ground so jacks supporting the template should not be placed very nearer to edge of pit.

(vii) Machines developing vibrations like concrete mixture, vibrator etc. should be placed away (minimum distance equal to the depth of the pit) from the edge of excavation to avoid development of cracks due to external vibrations.

(viii) During excavation availability of ladder of sound construction shall be ensure with extension of at least one metre above the ground-level for easy ingress and outgress of working personnels.

Tower Errection

Tower erection is one of the critical activity during construction of transmission line which requires utmost attention involving Supervision, Deployment of skilled man power, Safe rigging procedures, Use of healthy lifting tools and tackles being used during tower erection, Personal Protective Equipment, Training to staff, Safety Audit etc. to avoid mishaps.

Some of the safety aspects required to be taken care of during excavation work are as follows:

Supervision of Rigging and Pulling Arrangement

The main contractor whom the work of tower erection has been awarded sublet the work to subcontractor. The subcontractor also does not appoint worker or casual workers for supervision purpose but further sublets the works to another subcontractor on rate contract basis. The subcontractor further sublet the works to even individual or group of workers/ working gang on basis of rate of per tower erected. In such cases, contractor treats himself to be fully relieved of his responsibilities of supervision of works. The main contractor/sub-contractor issues only tower material parts and some minimal required T&P to his sub-contractor/working gang. In transmission line a contractor deploy only few supervisors for superficial/peripheral works. Supervision on material handling, way leave problem, measurement of works by POWERGRID and chasing of payments as well as other coordination problem. So there is always lack of manpower deployed for supervision of work executed safely by the workers.

Worker should use personal protective equipment like safety helmet, safety shoes.

Excavated soil should not be placed very near to edge of the pit.

Personal Protective Equipment

Use of Personal Protective Equipment

Use of personal safety equipment (PPEs) was neglected by the subcontractor/main contractor and resisted to implement them on the grounds that it affects the work progress. Mostly workers including skilled workers are uneducated and gain skills through their experience only, they fell inconvenient in use of safety belt/helmet in the beginning but after some time with their experience they realize that these equipments are meant only for their personal safety.

Negligence of Contractor in issue of Personnel Protective Equipment

Workers are not fully aware about importance of safety hence they had never insisted for issue of personal safety equipment. Main contractors don't bother about personal safety equipment for workers engaged through their subcontractor. It has been observed that the personal safety equipment were purchased by the contractor only after taking hard decision by POWERGRID for stopping the work.

Issue of non-Standard and Defective Personal Protective Equipment by the Contractor

During site visits/internal inspection, safety belts/safety helmets were found of non-standard quality. The reason behind procurement of Non-standard safety belt are as under:

(i) Very rare suppliers got ISI approval but it is difficult to enquire about the manufacturers supplying safety equipment conforming to Indian Standard. Numbers of manufacturers supply safety belts and helmets conforming to Indian Standard, but it came to notice that they have not been approved by IS.

(ii) The standard IS mark safety belts are costlier than ordinary one. Normally contractor procures cheapest Personal Protective Equipments available from local market. POWERGRID is insisting to use only quality Safety Belts, Safety Helmets being procured directly from reputed manufacturer get approval from POWERGRID before issuing it to the worker.

Negligence from workers side in use of Personal Protective Equipment

Mostly it is observed that workers in construction of transmission lines including skilled workers are uneducated and from very poor section of society and also do not come forward at their own for issue of safety equipments. They start working at very early age from materials handling at the ground level. Since they have not been trained for use of safety equipment and they are not really aware of the importance of safety and have been neglecting its use. Due to various reasons given above. The ultimate result is that the workers are not only negligent in use of personal protective equipment but try to oppose them for issue from subcontractor side or main contractor side.

Safe methods of work should be adopted during excavation.

Concrete mixture should not be placed near the edge of the pit.

Safe Rigging Arrangement

Transmission line towers are generally located in the remote areas. The work is scattered over long distances and there is no concentration of work at any single point, it is uneconomical to mechanize the whole process of erection. Moreover manual labour is quite cheap in India as such contractors finding it more economical and convenient to get the work done manually rather than mechanically. Skilled and experienced manpower should be deployed as hazards of accidents during tower erection are more.

The height of 400 KV transmission line tower varies from 30 Mtrs to over 50 Mtrs, more than 50 Mtrs. are special towers. For erection of towers at such heights, adequate rigging arrangement is to be made for lifting of single member or semi-assembled structures. In majority of the cases such structures are lifted through derrick and pulleys. Derricks are fixed appropriately with a pulley at its top for lifting structures upto the desired height. Under such conditions the bottom of the derrick is to be supported on some member of the tower already erected, top portion of the Derrick has to be anchored at 3 points in 3 different directions. Crow bars are driven in the ground at 3 points and matching with the guying angle to take care of full load coming on guy and Derrick is guyed with these crowbars through ropes. Deficiency has been found in the following aspects:

(a) The strength of the soil at site is known through general assumption by driving the crowbars in the ground by simple hammering on the crowbar by casual workers. By virtue of experience, they guess firmness of the crowbars during hammering or by their own hand. Angle of driven crowbar is also not checked and it is fixed by the workers simply by virtue of their experience.

(b) Proper tension in the ropes supporting the derrick are to be ensured when one end of the ropes is first fixed at the top of the derrick, tension is given to the ropes by pulling it from the second end through the crowbars. Assessment of tension in ropes is made by the workers by their experience and with hands only. Pulleys, slings and D-Shackles etc. are also not inspected very carefully before they are

Some snaps of tower erection, testing of lifting tools and tackles and Personal Protective equipment.

Educate worker before start of work

Supervise each activity for dangers and All workers must use personal protective equipment while working at height.

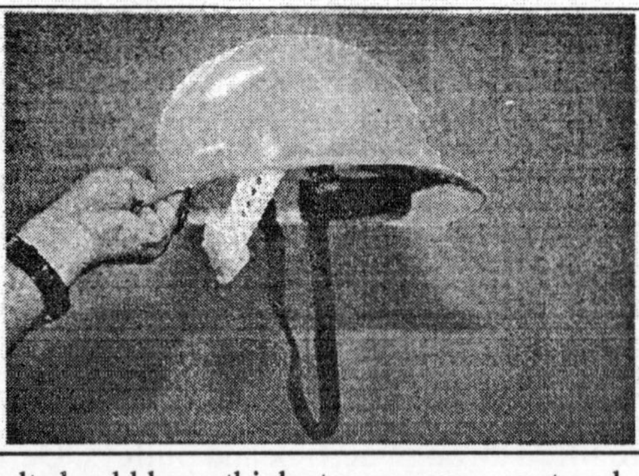

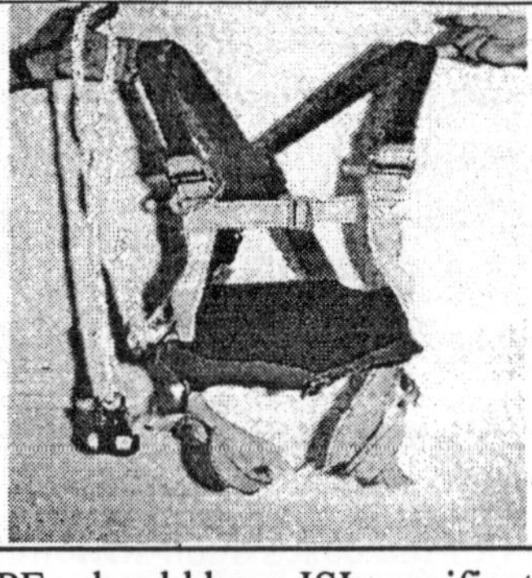

Safety Belt should have thigh strap arrangement and all PPEs should have ISI specifications.

actually fixed or used for tower erection. Direction of pulley is also decided by the convenient direction available for manual pulling or pulling with the help of tractor. No assessment is made for proper direction of pulley keeping in mind the strength of rigging and guying arrangement etc. of the tower. In view of the above, it can be said that rigging arrangement is very crude method of tower erection.

Some of the safety aspects required to be taken care of during tower errection are as follows:

End towers should be guyed

Dia. of guy wire rope should not be less than 16 mm

Do not over tension cross arm other wise it will buckle.

Use regulation winch machine during final sag.

(c) The lifting tools and tackles used should be tested by the competent person for the safe working load and its healthyness should be ensured before they are being used at site.

Continuous Training of Workers as Essential Safety Requirements

There are only a few transmission lines contractors in India, some of them, who can be treated amongst best and well established contractors, have training facilities for their supervisors and engineers in tower erection and other construction activities of transmission lines. However, basically due to labour problem and high wages of the departmental workers, contractors are switching over more and more towards subletting of work to very small contractors or directly to casual workers. There is absolutely no system available for training of such workers, who have practically become actual workers. It has been seen in majority of cases that none of the worker during tower erection including gang leader have gone through any formal training for construction of transmission lines including tower erection and stringing. These people use only a custom built method for tower erection and cannot analyze special feature of any location or meeting unusual occurrences. They are fully dependent on the T&P issued by the main contractor and don't have adequate training for scientific supervision/development of the skill.

(i) Check back filling has been done prior to erection activity.
(ii) Check the derrick used before structure to be erected has been checked for adequate strength/size and no joints are permitted (Test certificate are required apart from visual inspection).

(iii) Check that the pulleys used before structure erection/equipment erection has been checked for adequate strength/proper size (diameter), also in case of open type pulleys proper locking arrangements like providing of safety pin is made safe working load should be punched. (Test certificate are required apart from visual inspection).

(iv) Check that the rope used before structure erection/equipment erection has been checked for adequate strength/physical condition (free from break of strands and knots etc.). (Test certificate are required apart from visual inspection).

Safety Aspect During Stringing

To carry out work of stringing activity smoothly and safely one has to ensure that the following aspects has been taken care.

Supervision, Skilled and experience manpower, Adoption of safe work procedure, Use of healthy lifting tools and tackles, Earthing of LT lines, Erection of strong scaffoldings, Use of Personal Protective Equipment, Safety Audit and Training of staff.

To ensure safety during stringing more efforts are required to be taken by the contractor and more effective supervision by POWERGRID is essential.

Given below is the listing of precautions to be taken by contractors/subcontractors as well as by POWERGRID.

From Contractor Side

Tools and Plants

The quality of Tools & Plants being used and required for stringing are more costlier in comparison to T&P for the other work of transmission line. Due to heavy cost reflection in purchases of T&P for stringing, contractors are using old T&Ps, specially the pilot wire which may be defective due to cuts/dents during the stringing. Normally contractors do not turn up to purchase new pilot wires because of costly items. Pilot wires of better quality are to be imported. In view of the above mostly old pilot wires with minor repairing/making joints are being used which may lead to the accident. It has been seen that number of accidents cases have occurred due to failure of pilot wire.

Second sensitive T&P item is auto-comealong clamp, which has become most commonly being used in place of bolted type come along clamp. It has been observed through enquiry about the quality of clamp and came to know that these clamps were fabricated locally. Other auto-come along clamps were of imported quality from Italy. After observing the failure a decision was taken to put double clamps one auto and one bolted type specially for giving anchoring for a longer period of night hours.

Apart form above lifting tools and tackles items like D-shackle, rollers, slings, rope pulleys, ropes, rope slings, winch machines should also be of tested from quality point of view and of appropriate rating to withstand the safe working load. Moreover these Tools and Plants are to be tested from the competent authority.

Experienced Manpower

Normally stringing activity involves the adequate manpower including skilled/semiskilled workers. Minor mistakes of the puller/tensioner operator may lead to major accident. Therefore, the manpower involves in tension and pulling machine operation should be trained.

Effective Communication System

Communication between two puller and tensioner operations is the very important from the safety point of view. Normally contractors were doing the paying out of conductor by receiving indications through the flag operated by men deputed on each and every tower. Always there have been chances of mismatching and consequent accident.

Walky-talky sets are best alternative to operate between stringing machines tensioned and pullers on both sides of the stringing side also in between the tower along with the flag man for prompt communication and minimizes the misshappening but contractors are facing some time problems in getting permission from district authorities. In some cases POWERGRID manages and helping the contractors in obtaining the permission from district authorities for operating the walky-talky sets.

Erection of Strong Scaffolding

Stringing activity sometimes has to come across number of village roads, nallahs, small rivers, national highways and rail crossings etc. so as to cross these barriers erection of strong scaffolding is essential. Use of wooden *ballies* or iron girders and ropes is required to be ensured to build scaffolding strong enough to take the full load during laying and stringing of wire.

Adequate Personal Protective Equipment

Contactor has to ensure that all workmen working during tower stringing are being issued IS marked Personal Protective Equipment and they are using them at works.

From POWERGRID Side

POWERGRID has been managing the shutdown on LT/HT lines during stringing. No accident case was seen during HT lines shutdown because everyone is much more careful and also paying much attention during availing the shutdown on HT lines. But some accident cases have been reported during availing shutdown of LT lines. The reason was "No responsible persons were deputed on 33/11 KV substations or at the place of isolation by State Electricity Boards."

Instances has come to the notice that some SEBs Substations makes lot of irregularities while issuing shutdown. They did not keep off the feeder on which requisition was given and did not do the earthing to drain out induced voltages and gave the clearance, resulting, occurrence of serious accidents of electrocution. In some cases, they charged the feeder without getting return of shutdown in confusion or because sometimes of ignorance from local pressurizing peoples.

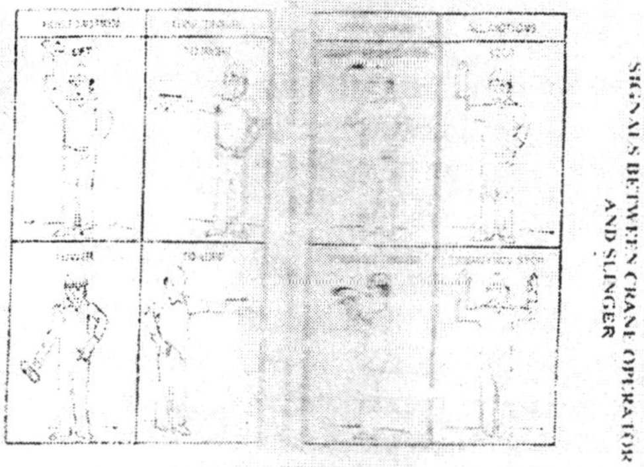

Follow rigging rules

Before stringing of insulator string check of Split lock in the disc. Insulators

Rigging arrangement should be checked before stringing.

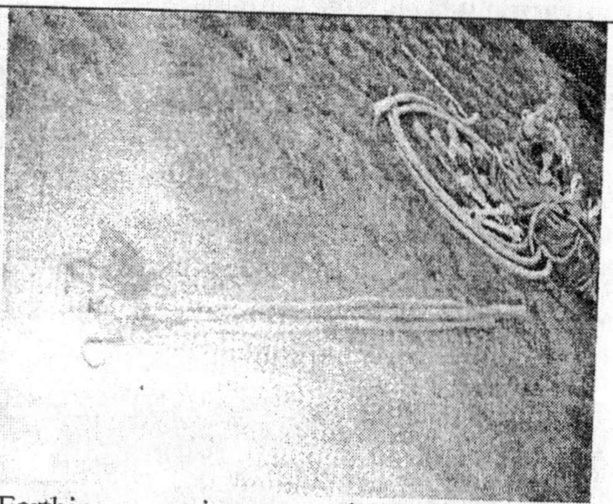

Earthing equipment should be of IS specification. Do not use local made earthing.

To avoid these type of misshappening, representative of POWERGRID is very much conscious during LT line shutdown and ensures that possibly one man is being deputed extremely for taking care of LT line shutdown.

LT Line is being earthed positively with discharge rod/earthing chain before starting work on line and remain effective till the end of the work or as per the work permit.

Some Safety Tips Required during Stringing Activities

(a) Ensure the back filling of the foundation has been done as per specifications.

(b) At very stage due care should be taken in stringing, while transporting insulators, hardware fittings, conductors, earth-wire adequate precaution must be taken.

(c) Operation of winch, tractor or tension puller should be done by skilled and trained operators while providing tension in conductor dynamometer should be used.

(d) When conductors shield wires, pilot wire or hauling wires are to be pulled out, the running blocks at suspension towers should be bonded to the tower cross arm from which they are suspended and should provide an efficient earth path from the conductor to the tower.

(e) PTW of crossing lines equipment is necessary local earthing must be provided both sides of the object under question.
(f) When conductors have been landed and jumpers have been connected, the jumpers must be earthed before the earths bridging the insulator string are removed.
(g) Electrical clearances are to be maintained.
(h) Safety - Register to be available at site.

T&P for lifting arrangement etc. So there is need of the hour to give formal training programmes for the workers of contractor.

As per regulations presently in force, contractors are responsible for supervision of quality work and also for safety of their own workers and the adjoining working conditions but the main responsibility of maintaining the safe working environment rests with Powergrid organization who is executing the work. So all out efforts are being maintained to maintain the safe working environment, healthy and safe working conditions of the personnel's deployed for supervision works by Powergrid Engineer and supervisors. For this POWERGRID has its own Human Resource Department in all the regions and have an annual training calendar. The staff of POWERGRID is being trained by in-house and outside faculty as per the annual training schedule. Employees at different level are being trained and developed from time to time. Practical training programmes at site are also being organized, apart from above the department also organized extra special training programmes including First Aid Techniques for the development of workers and engineers at all levels.

Safety awareness program at const. sites.

First Aid Training for all the gang leaders and supervisors.

Continuous Improvement of Safety Culture - Safety Audit

It is essential that the highest safety standards are maintained throughout the construction activities which can only be ensured through proper safety audit. Any improvement in the system can be judged by the way of safety audit for which Powergrid has developed the format for the Safety audit during construction of transmission lines. There is always scope of improvement in the system which can be detected and modified accordingly.

The safety audit should not be seen as a means of judging an individual's performance.

Conclusion

By adopting a mixture of activities and initiatives, workmen of contractors as well as those of POWERGRID have been geared up mentally to adopt safety measures while working. Meeting the statutory requirements as well as use of proper tools, tackles and other equipment have resulted in an actual reduction in the rate of accidents.

Acknowledgements

The authors are grateful to POWERGRID management for granting permission to write and present this paper. The views expressed in this paper are of the authors only and not of the management.

Bibliography

(i) Safety Manual - POWERGRID
(ii) O&M Manual of Transmission lines - CBIP
(iii) Construction Manual of Transmission lines - CBIP
(iv) IS 18001: 2000 - Occupational Health and Safety Management System-specification with guidance for use
(v) OHSAS 18001: 1999 - Occupational Health and Scifety Management System Specifications
(vi) J. Haque, Umesh Chandra and S.K. Agrawal, "Safety issues in power transmission sector" published in "Managing safety: Challenges ahead" Theme: Safety & Hazard Control held in February '2005 organized by Safety and Quality forum, Institution of Engineers - pp. 140 to 150

10

NATIONAL BUILDING CODE OF INDIA AND ITS RELEVANCE TO BUILDING CONSTRUCTION SECTOR

Sanjay Pant*

ABSTRACT

Buildings make an immense impact on quality of life. A holistic approach of building construction with overall aim to affect the quality of life positively on long-term basis has to take care of quality, safety, energy efficiency and conservation and environment protection all leading to sustainable development. It is imperative that a complete philosophy to take cognizance of the above concerns is consistently built in any endeavour towards streamlining the land and building development activity. The recently brought out National Building Code of India 2005 addresses these aspects in a coherent way while laying down provisions for different aspects of building activity such as planning, designing, construction, operation and maintenance, repairs and retrofitting, etc. The Code not only gives the complete network of provisions, information and guidelines but also provides for detailed administrative mechanism to ensure compliance to the same.

Introduction

Construction programmes are interwoven in a large measure in all sectors of development be it housing, transport, industry, irrigation, power, agriculture, education or health. Construction, both public and private, accounts for about fifty per cent of the total outlay in any five year Plan. Half of the total money spent on construction activities is spent on buildings for residential, industrial, commercial, administrative, education, medical, municipal and entertainment uses. It is estimated that about half of the total outlay on buildings would be on housing. It is imperative that for such a large national investment, optimum returns are assured and wastage in construction is avoided.

*Joint Director (Civil Engg) & Member-Secretary, National Building, Code Sectional Committee Bureau of Indian Standards, New Delhi.

Soon after the Third Plan, the Planning Commission decided that the whole gamut of operations involved in construction, such as administrative, organizational, financial and technical aspects, be studied in depth. For this study, a Panel of Experts was appointed in 1965 by the Planning Commission and its recommendations are found in the 'Report on Economies in Construction Costs' published in 1968. These studies led to conclusion that one of the important steps towards achieving economy is through the formulation of a unified building code at the national level, which would rationalize and unify building codes and bye-laws of various departments and local bodies respectively and which would reflect the latest trends in building construction activity. For this, it was recommended that a National Building Code be prepared to unify the building regulations throughout the country for use by government departments, municipal bodies and other construction agencies. The first version of the Code was published in 1970 by the then Indian Standards Institution (now Bureau of Indian Standards).

Since the publication in 1970 version of the National Building Code of India, a large number of comments and useful suggestions for modifications and additions to different parts and sections of the Code were received as a result of use of the Code by all concerned, and revision work of building bye-laws of some States. Based on the comments and suggestions received the National Building Code of India, 1970 was revised in 1983. Thereafter three major amendments were issued, two in 1987 and the third in 1997 to the Code.

The Revised Building Code

Considering a series of further developments in the field of building construction including the lessons learnt in the aftermath of number of natural calamities like devastating earthquakes and super cyclones witnessed by the country, a Project for comprehensive revision of NBC was taken up under the aegis of National Building Code Sectional Committee, CED 46 of BIS and its 18 expert Panels; involving as many as 400 experts. As a culmination of the Project, the revised NBC has been brought out in 2005 as National Building Code of India 2005 reflecting the state-of-the-art, contemporary applicable international practices and aspiration of the people of the country. The salient features of this latest revision of the Code are:

(1) Inclusion of a complete philosophy and direction for successfully accomplishing the building projects through Integrated Multi-disciplinary Approach right from conceptual stage through planning, designing, construction, operation and maintenance stages.
(2) A series of reforms in building permit process.
(3) Provisions for ensuring safety of buildings against natural disaster and certification of structural sufficiency by engineer and structural engineer.
(4) Provision for two stage permit for high rise residential and special buildings.
(5) Provision for periodic renewal certificate of occupied buildings from structural, fire, electrical health safety point of view.
(6) Provision for empowering engineers and architects for sanctioning plans of residential buildings up to 500 m^2.

(7) Inclusion of detailed town planning norms for various amenities such as educational facilities, medical facilities, distribution services, police, civil defence, fire services, etc.
(8) Revision of parking requirements for metro and mega cities.
(9) Updating of special requirements for low income housing for urban areas.
(10) Inclusion of special requirements for low income housing for rural habitat planning.
(11) Inclusion of guidelines for development planning for hilly areas.
(12) Revision of the provisions for buildings and facilities for physically challenged.
(13) Fire safety norms completely revamped through detailed provisions on Fire Prevention, Life Safety and Fire Protection.
(14) Inclusion of new categories of starred hotels, heritage structures and archaeological monuments for fire safety provisions.
(15) Substitution of halon based fire extinguishers/fire fighting system.
(16) Promotion to new/innovative building materials/technologies.
(17) Inclusion of latest provisions for earthquake resistant design and construction.
(18) Inclusion of details on multi-disaster prone districts.
(19) Inclusion of new chapter on design and construction using bamboo.
(20) Chapter on prefabricated and composite construction for speedier construction.
(21) Updating of provision of safety in construction.
(22) Complete revision of provision on building and plumbing services in line with applicable international practices.
(23) Provisions on rain water harvesting.
(24) Inclusion of new chapter to cover landscaping needs.

Actual Coverage of the Code

The National Building Code lays down a set of minimum provisions designed to protect the safety of the public with regard to structural sufficiency, fire safety and health aspects of buildings; so long as these basic requirements are met, the choice of material, methods of design and construction is left to the ingenuity of competent professionals. It covers, *inter alia* the following important aspects:

(a) Integrated approach through multi-disciplinary team work to obtain maximum benefits in terms of quality, timely completion and cost effectiveness by utilizing appropriate knowledge and experience of qualified professionals right from the conceptualization through construction and completion stages of a building project and in deed during the entire life cycle.
(b) Administrative provisions which pertain to the efficiency and effective application of the Code defining powers, duties and responsibilities of those concerned;
(c) Requirements to ensure safety from fire and health hazards related to the occupancy and use of buildings;
(d) Stipulations with regard to use of accepted and new building materials from consideration of safety, performance, compatibility, durability and economy;
(e) Design practices for structures as a whole using various materials like reinforced and prestressed concrete, structural steel, timber, bamboo, masonry, etc., and

guidelines for design of prefabricated structures and mixed/composite constructions, duly taking into account the various loads, forces and effects including due to natural calamities like earthquake;

(f) Measures to ensure safety of workers and public during construction;

(g) Provisions for safe and efficient design of lighting, ventilation, electrical and allied installations, air-conditioning, heating, lift and escalator installations, and acoustics systems; and

(h) Provisions with regard to the requirements of water supply, drainage and sanitation including solid waste management and the design of water supply and drainage system in buildings, and safety requirements for the installation of gas supply.

(j) Requirements regarding landscape planning and design, signs and outdoor display structures with a view to promoting safety and quality of outdoor built environment.

This information is brought out in 11 Parts, details of which are given below:

Part 0 Integrated Approach–Prerequisite for Applying Provisions of the Code
Part 1 Definitions
Part 2 Administration
Part 3 Development Control Rules and General Building Requirements
Part 4 Fire and Life Safety
Part 5 Building Materials
Part 6 Structural Design
- Section 1 Loads, Forces and Effects
- Section 2 Soils and Foundations
- Section 3 Timber and Bamboo
  - 3A Timber
  - 3B Bamboo
- Section 4 Masonry
- Section 5 Concrete
  - 5A Plain and Reinforced Concrete
  - 5B Prestressed Concrete
- Section 6 Steel
- Section 7 Prefabrication, Systems Building and Mixed/ Composite Construction
  - 7A Prefabricated Concrete
  - 7B Systems Building and Mixed/Composite Construction

Part 7 Constructional Practices and Safety
Part 8 Building Services
- Section 1 Lighting and Ventilation
- Section 2 Electrical and Allied Installations
- Section 3 Air-conditioning, Heating and Mechanical Ventilation
- Section 4 Acoustics, Sound Insulation and Noise Control
- Section 5 Installation of Lifts and Escalators

Part 9 Plumbing Services
- Section 1 Water Supply, Drainage and Sanitation (including Solid Waste Management)
- Section 2 Gas Supply

Part 10 Landscaping Signs and Outdoor Display Structures
- Section 1 Landscape Planning and Design
- Section 2 Signs and Outdoor Display Structures

Theme of the Code

The National Building Code of India is a single document in which, like a network, the information contained in various Indian Standards is woven into a pattern of continuity and cogency with the interdependent requirements of Parts/Sections of the Code carefully analyzed and fitted in to make the whole document a cogent continuous volume. Thus the Code gives all the information required by the architect, engineer, structural engineer, construction engineer, services engineers and other professionals from the early stages of planning to translating the building on to *terra firma*.

The provisions of the whole Code have been drafted with performance orientation, with a view to give full freedom to the ingenuity of the architects and engineers. However, in certain cases, these performance oriented clauses have been translated into empirical rules for easy implementation of such provisions.

The whole Code has been built around the four pillars of safety, namely, (i) structural safety, (ii) health safety, (iii) fire safety, and (iv) public safety (encompassing electrical safety and safety during construction). The various provisions of this Code have been specified after checking them against these safety requirements.

This Code strongly emphasizes the importance of preplanning in the construction activity and lays down areas where preplanning would have to be done in a more co-ordinated manner. A continuous thread of preplanning is woven which, in itself, contributes almost two-thirds of economics in construction particularly in building and plumbing services. The need for spaces and areas required for such services is brought out so that the same can be assessed at the planning stage and provided for.

The need for proper planning and coordination among professionals right from conceptualization to completion and subsequently in operation and maintenance, has been conspicuously brought out in Part 0 of this Code.

As this Code is intended to help regulate the building construction activity for the whole country, this would be applicable to municipal corporations, local urban bodies, public works departments and other construction departments and agencies dealing with construction. Therefore, the administrative bye-laws and technical provisions, which are required in these regulatory media, are both included in the Code.

The Code as now published represents the present state of knowledge on various aspects of building construction. The process of preparation of the Code has thrown a number of important issues which have been duly dealt with. However, a continuous programme is envisaged by which additional knowledge that is gained through technological evolution, users' views over a period of time pinpointing areas of clarification and coverage and results of research in various connected fields, would be incorporated in the Code from time to time to make it a living document.

Safety–The Prime Concern

India is a disaster-prone country with certain regions having multi-disaster vulnerability. The country has been witnessing a huge loss of life and property during the series of natural calamities such as earthquakes and super cyclones faced in last one and a half decade. It is important to have required preparedness to meet such challenges caused by nature. Then there are man-made disasters too like conflagration. While buildings are intended to provide safety and security, it is the inadequately conceived, designed and constructed buildings themselves which have proved to be death-traps in the event of an earthquake or cyclone or a fire. With vast stretches prone to high seismicity, the long coastline, high snow and rainfall regions, hilly regions with fragile ecosystem and urban agglomerates with mushrooming skyscrapers, disasters are waiting to happen. The scale of these disasters or calamities, or just the vulnerability to these, brings unmatched challenges to the profession of building construction. Properly designed and constructed houses and other buildings can substantially mitigate the miseries inflected by the fury of nature.

Notwithstanding these vulnerabilities, infrastructure development and importance of building construction would continue to be high on our national agenda. It is, therefore, imperative that, considering the well-being of people and the huge national investment involved, 'safety' along with economy should be given prime importance in the whole scheme of things. A considered approach towards safety perceptions and giving it its due precedence over other important considerations such as comfort and aesthetics, is the need of the hour. The tragic loss of human lives and property can indeed be prevented. Standardization and enforcement of standards hold the answer.

Standards in Civil Engineering make an enormous contribution for enabling a safer world. Safety considerations have immense importance, which need to be kept in mind and built-in at all stages such as planning, designing, construction, operation and maintenance of civil engineering projects. During the above stages, the aspects like orientation, lighting and ventilation; fire safety provisions; safety through structural design; safety during construction and safety in electrical/other services related aspects; etc., need to be taken care of. A series of Indian Standards have been developed to cover the whole gamut of safety considerations and necessary recommendations have been provided therein for guidance and implementation by all concerned, as follows:

On Health Safety - The aspects like orientation, lighting and ventilation and functionality have a bearing on hygiene and health of people including workers in industrial units, for which a number of Indian Standards have been formulated covering aspects like day lighting, ventilation, noise reduction, facilities for physically challenged, etc. as applicable to various building occupancy types. Similarly the standards on water supply, drainage and sanitation have an important role to play as regards health and hygiene of occupants/users of buildings.

On Fire Safety - Fire Safety is assuming an increasing importance in view of complexities now encountered in buildings and installations built to meet the challenging requirements of today. Indian Standards have, therefore, been developed in the vast area of fire safety covering provisions and guidelines on fire safety of buildings of various types including residential, educational, industrial, etc. and their further sub-categories.

On Structural Safety - Structural design of buildings and other structures takes care of various possible loads, forces and effects likely to be encountered during life cycle of building/structure, affecting strength, stability and safety. Loading Codes and Design Codes have, therefore, been developed providing comprehensive guidance to design a structure taking cognizance of dead load, imposed load, wind load, snow load, seismic forces, cyclone resistance and landslide control, and the load combination. Such comprehensive Design Codes are made available for design of safe and stable structures using various material streams like concrete, steel, timber, bamboo, masonry and even using prefabricated construction techniques.

On Public Safety - Safety during construction is another area which has been given the attention it deserves and a number of Indian Standards covering aspects like safety during excavation, blasting work, tunneling work, deep foundation work, while working at height, handling of materials likely to cause harm, etc., have been formulated. Safety from electrical and allied installations and in different building services has also been dealt with in number of standards developed in the field. Equally important are the provisions laid down regarding gas supply for ensuring safety.

Notwithstanding the above, the repeated onslaught of natural calamities such as earthquakes, cyclones, landslides, etc. faced by the country and the man-made disasters such as fire, has brought home the ever increasing need for the common guiding document to enable monitoring and implementation of sound technical provisions and practices through techno-administrative mechanism and comprehensive features built-in, in such a document. The NBC fulfills this need. All the relevant aspects and provisions specific to buildings, have been in-built and interwoven in the National Building Code of India 2005, which can be effectively used as an instrument for regulating the building activity in the country and thereby ensuring implementation of safety aspects dealt with in Indian Standards.

The whole Code has been built around the four pillars of safety, namely, (i) structural safety, (ii) health safety, (iii) fire safety, and (iv) public safety (encompassing electrical safety and safety during construction). The various provisions of NBC 2005 have been specified after checking them against these safety requirements. Particularly, the structural safety provisions take care of the latest technological advancements to meet the onslaught of natural calamities by designing and constructing the building to withstand the loads, forces and effect due to such natural calamities including devastating earthquakes and defining the responsibilities of competent professionals to carry out safe design and construction of buildings. The continuous thread of 'preplanning' woven itself contributes considerably safety in the construction of building and thereafter in safety of building and its occupants during its use.

The revised Code has the necessary ingredients for ensuring safe and orderly development of our villages, towns and cities. In a disaster-prone country like ours, NBC 2005 would serve as an effective tool for design and construction engineers, architects, government construction departments and other construction agencies, builders and developers and for administrators/local bodies to ensure safe, healthy and sustainable habitat for citizens of our country.

Sustainable Development

A closer look at nature provides key to developmental issues. The balance among various elements of nature has been developed in an excellent way over years and years of slow but continuous adaptation process, yet it remains to be fragile. Over and improper exploitation of natural resources have caused irreparable damage to our ecosystem. It is, therefore, imperative that a modern Code of building construction takes cognizance of such vital aspects and promotes maintaining ecological balance while ensuring safe and orderly land and building development. The National Building Code of India 2005 fulfills this need. The aspects like energy conservation, energy efficiency and sustainable development have been duly interwoven throughout the text of the Code. Particularly, the Code incorporates the necessary enabling provisions and the flexibility of adopting alternative building materials and design and construction methodologies subject to fulfillment of the minimum requirements of strength, stability, durability, fire resistance, aesthetics, energy efficiency, functionality, performance, environment protection, etc.

The Code provides for utilization of natural agencies for natural lighting and ventilation thus minimizing use of supplementary means. For supplementary lighting and ventilation, as may be required, it prescribes guidelines for utilization of efficient fixtures. Similarly for other building services aspects such as heating and air-conditioning, it provides for a complete energy efficient building management system.

The Code enlists a large number of Indian Standards for materials and their usage which effect substantial utilization of wastes such as fly ash, and various agriculture and industrial wastes. It provides complete guidelines for design and construction using bamboo which is a renewal material with low gestation period. Conservation of water is another issue which has been addressed to also encompassing therein the provisions for rain water harvesting.

In fact, a careful application of the provisions indicated above and many others enshrined in the Code would lead to sustainable land and building development scenario.

Implementation

The National Building Code of India is intended to serve as a model for adoption by PWDs and other construction departments, local bodies and other construction agencies. Existing PWD Codes, municipal bye-laws and other regulatory media could either be replaced by the National Building Code of India or suitably modified to cater to local conditions.

In the case of municipalities and other local bodies which are the main agencies to regulate the main building activity within the jurisdiction of the cities and towns, it is the administrative requirements and bye-laws provisions for the health safety aspects which should mainly constitute the coverage of their bye-laws. Guidelines on all these aspects are included in the National Building Code of India. The information cited above is mainly covered in Parts 2, 3, 4, 5 and 10 of the Code. The other parts of the Code are equally valid and should be referred to in the bye-laws.

In the case of Public Works Departments of the States and Centre, MES, Railways and other governmental construction agencies who would regulate the construction within their jurisdiction with the help of their handbooks, codes and specifications of works, it is the information contained in Parts 0, 5, 6, 7, 8 and 9 of the Code which should mainly be used/ adopted to modernize their regulatory media. The present PWD specifications and handbooks essentially deal with the materials specifications and the construction procedures for various items of work; these requirements are given in Part 5 and 7 of the Code. The structural design requirements and procedure for the design and installation of various services, etc., are not covered in detail in the above codes and detailed information on the same is given in Parts 6, 7 and 9 of the Code. Even though the essential contents of the departmental code should be aimed only for the design and construction of the buildings, there are certain planning requirements which should also be included in these codes, which are covered in Parts 3 and 4; depending upon the set up in each department, information from the above parts should be included in their regulations.

In the case of other constructional agencies like public sector projects, the whole Code would be applicable to them and implementation of the complete Code would result in substantial economies. Similarly the private construction agencies should make full use of the provisions of the Code.

Conclusion

Considering the national need for housing and infrastructure development, a large number of Indian Standards have been brought out in the important fields of planning, designing and construction of buildings, as also on the methodologies for enabling speedier construction and requirements for low income housing. Also, number of Indian Standards have been developed for ensuring sound practices and safety during construction and the durability and safety of structures. The focus has been, of late, on the earthquake resistant design and construction of buildings, for which series of Standards had been already available for design and construction engineers, including for strengthening and retrofitting of buildings.

Notwithstanding the above, the repeated onslaught of natural calamities such as earthquakes, cyclones, landslides, etc. faced by the country as also the need to provide holistic approach towards quality, safety, energy efficiency and conservation and environment protection all leading to sustainable development, has brought home the ever increasing need for the common guiding document to enable monitoring and implementation of sound technical provisions and practices through techno-administrative mechanism and comprehensive features built-in, in such a document. The NBC fulfils this need.

The unprecedented exercise of revision of the National Building Code of India through 18 expert panels and other groups involving 400 experts who in around 50 meetings spread over two years, worked consistently leading to a landmark second revision of the Code, reflective of the state-of-the-art, applicable international practices and aspirations of the citizens of the country. The revised Code has the necessary ingredients for ensuring safe and orderly development of our villages, towns and cities. In a disaster-prone country like ours blessed with the present infrastructure boom, NBC 2005 would serve as an effective tool for design and construction engineers, architects, government construction departments and other construction agencies, builders and developers and for administrators/local bodies to ensure safe, healthy and sustainable habitat for citizens of our country.

11

NATURAL DISASTERS IN INDIA AND ITS SAFETY MEASURES

Raju Sarkar*

ABSTRACT

India is a large country and prone to a number of natural disaster. Among all the natural disasters that country faces, river floods are the most frequent and often devastating. The shortfall in the rainfall causes droughts or drought like situation in various parts of the country. The country has faced some severe earthquakes causing widespread damage to the life and property. India has a coastline of about 8000 km which is prone to very severe cyclonic formations in the Arabian Sea and Bay of Bengal. Another major problem faced by the country is in the form of landslides and avalanches. In the present paper an attempt has been made to highlight few of the natural disasters that India faces along with safety measures before, during and after the calamity.

Introduction

Natural Disaster such as Flood, Fire, Earthquake, Tornado, and Windstorms affect thousands of people every year. Natural disasters are natural events that threaten lives, property, and other assets. These are inevitable. Disasters can be classified in several ways. A possible sub-division of disaster is: Natural Disasters, Human made disasters, Human induced disasters. Another sub-division is related to the main controlling factors leading to a disaster. These may be meteorological, geomorphological/geological, ecological, technological, global environmental and extra terrestrial. Another useful distinction that can be made between disasters is regarding their duration of impact and the time of forewarning. Some disasters strike within a short period with devastating outcomes; others have a slow onset period with equally or even more serious repercussions.

According to the available statistics 60 per cent of the total area of Indian subcontinent is venerable to seismic activity of varying intensities, 16 per cent of the country's total area is drought prone. In India 68 per cent of total sown area of the country is drought prone.

*Lecturer in Civil Engineering, G.B. Pant Polytechnic, New Delhi - 110 020. *E-mail :* sarkar_raju@yahoo.com

Coastal areas of India is exposed to tropical cyclones and among all the disaster occur in the country, river floods are the most frequent and often the most devastating.

We should know what our risks are from natural disasters and take sensible precautions to protect ourselves, our families, and our communities.

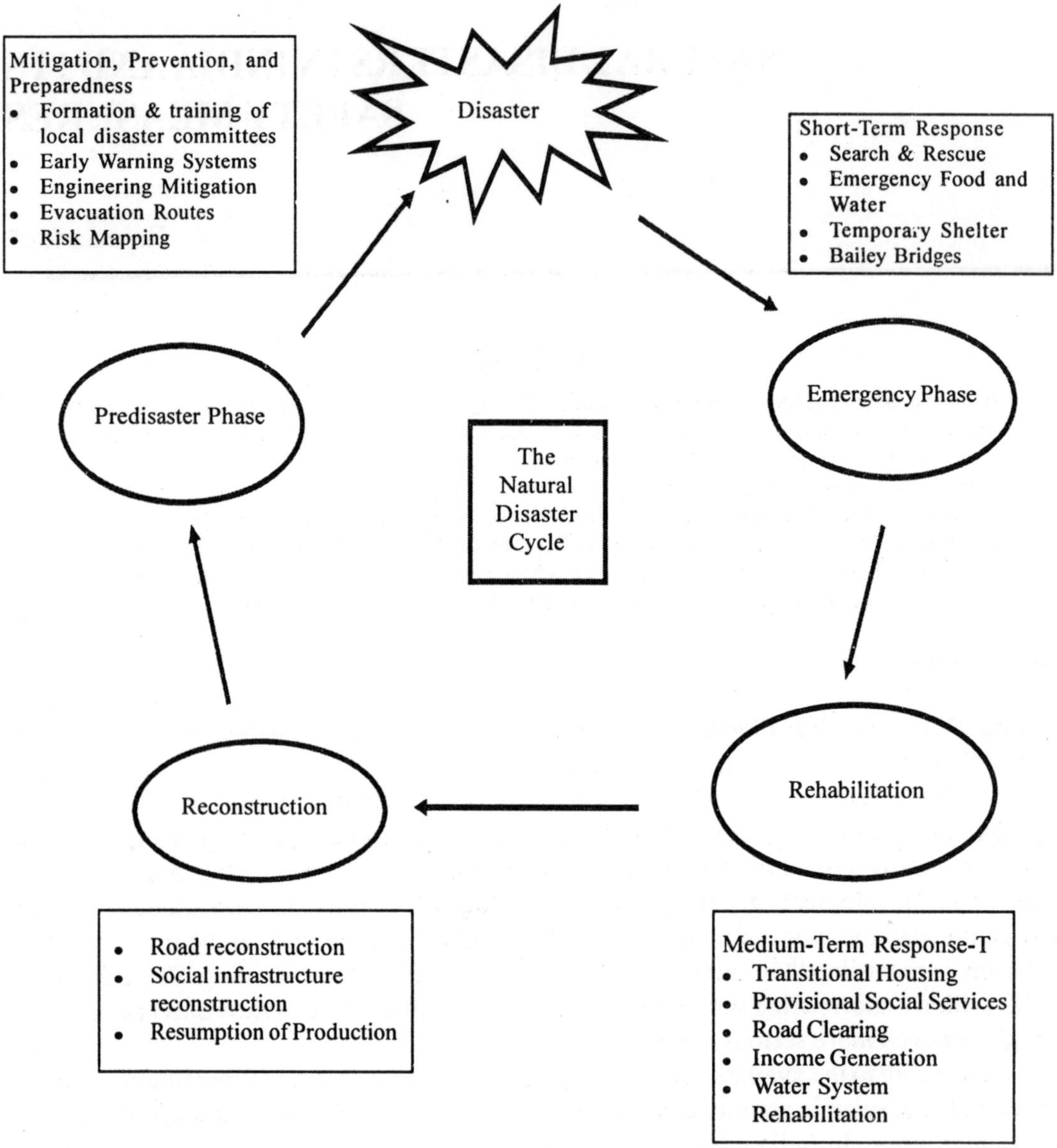

Fig. 1 : The Disaster Cycle

Few Natural Disasters in India and Their Safety Measures

Flood

Floods are one of the most common natural disasters in India. Flood effects can be local, impacting a neighbourhood or community, or very large, affecting entire river basins and multiple states. Floods directly or indirectly affect the economy of the country either in the form of natural resources, lives, property or infrastructures such as houses, roads, railways, pipelines, electricity and telecommunication network.

However, all floods are not alike. Some floods develop slowly, sometimes over a period of days. But flash floods can develop quickly, sometimes in just a few minutes and without any visible signs of rain. Flash floods often have a dangerous wall of roaring water that carries rocks, mud, and other debris and can sweep away most things in its path. Overland flooding occurs outside a define river or stream, such as when a levee is breached, but still can be destructive. Flooding can also occur when a dam breaks, producing effects similar to flash floods.

Beware of flood disaster no matter where we live, but especially if you live in a low-lying area, near water or downstream from dam. Even very small streams, gullies, creeks, culverts, dry streambeds, or low-lying ground that appears harmless in dry weather can flood. Every state is at risk from this hazard.

Safety Measures

Before a Flood : To prepare for a flood, the safety measures are :

- Avoid building in a floodplain unless you elevate and reinforce our home.
- Elevate the furnace, water heater, and electric panel if susceptible to flooding
- Install "check valves" in sewer traps to prevent flood water from backing up into the drains of our home.
- Construct barriers (levees, beams, floodwalls) to stop floodwater from entering the building.
- Seal walls in basements with water proofing compounds to avoid seepage.

During a Flood : If a flood is likely in a area, the safety measures are :

- Listen to the radio or television for information.
- Be aware that flash flooding can occur. If there is any possibility of a flood, move immediately to higher ground. Do not wait for instructions to move.
- Be aware of streams, drainage channels, canyons, and other areas known to flood suddenly. Flash floods can occur in these areas with or without such typical warnings as rain clouds or heavy rain.

After a Flood : The following are the guidelines for the period following a flood :

- Listen for news reports to learn whether the community's water supply is safe to drink.

- Avoid floodwaters; water may be contaminated by oil, gasoline, or raw sewage. Water may also be electrically charged from underground or downed power lines.
- Avoid moving water.
- Be aware of areas where floodwaters have receded. Roads may have weakened and could collapse under the weight of a car.
- Stay away from downed power lines, and report them to the power company.
- Return home only when authorities indicate it is safe.
- Stay out of any building if it is surrounded by floodwaters.
- Use extreme caution when entering buildings; there may be hidden damage, particularly in foundations.
- Service damaged septic tanks, cesspools, pits, and leaching systems as soon as possible. Damaged sewage systems are serious health hazards.

Earthquakes

Earthquakes are caused by the abrupt release of strain that has built up in the earth's crust. Most zones of maximum earthquake intensity and frequency occur at the boundaries between the moving plates that form the crust of the earth. Major earthquakes also occur within the interior of crystal plates such as those in China, Russia and the south-east United States. A considerable research has been carried out to predict earthquakes using conventional technologies, but the results to date are inconclusive. Seismic risk analysis based on historic earthquakes and the presence of active faults is an established method for locating and designing dams, power plants and other projects in seismically active areas. If the earthquake occurs in a populated area, it may cause many deaths and injuries and extensive property damage.

An earthquake does not cause the earth to split open and swallow up people and neighbourhoods. Shallow crevasses can form during earthquakes due to landslides or other types of ground failures. Faults, however, do not open up. Buildings do not automatically collapse in earthquakes. Earthquakes can occur at any time. They are not more common in certain seasons or in certain kinds of weather. No one can reliably predict an earthquake.

Safety Measures

Before an Earthquake : To prepare for an Earthquake, the following safety measures are to be taken to save ourselves, our families, and our property

- Repair defective electrical wiring, leaky gas lines, and inflexible utility connections. Get appropriate professional help. Do not work with gas or electrical lines.
- Anchor overhead lighting fixtures.
- Be sure the residence is firmly anchored to its foundation.
- Locate safe spots in each room under a sturdy table or against an inside wall. Reinforce this information by moving to these places during each drill.
- Place large or heavy objects on lower shelves. Fasten shelves, mirrors, and large picture frames to walls. Brace high and top-heavy objects.
- Store bottled foods, glass, china, and other breakables on low shelves or in cabinets that fasten shut.

During an Earthquake : During an earthquake, the safety measures are

Indoor

- Stay inside.
- Take cover under a heavy table, desk or any solid furniture and hold on.
- If can't get under something strong, or if in a hallway, flatten or crouch against an interior wall.
- Stay away from windows, glass partitions, mirrors, fireplaces, bookcases, tall furniture and light fixtures. In an earthquake, a person could be hurt by shattered glass or heavy objects thrown around by the shaking.
- If in a shopping mall, go into the nearest store. Stay away from windows, skylights and shelves with heavy objects.
- Avoid doorways. Doors may slam shut and cause injuries.
- If at school, get under a desk or table and hold on. Face away from windows.
- Wherever are, protect head, face and neck.

Outdoor

- Stay outside.
- Go to an open area away from buildings. Sidewalks next to tall buildings are especially dangerous.
- Stay away from windows, buildings (or any other structure that could collapse), overhead wires, downed electrical wires, power lines and telephone poles.
- Remember that broken gas mains and fallen chimneys can cause fires. Downed power lines and broken water mains can also wreak havoc.
- Stay at least 10 metres away from downed power lines.

In a vehicle

- Avoid bridges, overpasses, underpasses, buildings or anything that could collapse on you and your car.
- Listen to your car radio for instructions from emergency officials.
- Do not attempt to get out of your car if downed power lines are across it. Wait to be rescued.
- Place a HELP sign in your window if you need assistance.
- Keep roads clear for rescue and emergency vehicles.
- If you are on a bus, stay in your seat until the bus stops. Take cover in a protected place. If you can't take cover, sit in a crouched position and protect your head from falling debris until the shaking stops.

After an Earthquake : The following are the guidelines for the period following an Earthquake

- Be prepared for aftershocks. These secondary shockwaves are usually less violent than the main quake but can be strong enough to do additional damage to weakened structures.

- Open cabinets cautiously. Beware of objects that can fall off shelves.
- Stay away from damaged areas unless your assistance has been specifically requested by police, fire, or relief organizations.
- Be aware of possible tsunamis if living in coastal areas. When local authorities issue a tsunami warning, assume that a series of dangerous waves is on the way. Stay away from the beach.

Landslides

Outward and downward movement of mass, consisting of rock and soils, due to natural or man-made causes is termed as landslide. As long as landslides occur in remote, unpopulated regions, they are treated as just another denudation process sculpting the landscape, but when occur in populated regions, they become subjects of serious study. Most of the landslides occur due to exhaustive deforestation for the development of urbanization and plantation. In these areas rainwater directly penetrates into the soil and cause landslides.

Most of the landslides occur due to exhaustive deforestation for the development of urbanization and plantation. In these areas rainwater directly penetrates into the soil and cause landslides. In spite of the fact that the landslide is more manageable and more forecastable as compared with other natural calamities like earthquake and flood, there are few areas of the country that have the landslide maps and few landslide stability potential maps have been prepared.

Safety Measures

Before a Landslide : The following steps can be adopted to protect from the effects of landslide

- Do not build steep slopes close to mountain edges, near drainage ways, or natural erosion valleys.
- Get a ground assessment of your property.
- Consult an appropriate professional expert for advice on corrective measures.
- Minimize home hazards by having flexible pipe fittings installed to avoid gas or water leaks, as flexible fittings are more resistant to breakage.

During a Landslide : The following are the guidelines to be followed during a landslide

- Move away from the path of a landslide as quickly as possible.
- Curl into a tight ball and protect head if escape is not possible.

After a Landslide : The following are the guidelines for the period following a landslide

- Stay away from the slide area.
- Check for injured and trapped persons near the slide, without entering the direct slide area. Direct rescuers to their locations.

- Help a neighbour who may require special assistance - infants, elderly people, and people with disabilities.
- Listen to local radio or television stations for the latest emergency information.
- Watch for flooding, which may occur after a landslide or debris flow.
- Look for and report broken utility lines to appropriate authorities.
- Check the building foundation, chimney, and surrounding land for damage.
- Replant damaged ground as soon as possible since erosion caused by loss of ground cover can lead to flash flooding.
- Seek the advice of a Geotechnical expert for evaluating landslide hazards or designing corrective techniques to reduce landslide risk.

Fire

Fire spreads quickly, there is no time to gather valuables or make a phone call. In first two minutes, a fire can become life threatening. In five minutes, a residence can be engulfed in flames. Heat and smoke from fire can be more dangerous than the flames. Inhaling the super hot air can sear lungs. Fire produces poisonous gases that make disoriented and drowsy. Instead of being awakened by a fire, you may fall into a deeper sleep. Asphyxiation is the leading cause of fire deaths, exceeding burns by a 3:1 ratio.

Safety Measures

Before a Fire : The following steps can be adopted to protect from the effects of Fire

- Install smoke alarms. Properly working smoke alarms decrease chances of dying in a fire by half.
- Review escape routes.
- Clean out storage areas. Do not let trash, such as old newspaper and magazines, accumulate.
- Never use gasoline, benzene, naphtha, or similar flammable liquids indoors.
- Place heaters at least three feet away from flammable materials. Make sure the floor and nearby walls are properly insulated.
- Never smoke in bed or when drowsy or medicated. Provide smokers with deep, sturdy ashtrays. Douse cigarette and cigar butts with water before disposal.
- Have the electrical wiring in residence checked by an electrician.
- Ask local fire department to inspect residence for the safety and prevention.

During a Fire : The following are the guidelines to be followed during a fire

- If cloths catch fire, stop, drop and roll until the fire is extinguished. Running only makes the fire burn faster.
- To escape a fire, check closed doors for heat before open. If escaping through a closed door, use the back of the hand to feel the top of the door, the doorknob, and the crack between the door and door frame before open it. Never use the palm of hand or fingers to test for heat-burning those areas could impair ability to escape a fire.

- Crawl low under any smoke to exitheavy smoke and poisonous gases collect first along the ceiling.
- Stay out once safely out, don't re-enter.

After a Fire : Guidelines for different circumstances in the period following a fire are

- For burn victims, cool and cover burns to reduce chance of further injury or infection.
- If detect heat or smoke when entering a damaged building, evacuate immediately.
- If any safe and strong box available, don't try to open it. It can hold intense heat for several hours. If the door is opened before the box has cooled, the contents could burst into flames.
- Ask someone close to watch the property, if fire department says the building is unsafe, before leaving.

Tsunamis

Tsunami is a Japanese word with the English translation, "harbor wave". Represented by two characters, the top character, "tsu", means harbor, while the bottom character, "nami", means "wave". Tsunamis can be generated when the sea floor abruptly deforms and vertically displaces the overlying water. Tectonic earthquakes are a particular kind of earthquake that are associated with the earth's crustal deformation; when these earthquakes occur beneath the sea, the water above the deformed area is displaced from its equilibrium position. Waves are formed as the displaced water mass, which acts under the influence of gravity, attempts to regain its equilibrium. When large areas of the sea floor elevate or subside, a tsunami can be created. A tsunami can move hundreds of miles per hour in the open ocean and smash into land with waves as high as 100 feet.

From the area where the tsunami originates, waves travel outward in all directions. Once the wave approaches the shore, it builds in height. The topography of the coastline and the ocean floor will influence the size of the wave. There may be more than one wave and the succeeding one may be larger than the one before. That is why a small tsunami at one beach can be a giant wave a few miles away.

Safety Measures

Before a Tsunami : The following are the guidelines for a tsunami if it is likely in a particular area

- Turn on the radio to learn if there is a tsunami warning if an earthquake occurs and you are in a coastal area.
- Move inland to higher ground immediately and stay there.
- If there is noticeable recession in water away from the shoreline this is nature's tsunami warning and it should be heeded. So move away immediately.

After a Tsunami : The following are guidelines for the period following a tsunami

- Stay away from flooded and damaged areas until officials say it is safe to return.
- Stay away from debris in the water; it may pose a safety hazard to boats and people.

Extreme Heat

Heat kills by pushing the human body beyond its limits. In extreme heat and high humidity, evaporation is slowed and the body must work extra hard to maintain a normal temperature.

Most heat disorders occur because the victim has been overexposed to heat or has over exercised for his or her age and physical condition. Older adults, young children, and those who are sick or overweight are more likely to succumb to extreme heat.

Conditions that can induce heat related illnesses include stagnant atmospheric conditions and poor air quality. Consequently, people living in urban areas may be at greater risk from the effects of a prolonged heat wave then those living in rural areas. Also, asphalt and concrete store heat longer and gradually release heat at night, which can produce higher nighttime temperatures known as the "urban heat island effect".

Safety Measures

Before Extreme Heat : The following are the guidelines for a extreme heat if it is likely in a particular area

- Install window air conditioners or coolers snugly. Insulate if necessary.
- Check air conditioning ducts for proper insulation.
- Weather-strip doors and sills to keep cool air in.
- Cover windows that receive morning or afternoon sun drapes, shades, awnings, or louvers.

During Extreme Heat : The following are the guidelines to be followed during a landslide

- Stay indoors as much as possible and limit exposure to the sun.
- Stay on the lowest floor out of the sunshine if air conditioning is not available.
- Consider spending the warmest part of the day in public buildings such as libraries, schools, movie theatres, shopping malls, and other community facilities.
- Eat well-balanced, light, and regular meals. Avoid using salt tablets unless directed to do so by a physician.
- Drink plenty of water.
- Limit intake of alcoholic beverages.
- Protect face and head by wearing a wide brimmed hat.

Drought

Drought is defined as a deficiency of precipitation over an extended period of time resulting in water shortage and extensive damages to crops resulting in loss of yield. Drought is the single most important weather-related natural disaster often aggravated by human action. Drought's beginning is subtle, its progress is insidious and its effects can be devastating. Drought may start any time, last indefinitely and attain many degrees of severity. Since it affects very large areas for months and years it has a serious impact on economy, destruction of ecological resources, food shortages and starvation of millions of people. It begins with agriculture section (heavy dependence on soil moisture/water) as well as people dependent on source of water. It diminishes with agriculture sector, soil moisture/water and source of water. Its impact on society result from the interplay between a natural event (less precipitation than expected resulting from climatic variability) and demand people place on water supply. The demand for economic goods increases with increase in population and per capita consumption.

Safety Measures

Before a Drought

- An emergency water shortage can be caused by prolonged drought, poor water supply management, or contamination of a surface water supply source or aquifer. So awareness campaign for the conserving water should be made among the people of the possible effected area.

After a Drought

- Drought creates environmental conditions that increase the risk of other disaster such as fire, flash flood, and possible landslides. So safety measures for the said disaster to be taken immediately during the drought or after the drought.

Cyclone

The intense tropical storms are known in different part of the world by different names. In the Pacific Ocean, they are called 'typhoons', in the Indian Ocean they are called 'cyclones' and over North Atlantic, they are called 'hurricane'. Among various natural calamities, tropical cyclones are known to claim a higher share of deaths and destruction worldover. Records show that about 80 tropical cyclones form over the globe every year. India has a vast coast line which is frequently affected by tropical cyclones causing heavy loss of human lives and property. Cyclones occur usually between April and May (called pre-monsoon cyclonic storms) and between October and December (called post-monsoon cyclonic storms). While cyclonic storms cannot be prevented, the loss of lives and damage to the properties can be mitigated if prompt action is taken after receiving timely warnings.

Safety Measures

Before a Cyclone: Following measures should be taken to prepare for a cyclone

- Make plan to secure property. Permanent storm shutters offer the best protection for windows.
- Install straps or additional clips to securely fasten roof to the frame structure. This will reduce roof damage.
- Be sure trees and shrubs around home are well trimmed.
- Clear loose and clogged rain gutters and downspouts.

During a Cyclone: If a cyclone is likely in a area, the steps to be taken

- Listen to the radio or television for information.
- Secure home, close storm shutters, and secure outdoor objects or bring them indoors.
- Avoid using the phone, except for serious emergencies.
- Ensure supply of water for sanitary purposes such as cleaning and flushing toilets. Fill the bathtub and other large containers with water.
- Stay indoors during the cyclone and away from windows and glass doors.
- Lie on the floor under a table or another sturdy object.

Conclusion

The safety measures that should be taken during emergency are absolutely essential for the common person. Therefore, citizens regardless of their age, sex and social status should know certain elementary precautions, which would save them. In particular children who become vulnerable during emergencies should be exposed to training and information as is being done very effectively in developed countries.

The common precautions to be followed by all are:

(1) Please keep the antidotes for use during any Medical Emergency and use it in consultation with a doctor.

(2) Children are vulnerable for any airborne contaminants. During emergency like fire/collapse or subsidence of structure, lot of airborne particulate matter will be released. As they breathe more air, they need to be protected to prevent inhalation of dust and particulate matter.

(3) Please conduct in a disciplined, organized and responsible manner during emergencies.

(4) During emergency, the authorities concerned would always make available emergency contact numbers or would provide information and instruction for the benefit of the general public. Listen to it carefully and act accordingly.

(5) Cooperate fully with public safety officials. Respond to requests for volunteer assistance from police, fire fighters, emergency management officials, and relief organizations, but do not go into damaged areas unless assistance has been requested.

REFERENCES

Carter, W.N., (1992): *Disaster Management: A Disaster Manager's Handbook*, Asian Development Bank, Manila.

Adult Coping With Disasters, (1996): Los Angeles City Fire Department, Earthquake Preparedness Handbook.

Natural Disaster Reduction, (1994): South Asian Regional Report, Proceedings of the SAARC Workshop on Natural Disaster Reduction.

Natural Disaster and Disaster Risk Reduction Measures, (2005): Draft Final Report, Department of International Development, Environmental Resource Management.

Natural Hazards, (2002): FEMA Publications, Volume 2 and 3.

Rao, D.P., (2000): *Disaster Management*, Map India, 2000.

Smith, K., (1996): *Environmental Hazards, Assessing Risk & Reducing Disaster*, II Edition, London and New York, Routledge.

Sarkar, Raju (2004), 'Uttarkashi Landslides - A Case Study', Presented paper Hazards 2004 Conference (10th International Symposium on Natural and Human-Induced Hazards and 3rd Workshop of the IUGG Commission on Geophysical Risk and Sustainability), Hyderabad, India.

Petterson, Jeanine (1999), 'A Review of the Literature and Programs on Local Recovery from Disaster', Natural Hazards Research Working Paper, Federal Emergency Management Agency.

Section–IV

Safety in Energy Sector

12

OCCUPATIONAL HEALTH MONITORING IN INDIAN OIL CORPORATION LIMITED – AN EXPERIENCE AT GUJARAT REFINERY

R.C. Saxena* and S. Kaul**

ABSTRACT

A company is recognised by its production, profit and product quality. To achieve all this to its maximum, right input in the form of best material, adequate investment and highly skilled manpower is required. Healthy worker is an asset to the management as only a healthy worker can give his maximum output in terms of productivity. Loss of human resource will bring about diminished production and as well reputation of company. Progressive modernization in our country is simultaneously changing the type and nature of work related hazards and ill health problems among the workers. Manifested health problems may be acute or chronic in nature, affecting one or multiple systems of our body.

Most management realise that health is an important factor; hence they see to it that they employ healthy workers, by subjecting the selected workers to pre-employment medical examinations and they are taken on job only when they are medically fit. Hence it is the responsibility of the management to see to it that fit worker does not suffer from any illness on account of his work. Health of the worker is influenced by factors, which are occupational as well as non-occupational. The interaction of the worker with his working environment may result in impairment of his health leading to his work related illnesses also known as occupational diseases. These diseases are those, which may arise out of or in the course of employment. The working environment has got direct effects on the health of persons who are present in the area. The environment may be responsible in causation of occupational diseases or exacerbation of other non-occupational diseases. The state of health of the worker can influence his ability to work safely and efficiently.

Gujarat Refinery is one of the prestigious Refineries having thru-put of 13.3 MMT. This Refinery has established a landmark as No. 1 in India and has achieved various certifications and awards. Refinery has 2200 employees, working in this modern and complex plant of Petroleum Refining, having average mean age of worker as 47.3 years. Establishment of full-fledged OH Services to monitor the health hazard on continuous basis is the crux of human health preservation. It is a long-term gain to employer. A systematic approach of environmental surveillance to identify OH hazards at workplace and their monitoring is of great importance. This is done by a competent

*ACMO, Gujarat Refinery
**CM (S, H & E), CO.

Hygienist who monitors workplace at breathing zone to know actual TLV of various hazards on daily basis. Planning of medical check up of all identified employees exposed to hazards like toxic gases, noise, vibration, heat etc. fall next into health surveillance programme. Each employee is subjected to periodic check up with all routine, specialized and target organ assessment. Each check up is analysed and advices are given on lifestyle modification. Analysis of group and disease trend is performed to assess emergence of any occupational or non-occupational disease. These organized activities of OHC of Gujarat Refinery have brought the Centre as a model OH Centre, bringing standards to OHSAS-18001 guidelines.

During the course of employment, not only that worker may contract occupational disease, he may also develop non-occupational metabolic diseases like diabetes, hypertension etc. Proper analysis of these diseases is very vital in nature. So for no occupational illness has been found from the inception of OH services but metabolic diseases are detected, for which various health programmes are in place. A good hygienic condition, safe working condition, periodic work place monitoring and regular health check ups keep the worker healthy and productive thorough out his life. As employer reaps the productivity of worker, the worker enjoys the fruits of life with his family.

Introduction

A company is recognised by its production, profit, product quality and concern for safety, health and environment. To achieve all this to its maximum, right input in the form of best material, adequate investment and skilled manpower is required. Healthy worker is an asset to the management as only a healthy worker can give his maximum output in terms of productivity. Loss of human resource will bring about diminished production and as well reputation of company. Progressive modernization in our country is simultaneously changing the type and nature of work related hazards and ill health problems among the workers. Manifested health problems may be acute or chronic in nature, affecting one or multiple systems of our body.

Health of the worker is influenced by factors, which are occupational as well as non-occupational. The interaction of the worker with his working environment may result in impairment of his health leading to his work related illnesses also known as occupational diseases. These diseases are those, which may arise out of or in the course of employment. The working environment has got direct effects on the health of persons who are present in the area. The environment may be responsible in causation of occupational diseases or exacerbation of other non-occupational diseases. The state of health of the worker can influence his ability to work safely and efficiently.

Different industrial processes present a wide range of hazards to the health of the workers. Modernization, which is in progress in our country, is changing the type and nature of work related hazards and ill health problems among the workers. If we consider the human resources as the essential input in any process, its conservation becomes the moral obligation of the employer. Therefore, a progressive company must adopt the policy of human resource conservation by promoting their safety, health and environment. After Bhopal disaster and the amendment of Factories Act, 1987, the responsibility of the employee working in factory has been squarely fixed on the occupier. The role of Occupational Health Centre (OHC) at this juncture is very critical and the role of the OH services is aimed at harmoniously combining environmental protection and health promotion of the employees.

Indian Oil has always believed that the man behind the machine is more important and therefore considers their health and well being a valuable asset to the corporation. Keeping this in mind, Occupational Health Centres were set up at all Refinery Units in 1994 and doctors and paramedics were specially trained for the purpose. All these OHCs are certified under OHSAS-18001 by DNV. At Marketing, Pipeline and other locations, similar activities are undertaken with the help of retainer doctors, which are currently being reviewed at Divisional and Corporate level.

Occupational Environment and Hazards

Work environment can be broadly divided into physical, chemical, biological, behavioural and ergonomical hazards. Occupational health hazards are -

1. *Physical Agents:* Heat, light, noise, radiation, vibration, humidity, decompression.
2. *Chemical Agents:* More than 2 lac chemicals are being used by industries. Every year some 1000 new chemicals emerge and are being used by different industries. Chemicals are categorised as:

   Metals:
   - Ancient metals: Lead, TEL, Hg and its compounds.
   - Other metals: As, Phosphorous, Zn
   - New metals: Be, Cd, Cr, Ni, Co, Pl, Se, Ur, Th

   Aromatic compounds: Benzene, Toluene, Phenol, Quinon, Amino and Pyridium derivatives.
   Aliphatic compounds: Methyl alcohol, Nitro-glycerine, Dimethyl, and Vinyl chloride.
   Noxious gases: Simple asphyxiant - N_2, CH_4, and CO_2
   Chemical asphyxiant - CO, H_2S, HCN
   Irritant gases - NH_3, SO_2, Cl_2, $COCl_2$
   Systemic poison - CS_2, Nickel carbonyl, Phosgene
   Dusts: Pneumoconiosis, Occupational asthma, Occupational cancer, Extrinsic allergic alveolitis

3. *Biological Agents:* Anthrax, Weil's disease, Virus, Fungi, molds, mites, insects
4. *Behavioural:* Absenteeism, alcoholism, accidents, boredom etc.
5. *Ergonomical*: Awkward or static postures, heavy lifting, fatigue, over exertion, monotony, Reaching beyond body, Repeated jobs

Routes of Entry in the Body

It is important to know how the harmful substances that industrial workers are exposed to pass through the body's defence barriers and enter the system.

Skin

The skin has a protective coating of oils and proteins. But some chemicals, like phenol or carbolic acid, can penetrate the skin without being felt, or else, like Triflouroacetic acid, burn their way through the skin barrier. Sometimes a substance may react with the proteins of the skin and cause an allergy. When a chemical passes right through the skin, it can be absorbed into the bloodstream and carried throughout the body. For example, Aniline, a common dye, can be absorbed through the worker's skin (sometimes coming right through shoes and clothes) and after reacting with the blood, can cause the whites of the eyes, the lips, and the fingers to turn blue, as well as seriously damage other organs of the body.

Inhalation

Majority of poisons that affect the internal organs enters the body by being breathed in. Chlorine and Ammonia can cause local irritation, other substances may be absorbed from the lungs into the blood and cause damage to other organs. These are called soluble substances because they dissolve in the blood. Finally, insoluble substances that do not dissolve in the blood or dissolve only in small amounts tend to remain in the lungs for long periods of time. There they may cause serious local reactions either immediately or many years after the initial exposure. Among these substances are dusts like Silica, Asbestos and Beryllium.

Ingestion

Once swallowed, the substances enter the digestive tract. Not everything that is eaten enters the blood system right away. However, once absorbed into the bloodstream, the toxic substance goes directly to the liver, which then attempts to change the substance chemically to make it harmless to the body.

Physical Health Hazards

Physical hazards are often thought to be less important than chemical but this is not so. They can and do cause severe health problems, injuries or even death. The nature of physical agents is wide and should not be underrated but the main ones capable of causing occupational disorders or injuries are:

Heat

Disorders due to heat are -

(a) *Systemic:* - Heat stroke, Heat exhaustion, Heat syncope, Heat cramp, Dehydration.
(b) *Skin:* - Prickly heat, Milliaria rubra, Cancer, Rodent ulcer.
(c) *Psychoneurotic:* - Heat fatigue, Loss of emotional control.

Noise

Normal permissible limit for 8 hours continuous exposure has been recommended to be maximum of 90 dBA. In situations where the noise level is high, workers get ill effects like temporary hearing loss, permanent hearing loss, rupture of the membrane and also non-auditory ill effects - speech interference, variation in blood pressure, dilatation of pupils, BP, annoyance.

Vibration

Prolonged exposure to vibration leads to these diseases like White fingers, Polyneuritis, frequent fractures.

Illumination

The man is having a high position in the evolutionary scale only due to acuity of his sight, the accuracy of thumb and finger movement and the co-ordination of the eye and hand by the brain. This biological fact alone makes the importance of illumination in day-to-day work. The ill effects due to defective illumination are accidents, decrease in visual acuity, eye fatigue and headache. Stimulation of nervous system is also reported. Glare can cause visual discomfort and irritability.

Colour

Each colour gives a special psychological appreciation on the human and moderates the behaviour accordingly. Psychological effects of colours are - Red: stimulates, warm feeling; Purple : depression; Yellow : freshening, warm feeling; Orange: tension producing; Light green and blue : relaxed, cool feeling; White: stimulating.

Radiation

Ionising radiation can affect the workers depending upon from where it comes. In industries, external radiation is common. The amount of tissue damage depends on the energy absorbed per unit mass of the tissue. Various types of radiations are - Alpha particles, Beta particles, Gamma rays, X-rays, Neutrons etc. ionising radiation causes cancer of skin and blood forming organs.
Ultraviolet radiations: UV rays affect the skin causing burn, skin cancer and conjunctivitis. In welders it may cause "Arc eye". Other such radiations are - Infrared radiation, Microwave radiation and Laser beams.

Air Pressure

A. *High air pressure* - In operations like tunnelling, diving etc. high air pressure is exerted on the body. Problems like pain in muscles, bones and joints are felt due to decompression phenomenon.

B. *Low air pressure* - Lack of O_2 can lead to black out or behavioural changes at high altitudes.

Defective Layout/Bad Housekeeping

If the layouts are not made properly the health hazards may appear. Planning and making good layout is necessary. Good housekeeping prevents majority of accidents at work place.

Behavioural/Psychosocial Aspects of Occupational Health

It is unfortunate that the role of extrinsic psychosocial stimuli is not so clear. In the context of stress at work, psychosocial stimuli originates in a social process within a social structure and affects the organism through the mediation of perception and experience - the higher nervous processes. Well-being is a dynamic state of mind characterised by reasonable harmony between a worker's abilities, needs and expectations and environmental demands and opportunities. Among psychosocial aspects, the variables generally studied are those related to job stress. These include such as work load, degree of attention, complexity of job, place of work, degree of control, thoroughness which have a psychological bearing in the sense that they effect job satisfaction, general well-being and mental health.

Work Stress

Job with no stress is not a work at all. Very low job demands (boredom) and very high job demands (works overload) create psychological and physical consequences. However, their effect is moderated or influenced by non-work situation, individual characteristics and importantly by work stress moderators.

Occupational Stress

Occupational stress refers to any characteristics of the job environment, which poses a threat to the individual. In organisations, two types of threats are generally experienced:

1. Job demand, which the individual may not be able to meet the extent to which the person's skill and abilities match the demands and requirements of the job.
2. Insufficient supply to meet the individuals needs, i.e. the extent to which the person's needs are supplied/satisfied in the job environment. As indicated, it has been found that when workload is very high, and decision latitude is low (need for control is not satisfied) job stress is experienced.

General Principles in the Control of Occupational Health Hazard

The control measures can be at three different points, i.e. source, air path and receiver -

1. *Source* - During planning and designing the plant, newer technology machine should be adopted.

Substitution, e.g. Silicon carbide in place of silica in grinding stone.
Change of process
Enclosure of process
Wet methods to prevent dusty environment
Local exhaust ventilation (capturing at the source)
Adequate preventive maintenance programme

2. *Air Path* - Good house-keeping
General exhaust ventilation
Dilution of ventilation
Increasing distance between source and receiver (semi-automatic/remote ctrl)
Continuous area monitoring (Pre-set alarms)
Adequate maintenance programme

3. *Receiver* - Training and education
Rotation of workers (split up of dose)
Enclosure of workers (Air conditioned overhead cranes)
Personal monitoring device (Dosimeter)
Personal protective devices
Medical check ups for early detection.

Gujarat Refinery is one of the prestigious Refineries having thru-put of 13.3 MMT. This Refinery has established a landmark as No. 1 in India and has achieved various certifications and awards. Refinery has 2200 employees, working in this modern and complex plant of Petroleum Refining, having average mean age of employee as 47.3 years. Establishment of full-fledged OH Services to monitor the health of employee on continuous basis is the crux of human health preservation. This has been also emphasised and stressed by Indian Factories Acts as statutory requirement. Functions of OH Services are - Environmental surveillance to assess hygienic conditions, health surveillance to assess any early sign of health hazard on worker, trend analysis of diseases, result interpretation and presenting data to employer and government. It is a long-term gain to employer. A systematic approach of environmental surveillance to identify OH hazards at workplace and their monitoring is of great importance.

OH Services at Gujarat Refinery

Gujarat Refinery has established full-fledged Occupational Health Centre situated next to hospital building. It meets all statutory requirements of Factories Act. OHC was inaugurated in December 1994.

The staff of OHC had been given exhaustive training at BHEL (Trichy) and MRL (Madras) to handle various equipment, appliances. OHC conducts various medical check-ups for pre-employment, pre-placement, executive, well person screening and all occupational health check-ups. Regular check-ups are supported with instruments like:

Spirometry
Audiometry

Refraction of eyes
CO monitor
12 channel ECG.

Cardiac treadmill test is performed by cardiologists to all employees above 40 years of age. Hygiene work includes environmental monitoring in the Refinery premises by use of Gas detectors, Sound level meter, Gas chromatograph and other relevant equipments. These medical check-ups are backed up with biological monitoring.

Functions of OHC

- Identification of occupational health hazards of those specified in Schedule-I of Factories Act either hazardous substances or dangerous operations.
  - — Those handling hazardous materials like Benzene, CO, Cl_2, H_2S, SO_2, LPG in different sections of plant.
  - — Those doing operation like Welders, Loco operator, Drivers, Radiographers.
- Identification of employees identified under target groups for periodical check-up.
- Pre-employment screening, choosing right person for right job.
- Periodical check up of Executives above 40 years of age.
- Comprehensive lung function testing of target group.
- Audiometry of employees working in high noise areas (Turbines, Boilers, Steam-air line, Pump houses).
- Vision testing of all employees.
- Work environment monitoring.
- Imparting occupational health education training to the employees through one day training (6 such trainings/year) modules, bulletins, journals and cable TV (We have video cassettes on occupational safety and health from National Film Education.)
- Maintaining up-to-date health records of each employee and analyse them.
  - — Early detection of BP, Diabetes, IHD, Hypertriglyceridemia.
  - — Follow up curative advices to employee.
  - — Early detection of stress reaction of Executives and high noise area employees.

Activities in OHC for the Year 2005-06

- 3 Batch of 15-20 "Medical Attendant" of different Industries from Vadodara had come to attend practical training as a part of their curriculum.
- Practical classes for Post-graduate Diploma in Industrial Safety were started at our OHC for every Saturday approved by Directorate of Factories, Gujarat.
- Students undergoing post-graduation in DIH from SSG Medical College, Baroda had come to attend 21 days exhaustive training at our OHC as part of their curriculum. 20 Samples for blood Lead estimation on payment were done for Narmada Videocon.
- 15 Doctors undergoing CIH course from GLI, Ahmedabad had come to get acquainted with various standards and practices of OHC.
- 25 students from SSG Medical College and 40 students from Jatin Modi Nursing Institute visited GR hospital and OHC to understand the functioning of OHC.

- Ex.Chairman Railway Board along with Director-R Mr. Jaspal Singh visited this prestigious Occupational Health Centre of GR.
- Dr. Saxena imparted a deliberation on OH in CII conference of Safety, Baroda.
- Illumination survey of whole Refinery was done by OHC twice.
- Sound Level Monitoring was done at boundary wall of Refinery premises battery area complying Air Pollution Act. This was in addition to normal workplace monitoring.
- Dr. Saxena rendered faculty assistance on OH to DNV's LEAD Auditor's course and delivered a talk on "OSHAS *vs.* Factories Acts" at Panelav Halol organised by Directorate of Factories. He also rendered faculty assistance at Surat for "Medical Attendant" course organised by IAOH, Baroda.
- Doctors from APOLLO TYRES had come to see functioning of OHC.
- As requested by Panipat/HQ, 40 Pre-employment medical examinations were done for Panipat Refinery.
- One-day seminar on "Noise, Industry & you" was organised by IAOH Baroda at Hotel Swagat, Dr. Saxena talked on "Audiometry & Audiogram".
- A team of AFMC doctors from Pune accompanied by Col. S. Chawla visited OHC, Shri HP Singh, the then ED briefed about Refinery functioning. Dr. Saxena made a presentation on OH activities.

Conclusion

OHSAS guidelines, which Gujarat Refinery has adopted, regarding Occupational Health is critical to the health and well being of all employees. Extreme care and commitment is demonstrated from all levels of management when planning, organising and leading health related activities. During the course of employment, not only that worker may contract occupational disease, he may also develop non-occupational metabolic diseases like diabetes, hypertension etc. Proper analysis of these diseases are very vital in nature. So far no occupational illness has been found from the inception of OH services but metabolic diseases are detected, for which various health programmes are in place. A good hygienic condition, safe working condition, periodic work place monitoring and regular health check ups keep the worker healthy and productive through out his life. As employer reaps the productivity of worker, the worker enjoys the fruits of life with his family.

REFERENCES

Amendment of Factories Act, 1987

Archives of Occupational Health Centre of Gujarat Refinery of IOCL

International Labour Organisation (ILO) guidelines on Occupational Health & Safety

Oil Industry Safety Directorate (OISD) guidelines on Occuaptonal Health Monitoring in Oil & Gas industry (OISD-GDN-166) published in July 1997

Occupational Health Manual of Indian Oil published in March 2004

13

HOLISTIC APPROACH TO PROCESS SAFETY

G.B. Tolmare*

ABSTRACT

Process safety incidents are less frequent than, say, traffic accidents, but they are of great concern because of associated high consequences. The concern arises mainly from their unpredictability in terms of where and when they will happen and their scale of impact. Process Safety related major hazard in a process plant usually materializes due to loss of containment. The three big major hazards are fire, explosion and toxic release. In past, we have seen the occurrence of a number of process safety related incidents that have had major impacts on surrounding communities.

The paper emphasise that compared to personal safety, management of process safety has to deal with number of engineering issues that require knowledge and experience in various disciplines of engineering, and suggest for "Technical Management of Process safety" approach based on CCPS books on process safety.

Key Words: Process Safety, Lines of Defence, Independent Protection Layers, SIL.

Introduction

There is no such thing as "zero risk" to individual, society, or the environment. No matter how people occupy their time, whether at home or in a hazardous industry, they are exposed to number of hazards and risks. In a wide variety of industries, many of which have been benefited from many years of design evolution and operational experience, there remains a residual risk, which must be consciously managed and controlled.

Process operations are one of a number of activities, which are of concern to communities and governments. In particular, high technology, which sometimes brings unforeseen hazards, causes some unease. High technology plants tend to be vulnerable to failures of all kinds. There is only one way in which they can go right, but many in which they can go wrong.

*Chief Manager (S, H & E), Indian Oil Corporation Limited.

Process Safety related major hazard in a process plant usually materializes due to loss of containment. The three big major hazards are fire, explosion and toxic release. In past, we have seen the occurrence of a number of process safety related incidents that have had major impacts on surrounding communities. A few of these incidents, which have become "household words" as symbol of the potential flipside of technologies, are given below.

Incident	*Impact*
Flixborough (1974) Vapour cloud explosion	28 fatalities on-site; $232 million damage; damage to homes off-site
Seveso (1976) Toxic material release	Widespread contamination on-site and off-site
Mexico City LPG (1984) LPG explosion	300 fatalities, mostly off-site; $20 million damage
Bhopal (1984) Toxic material release	2500 fatalities off-site, many others injured off-site
Chernobyl (1986) Fire and radiation release	31 fatalities; 300 square miles evacuated; widespread contamination

The chemical industry was generally assumed as a safe industry because of relatively low accident rate. This impression, however, was proved unfounded by the explosion in Flixborough, UK in 1974, which killed 28 workers, injured many others and devasted the plant, and by the toxic release in Seveso, Italy in 1976, which caused extensive damage to the surrounding environment.

The worst industrial accident ever, involving the catastrophic release of extremely toxic Methyl Isocyanate (MIC) from pesticide manufacturing plant, occurred in Bhopal on 3rd December, 1984, killing more than 2,500 people and affecting the health of several thousand of people. The incident drew much attention to the problem of major hazards associated with the operation of certain chemical plants.

Process Safety Incidents are low frequency and high consequences events. Therefore, safety performance data and existence of SMS creates illusion/generates complacency. Most of the industries adopt the strategy of winning awards for reduction in minor injuries and underemphasize sources of major accidents and disasters. Such a tendency can mislead the management. Other option is adoption of strategy that specifically address major accident/disaster potential in every aspect of safety management - from initial design through dismantling and disposition. The strategy is realised through management of "Process Safety" which differs from the conventional safety activities of industries other than Chemical industries.

What is Process Safety?

Process Safety is the operation of facilities that handle, use, process, or store hazardous materials in a manner free from episodic or catastrophic incidents. However, the handling, use, processing, and storage of materials with inherent hazardous properties can never been done in the total absence of risk. In other words, process safety is an ideal condition to achieve. It is a dynamic condition, which involve the technology, materials, people, and equipment that comprise a facility.

Process Safety does not include personal safety issues (e.g. slips, trips, and falls) or security issues (e.g. theft/sabotage) that may occur at chemical process operation, nor does it encompass chronic releases to the environment.

What is PSM?

Process Safety Management (PSM) differs from the personal safety activities that have been in place for many years. The essential difference is the much greater engineering content of PSM.

PSM provides a framework, which can be used to minimise the number of uncontrolled deviations from design or operating intent. It ensures that a properly designed facility is kept that way, and is operated according to the safe manner intended.

PSM is the application of management systems to the identification, understanding, and control of process hazards to prevent process-related injuries and incidents.

Process Safety Management Systems are comprehensive sets of policies, procedures, and practices designed to ensure that control measures/barriers to major accidents are in place, in use, and effective.

PSM addresses the need for managing the process safety-related aspects of technology, facilities, personnel, hazardous material, and emergency responses. Management of "Process Safety", therefore, is a gamut of different elements of safety.

Key Steps to Manage Process Safety, therefore, are:

- Manage process safety-related aspects of technology and facilities during design for adoption of appropriate control measures for reducing the risk associated with major hazard(s).
- Ensure implementation of control measures envisaged in design during construction. Minimise number of uncontrolled deviations from design intent by way of compliance checking.
- Verify the existence of control measures during commissioning/pre-start up.
- Operate according to safe manner as intended in design by ensuring that control measures are in place, in use and effective. Minimise uncontrolled deviations from design or operating intent.

The essence, therefore, is:

— Adopt appropriate control measures by proper design of the facility,

— keep it the way intended in design, and
— operate it safely as intended without any deviation from design intent.

What are Control Measures?

Control measures are the Engineering, Administrative, Procedural means of reducing the risk (likelihood and consequences) associated with major hazard/incident. They eliminate, prevent, reduce or mitigate the major hazard and/or consequences.

What are Main Lines of Defence for Process Safety?

The traditional lines of defence adopted for avoiding/minimizing accidents are known to almost all persons e.g. Barricading, Means of egress/exit etc. because these are obvious. The lines of defence for process safety consist of layers of control measures. These lines of defence for process safety/major hazards are not that obvious and calls for knowledge and experience in various disciplines of engineering. The problem of avoiding major hazards is essentially that of avoiding loss of containment. It is thus evident that the lines of defence must avoid/minimize the possibility of episodic release to prevent catastrophic incidents.

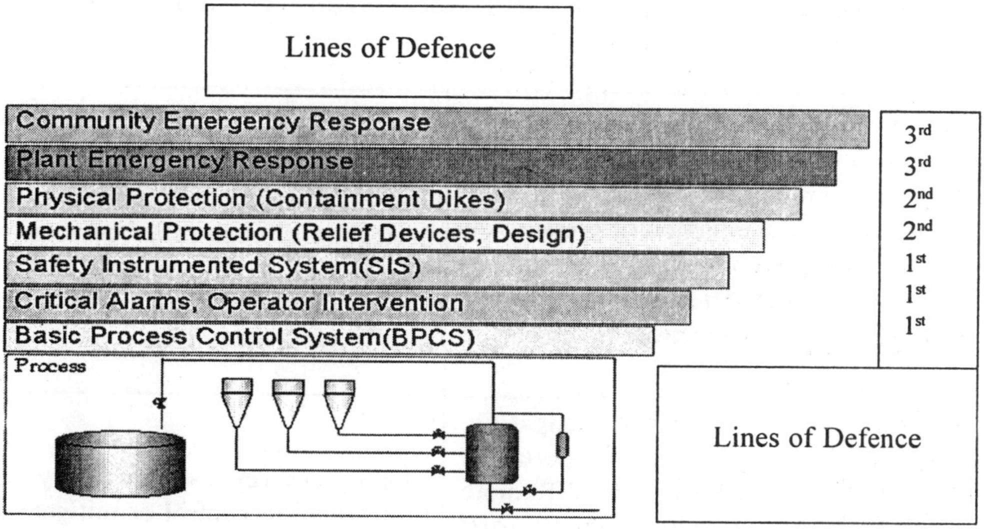

1st Line of Defence

For process safety, the first line of defence is to operate and maintain the process as designed, and keep the chemicals contained. The 1st line of defence consists of various layers with their defined role as given below:

1st Layer Basic Process Control Systems (BPCS) e.g. Pressure/Level Control	To control parameters of process within design limits.
2nd Layer Critical Alarms and Operator Intervention	To alert when 1st Layer fails to do its intended function.
3rd Layer Safety Instrumented Systems (SIS) (Emergency S/down Systems, Safety Systems)	Brings the process to a safe state when predetermined conditions are violated due to failure of both 1st and 2nd Layers.

The 1st line has a potential to avoid the release of chemicals. It is therefore prudent to pay utmost attention to the different layers of this line in design engineering stage.

2nd Line of Defence

1st line of defence is backed by 2nd line of defence with two layers, one prevents unwanted release and other control or mitigate the consequences in case there is a unwanted release.

Primary layers to prevent unwanted release. Some examples • Vapour Depressurising System e.g. flare system for rapid reduction of pressure on equipments by withdrawal of vapour. • Blow-down facilities for emergency removal of liquid from process vessels.	The layer represents a Mechanical Protection through relief devices and proper design of pressure parts to prevent unwanted release when 1st line fails to avoid the release.
Secondary layers for control or mitigation Some examples (Mostly in order of importance) • Remote Operated Valves ROV/Remote Switch-off provision for Fuel Cut-off/ Isolation. • Dykes, Catch Basins, Drainage System for fuel Containment.0000 • Fire Stops/Barriers for fuel Segregation. • Structural Fire proofing to delay the onset of fire. • Fire Protection Systems (Water Spray Systems etc.) to mitigate the fire.	The layers represent a "Physical Protection" to control or mitigate the consequences when both 1st line and primary layer of 2nd line fail.

3rd Line of Defence

Plant Emergency Response Community Emergency Response	This is "Emergency Preparedness (Disaster Management) Plan" both on site and off site.

3rd line of defence along with secondary layers of 2nd line of defence is required only when all other lines of defence fail.

What is an Independent Protection Layer (IPL) and a Safeguard?

A protection layer is a control measure. An Independent Protection Layer (IPL) is a device, system, or action that is capable of preventing a scenario from proceeding to its undesired consequence independent of the initiating event or the action of any other layer of protection associated with the scenario. The effectiveness and independence of an IPL must be auditable.

The effectiveness of an IPL is quantified in terms of its probability of failure on demand (PFD), which is defined as the probability that a system (in this case the IPL) will fail to perform a specified function on demand. The PFD is a dimensionless number between 0 to 1. The smaller the value of the PFD, the larger the reduction in frequency of the consequence for a given initiating event frequency. The "reduction in frequency" achieved by an IPL is sometimes termed the "risk reduction factor". IPLs are assigned "Safety Integrity Levels (SIL) as per IEC 61508.

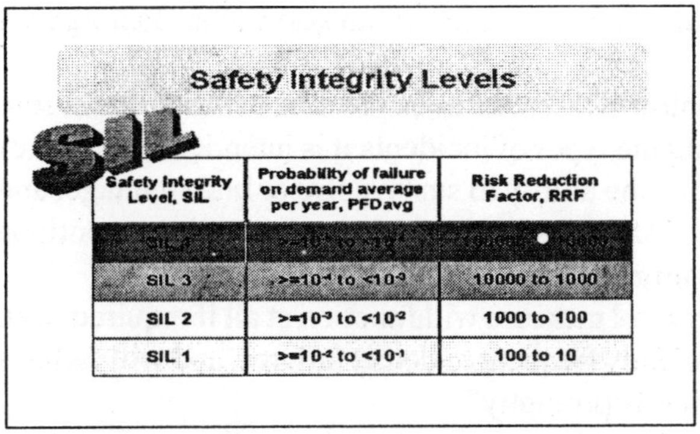
Safety Integrity Levels

SIL

Safety Integrity Level, SIL	Probability of failure on demand average per year, PFDavg	Risk Reduction Factor, RRF
SIL 4	>=10^{-5} to <10^{-4}	100000 to 10000
SIL 3	>=10^{-4} to <10^{-3}	10000 to 1000
SIL 2	>=10^{-3} to <10^{-2}	1000 to 100
SIL 1	>=10^{-2} to <10^{-1}	100 to 10

What does SIL mean?

It is simply statistical representation of the integrity of the control measure when process demand occurs.

For example consider the installation of a SIL 1 high level trip in a liquid tank. For PFD= 10^{-1}, the SIL 1 means that out of every 10 times that level reached the high level trip point, there would be one predicted failure and subsequent overflow of the tank.

For PFD= 10^{-2}, the SIL 1 means that out of every 100 times that level reached the high level trip point, there would be one predicted failure and subsequent overflow of the tank.

In order to be considered an IPL, a device, system, or action must be

- Effective in preventing the consequence when it functions as designed.
- Independent of the initiating event and the components of any other IPL already claimed for the same scenario.
- Auditable, the assumed effectiveness in terms of consequence prevention and PFD must be capable of validation in some manner (by documentation, review, testing, etc.).

The distinction between an IPL and a safeguard is important. A safeguard is any device, system, or action that would likely interrupt the chain of events following an initiating event. However, the effectiveness of some safeguards cannot be quantified due to lack of data, uncertainty as to independence or effectiveness, or other factors.

What is the Criterion for Effectiveness of Control Measure?

Effectiveness is a measure of how well the control measure performs, or is likely to perform, and can be defined in terms of: functionality, reliability including reliance on people, survivability. To a great extent, effectiveness of control measure depends on whether it is a proven approach or technology. In this regard, it must be recognized that the control measure when widely used does not mean that it is a proven approach or technology.

Effectiveness Criteria

- What is the functionality of a control measure against the relevant hazards? Is it sufficient to control the hazard in the intended manner, i.e. is it fit for purpose, will it suppress the hazard completely, prevent escalation or simply mitigate effects? Functionality can include a wide range of performance characteristics, for example, rate of application of foam and time of application for rim seal fire in floating roof tank.
- What is the survivability of the control measure in an incident? Is the control measure able to function as intended during the types of incidents it is intended to reduce or mitigate? Survivability can include the ability to survive fire or blast damage, and the other possible consequences of Major Incidents, and also the ability to continue to function as intended under abnormal process conditions.
- Reliability dictates whether the control measure will function at all if required in an incident. Is function testing sufficiently frequent to detect failures, and will failures once detected be rectified sufficiently promptly?
- Cost - Does this control measure provide sufficient benefit for the cost? Is there something, which would be better for the same or lower cost?

Holistic Approach to Process Safety

Process Safety Management is nothing but a defence mechanism to prevent and mitigate the consequences of episodic release of highly hazardous chemicals. The lines of defence play a crucial role to meet the objective/purpose of various standards on process safety because they provide the defence in depth. These lines of defence consist of layers of control measures. It is, therefore, essential to ensure that appropriate control measures are not only in place but also are operative.

The success for Process Safety lies in the way defence in depth is handled in different stages of Design, Construction, Operation and Maintenance. Hence what to do is evident?

1. Manage process safety-related aspects of technology and facility in design and adopt adequate control measure(s) in relation to major hazard.
2. Establish, implement and use SMS, which provides a "Comprehensive & Integrated System" for the management of all aspects of all adopted major hazard control measures for process safety.

Success of managing process safety greatly depends on "What is done in design, construction and commissioning?" and "What is the effectiveness of SMS? It is, therefore, a complex subject that involves many technical issues. In nutshell, it is better to call "Technical Management of Process Safety" instead of "Process Safety Management" as usually addressed in the industry.

CCPS (Centre for Chemical Process Safety) of AIChE (American Institute of Chemical Engineers) was established by AIChE in 1985 as a focal point to further the development and communication of improved safety methods, practices, designs, and procedures in the chemical process industry.

CCPS established a multifaceted programme to address the need for technical management commitment and technical management systems to reduce the potential for exposures to the public and the environment. One of the goals of the CCPS has been to prepare a series of books, which cover different aspects of process safety in order to provide a means of sharing approaches that have proved to be successful with the rest of the industry. The subject-matter of these books ranges from procedures for identifying and evaluating hazards to safe ways of storing and handling highly toxic materials. CCPS has published number of books on process safety. These books can be considered as resources for "What to do in design?" and "What to do for effective SMS?"

CCPS Books

(1) Guidelines for Technical Management of Chemical Process Safety.
(2) Guidelines for Vapour Release Mitigation.
(3) Guidelines for Safe storage and Handling of High Toxic Hazard materials.
(4) Guidelines for Safe Automation of Chemical Processes.
(5) Layers of Protection Analysis (LOPA) - Simplified Process Risk Assessment.
(6) Guidelines for Hazard Evaluation Procedures.
(7) Guidelines for Chemical Process Quantified Risk Analysis (CPQRA).
(8) Guidelines for Design Solutions for Process Equipment Failures.

Many safety programmes/books include personal safety issues. CCPS books, however do not directly address either personal injuries or industrial hygiene issues. CCPS recognises the importance of emergency preparedness programme. However, CCPS books do not address these necessary activities with outside community. The thrust of CCPS books is on 1st line of defence and 2nd line of defence.

The author believes that SMS of most of the companies, apart from process safety, focus on wide range of issues like production, quality, control of emissions, personal safety and industrial hygiene. Therefore, process safety related issues/aspects either get neglected or obscured. Hence industries should examine the effectiveness of SMS for process safety in the light of issues dealt in CCPS books.

REFERENCES

Guidelines for Technical Management of Chemical Process Safety.

Layers of Protection Analysis (LOPA) - Simplified Process Risk Assessment.

14

DEVELOPMENT OF SAFETY CULTURE

Amar Nath*

ABSTRACT

A well-designed safety management system can help to reduce injuries along with the associated hidden costs. But, many managers cannot tell you how to develop and enhance their safety management systems. As traditional way of managing safety does not bring desired results, managers are trying to find other methodologies to improve safety standard of their organizations. This paper discusses some ways to develop Safety Culture to achieve the desired results. Safety culture is about good safety attitudes in people but it is also about good safety management established by organizations. Good Safety Culture means giving the highest priority to safety. Good Safety culture implies a constant assessment of the safety significance of events and issues, in order that the appropriate level of attention can be given.

Introduction

In high reliability industries, there has been an increasing recognition of the importance of the cultural and the behavioural aspects of safety management. Investigations into major disasters have revealed that complex systems broke down disastrously, despite the adoption of the full range of engineering and technical safeguards, because people failed to do what they were supposed to do.

Management has come to realize the general likelihood of an accident occurring in their plant depends not just on the actions of individual employees but also on the safety culture of the organisation. The term 'safety culture' has arisen out of the report on the 1986 Chernobyl accident, where the errors and violations of the operating procedures that contributed to the accident were seen as the poor safety culture at the plant.

The concept of safety culture is defined in INSAG-4 as follows:

> *"Safety culture is that assembly of characteristics and attitudes in organizations and individuals which establishes that, as an overriding priority, nuclear plant safety issues receive the attention warranted by their significance."*

---

*Head, Industrial Safety and Fire, Narora Atomic Power Station.

Organizations with a positive safety culture are characterized by "communications founded on mutual trust, by shared perceptions of the importance of safety and by the efficacy of preventive measures".

In order to operate a nuclear installation safely, it is not enough to have a technically safe system. For safe operation it is also equally important that the operating personnel should have a proper attitude to safety and the management, as well as the workers must be committed to safety and must realize that safety has the highest priority above all.

Safety culture applies to conventional and personal safety as well as nuclear safety. All safety considerations are affected by common points of beliefs, attitudes, behaviour, and cultural differences, closely linked to a shared system of values and standards.

An organization with a good safety culture relies on close interdependence between technical safety and organizational processes. In practice, a high level of safety culture means the systematic organization and implementation of activities aimed at creating high quality technical, human and organizational systems. Whatever the level of technical sophistication, a mature safety culture can offer a defence in depth against the risk of accidents.

If one wishes to summarize the relationship between the behaviour of individuals and safety culture, one can say: the response of all those who strive for excellence in matters affecting nuclear safety should be characterized by:

A QUESTIONING ATTITUDE
plus
A RIGOROUS AND PRUDENT APPROACH
plus
COMMUNICATION
The result will be a major contribution to:
SAFETY

Stages of Development of Safety Culture

IAEA Safety Report has indicated that three stages of development seem to emerge, each displaying a different awareness of and receptiveness to the effect on safety of human behaviour and attitudes. The characteristics of each stage, identified below, provide organizations with a basis for self-diagnosis.

STAGE I—Safety Based Solely on Rules and Regulations

At this stage, the organization sees safety as an external requirement and not as an aspect of conduct that will help the organization to succeed. The external requirements are those of national governments, regional authorities, or regulatory bodies. There is little awareness of behavioural and attitudinal aspects of safety performance, and no willingness to consider such issues. Safety is seen very much as a technical issue; mere compliance with rules and regulations is considered adequate.

Following characteristics may be observed:

- Problems are not anticipated; the organization reacts to each one as it occurs.
- The decisions taken by departments and functions concentrate upon little more than the need to comply with rules.
- People who make mistakes are simply blamed for their failure to comply with the rules.
- The role of management is seen as endorsing the rules, pushing employees and expecting results.
- There is not much listening or learning inside or outside the organization, which adopts a defensive posture when criticized.
- Safety is viewed as a required nuisance.
- Regulators, customers, suppliers and contractors are treated cautiously or in an adversarial manner.
- Short-term profits are seen as all-important.
- People are viewed as 'system components' - they are defined and valued solely in terms of what they do.
- People are rewarded for obedience and results, regardless of long-term consequences.

STAGE II—Good Safety Performance Becomes an Organizational Goal

An organization at this stage has a management, which perceives safety performance as important even in the absence of regulatory pressure. Safety performance is dealt with, along with other aspects of the business, in terms of targets or goals. The organization begins to look at the reasons why safety performance reaches a plateau and is willing to seek the advice of other organizations.

- The organization concentrates primarily on day to day matters. There is little in the way of strategy.
- Decisions are often centered on cost and function.
- Management's response to mistakes is to put more controls in place via procedures and retraining. There is a little less blaming.
- Conflict is disturbing and is discouraged in the name of teamwork.
- Safety, cost and productivity are seen as detracting from one another. Safety is thought to imply higher cost and reduced production.
- The organization's relationship with regulators, customers, suppliers and contractors is distant rather than close; there is a cautious approach where trust has to be earned.
- There is growing awareness of the impact of cultural issues in the work place. It is not understood why added controls do not yield the expected results in safety performance.

STAGE III— Safety Performance can Always be Improved

An organization at Stage III has adopted the idea of continuous improvement and applied the concept to safety performance. There is a strong emphasis on communications, training, management style, and improving efficiency and effectiveness.

The level of awareness of behavioural and attitudinal issues is high, and measures are being taken to improve behaviour. Progress is made one step at a time and never stops. The organization asks how it might help other companies.

- The organization begins to act strategically with a focus on the longer term as well as awareness of the present. It anticipates problems and deals with their causes before they happen.
- Decisions are made in the full knowledge of their safety impact on work or business processes as well as on departments and functions.
- There is no goal conflict between safety and production performance, so that safety is not jeopardized in pursuit of production targets.
- Almost all mistakes are viewed in terms of work process variability. It is more important to understand what has happened than to find someone to blame. This understanding is used to modify the work process.
- Management's role is seen as coaching people to improve business performance.
- Learning from others both inside and outside the organization is valued. Time is made available and devoted to adapting such knowledge to improve business performance.
- Safety and production are seen as inter-dependent.
- Collaborative relationships are developed between the organization and regulators, suppliers, customers and contractors.
- People are respected and valued for their contribution.
- People are aware of the impact of cultural issues, and these are factors considered in key decisions.
- The organization rewards not only those who 'produce' but also those who support the work of others. People are also rewarded for improving processes as well as results.

Linking Practices to the Development Stages of Safety Culture

Some general advice on practices, which may be particularly appropriate at given stages, is given below:

Stage I

- Senior managers commit the organization to improving its safety performance and agree on a safety vision.
- Senior managers review or formulate safety policy and communicate it to the workforce.

- Managers review safety training and start to develop employee participation by inviting employees to identify training needs.
- Managers establish safety performance measures and analyze statistics to establish trends. They share information with employees.
- Joint management/employee safety meetings are held to discuss safety issues in a non-adversarial way.
- Managers introduce regular review and audit of safety in order to identify areas for improvement.
- Managers seek suggestions from employees on how to improve safety.

Stage II

- Senior managers make managers aware that values, attitudes and behaviour of employees are important factors in achieving good safety performance and help employees to contribute to improving safety performance.
- Managers make employees aware of other organizations, which have successfully improved their safety performance in order to demonstrate that this can be achieved. Employees are thus introduced to external ideas, which may be worth adapting.
- Managers seek active involvement of employees in improving safety.
- Managers review contractors' safety performance.
- Senior managers make managers aware of human factors and introduce root cause analysis.
- Senior managers introduce positive safety performance measures.
- Managers introduce self-assessment of safety performance and ensure that there is a comprehensive corrective action programme.
- Senior managers encourage managers' awareness that good safety performance is good for business.

Stage III

- Senior managers remain alert to the possibility of learning from other organizations and establish systems for doing this. They recognize the effects of processes on safety results.
- Managers review safety targets and objectives. They remain alert to potential safety improvements.
- Managers co-operate with suppliers and contractors to improve their safety performance.
- Senior managers introduce organizational cultural indicators (e.g. standards of housekeeping, reporting of 'near misses') that have a bearing on safety performance.
- Senior managers make comparisons with external organizations chosen as benchmarks.
- Senior managers communicate with the public on safety issues.
- Managers encourage employees to assist in the further improvement of existing processes.

Practices for Senior Management

The involvement and commitment of senior management in pursuing high standards of safety is essential. Without a visible and genuine demonstration of this commitment by personal behaviour and leadership by senior managers, other workers in the organization will not be convinced of the importance of safety compared to other organizational issues. Words without deeds will create an illusion of safety that will result in the development of a superficial safety culture.

To support the development of a good safety culture, senior managers can contribute by:

- Gaining understanding of safety culture concepts and practices through appropriate training;
- Demonstrating a leadership style with an appropriate balance between caring and controlling;
- Being visibly interested in safety;
- Having safety as a priority item on the agenda at meetings;
- Encouraging employees to have a questioning attitude on safety issues;
- Ensuring that safety is addressed in the strategic plans of their organization;
- Having personal objectives for directly improving aspects of safety in their areas of responsibility;
- Monitoring safety trends to ensure that safety objectives are being achieved;
- Taking a genuine interest in safety improvements, giving recognition to those who achieve them, and not restricting their interest to situations where there is a safety problem.

Senior management should ensure that their organization has a safety management system that provides a structured systematic means of achieving and maintaining high standards of safety performance.

Safety Performance Indicators

As per the IAEA Safety Report traditionally, most organizations record the number of accidents and safety related events. Whilst providing important trend information, these indicators are of a passive nature and their exclusive use can be demotivating to the workforce. Some organizations use indicators of a more positive nature to complement the traditional passive indicators. Positive safety indicators include:

- Percentage of employees who have received safety refresher training during the previous month/quarter;
- Percentage of safety improvement proposals implemented during the previous month/quarter;
- Percentage of improvement teams involved in determining solutions to safety related problems;

- Percentage of communication briefs that include safety information;
- Number of safety inspections conducted by senior managers/managers/ supervisors during the previous week/month (a safety inspection may be combined with a housekeeping inspection);
- Percentage of employees' suggestions relating to safety improvement;
- Percentage of routine organizational meetings with safety on the agenda.

The value of positive safety indicators is that they serve as a mechanism for awarding recognition to employees who are endeavouring to improve safety by thought, action or commitment. Recognition for achievement is a powerful motivating force to encourage continued improvement.

Concluding Remarks

There is no consistent and visible prescriptive formula for developing a strong safety culture. However, a prerequisite is genuine and consistent commitment by the top management of an organization to improve safety. Provided this commitment exists, the best recommendation is to do something tangible and visible to improve safety, preferably involving employees from the outset.

REFERENCE

Developing Safety Culture in Nuclear Activities, practical suggestions to assist progress; IAEA Safety Reports Series No. 11.

IMPROVING OCCUPATIONAL HEALTH AND SAFETY ASPECTS
A Case Study

S.K. Agrawal*, Pankaj Kumar**, Rajeev Kumar*** and R.G. Yadav****

ABSTRACT

There is a global endeavour to adopt an Occupational Health and Safety Management System (OHSAS 18001) to identify/minimize work related Health and Safety hazards. An Occupational Health and Safety Management System is a structured process to minimize potentials of work related fatalities, injuries and illness, to increase productivity by reducing the direct and indirect costs associated with accidents, and to enhance the usefulness of products and/or services.

POWERGRID, being the leader in advancement of technology, always utilizes state of the art technologies in every field including Occupational Health and Safety. In this endeavour, POWERGRID is committed to provide good Occupational Health to its employees; other associated stakeholders and minimize risks in area of its operation. Implementation of Occupational Health and Management System (OHSAS 18001: 1999) has enabled to identify the areas of improvement and measures required. It identified the risks towards consequences for Safety in all works of activity, especially at work places has created eagerness to take proactive steps for Safety.

This paper shares POWERGRID's experience in improving occupational health and safety aspects. In this paper, core issues for seamless integration of various diverse management systems like ISO 9001: 2000, ISO 14001: 1996 and OHSAS 18001: 1999 into one coherent system to achieve desired objectives are also discussed. It is concluded that a common holistic framework provides opportunities for continually improved performance.

Key Words

Continual Improvement, Certification Process, Hazard and Risk Control, Integrated Management System, Occupational Health and Safety Management System, Non-Conformity.

*GM (OS), Power Grid Corporation of India Ltd., Saudamini, Plot No. 2, Sector 29, Gurgaon-122001.
**DGM (OS), Power Grid Corporation of India Ltd., Saudamini, Plot No. 2, Sector 29, Gurgaon-122001.
***Manager (OS), Power Grid Corporation of India Ltd., Saudamini, Plot No. 2, Sector 29, Gurgaon-122001.
****Executive Director (OS), Power Grid Corporation of India Ltd., Saudamini, Plot No. 2, Sector 29, Gurgaon-122001.

Introduction

Power Grid Corporation of India Ltd., one of the largest transmission utility of the World is operating and maintaining 56317 ckt km of EHV transmission lines and 95 Sub-stations having transformation capacity of 55322 MVA with transmission system availability nearly 99 per cent. POWERGRID was certified to ISO-9001:1994 in July 1995 and became the first utility in Power Sector to be bestowed with this distinction. Subsequently, after revision of ISO 9001, POWERGRID aligned its QMS as per ISO 9001: 2000 and the certificate was revalidated up to November 2005 after regular surveillance audits by certification bodies.

The Quality Standard ISO 9001:2000 is compatible with ISO 14001:1996. It has triggered the blending of an organization's quality and environment management systems to address the short-term and long-term impact on quality and environment through its products, processes and services.

In the changed global scenario of continuous improvement, there is a drive for competitiveness based on improved quality and higher concern for Occupational Health & Safety and Environmental aspects. There is a renewed trust for a suitable global framework to implement cost effective Occupational Health & Safety Delivery System to prevent work-place ailments and promote the health and welfare of the employees. Further, organizational outlook towards consequences of not adhering to Safety norms in work places has created eagerness to take proactive steps for developing safety culture. The need is felt by the organizations to bring a dynamic balance between conflicting interests of the Nation, Organizations and individuals to achieve objectives of Occupational Health and Safety. There is a global trend of adopting Occupational Health and Safety Management System (OHSAS 18001) to identify and minimize work related Health and Safety hazards.

In this context, POWERGRID has developed and implemented systems and procedures aligned to the integrated requirements of ISO 9001: 2000 (Quality Management System), ISO 14001: 1996 (Environmental Management System) and OHSAS 18001: 1999 (Occupational Health and Safety Management System) in 2005 and certified to the above standards by British Standard Institution. The certification is continued after successful compliance to routine surveillance audits.

What is OHSAS

OHSAS is a structured management system to minimize potentials of work related fatalities, injuries and illness to increase productivity by reducing the direct and indirect cost associated with accidents, and to increase the quality of products and/or services. In order to achieve these objectives, voluntarily organizations have gone for implementation of Occupational Health and Safety Management System Standard (OHSAS 18001:1999) and got themselves certified by independent agencies.

Primarily, effective management of employee safety and health protection is a decisive factor in reducing work-related injuries and illnesses. OHSAS management system provides a structured process to minimize work related injuries and illnesses, and reduce the direct and indirect costs associated with accidents. Also, it provides a direction to health and safety requirements, with reference to organizational policies, regulatory requirements, recommended guidelines, industry practices and standards. Therefore, conforming to OHSAS 18001:1999 management system is of significant value for the organizations.

OHSAS 18001:1999 is a specification against which certification can be obtained. The OHSAS is a management system that enables an organization to control the impact of their activities, products and/or services in Occupational Health and Safety. The organizations which effectively established, implemented and maintained OHSAS standard requirements are eligible to apply for certification. The certification scheme was established with the objective that while making effort and upon receiving the certification; the organization will become more self-regulatory in promoting Occupational Health & Safety at work places. This standard provides the framework to establish a strategic approach by:

- Implementing the management system at various levels of OHSAS maturity.
- Demonstrating compliance with applicable OHSAS legislation and regulations, with a commitment to continuous improvement.

This standard has been developed to be compatible with ISO: 9001:1994 and ISO 14001:1996, in order to facilitate the integration of three standards. The system components in OHSAS are given in figure 1.0 below:

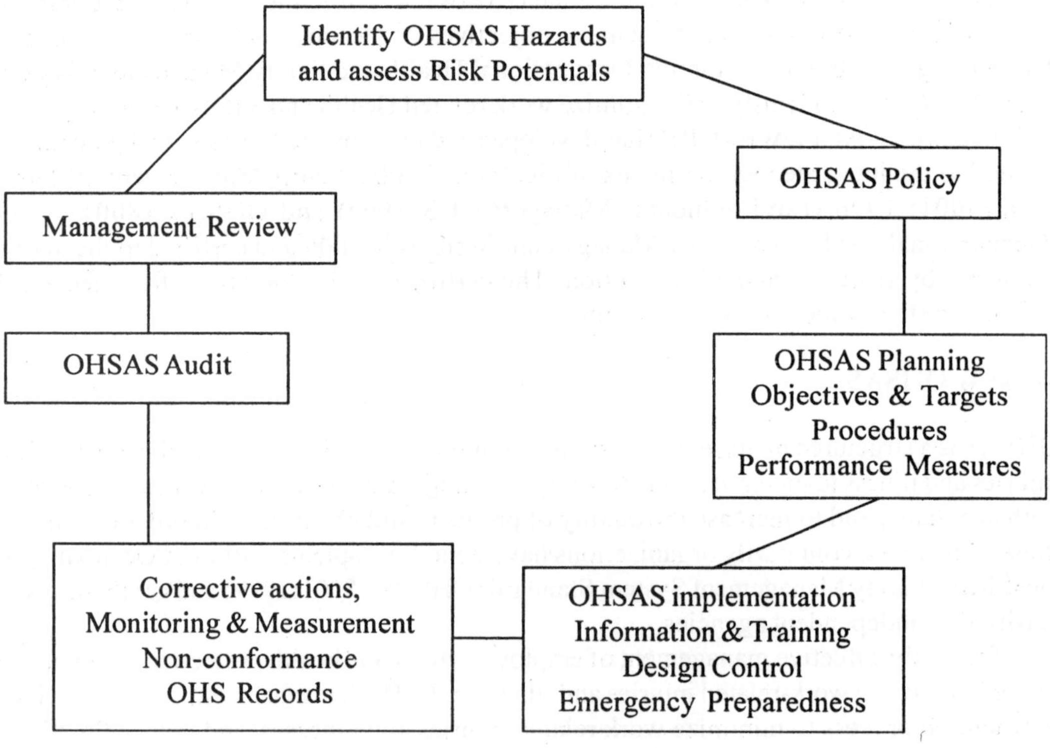

Fig. 1: System Components of OHSAS

Requirements for Implementation of OHSAS: 18001

For implementation of OHSAS: 18001, the following requirements are to be considered:

- Policy Statement for safety and health protection of the employees.
- Occupational Health & Safety Policy Objectives.
- Occupational Health & Safety measurable goals and objectives.
- Identification of health and safety hazards and assessment of Risk potentials.
- Legal & Statutory Labour laws.
- Concepts of Hazards Prevention and Continual improvement.
- Handling, Storage and Packaging of Hazardous materials.
- Emergency Preparedness & Response Plan.
- Implementation of a medical surveillance programme with competent medical services.

To integrate Occupational Safety and Management System with existing Quality Management System, the organization should provide systematic policies, procedures and practices to protect employees from, and allow them to recognize work related health and safety hazards. An effective programme includes the provision of identification, evaluation and control of general work place hazards, specific job hazards, and potential hazards. The major elements of the guidelines are:

- Management commitment and employee involvement.
- Work place analysis.
- Hazard prevention and control.
- Safety and health training.

Management Commitment and Employee Involvement

Management commitment is must to motivate the employees and provide resources for organizing and controlling the activities within the organization. The management must regard the safety and health of the employees as fundamental value of the organization and should be committed to the safety and health of employees like other organizational goals. Involvement of employees provides the commitment to the health and safety of themselves as well as of colleagues. Some of the recommended actions are:

- Clearly state a worksite policy on safe and healthy working conditions. All the personnel should clearly understand the priority and importance of safety and health protection in the organization.
- Provide top management involvement in implementing the programme.
- Encourage employees to follow safe practices and avoid shortcuts.
- Assign and communicate responsibility for all aspects of the programme so that the employees at different levels understand their expected performance level.
- Review the programme at regular interval to evaluate the progress in meeting the goals and objectives and initiate preventive/ corrective actions for the shortcomings.

Work Place Analysis

Work place analysis involves the examination of work place to identify the existing hazards/ near misses and conditions/operations which might create new hazards. The following measures are recommended to identify existing and potential hazards:

- Conduct a comprehensive work place survey and periodically update surveys.
- Analyze existing and planned facilities, processes, material and equipment.
- Perform routine job hazard analysis.
- Assess risk factors/near misses.
- Investigate accidents and near miss incidents. Analyze injury and illness trends over time, to identify and prevent common causes.

Hazard Prevention and Control

Elimination/control of work place hazards must be completed in a time-bound manner after recognizing the hazard and near misses. The risk control procedure should include:

- Use of engineering technique where feasible and appropriate.
- Establish safe work practices and procedures. These should be understood and followed by all the affected parties.
- Provide personal protective equipment.
- Plan and prepare for emergencies and conduct emergency drills periodically.
- Provide first-aid onsite and emergency medical care to minimize the risk.

Safety and Health Training

Safety and health training is an important tool to make the employees aware about safe practices and medical help. The training should be designed to ensure that all employees are aware of the hazards to which they are exposed and proper methods for avoiding such hazards. The supervisors should understand their role and carry out their responsibility effectively like analysis of work to anticipate and identify potential hazards, maintenance of physical protection at work sites etc.

Implementation of OHSAS

POWERGRID was certified to ISO-9001:1994 in July 1995 became the first Utility in Power Sector to be bestowed with this distinction. Considering the importance of Quality Management System and Occupational Health and Safety Management Systems, POWERGRID had decided to integrate Quality Management System with these Management Systems in December 2004.

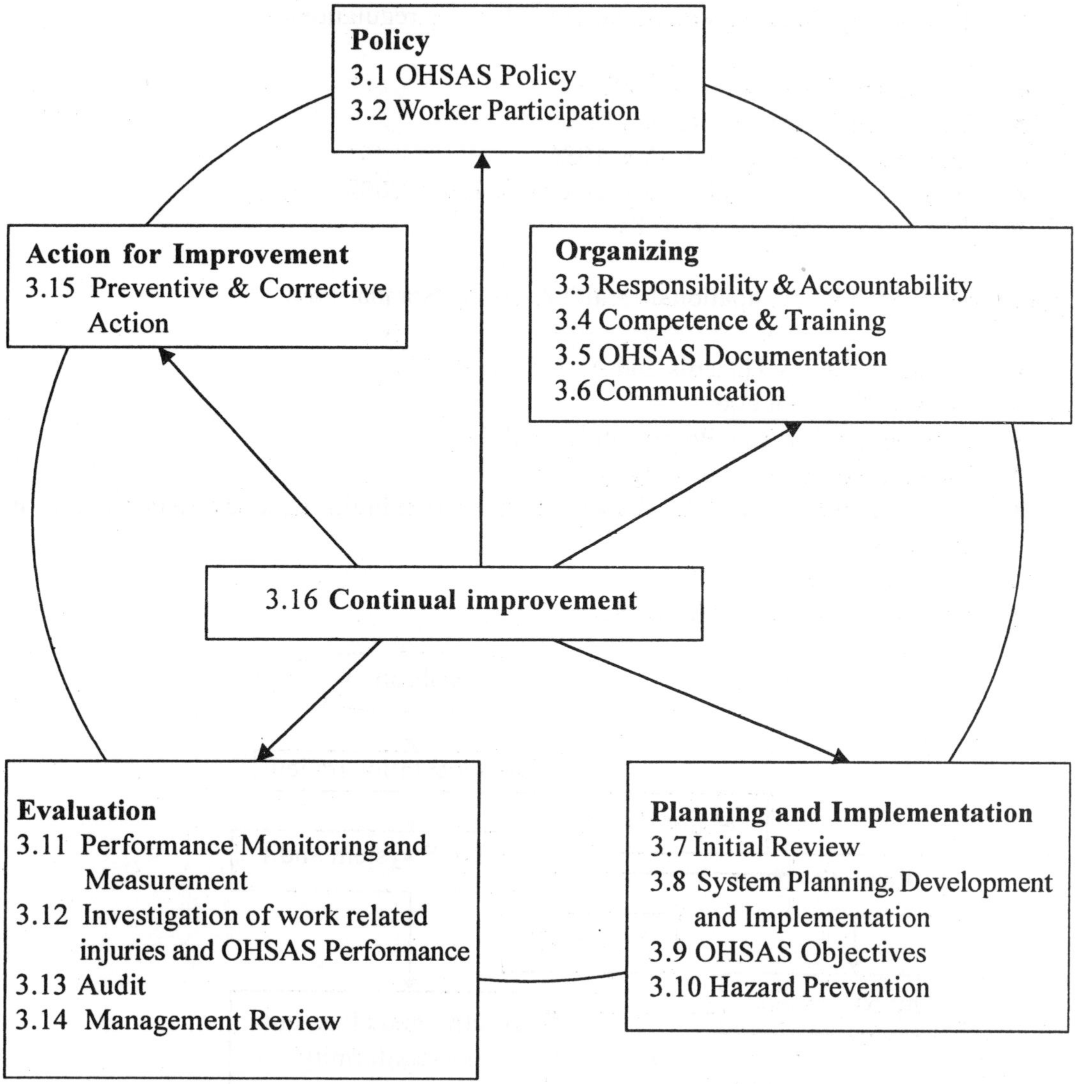

Fig 2.0: Main Elements of Occupational Health and Safety Management System

Steering committee comprising of representatives from concerned Departments was constituted and the plan for integration was finalized in its initial meetings. Gap analysis was carried out to find the difference in above Management Systems. Several awareness programmes were organized to aware the employees about the management systems being integrated. Training for internal audit of IMS was imparted to the employees.

Hazard and Risk analysis was carried out as per the requirement of OHSAS 18001. Operational control procedures were prepared to improve the practices and reduce the risks. Level-I, Level-II and Level-III documents were developed. Some of the procedures developed are as under:

Applicable Statutory Requirements as per the following regulations:

- The Indian Electricity Act, 2003.
- The Indian Electricity Rules, 1956.
- Environment (Protection) Act, 1986.
- Noise Pollution (Regulation and Control) Rules, 2000.
- The Gas Cylinder Rules, 1981.

Procedures related to Occupational Health & Safety Standard are

- Health & Safety Hazards and Associated Risks.
- OH&S Requirements.
- Emergency/Disaster Preparedness and Response.
- Material/equipment handling by crane.
- Working on high altitudes (Towers/multi storied buildings/overhead structures in switchyards).
- Drinking water.
- Management of electric shock.

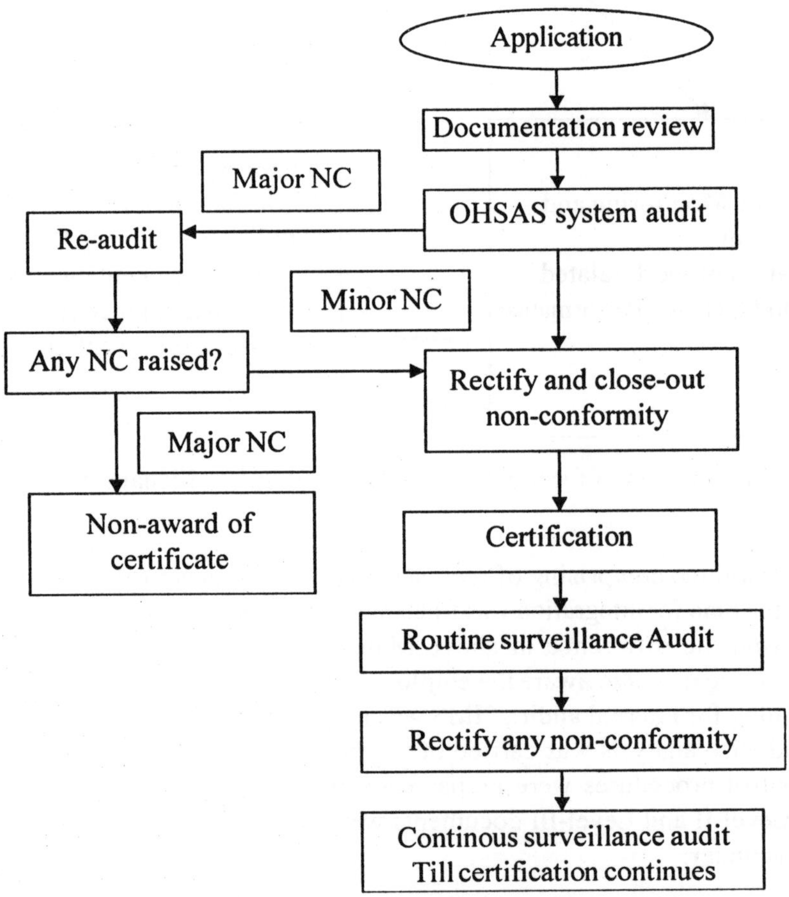

Fig. 3: Process of certification of Integrated Management System

Extensive Internal audits were carried out to find the area of concern and initiating corrective actions. Adequacy audit was carried out to check the adequacy of Level-I, Level-II and Level-III documents. After taking the corrective action, Final Assessment and Certification audit was carried out. Flow chart of the processes involved is as per Figure 3 above.

Indian Scenario

Large organizations are subjected to compliance of regulatory instruments like Environment (Protection) Act, Factory Act and other applicable act and rules. Considering the ever growing development, pressure of regulatory compliance on employment and industries will call for well defined occupational and environmental health guidelines. Traditional work pattern involving dependence on human being is being replaced with high automation and technological surges. Therefore, comprehensive analysis of technology application and human factors identify potential accident and safety risks. Integrating ergonomic and other control measures in planning and design helps to reduce capital cost, compensation and operational delays.

In changing scenario, social awareness about the environment and occupational health has brought a good impact on conservation of environment as well as safety awareness. Safety at work places and occupational health is also getting the importance. Being the 2nd largest population with limited economic resources, we have to face the challenges of following safe and healthy work practices comparable with international standard.

Future Perspective

It is being realized by organizations that implementing OHSAS have positive impact on organizational sustainability and create a positive perception of prevention of work place hazards. If, we calculate the total costs resulting from injury, illness and disability, the true cost of production will be higher than the production cost calculated after implementing the safe practices. Therefore, it is necessary to integrate the OHSAS requirements in the manufacturing/service processes.

Safety, health and environmental issues are the integral element of other management system and mandatory regulations. As per clause No. 6.4 of ISO 9001:2000, the organization shall identify and manage those human and physical factors of the work environment needed to achieve conformity of product and processes, as suitable. Therefore, we have to provide healthy working environment to the employees to meet the requirement of other management systems as well as mandatory regulations.

Conclusion

POWERGRID's experience with implementation of IMS is quite encouraging. IMS was implemented in Corporate office during 2004. Subsequently, two more regions, namely SRTS-I and NRTS-II have been certified for IMS during 2005-2006. By implementation of IMS, safety awareness amongst the employees and workers has been enhanced. This has resulted in improvement of working atmosphere as well as the quality and productivity of work.

Acknowledgements

The authors are grateful to POWERGRID management for granting permission to write and present this paper. The views expressed in this paper are of the authors only and not of the management.

Bibliography

IS 18001: 2000 - Occupational Health and Safety Management System - specification with guidance for use.

OHSAS 18001: 1999 - Occupational Health and Safety Management System - Specifications.

J. Haque, Umesh Chandra and S.K. Agrawal "Safety issues in power transmission sector" published in "Managing safety: Challenges ahead" Theme: Safety and Hazard control held in February' 2005 organized by Safety and Quality forum, Institution of Engineers, pp. 140 to 150.

16

ROLE OF ELECTRICAL SAFETY ON INDIAN RAILWAYS

R.S. Grover*

ABSTRACT

Indian Railways are the third largest railway system in the world under a single management and is the principal mode of transportation for bulk freight and long distance passenger traffic. It handles daily about 1.7 million tonnes freight and 15 million passengers across the country. Therefore, safety is *sine qua non* for train operation on this gigantic railway system covering 63,500 Rkms. With emphasis on prevention of accidents on Indian Railways, avoidance of Electrical accidents is one critical area, which needs to be addressed with due seriousness and importance. Electricity if not handled with due care, may lead to heavy damages and casualty. Indian Railways have formulated legislations and laid down rules/regulations to ensure public safety due to electrical equipments in locomotives, coaches and railway stations/installations. These regulations are derived from Electricity Act and accordingly appropriate Electricity Rules are made. There also exists a suitable link between Electricity Act/Rules with Indian Railway Act. Railways have special requirements in train operations, certain amount of discretion has been provided in the IE Act as well as IE Rules, which in turn are expected to be taken care of in IR Act. Additional Member Electrical at apex level, i.e. Ministry of Railways and Chief Electrical Engineers of Zonal Railways have also been assigned role of Electrical Inspector - a statutory authority under the IE Act.

This paper is an effort to bring out obligations and responsibilities stipulated in these Regulations and to assess level of compliance at present, and also to identify areas where implementation needs to be streamlined and suggest modalities for strengthening the institution of Electrical Inspector in accordance with the Electricity Act/Rules as part of corporate responsibility.

Introduction

Indian Railways is the principal mode of transport of the country and have completed 150 years of service to the nation. It has played a vital role in the overall development of the

*Advisor Electrical, Rail Vikas Nigam Ltd., New Delhi. Former Addl. Member Electrical, Rly. Board, Ministry of Railways.

country and national integration. During 2004-05, Indian Railways had carried 626 million tonnes of freight and 5513 million passengers. Therefore safety in train operation is one of the important mission areas of Indian Railways. Accordingly steps have been taken to reduce train accidents and tangible results have been achieved during last 2 decades. One of important area of concern is electrical safety in train operation and maintenance of rolling stock and other fixed assets.

Indian Railways—Use of Electricity

The Indian Railways use various types of carriages and vehicles (referred to as Rolling Stock) that have electrical equipment for traction and controls, lighting, ventilation, air-conditioning and other passenger amenities. In addition electrical power is required for various other fixed installations for convenience of passengers at railway station, besides maintenance of various assets. Some of the important applications are as under:

- Passenger carriages are provided with electrical equipments for generation and distribution of electricity at various voltages, e.g. 110 V AC and DC, 230 V AC, 415 V AC, 750 V AC etc., for lighting, ventilation, air-conditioning, heating and various types of pantry car equipment. Further, the development of equipment using high voltage and power-electronics system of capacity up to 500 kW is in progress.
- In Electrical/Diesel locomotives and Electrical Multiple Units and Diesel Multiple Units, high, medium and low voltage systems for traction and controls.
- 25 kV AC and 1500 V DC system traction Over Head Equipment as well as 750 V DC third rail system for feeding power to locomotives and electrical rolling stock.
- Railway traction sub-stations are fed at 132/220 kV for traction and 66/33/11 kV for general services. Supply of power supply for lighting and ventilation in Railway stations, workshops, maintenance yards, goods sheds, administrative and ancillary offices, pumping and sewage installations, signalling and telecommunication equipments, computer installations for operations, commercial and other purposes, construction equipments, etc. With technological improvements and need for automation, electrically operated equipments are increasing use in various applications. Supply is either taken from the local electricity supply authorities, or OHE and supplemented with other sources such as diesel generating sets, uninterrupted power supply systems, etc.

Electrical Safety Regulations

Provision in the Act

Basic provision in Indian Electricity Act for ensuring electrical safety is Section 53 which empowers the Central Electricity Authority to specify suitable measures for:

> "Protecting the public from dangers arising of electricity and specifying action to be taken in relation to any electric line or electrical plant, or any electrical appliance

under the control of a consumer for the purpose of eliminating or reducing the risk of personal injury or damage to property or interference with its use."

Chief Electrical Inspector and Electrical Inspector are authorities who are to be appointed by Appropriate Government under Section 162 of Act to ensure enforcement of provisions of Act and Rules.

In respect of Railways, the Chief Electrical Engineers are also the Electrical Inspectors to the Government, as decided by the Appropriate Government. In addition to this the Additional Member Electrical of Ministry of Railways is also designated as the Chief Electrical Inspector for Ministry of Railways.

Applicability and Extent of Compliance

With dual role of Chief Electrical Engineer and Electrical Inspector, enforcement of various provisions in Act and Rule are by and large followed and in-built with regard to electrical equipments and works directly under technical and administrative control of Chief Electrical Engineer. In respect of fixed installations, there exists a practice of concerned officers and staff making a formal application with all related documents to Electrical Inspector for commissioning of new and modified electrical works.

Strict compliance of the following sections of the Act and the Rule are not being observed by the Railways:

(a) Section 45 of Rules titled Precautions to be adopted by consumers, owners, occupants, electrical contractors, electrical workmen and suppliers stipulates:
"No electrical installation work should be done by a person not holding a certificate of competency and by a person not holding a permit issued or recognized by the State Government."
"No electrical installation work which has been carried out in contravention of sub-rule (1) shall either be energized or connected to the works of any supplier."
No exemption has been officially notified by the Railways under this section and there are several areas where electrical works are sometimes executed by persons not having the requisite permit and are also not supervised by competent personnel.

(b) Section 5 of Rules titled "Entry and Inspection" authorizes the Electrical Inspector or any other officer appointed to assist him to enter into any place, carriage or vessel where there is an electrical equipment or apparatus for generation, transmission, transformation, conversion, distribution or use of energy takes place and carry out tests therein and check observance of provisions of the Act.
No set practice exists in the Railways presently to cover all such areas indicated above under the purview of the Electrical Inspector or his assistant.

(c) Section 47(A) of the Rules titled "Installation and testing of generating units" stipulates:
Any consumer or occupier installs a generating plant, he shall give a thirty days' notice of his intention to commission the plant to the supplier as well as the Inspector and shall not commission his generating plant of a capacity exceeding 10 kW without the approval in writing of the Inspector.

Strict compliance of this provision is not being followed at times, especially with regard to Rolling Stock applications.

(d) Section 161 of the Act titled Notice of Accidents and Inquiries stipulates prompt reporting of electrical accidents by person in charge of equipment to Electrical Inspector.

Strict compliance of this provision is also not being followed, again especially with regard to Rolling Stock applications.

Special Provisions for Railways

A specific case is regarding the exemption of Railways Rolling stock from the applicability of Chapter IX (Electric Traction) of the Rules as detailed in Section 94:

Section 94: Additional rules for electric traction: The rules in this Chapter apply only where energy is used for purposes of traction.

The items covered under this chapter pertain to the conductors used for electric traction and for the Railways; these items are in turn covered elaborately in the AC Traction Manual.

Another case is the exemption of Railways from issue of advance notice to prior to transmission or use of electricity in public places, as detailed in Section 54 of the Act:

Section 54: Control of Transmission and Use of Electricity: no person other than the Central Transmission Utility or a State Transmission Utility, or a licensee shall transmit or use electricity at a rate exceeding two hundred and fifty watts and one hundred volts in any street, or in any place in which one hundred or more persons are ordinarily likely to be assembled; or which is a factory within the meaning of the Factories Act, 1948 or a mine within the meaning of the Mines Act of 1952, or

In this case also, with regard to fixed installations Railways have taken adequate precautions under the AC Traction Manual and other laid down procedures. But with regard to Rolling Stock, adequate steps have to be taken by the Railways.

Role of Electrical Inspector in Electrical Safety of Rolling Stock

Railways have laid down a detailed procedure for opening of new lines, introduction of new rolling stock, etc., *vide* Gazette notification dated 21st July, 2000. However, the role of Electrical Inspector is defined clearly only in case of approval of electric traction equipment.

As regards use of new types of locomotive or rolling stock, an application is required to be made to the Government through Commissioner along with six items. One of six items is a Safety certificate, to be jointly signed by Chief Engineer, Chief Mechanical Engineer and Chief Electrical Engineer (for Electric stock). Chief Signal and Telecommunication Engineer and Chief Operations Manager are also required to sign certificate for certain specified cases. However, definition of Electric stock is absent in the document. Also since the certificate is to be issued by the Chief Electrical Engineer as different from the Electrical Inspector, it is presumed that the maintenance aspects and interference with OHE etc., only are taken care of and not the fundamental issue of Electrical safety. There is an urgent need to include a separate certification from the Electrical Inspector clearing the electrical safety of rolling stock additionally, while making the application to the Commissioner.

Penalties

Another important aspect in the Act, as provided under Section 148, is the applicability of penalty for non-conformity to the provisions, even for works pertaining to the Appropriate Government, as detailed below:

Section 148 Penalty where works belong to Government: The provisions of this Act shall, so far as they are applicable, be deemed to apply also when the acts made punishable there under are committed in the case of electricity supplied by or of works belonging to the Appropriate Government.

This makes it all the more imperative that a proper machinery be installed for proper monitoring and implementation of all the applicable provisions in the Act.

Responsibility of Railways

From the foregoing, it is evident that there is a definite responsibility on Indian Railways not only as a public service provider involved in generation, transmission, distribution and utilization of electricity, but also as Appropriate Government, to institute adequate machineries and lay down rules, regulations and procedures for strict compliance of various provisions of Indian Electricity Act and Indian Electricity Rules truly in letter and spirit.

In this context, some of the observations made by the Hon'ble High Court of Delhi while delivering the judgment on the *Association of victims of Uphaar Tragedy and Others* vs. *Union of India and Others* are very pertinent and relevant.

The Government and its agencies would also be liable for not having ensured strict compliance with Rules and Regulations which have been created to ensure safety.

Safety is the first aspect which has to be looked into by all concerned including the Board and even if there is any apprehension of the safety standards having not been followed, the transformer ought not have been made functional.

This litigation has highlighted the malaise of indifference, sloth and indeed "*chalta hai*" attitude, which affected the statutory authorities required to ensure and guarantee public safety. It is very clear that the tragic loss of innocent lives could have been avoided/ reduced if rules for public safety were given the importance, which the legislature intended, and the executive disregarded.

Functions of Electrical Inspector to the Government on the Railways

Presently Chief Electrical Engineers of Zonal Railways are expected to discharge functions of Electrical Inspector in Railways. The duality of role both as a maintainer and as an enforcer of rules creates a situation of complicity for items under his technical and administrative control. A similar situation existed in State Governments but now they have established an independent institution of Electrical Inspectorate to deal with issue of electrical safety exclusively.

The present system of implementing institution of Electrical Inspector on Railways is becoming increasingly inadequate and ineffective on account of large number of electrically operated equipments getting introduced into system as already explained and number of agencies involved, many of them technically and professionally not competent to operate and maintain such assets safely. With volume and complexity of electrical assets increasing manifold and need for exercising adequate control over various agencies involved with such assets, there is a pressing need for augmenting, if not separating institution of Electrical Inspector on Indian Railways, before system goes out of control leading to public trauma and tragedy of a magnitude witnessed as in case of Uphaar Cinema fire disaster.

Operative Mechanism

Various options are available for organizational structure of Institution of Electrical Inspector on the Indian Railways

- Maintain existing system with necessary augmentation.
- Modify existing system to extent of creating a separate and exclusive identity of Electrical Inspector under the Chief Electrical Engineer.
- Differentiate the functions of Chief Electrical Engineer and Electrical Inspector by setting up a separate entity:

In addition to structure of organization, several additional systems, regulations, procedures and instructions need to be introduced to take care of various safety aspects and statutory obligations brought out above, which have so far either not been addressed or implemented adequately.

Conclusion

Railways are a gigantic organization who are involved in transportation of men and material therefore safety is of paramount importance. In order to get out of the complicity arising out of the dual roles and also loss of objectivity arising out of common administrative control of Electrical Inspector and Chief Electrical Inspector, it would always be preferable to have a separate entity who will be directly under the Ministry of Railways.

17

HEALTH HAZARDS IN EXPLORATORY/ DEVELOPMENTAL MINING
Safety Practices in MECL

A.K. Lomas* and D.S. Mathur**

Mineral Exploration Corporation Ltd. (MECL) is engaged in the exploration of minerals and have projects at remote areas, with objectives of proving the exploitable mineral wealth of the country. It carries out drilling and exploratory mining, prospecting operations, estimation of reserves of minerals etc. Besides this it also executes the work like contractual mining, coal sampling and supply of Ballast to railways.

The exploration campaigns are brought to efficient fruition with the help of streamlined macro as well as micro planning at different levels of all disciplines, periodic inter-disciplinary interactions, systematic supervision and monitoring by Comprehensive Management Information System.

Safety training programs are conducted, both in-house and externally to update the knowledge of executives as well as the staff for the purpose of proper orientation of the recruits. The employees are encouraged to participate in the national as well as international seminars/workshops that are based on exploration, management techniques and job oriented safety so as to ensure exposure to new concepts and practices. This gives a splendid opportunity to the geo-scientists of MECL to interact with the cream in discipline.

For the purpose of safety convention 2006 focus has to be made as to what one should observe deeply in each operation so that we may achieve the ultimate goal of 100 per cent safety with production. For this purpose MECL has introduced the concept of operational safety under which we study the safe procedure for the operation of each mining equipment. This concept of operational safety includes perpetual preaching to each and every worker who is engaged in mines for the developmental and product ional activities of the mines.

MECL has contributed a long way for the exploration and exploitation of mineral wealth of the country. Some of the highlights of the mining activities are given below:

---

*CMD Mineral Exploration Corporation Ltd., Nagpur.
**Sr. Manager (Mining), M.E.C. Ltd., Nagpur.

- The magnitude of total exploration inputs in the last 25 years of existence include about 5 million meters of drilling, over 0.8 million meters of geophysical logging, 3000 sq. kms. of detailed geological mapping and surveying and 0.2 million meters of exploratory and developmental mining.
- MECL has constructed a 600 meters long incline at Balaria Lead-Zinc mine (Rajasthan), one of the longest in the country. India's longest raise of 143 meters was also constructed by MECL at Zawar.
- Four pairs of inclines with heavy support were successfully constructed in very loose ground conditions for Singareni Colleries Company Limited in Andhra Pradesh.

Presently MECL has completed mine construction projects of GDK-9 incline having two pairs of incline with heavy support at SCCL's Vakilpalli block.

Besides these other running projects for mine development are at Khetri Copper Complex and UCIL. At Jaduguda, Narwapahar, Turmadih and Bagjata, jobs like mine drivage, raising, winzing, etc. are in progress.

Operational Safety

In general, for any development, whether horizontal or vertical, mining processes like drilling, blasting, mucking and transportation of the muck for the disposal inside or outside the mine are involved. Each operation has got its due considerations for higher productivity and safety. Besides this there are some considerations that are necessary in working inside a mine viz.

1. Attendance is a must before entering in a mine and for visitors permission from manager should be obtained observing normal procedure of that mine.
2. Before entering inside the mine, cap lamp, safety shoes, helmets, etc. should be put on.
3. Loose clothes should be avoided.
4. Enter through the man way not by haulage road.
5. During the movement of tubs or mine cars take shelter in the man ways.
6. While moving on slopes use the handrails for support.
7. Do not touch any wire or cable while going down or coming up.

In various projects the Corporation has deployed different mining equipments for the execution of the job. We are providing safety instructions to operation and maintenance crews. Some of which some are given below: -

Drilling Process

There are certain safety procedures to be followed while drilling is being done which are as follows:

1. Before starting the work, drill machine, air leg and hosepipes are checked and if something like nut-bolts, etc. is found loose, it is tightened.

2. Drill steels are to be sharpened before they are reused. This helps in drilling the hole within time.
3. Use of ungrounded or blunt drill steel results in time and energy loss.
4. Before starting drilling face should be washed, loose rocks are properly dressed and position of holes is marked on the face. This ensures proper marking of drill pattern for good quality drilling.
5. No drilling should be done inside the sockets (partly broken holes) as there might be some unblasted explosives hidden, which due to drilling on that may explode, and result into an accident. This is also strictly prohibited as per mines act and regulations.
6. If sockets are present, they should be cleaned and blown by compressed air and water.
7. For better fragmentation and to break the rock in proper size (other than very small or too large), number of holes, their depth, and drill pattern is decided previously.
8. Before operating the drill machine lubricator is filled with proper quantity of lubricating oil, otherwise the machine may get heated resulting in more wear and tear. Wrong procedure of using lubricating oil may result in production of gas, which is harmful.
9. Drilling is done as per the instructions and guidelines of foreman or mining mate (supervisors).
10. Holes are blown during drilling otherwise dust that is produced due to cutting and chopping action of drill steel may get deposited inside the hole and may also result in jamming of drill rod inside the hole.
11. Dry drilling is strictly prohibited in undergrounds because the dust so produced may result into choking of respiratory system and poor visibility.
12. After drilling is over the machine, air leg, hosepipes, etc. are not allowed to remain there as they may get damaged due to wet mud and flying rock fragments (produced as a result of blasting).
13. Every drilling accessories like machine, air leg, hosepipes, etc. should be washed, cleaned, dried and hanged at proper in next cycle of operation.
14. Good equipment condition ensures more safety specially when motive power is compressed air.

Loading Process

1. Before starting the work get the working place checked by the first line supervisor Mining mate or Mine Sardar.
2. Get the loose rock dressed properly.
3. Look for the unblasted or partly blasted explosive or detonators. If available remove them and keep at a safe place to send it out of the mines.
4. All the hosepipes before using compressed air so that no dust or foreign body goes inside the loader should blow use.
5. Nut bolts of wheel; chain and rope bucket should be checked.
6. Inform at appropriate places before starting loading machine. Do not fill big boulders (by lifting them through loader bucket) inside the tubs.

7. Tubs/mine cars should be connected with each other by approved type of links. Use stoppers to avoid accidental movement of tubs during filling of muck by loader operator.
8. Oiling, greasing to be done as per instructions given in the manual of that machine.
9. Do not leave the loader in running condition.
10. Shut the compressed air/power of the machine.
11. At the end of work clean the loading machine, keep it at proper place and shut the compressed air/power.

Transportation of Muck by Locomotive

Mineral/muck after loading into tubs is carried away outside or inside the mine for dumping by means of loco-mine cars set. Locomotives, which are used in underground, are either battery loco or Trolley wire loco. (Operating at low voltage electric current being provided by a hanging wire along roadways) For transportation by loco, following precautions are being observed:

1. Before starting a locomotive operator gets it checked with the help of a mechanic and an electrician who are deputed for the purpose at loco-shed.
2. All safety devices like loco-bell; brakes, sand spraying device, light, seat, horn, etc. are properly checked.
3. Maximum number of mine cars/Trolleys to be attached with locomotive is fixed by manager of mine and it is religiously followed.
4. To link the loco with mine cars/Trolleys only standard approved type links are used.
5. Maximum speed of the loco is also fixed by manager of mine and is never exceeded.
6. Red lamp is attached at the end of last mine car to avoid accidental collision.
7. No fitting into tub is allowed when the loco car set is in motion.
8. Track line, gauge, crossings, etc. are checked as a routine check up.
9. No grease, jute, waste cloth or inflammable substance is kept in the vicinity of loco or its parking place.
10. Fire extinguishers are kept at appropriate place so that it is available for use in case of emergency.
11. After finishing the work it is cleaned/dedusted by dry cloth and daily report is written in a bound paged book for information to next shift.
12. It is parked inside the closed loco shade. It is not kept outside in workable/usable condition and key is deposited to supervisor.
13. During shunting horn is sounded.
14. Report is to be given to next shift loco operator by previous shift loco operator.

Hand Tramming Operation

Tubs after filling require manual tramming inside or outside the mine for making them empty at dumping place for reuse in next cycle of operation:

1. Haulage way is thoroughly inspected by supervisor for proper Track guage,

cleanliness, signaling wires, etc. Signaling lights are checked and fused bulb, loose connections, and etc. are also corrected.

2. Tub is never pushed from sides but it is pushed from front with proper safety precautions especially on slopes.
3. Inspect the tippler for tipping the tubs regularly after the end of shift and beginning of shift.
4. Use strap when the tubes are being handled up the machine. Red light and horn is used when tubs are being handled down the incline.
5. Tubs/mine cars are joined with approved type of links.
6. Loaded and empty tubs or mine cars are coupled or decoupled at plane surfaces and not on slopes.
7. Maintain a distance of 10 mts. whenever tubs are being lowered or raised or being pulled or pushed.
8. While coupling two tubs or loco, do not allow your head to come in between the two.
9. While loading material like *ballies*, pegs, poles or rail pieces inside the tub for lowering or raising, it should be properly tied with rope to avoid its accidental fallout.
10. Use stop block, run away switch, buffer etc. as per need.

Safety in the Workplace

MECL is working in metal and coal mines for mine development work at khetri mines of M/s. HCL (Hindustan Copper Limited) and Jaduguda, Narva Pahar, Turamdih and Bagjata mines of M/s. UCIL (Uranium Corporation of India Limited) in underground, there are some places which are situated in the return airway and are hot & humid. The working places, which are in the intake side of ventilation current, are cold and dry. Miners face lots of stress due to such environmental condition inside the mine.

An excess of heat or deficit - cold - is termed thermal stress. Heat is exchanged between the body and the environment, using physiological processes. Environmental factors determining the level of heat stress include:

- Air temperature;
- Relative humidity;
- Air movement; and
- Radiant temperature of the surroundings.

Heat stress is high in an environment characterized by high ambient temperatures, high humidity and low air movement such as in a sauna. Cold stress is associated with low temperature, high air movement and humidity, for example, from a blast of cold, wet wind.

Hot work induces heat stress when more heat is absorbed into the body than can be dissipated. The short-term effects of heat stress are to:

- Reduce concentration and thus promote accidents;
- Aggravate effects of other work place hazards; and
- Induce heat illness.

Heat illness manifests itself as skin conditions (prickly heat), as heat exhaustion (fainting, syncope), or as heat cramps (if body water and salt balance is incorrect). The long-term effects of heat stress include chronic heat exhaustion or birth deformities and other reproductive problems.

Our bodies are unable to acclimatize to cold in the same manner that they can adapt to heat. Lowering of body temperature (hypothermia) has an effect on the brain, causing erratic behaviour and numbness, muscular weakness and cramps. Localised exposure to cold may cause frostbite and chilblains.

Long-term effects of working in the cold include arthritis, rheumatism, chest complaints and heart disease, because of the strain on the heart caused by circulatory changes.

The range of thermal comfort for workers has been found to be 19°C to 30°C. Control of heat and cold should aim to lower or raise working temperatures to within this range. Measures available include:

- Insulation;
- Ventilation;
- Heating;
- Isolation;
- Shielding of the source or the operator;
- Job modification and work rotation; and
- Protective clothing.

Extremes of Temperature

Heat effects are

1. Dehydration.
2. Heat syncope.
3. Heat exhaustion.
4. Heat cramps.
5. Prickly heat.
6. Heat strokes.
7. Heat hyper pyrexia.
8. Cancer of skin.

Prevention and Treatment

1. Maintain thermal comfort zone i.e. temperatures from 55-60° Fahrenheit with humidity of 30-60%.
2. Regulation of working hours.
3. Protective clothing.
4. PPE
5. Regular intake of water (1litre/hour) in order to prevent dehydration with salt replacement.

6. If heat syncope, lie the patient in a shade with head slightly down and legs raised to an angle of 45°.
7. If heat stroke-rapidly cool body by water and ice packs in axilla, hospitalize.

Cold

Cold injuries can be local or systemic

Local injuries

1. Immersion foot or trench foot.
2. Frost bite-freezing injury with numbness. Prickling. The skin is often white and swollen.

Systemic

Hypothermia

Treatment consists of rapid rewarming of affected part. And if hypothermia the person.

Other Physical Hazards Faced by Miners and Methods to Overcome

Noise

The term noise covers all sounds that can result in hearing impairment or be harmful to health or otherwise dangerous.

MECL workers face tremendous noise problems during operation of Hopper loader and 824 loader in the confined space at sub-levels and in drive and crosscuts. Frequent blasting in nearby areas and use of rotatory percussive hand drills further aggravates the problem.

Prevention

1. Measurement of noise exposure carried out as traditional Industrial Hygiene function by means of sound level meter.
2. Control of noise at source by Engineering Control Methods applied to men machine and environment.
3. Use of personal protective equipments like earplugs or earmuff.
4. Periodic medical examination along with audiometric examinations.

Vibration

Vibration refers to the mechanical oscillation of a surface around its reference points. The vibrations of 2 to 1000 Hz at frequency are causing health hazard. Vibration may effect

1. Whole body vibration : It can affect vision low back pain, headache, and irritability.

2. Segmental vibration: It causes physical damage to part of the body that is directly exposed to the vibration. Pneumatic tools causes raynaud's phenomenon in which blood supply to finger is reduced. The sensations are reduced and there can be ulcers.

Compressed air operated rotatory percussive hand drills that are used in underground as a daily routine provides sufficient vibrations to the drillers of MECL. Few preventive measures are given below:

1. Using well designed vibrating tools.
2. Wearing gloves to minimize vibration and keep the hands warm.
3. Proper maintenance of instruments.
4. Following a work rest schedule that prevents long period of exposure to vibration.
5. Pre-employment and periodic medical examination.

Radiation

MECL is having four projects in Uranium Corporation of India Limited, development of which is for the purpose of obtaining radioactive mineral. This is a health hazard and the prolonged exposure of which may cause following deleterious effects on the human body:

1. Blood Cancer
2. Breast Cancer
3. Thyroid Cancer
4. Bone Sarcoma
5. Lung Carcinoma

Radiation Injuries can be

1. Total body radiation resulting in bone marrow syndrome, Gastro Intestinal Syndrome, Neuro Vascular Syndrome.
2. Localized Exposure causes - Burn of skin in the form of Redness' Loss of hairs, Ulcer and degeneration of skin. The treatment consists of application of Steroid ointments, analgesics and sedatives.
3. Radio active contaminated - It can be external contamination or internal contamination resulting form accidental ingestion, inhalation and absorption of radioactive isotopes.
   Treatment consist of decontamination measures which consists of gently scrubbing the skin with soap and warm water and if necessary cutting the hairs. The internal contamination is treated by inducing vomiting, giving purgatives and chelating agent depending on the type of contamination for alpha emitters' diethyl triaminepentacetic acid (DTPA).

Abnormal Air Pressure

In all the mining projects, compressed air is being used for the operation of hand drills, hopper loader and 824 loader as a motive power. Thus during the operation of these equipments, miners face ABNORMAL AIR PRESSURE.

ABNORMAL AIR PRESSURE can be high air pressure or low air pressure

High Air Pressure

In mining work where persons have to work in compressed air which is at higher air pressure than normal. Exposure to compressed air may cause rupture of Eardrum, burst lung, air embolism in blood vessels of brain causing unconsciousness, convulsions and paralysis of limbs. It can also cause necrosis of bones and joints.

Decompression Sickness: At some places there is no alternative rather than to use some compressed air for getting relief from hot and humid mine environment at the working place and workers remain in this condition during work for full shift. After the job is done they come to the surface. If this is done rapidly or suddenly in some incidences, the nitrogen dissolved in the blood forms bubbles in the blood and tissue, causing damage to the blood circulation and local tissue. In extreme cases this may be very severe to cause shock and death.

Prevention and Treatment

1. Careful adherence to the prescribe decompression work practices.
2. Periodical Health check up to the employee with reference to nervous system, Circulatory System and Ears.
3. Immediate First Aid is given by administering 100 per cent Oxygen and aspirin may be given for pain. After this the patients should be transported rapidly to an emergency facility that has a hyper baric chamber for recompression and decompression.

Lower Air Pressure

Sometimes MECL gets projects in remote areas that are situated at high altitudes. Here, the pressure of the atmosphere gradually diminishes, hence reducing the partial pressure of Oxygen in atmosphere. This reduces the rate of oxygenation of blood in the lungs, producing hypoxia. It reduces the working efficiency of the person at high altitude. Altitude sickness occurs in accustomed workers at high altitudes. In this breathlessness in accompanied with headache, tingling sound in the ear, nausea, vomiting, etc. Hence, workers, who intend to work at high altitudes, should acclimatize themselves before beginning work. After onset of the disease, rapid descent to the lower altitudes and intensive care are required for treatment.

Prevention and Treatment

1. Gradual acclimatization.

2. Pressure suits also help in preventing altitude sickness.

Occupation Health Services in MECL

1. Pre-employment medical checkup of employees.
2. Periodic/Annual health check up.
3. Pre-placement health check up.
4. Maintenance of Industrial Hygiene at work place.
5. Risk assessment in the form of important activities, possible health hazards associated with that particular activity, target human system assessment during health check ups. This data pertaining to accident statistics and risk assessment is maintained and is provided to DGMS whenever asked.
6. The result of all health check ups is maintained. The management gets information about health status of the employees for any corrective or proactive interventions. The medical bills for any sickness are reimbursed to the employees.
7. The corporation is trying for OHSAS 180001 certification.

The Corporation has achieved highest safety standards which is evident from zero fetal accident record in past ten years.

REFERENCES

Safety records of Mineral Exploration Corporation Limited.

DGMS circulars and regulations.

Operational Instructions of MEC Limited.

Preventive & Social Medicines, by Park & Park.

Hand Book of Occupational Medicines.

18

IMPLEMENTATION OF SAFETY IN CONSTRUCTION THROUGH INNOVATIVE MEASURES

P.K. Khare*

ABSTRACT

Construction sector has many inherent and inevitable hazards associated with it which gives rise to lot of concern for the safety of the workers. One of the prime reasons behind slackness in implementation of safety aspects in construction sector is the involvement of enormous number of labours with very low literacy and awareness. At 2 × 1000 MWe Kudankulam Nuclear Power Project (KKNPP), where India's largest nuclear power station is under construction, some innovative ideas have been introduced to improve the safety at workplaces by the active and enthusiastic involvement of the vast labour force.

With an intention of establishing direct communication with the workers novel ideas like Mobile Safety Talks (MST) and Safety Enrichment Talk (SET) were implemented. These concepts proved to be effective in gaining the confidence of the workers and motivating them in adopting safe work practices. As awareness spread into the masses, the incidences of unsafe acts at work places reduced considerably. The workers began to come out with the problems they face at the work site and even suggested solutions for the problems. Some motivational activities like declaration of safe workers of the month and presenting them with token gifts too helped in encouraging the workers further towards the cause of their safety and that of their fellow workers.

Considering the risk associated with working at height, a system of issue of height pass was introduced. A procedure was prepared and issued to all concerned for information and implementation. This system ensured that only those workers who are medically and physically fit are allowed to carryout work at higher elevations. Training on proper use of safety belts and ensuring issue of safety belts to all was also being ensured during implementation of the system.

Fieldwork permit system for works involving higher risk potential such as, rock blasting and work in confined space plays its role in reducing the inherent hazards. A construction safety work permit system is also implemented before commencement of work.

Our experience at KKNPP had led us to feel that involvement of workers in safety is the most effective way of minimizing the accidents in construction sites.

*Head, Industrial Safety and Fire, PFSO, Kudankulam Nuclear Power Project, PO, Kudankulam Radhapuram Taluk, Tirunelveli District, Tamil Nadu-627 106. *Email* : pkkhare@kknpp.com

Keywords

Mobile Safety Talks
Safety Enrichment Talks
Height pass system
Physical ability test rig
Construction safety permit
Fieldwork permit system

Prelude

Construction sector, which enjoys the reputation of being the second largest industrial activity involving millions of people worldwide, is also notorious for its alarmingly high rates of accidents. Although a lot of efforts are being made towards ensuring the safety of construction workers in developed countries, a precious little is visible in the developing countries, including India. The enactment of The Building and Other Construction Workers (Regulation of Employment and Conditions of Service) Act, 1996 has been the first major initiative taken by the Government of India to address the problem.

The major difficulties in effective implementation of safety in construction sector can be enumerated as follows

(a) involvement of very large number of workers with low rate of literacy
(b) lack of awareness among the workers
(c) subletting of the work by contractors to sub-contractors and further
(d) laxity in implementation of statutory requirements

With the effects of globalization getting increasingly visible in construction sector, a much awaited welcome change is slowly emerging in the safety considerations too. A visit to any major construction site now gives a fair glimpse of the improvement in use of personal protective equipment by the workers. But evidently, use of personal protective measures alone cannot ensure safety of the workers. A lot of sincere, effective and innovative measures are required to be integrated in the construction works to ensure the safety of the vast number of workmen involved in it.

All such considerations were particularly thought out since the incipient stage of Kudankulam Nuclear Power Project (KKNPP), India's largest nuclear power station under construction at the coast of Bay of Bengal in the state of Tamil Nadu. In line with the thoughts of Dr. H.J. Bhabha, the father of Indian nuclear industry, safety has been the top priority in all activities undertaken at KKNPP. Around 8000 workers have been working to construct this mega project. Involvement of such an enormous number of workers led to a lot of brainstorming by the management of KKNPP to effectively implement safety at the work sites. It was decided that apart from the conventional practices, some innovative and unconventional practices shall also be needed to be implemented at KKNPP to evolve a better safety culture. In order to achieve it, the workers were considered as the prime target.

Safety Awareness - A Right of the Worker

The major section of the workers involved in construction activities are from poor economic background with very low level of literacy or even not at all. Inculcating safety awareness among such people by motivating them to adopt safe work practices and appropriate use of personal protective equipment is a very difficult task. Conventional safety measures are more inclined towards enforcement actions, which of course are not helpful to create and sustain safety culture at worksite.

Since the beginning of the project, it was the firm belief at KKNPP that safety cannot be implemented by enforcement measures. Unless the urge comes from the heart, it is impossible to make someone follow your directions sincerely. Hence at KKNPP, the key words of safety became - awareness and motivation. It was considered that safety awareness is a right of every worker and hence, it was ensured that each and every worker who comes to KKNPP for work, undergoes basic safety induction training before being put on job. During the safety induction training, the workers are introduced to the anticipated hazards at work place where they are going to work, how they can protect themselves against those hazards, what are the general personal protective equipment to be used and what is the correct method of using them and what are the general safety rules they are expected to follow during the work. A simple and effective way adopted to ensure cent-per-cent safety induction training is by issuing personal protective equipment like safety helmets, shoes and safety belts to the workers only after the training. Language has also been a hurdle in the path of effective communication as workers were not only from various areas of Tamil Nadu, they had came from as far as Orissa, Uttar Pradesh, West Bengal and Bihar. Therefore, it became necessary to ensure that safety induction trainings are conducted in a language understandable to them. Refresher safety training, job specific training, tool box talks, pep talks etc. too have been made a regular feature to keep on reminding the workers on adopting safe working habits.

Innovative Awareness Measures

During the course of imparting training to the vast workforce of KKNPP it was felt that conventional training methods were not giving the effective results as the workers were not feeling belongingness towards the training measures. So, a new training methodology was developed and named as *Mobile Safety Talks*. Public address system was mounted on a jeep and the trainers started going to the work spots. During the programme, the workers at the work spot were assembled and a motivational talk on safety was first delivered to the workers in the language understandable by them. The launch of the mobile safety talks programme was carried out by the Project Director of KKNPP, who went among the workers and motivated them to adopt safe work practices and assured that the management of KKNPP shall always be committed towards the safety of the workers. During the mobile safety talks, the workers were motivated to talk about the safety problems they face during the work and also to suggest remedial measures. Some of the workers were also motivated to talk on workplace safety based on there own experiences.

Mobile safety talks had been very successful in achieving workers' participation in safety awareness campaign. Slowly the workers started looking forward towards attending mobile safety talks, which became popular as MST. Workers started discussing their problems pertaining to safety aspects and also began to feel that KKNPP as well as the contractors' management are very concerned about their well being. It was also ensured that the problems raised by the workers were attended and the result was communicated to them during successive mobile safety talks. Till date around 52 mobile safety talks have been conducted at various work spots involving around 3000 workers.

After the successful implementation of mobile safety talks programme, a new concept was devised as its extension, which was termed as *Safety Enrichment Talk.* A workmen training centre was made in one of the halls at the workplace and personal protective equipment, fire extinguishers, safety posters, demonstration arrangement for use of safety belt and fall arrester system etc. were displayed in it. PC with speakers and LCD projector was installed for providing sharing workers views with the aid of audio-visual means. During safety enrichment training, the workers are introduced to various personal protective equipment, fire extinguishers etc. With the aid of dummy, workers are trained on proper method of using safety belts and fall arrestor system. They are also informed about various safety signage and caution signs. Further, they are given a safety motivational talk with the aid of audio-visual media. At the end of the session a quiz is conducted on the aspects that had been told to them and small gifts are given to the workers giving right answers. More than 2000 workers have participated in safety enrichment training programme so far.

Safety enrichment talks which is purely based on "for the worker by the worker of the worker" too has been well received by the workers. The success of the programme could be assessed by the enthusiasm with which the workers ask questions to the trainer on various aspects that they had learnt during the talk, just before the beginning of the quiz.

Innovative Motivational Measures

When it comes to implementation of safety at workplace, motivating workers to follow safety regulations becomes a concern of the management of any organization. In construction sector, the gravity of the situation increases to a higher degree because, owing to the lower literacy rates among the construction workers and the tendency of fatalistic thinking, making them understand the necessity and importance of enhancing safety at workplaces becomes very difficult. Taking this aspect into consideration, some innovative motivational measures were taken up at KKNPP to encourage the workers participation in safety.

As a new initiative towards inspiring the workers, a monthly safety award scheme has been introduced. Every morning, before going to the work sites, the workers assemble at a location where one of the workers administers safety oath to the gathering and another worker talks about the need of adopting safe practices in workplaces. At the end of the month during the same routine, judged workers are presented with token awards declaring them as safe workers of the month. This simple system has proven to be very effective in motivating the workers. Now, a healthy competition is emerging among the workers to become safe worker of the month, with awareness that they shall not be considered for the title if they are found violating any safety regulations at their workplace.

Safety slogans, posters and signage displayed at conspicuous locations around the workplaces play a big role in keep on reminding the workers on the importance of safety. At KKNPP, a large number of slogan boards with catchy slogans in Hindi, English and Tamil languages have been placed on street lighting poles along the major roads. Apart from the conventional posters, many innovative and appealing safety posters were developed and displayed at prominent places in the work areas. Display of interesting and catchy slogans and posters with safety messages do help in sending the information to the subconscious mind the same way as commercial advertisements in TV and other media lure us in buying the products.

Engineering Interventions

From the analysis of the accidents at construction sites, it becomes evident that a major percentage of serious accidents are attributable to fall of persons from height. Since construction of high-rise buildings and other tall structures demand elevated scaffolding arrangements and a large number of working platforms at height, the hazard of fall of workers is omnipresent. The temporary nature of construction arrangements increases the hazard exponentially. Although safety belts are gradually becoming a safety ornaments to the workers working at height, yet safety belts alone cannot ensure safety at height.

As an effort towards ensuring safety of workers working at height, a permit system has been introduced for work at height. The primary aim of the *height pass system* as it is known popularly is to ensure that workers shall be allowed to work at height beyond 3.5m only after ascertaining their medical and physical fitness. The workers who are required to carry out work at height first undergo medical examination by a doctor. After being declared medically fit, they go through a physical fitness examination on specially designed *physical ability test rigs* installed at various locations. On these test rigs, the workers are required to climb up a vertical ladder and walk freely on a narrow walkway at a height of about 10 ft. They are taught on proper use of safety belts during the physical test. Immediately after the physical test, the blood pressure of the workers is monitored and they are observed for any indication of suffering from vertigo. The workers successfully completing medical and physical examination are issued with a height pass card with a validity of six months. It is being strictly ensured that no worker is allowed to work at height without possessing height pass and of course safety belts. Till date, more than 22,600 height passes have been issued at KKNPP and the process is going on.

Construction work involves many other activities with inherent potential of hazards. One of such activity is rock blasting. One of the uncommon situations faced at KKNPP was the need of carrying out rock blasting operations along with the ongoing construction activities which called for higher safety considerations for blasting activities. A *work permit system* was implemented for blasting activities, with specific consideration for the site related safety aspects. Peak particle velocity measurement was carried out to assess the impact of shock waves on the structures and buildings in the vicinity and accordingly safe charges for blasting were calculated for various areas. In order to ensure safety further, advanced delay detonation system was employed for the job and with the permit system it was ensured that all blasting operations are carried out under the supervision of qualified blasting engineers. More than 1800 blasting operations have been carried out at KKNPP without the occurrence of even a minor untoward incident.

Work permit system is also followed for other works with potential risk factor such as, work in confined areas and excavation works. Another work permit system in place requires permit for removal of guards and handrails provided along floor openings.

Conclusion

Regardless of the inevitable and inherent hazards associated with construction industry, the safety of the workers can be improved considerably with improving the association and involvement of the workers for the cause of their own safety. From personal experience at KKNPP, the authority feels that positive and effective efforts implemented with a little imagination and ingenuity can go a long way in improving safety in construction sites.

OCCUPATIONAL SAFETY, HEALTH AND ENVIRONMENT MANAGEMENT IN MINERAL EXPLORATION PROJECTS

Deep Prakash* and Naresh Nautiyal**

ABSTRACT

Minerals are the most important raw materials for industrial growth of a country. Their resources are finite and to keep pace between total mineral resource availability vis-à-vis consumption, exploration is required to be carried out on continuous basis to locate/establish new prospects. Exploration is a hazardous profession, and there is a need to maintain risk/hazards to an acceptable, level, since zero level is not feasible. MECL during last three decades has played a vital role in the development/expansion of mineral industry and it has the necessary infrastructure to provide high quality cost effective, time bound geo-scientific services for exploration and exploitation of minerals. The drilling and developmental mining, the main tool for exploration need involvement of human resources coupled with large number of plant and machineries. Success of exploration programme depends on safety of work force, plant and machineries with minimum impact on environment around the work place. MECL has taken appropriate steps to standardize suitable exploration strategies with due emphasis on health, safety and environment protection to minimize the risk and hazards thereof. MECL is committed to conduct exploration activities by maintaining a proper balance between exploration and the environment for the sustainable development of minerals in the country.

Introduction

Minerals are the important raw materials for the economic development of a nation and play a major role in improving the quality of life of the mankind. The per capita consumption of the mineral resources is one of the indices for assessment of the development/industrial growth of the country.

It is a well known fact that the mineral deposit(s) is not created by itself, but exist in the bowl of the mother earth. Mineral exploration is a basic and vital tool for evaluation of

*Sr. Manager (Geology), Mineral Exploration Corporation Limited.
**Head (Business Development), Mineral Exploration Corporation Limited.

a deposit(s) for its eventual exploitation. It is a dynamic activity and has no alternative. We are all aware that the exploration existed in the past, exists in the present and will continue to exist in future also as it is the life line for the mineral based industries.

Prior to India's independence, the total production of minerals in the country was very limited and mainly dominated by private sector and other many small mine owners. During Post-independence period, a phenomenal growth has been registered in terms of number and value of minerals produced. It has increased by leaps and bounds from a level of Rs. 58 crores (22 minerals) in 1947 to over Rs. 69583 crores (64 minerals) in 2003-04. The phenomenal increase is due to the pace of exploration activities during successive five year plans periods coupled with the Industrial Policy Resolution in 1956.

Notwithstanding the fact that the mineral wealth is finite, non-renewable and wasting asset , its fast depletion poses a serious problem to mankind and threat to the future generation. Exploration itself is an extremely high risk venture. It is presumed as nothing but a gamble with nature, where millions are spent before billions are won. Hence, there is an urgent need for pursuing integrated efforts with modern concepts and tools to attain necessary levels of efficiency, economy, environmental protection and conservation of resources. Moreover the exploration is hazardous profession and there is need to bring down the risk and hazards to an acceptable, level since zero level is not feasible. Efforts are needed to keep the work force the main input not only safe but healthy & happy also.

MECL's Role in Mineral Exploration

To accelerate the pace of mineral exploration activities in conformity with the industrialization in the country, Government of India, created MECL in 1972. It is assigned with the task of detailed exploration of minerals, on a commercial basis, in order to reduce the time lag between the initial discovery of a mineral prospect and its eventual exploitation. On creation of the company, the following two fold objectives were set:

- To plan, promote, organise and implement mineral exploration programme by the Central Government from time to time in order to establish viable deposits for commercial exploitation in and outside the country, and
- To undertake contract jobs in various fields of mineral exploration and also to take up drilling and mining contracts for purposes other than mineral exploration.

With this mandate, MECL has progressively grown manifold with the induction of a vast pool of professional experts in the different fields and by adopting modern technologies of exploration and resorting to innovation as per dictates of the situation. It is established as the only organisation both in Government and private sector, possessing all the exploration facilities and other allied services under one umbrella. Now, it has emerged as the premier exploration agency in the country, catering to the needs of the mineral industry within and outside India.

MECL has played a major role in the development of mineral industry through the most fascinating journey of more than three decades. It has completed about 1050 projects for mineral exploration, mine development, foundation engineering studies, tube well construction, restoration of archeological monuments, geo-technical studies in high attitude areas etc.

The magnitude of exploration inputs include 6.57 million metres of drilling, 1.88 million metres of geophysical logging, 4657 sq.km. of detailed geological mapping and surveying and 0.21 million metres of exploratory and developmental mining. So far, it has established over 1,24,408 million tonnes of reserves mainly for coal and lignite, base metals, bauxite gold, iron and manganese ore, phosphorite, limestone, molybdenite, rare metals, dolomite, etc. and 471 cum of CBM resources.

Over the period, MECL has developed the necessary infrastructure for mineral exploration activities, which includes geology, drilling, mining, geophysics, integrated laboratory and IT enabled services. MECL is committed to achieve the Mission of "Providing High quality, cost effect effective and time bound geo-scientific services for exploration and exploitation of minerals" with due priority assigned to the health and safety of the work force, equipments and environmental protection parameters.

Stages of Exploration vis-à-vis Risk Involved

Notwithstanding the fact that mineral exploration is the basic tool for evaluation of a mineral prospect for its eventual exploitation, any development activity, including exploration, is bound to create an imbalance in the environmental setting of the area, where natural resources exist. In fact, the development and environment are two sides of the same coin and emphasis on one of them will have significant impact on the other.

The exploration activity, as it implies, consists of multi-stage operations namely :

- Reconnaissance stage
- Prospecting stage
- Detailed exploration stage
- Pre-mine development stage

The risk hazards and uncertainties vary widely in terms of nature and magnitude from one stage to another.

As already explained MECL undertakes detailed exploration basically through exploratory drilling and mining with associated activity. The drilling activities are generally restricted to smaller surface area at each site location, whereas mining work is largely confined to relatively bigger surface area with surface and/or underground working. The operations are site-specific in diverse geo-environments, spreading across the length and breadth of the country.

The drilling and developmental mining activities need involvement of human resources together with the various plants and machineries, their handling, transportation and maintenance at different work places. The success of exploration programme depends on the safety of the workforce and the machineries, with minimum impact on environment around the work places. However, the possible risk/hazard involved in the exploration projects, as envisaged and also experienced by MECL can be grouped under two main categories.

(i) Hazards due to surface activities.
(ii) Hazards due to underground activities.

The hazards attributable to surface activities are mainly during topographic survey and geological mapping and drilling activities, shallow pitting/trenching etc.

As a part of underground activities, the exploratory mine development work is carried out for three dimensional evaluation of the deposit, to ascertain the reliability of exploratory drilling. Surface surveys and other tests for pre-feasibility studies, involves the likely set of hazards/risks. These risks are more or less identical to those being faced during actual mining operation but the magnitude of their after effects is lesser in extent. These hazards are related to drilling, blasting, mucking and transportation of material, hoisting to the surface, side/roof collapse, errection of plants and machineries, problem due to dust, surface water inundation, underground water flooding, release of harmful gases in mines and also due to electricity, compressed air and other allied works.

The hazards pertaining to workforce, plants and equipments are mainly related to occupational health and safety. They are influenced by shifting of plants and equipments, their repairs and maintenance, storage and handling of explosives, factor causing air and water pollution, airborne dust from road traffic, drilling, excavation and site clearing, noise and emissions from equipments and other operations and unsafe working conditions etc. The health related hazards are :

- Head injury.
- Dislocation of bones/joints.
- Severe bleeding due to major wounds.
- Snake bites, burns.
- Stroke due to exposure to extreme climatic condition.
- Frost bite.

The environment related hazards include :

- Destruction to land form due to excavation, pits, boreholes, shafts, access road etc.
- Cutting of trees and bushes for road making and pit/trench/BH sites in forest land (use of forest land for non-forest purpose).
- Displacement of people, reallocation of social conflict, alternate land use pattern, building roads, opening sensitive ecosystem to unplanned population influxes.
- Accidents due to non-reclamation of deep pits/shafts/large dia. boreholes etc. to local habitat and flora/fauna and their displacement.
- Land degradation in eco-fragile areas and threat to local/tribal population in sensitive belts.
- Disturbance/damage to soil, vegetation, cultural and/or historical resources.
- Conflict with other land user.
- Disturbance/pollution of water regime.

Risk Hazard Management

Keeping in view the probable areas of risk/uncertainties during the course of exploration and the importance to safety, MECL has taken appropriate steps and standardized the suitable exploration strategies under diverse geological and adverse terrain conditions with due emphasis on health, safety and environment protection/measures to facilitate eco-friendly exploration activities.

Because of the inherently hazardous nature of the exploratory drilling and mining activities, it may never be possible to completely prevent accident and serious injury in this field. All the more stress, therefore, should be put on safety and accident prevention to try to reduce the number of accidents. Safety is not the responsibility of one person. Safety is everybody's job.

Accidents don't "just happen": they are caused. No body wants accidents to happen. Accidents cause inconvenience, hardship, loss of time, suffering, and in extreme cases permanent physical injury. Most accidents can be prevented.

In order to reduce/minimize the accidents/injuries and the impact on work place surroundings, guidelines have been drawn. Some of them are described below :

- Awareness for precautions in transportation, handling of equipments, tools and tackles, lifting and moving of heavy objects/equipments during site preparations.
- Safe storage and handling of POL, mud and other chemicals, explosives, etc.
- Use of approved machines, equipments, tools and tackles.
- Maintain overall cleanliness of work place and its surroundings to facilitate trouble place working.
- Restoration/Reclamation of disturbed landforms after exploration.
- Providing proper clothing and other safety wares to all workmen.
- Awareness for emergency treatment/rescue operations and first-aid kit.
- Spot inspection of different aspects of mining activities for immediate compliance.
- Strengthening with adequate support system in mine working to prevent roof/side collapsing and maintenance of proper signaling system.
- Separation of dust formations and poisonous & harmful gases.
- Installation of fire extinguisher at critical points.
- Proper arrangements for storage and discharge of water during mining to prevent water flooding in mines/disasters.
- Follow Rules, Regulations and other statutes and their strict compliance.

Conclusion

Since mineral resources are non-renewable, the exploration programmes are required to be carried out with due emphasis on health and safety of workforce and minimum damage to environment is the need of the hour.

Any mining project, that is developed on scientific exploration, operated & closed in an environmentally and socially acceptable manner, could be seen as a contribution towards the sustainable development, for the socio-economic benefits of the people and the region.

The scientific exploration with safety of work force in an eco-friendly environment will serve the dual purpose of performance improvement and development and conservation of natural mineral resources as well as nature itself, under the ambit of Mines and Minerals (Development & Regulation) Act and Rules/Laws for mine safety and Forest and Environment Protection.

To sum up, MECL has taken adequate steps to strike a proper harmony between exploration and the environment for the sustainable development in real perspective.

REFERENCE

Indian Mineral Year Book-2004.

Section–V
Disaster Management & Safety

20

FAILURE OF ENGINEERED STRUCTURES DURING EARTHQUAKE IN URBAN GUJARAT
A Hazard Analysis Study

Subrata Gupta* and G.K. Sinha**

ABSTRACT

First time in the history of the urban India, structures created with inputs of engineering efforts failed during an earthquake struck Gujarat on 26.1.2001. Here an attempt has been made to identify and analyze the hazards with reasons, of the different kind of failures, which occurred and to create a general safety awareness on resistance to earthquake for the users as well as the builders.

The behaviour of earthquake forces are quite different from those of gravitational forces. This necessitates the structures to have adequate ductility to survive against failure. Types and reasons of failure reveal the inadequacy in the structures to address the failure mechanism, wherein certain structures even behaved like inverted pendulum. A safe earthquake resistant structure can be created with marginal cost increment with the provision like shear wall etc. Clear understanding of the behaviour of the structure, simple geometry, failure mechanism, load transfer location of the structure, etc. are essential in creating a safe structure. Lessons learned from the failures should be practiced while creating the future structures by all concerned to prevent avoidable loss to society.

Introduction

A structure created with the application of proven technology in conceiving, designing and implementation is considered as Engineered Structure. The low frequency of natural disasters could be one of the reasons for the development of a habitat at any place and its further flourishment into an urban nature. The emergence of civilized urban habitats necessitates the creation of the structures in a scientific manner which gave birth to the engineered structures. The history of Indian urban habitats will reveal a fact that engineered structures have faced seldom damages during a natural calamity like earthquake or cyclone due to scientific inputs provided in creating them. The major disaster to the urban habitats of

---

*BCE (Hons.), FIE, Chartered Engineer, Chief Engineer (Civil), IEOT, ONGC.
**BE (Civil), MBA, Superintending Engineer (C & M), IEOT.

Gujarat due to an earthquake of marginal intensity on 26th January, 2001 has changed the history.

Earthquake Resistant Structures

The scientific information about the siesmic activity in the Indian subcontinent is now well recorded from the past experiences and the siesmic zones are clearly identified even though earthquakes are not predictable. The technology is very well developed in creating an earthquake resistant structure whereas, creation of an earthquake proof structure may not be economically viable in most of the cases.

This discussion on the behaviour and failure of structures during an earthquake is limited to the concrete building structures.

The abnormally high cost of land forces a common citizen to depend on a third party (builder) for the fulfilment of his desire of owning a home in an urban area. So the knowledge of the basic requirements of a seismic resistant structure, will help in identifying a safe structure, being created by the third party.

This paper tries to bring out certain factors learnt from the failures of the engineered structures during the earthquake which, hopefully, will be able to create an awareness on the requirements of earthquake resistant structures, to ensure safety of one's life and property in future.

Behaviour of Structure

The behaviour of a structure due to dynamic seismic loads are quite different from those due to the static loads. The seismic loads act horizontally and are cyclic in nature. The capability of a structure in resisting the lateral deflections due to seismic lateral forces, known as "STIFFNESS" and the capability of a structure to absorb the deformations beyond the normal elastic limit by virtue of the whole structure acting as a single elastic body, known as "DUCTILITY". In mathematical term, it refers to the ratio of the displacement just prior to collapse to the displacement at first damage or yield. Ductility signifies the ability of the structure to sustain large displacements without collapse and is the most desirable quality for good earthquake performance of the building. The failure in providing the considerations of these factors in either designing or creating a structure will make it vulnerable to earthquake forces.

Failure Mechanism

A structure during an earthquake can generally be failed either due to Flexure/Shear or by Torsion. The shear failures are brittle in nature and are sudden whereas the flexural failures are ductile in nature and is slow with enough indication of the impending failure. Hence, for the safety of life and property, it is necessary to ensure that the structure should not fail in shear.

Load Transfer

The loads acting on a structure should be transferred effectively and efficiently to the foundations and further to the ground for the stability of the structure. The geometry and configuration of the structure play a major role in proper load transfer.

Mass of Structure

Seismic forces acting on the structure is directly proportional to the dead weight of it, i.e. heavier the structure, higher is the seismic forces. Also the non-uniformity or variation in the weight of the structure at different level attributes to seismic sensitivity.

Nature of Failure

The failures occurred during the above referred earthquake in urban Gujarat are categorized and discussed based on the reasons of failures attributable to the above features.

The factors contributing to the failures are :-

- Soft Storey
- Floating Column
- Weak Column and Strong Beams
- Lack of Ductility
- High Variation of Stiffness
- Geometry of Structure
- Selection of Site for Sound Foundation
- Ignorance or Violation of Basic Codal Provisions
- Deviation from Structural Design/Planned Load
- Quality of Construction, and
- Inadequate Design without incorporating Seismic Requirements

Each of the above factors are discussed below in details.

Soft Storey

In urban housing, the land is always a constraint and the ground floor of the building is either partially or fully utilized for car/scooter parking. Due to the exclusion of brick walls, the stiffness of the floor is reduced and varies tremendously in comparison with the other floors resulting in an uneven displacement of the columns of this floor compared to the other floors leading to failure. In this case the brick in-fill walls provided in the upper floors absorb lot of lateral seismic forces but will not be able to transfer this to the foundation uniformly due to the discontinuation of these shear resistant walls. This causes shear concentration in the columns in the ground floor resulting into sudden collapse of the weak column, if not designed adequately to absorb these shear forces.

Floating Column

In order to save the construction floor area while calculating FSI (Floor Space Index) as per the prevailing municipal regulations, the ground floor boundary columns of the structure are shifted internally which ultimately results in discontinuity of the upper floor columns (in order to avoid the appearance of the columns in the middle of a room). Thus the upper floor columns rest on the cantilever beams of the ground floor. This is called "Floating Column". In such situation the load transfer of even the gravity loads are not proper and the condition becomes worst in case of earthquake load.

Weak Columns and Strong Beams

Due to various factors, the strength of the columns are observed as weak compared to the beams supporting the structure. Due to this reason the shear or the brittle failure of the column becomes inevitable. This is due to the formation of plastic hinges in the column. In majority of the cases, the restriction in the size of the column for architectural reasons, inadequate compaction of concrete within, congestion of reinforcement, etc. are the reasons for the weak columns in addition to the design deficiency.

Lack of Ductility

Ductility of a structure means the capability of a structure to absorb the deformations beyond the normal elastic limit. This characteristic can be developed by increasing the ductility of individual members and improving the ductility of connections between the structural members.

Majority of the structures, damaged during the above earthquake, were having very weak connections between the structural members, viz. weak column-beam joints and weak joint between stair case and lift wall, either due to bad practices or inadequate detailing in the working drawings. The inter-connection of foundations either at the footing level or at the plinth level were also missing in certain cases. Under the circumstances, the members of the structure acted independently leading to failure.

High Variation of Stiffness

In certain cases the structures behaved like inverted pendulum as the structures were subjected to unthinkable additional load, subsequent to completion of the structure, at a later date, as per the whims and fancy of the user.

The 'Mansi' Tower at Vastrapur (Ahmedabad) was an unique example where a 60,000 litre swimming pool and a terrace garden with considerable earth filling were added at a later date without any approval from competent regulatory authority or without giving any technical thought on the danger of doing so. As a result, this 14 storied building collapsed like a pack of cards leading to considerable loss of life and property.

Geometry of the Structure

Simple geometric design and load transfer methodology are also essential to an economical earthquake resistant structure. Architectural gimmicks to provide an unsymmetrical structure will lead to either uneconomical or unsafe structure. Structures having shape of 'L', 'T', 'U', 'H', '+' or their combinations have re-entrant corners which are very much vulnerable to seismic forces. Vertical dissimilarity such as overhangs etc. are also equally undesirable.

Performance of a structure in earthquake depends on its overall configuration, lateral stiffness, ductility and lateral strength. Building with simple and regular configuration with direct load transfer path perform better during shaking of earth. Irregular or complicated geometry leads to more complicated and additional structural analysis requirements, even though the sophistication in analysis is not necessarily a solution to the problem caused by irregular configuration. The unsymmetrical structure causes torsion which results in an undesirable twist of the structure. This is primarily due to eccentricity between the centre of mass and the centre of stiffness. Hence, configuration becomes an important consideration at the stage of Architectural planning of a structure and it is said that simplicity is the best approach. The cost of compliance with seismic code provision also depends largely on the configuration of a structure.

Selection of Site for Sound Foundation

Selection of site for providing sound foundation is a key factor to have a good performance of the building during earthquake. If the soil consists of very loose sand or sensitive clays, such soils are liable to be destroyed during earthquake due to compaction and foundation may fail due to large unequal settlement. If the loose cohesion less soils is saturated with water, they may loose their shear resistance during shaking and get liquefied.

Hence, a site with sufficient bearing capacity should be chosen and its drainage condition to be improved so that no water accumulation occurs which can saturate the ground close to footing level. Sometimes over looking of this vital aspect lead to foundation collapse even for a perfectly designed ductile frame.

Ignorance or Violation of Basic Codal Provisions

The seismic maps of these urban areas were established and well recorded. These cities fell under Zone-III, which were clearly earthquake sensitive and the provisions required to be provided in the relevant earthquake resistant structure were well documented and in vogue. Either due to lack of enforcement of these provisions or mere ignorance of them resulted in the failure of most of the structures.

The major factors influencing the cost of complying with codal provisions are :

- Complexity of the shape and structural framing system of the structure.
- Cost of the additional structural inputs in relation to the total cost.
- Choice of configuration as well as materials of construction in the beginning to ensure earthquake resistance.

Deviation from Structural Design/Planned Load

It was observed that in many cases the designs of similar structures, constructed elsewhere in the same locality, have been blatantly copied without looking into the deviations in the soil condition. Due to this, the required depth of foundations have been deviated, ignoring the changes required to be incorporated in the structural details due to increased depth of footing and increased height of columns. In addition, number of floors and even floor heights have been increased or deviated from the original design during execution, resulting into failure of those structures during earthquake.

Quality of Construction

The designs are based on certain assumptions on the strength of concrete and steel reinforcement to be provided in the structures. It was observed that constructions have been carried out in many places in the conventional method without looking into the strength requirement, based on the design.

Inadequate Design without incorporating Seismic Requirements

The excuses of a builder or an inexperienced designer for not incorporating the seismic provision in the construction of a structure, is the high cost involved in it. It is well established that the increase in cost due to provisioning of seismic requirements in the design is marginal and may be in the order of 5-6 per cent only, compared to that of the static load design. This need not be avoided looking into the catastrophic effect of an earthquake. The various techniques, normally adopted to absorb the earthquake forces in design, are :-

- Replacement of certain members of the moment resistant frames with RCC shear wall.
- Consideration of shear resistance of the brick in-fill wall while designing a structure, which are normally ignored.
- Consideration of the diaphragm action of horizontal floor slabs while modelling the structure.
- Due consideration towards the connectivity of the lift cabin walls and its shear capacity in the design.
- Adoption of 'strong column - weak beam' philosophy to avoid shear failure of columns. Formation of plastic hinges in the beam shall be preferred to that of column, by which the collapse of the structure can be avoided..

These are certain factors which will help economizing the earthquake resistant design of a structure. In fact, it was observed that, most of the structures, which survived the earthquake in spite of not being designed as earthquake resistant structures, were due to the presence of the brick in-fill wall.

It has been observed that money spent on constructing the concrete lift wall has not been utilized properly. The weak joint between these walls with the rest of the structure resulted in shearing off of the structures from the walls, without any damage to the RCC lift wall. So many structures failed due to this.

Walls are very good shear resistant members when they are provided perpendicular to the direction of the earthquake forces. Hence, few RCC shear walls, in appropriate locations and directions, can absorb a major portion of the earthquake forces by which the other RCC frames can be provided economically. Due to this, the 'Shear Wall' has become synonymous to an economic earthquake resistant structure. It has been substantially proved that that an economical seismic resistant construction is not possible without the provision of shear walls in a RCC moment resistant framed construction.

Recommendations from Study

1. Consider designing a structure after ascertaining whether the structure is located in a seismically sensitive zone or not. Detailing for additional requirement for seismic considerations, may be made clear in the structural drawings.
2. Consider provision of 'RCC Shear Wall' from foundation to the top.
3. Consider structural members to be adequately connected physically from foundation to the roof.
4. Consider uniformity in the geometry of the structure in both vertical and horizontal direction.
5. Consider avoiding floating column.
6. Consider construction of RCC core wall of the lift shaft (which serves as a good shear wall) together with the adjoining members of the structure, i.e. stair case etc. Both should remain well connected.
7. Consider extending the reinforcement bars of the beams adequately into the columns at the column-beam junctions.
8. Consider avoiding joints of column reinforcing bars within the column-beam junctions.
9. Consider the column of a structure to have not less than six vertical bars of diameter 12 mm or more and stirrups/rings spacing properly throughout the column height.
10. Consider use of specified quality of steel and concrete (as per design/specifications) during construction.

Conclusion

This paper tried to establish inconsistencies and inaccuracies commonly accepted by the design profession and highlighted some simple solutions which could play a major role in preventing seismic failures of the engineered structures to a great extent. The Gujarat earthquake of 2001 as well as the recent earthquake in Jammu & Kashmir should act as an eye opener to our civil engineering fraternity as a whole, be it in the role of a designer/constructor or a member of the regulatory body; as we are responsible to provide safety to the innocent users of the structures.

21

BHOPAL DISASTER—A PERSONAL EXPERIENCE

J.K. Gehlawat*

ABSTRACT

Bhopal Tragedy was the worst industrial accident in the world where several thousand persons lost their lives. It occurred at the Union Carbide plant located inside the city of Bhopal and close to the railway station, at mid-night of December 2-3, 1984 due to the leakage of a MIC gas which took the local sleeping and floating population unaware.

This paper describes the experience of a transit passenger who reached the Bhopal Railway Station by train at about the same time when the deadly gas leakage occurred.

Introduction

Safety in the operations of chemical plants, where toxic gaseous substances are handled, is of prime importance. Safety aspects begin right at the stage of designing a chemical plant. Foolproof construction and meticulous drills for the prevention of any accident during operations of the plant are mandatory. Author had an opportunity of working at the pilot plants of a leading chemical production unit at Bombay where gas-liquid reactions involving toxic gases like ammonia, chlorine and sulphur dioxide were carried out. He was well familiar with the safety programmes and training.

He had personally known the Site-Chief at the Bhopal Plant of Union Carbide, Dr. Roy Choudhary and their Regional Marketing Manager at Delhi, Dr. U.V. Singh. Hence, he was aware of the activities at the Bhopal plant and that methyl isocyanate (MIC), a toxic reactant, was stored in underground storage tanks in tonnage quantity.

He was working as a consultant to a new project at Indore which is about 160 km from Bhopal by road. He used to visit this client once in a month. He was on his way to Indore when his train from Kanpur reached Bhopal at about mid-night of December 2-3, 1984 when the deadly gas leakage had occurred at the Union Carbide plant. The factory

*Former Professor, IIT Kanpur, President, People Oriented Science &Technology Society, 248, Ram Krishna Vihar, 29, I.P. Extension, Delhi - 110092, India. *Email :* gehlawat@hotmail.com

was situated in a thickly populated locality at a distance of about 1 km from the railway station. Fig. 1 shows the plant location and the gas affected areas of the town. Other details including compensation paid upto July 19, 2004 are shown in Fig. 2.

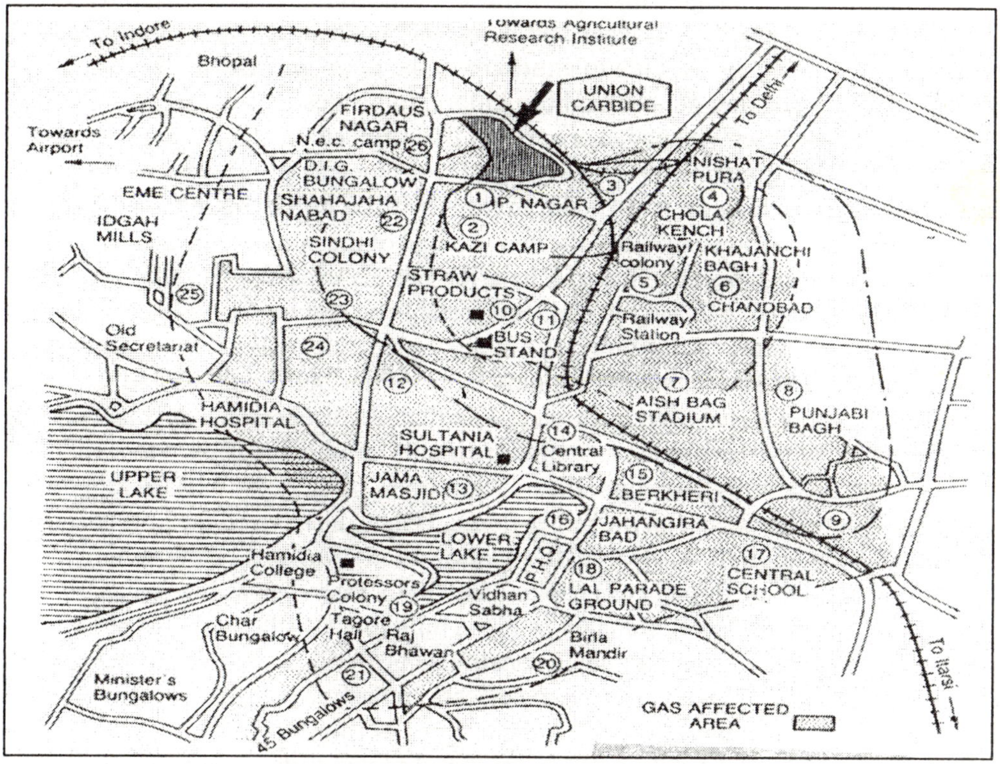

Fig. 1: Gas Affected Area of Bhopal

Gas Affected Area of Bhopal

- Wards in Bhopal Municipal Corporation (1984) - 56
- Gas affected wards - 36
- Estimated Population of Bhopal Municipal Corporation (1984) - 8,94,539
- Estimated Population of the 36 gas affected wards - 5,59,835

Night of December 2-3, 1984

- Methyl isocyanate (MIC) gas leaked from Union Carbide factory as Bhopal slept.
- Immediate toll stood at over 3000 with thousands impaired in various degrees. Toll continued to mount over the coming years.
- Union Carbide deposited US $ 470 million with Reserve Bank of India in settlement of claims in February 1989.
- Over the years part of the money distributed to victims, but a large amount is held up due to legal complications.

July 19, 2004

- Supreme Court orders the full amount, which has grown to Rs. 1,503 crores with interest, to be released to victims.

Fig. 2: Relief for Bhopal Gas Victims

A Frightening Personal Experience

Author's train reached Bhopal railway station amidst great chaos due to the leakage and heavy spread of the nasty pungent toxic gas in the atmosphere. There was no coolie (baggage handler), no taxi, no one to tell what had happened - except the cry all-around among suffocation and burning eyes owing to exposure to the toxic gas. On another occasion he would have taken a taxi and gone straight to Indore, to his destination. But on that fateful night he had to walk down with baggage to Hotel Bharati located at a distance of about 350 metres from the railway station across a flyover. He decided to go there because the owner of the Hotel was from Kanpur and known to him. It was a horrifying experience to walk down the distance upto the Hotel since the heavy cloud of the pungent gas not only affected the respiratory system adversely due to inhalation but his eyes also became sore and red like it happens with a tear gas. He felt a bit comfortable on reaching the Hotel. It is a three-storey high but small hotel.

There were about 20 occupants. As pointed out earlier in the text, he had worked in a chemical plant where toxic chemicals were handled. As a chemical engineer and as a teacher he knew that many gaseous reactants are highly soluble in water. Most are heavier than air and that on a chilly mid-night the concentration of the toxic MIC would be much higher at the ground level than on the upper floors. Hence, he advised the hotel occupants: (i) to shift to the top floor, (ii) to close all the windows, (iii) to switch on the ceiling fans and exhaust fans, (iv) to breath through wet napkins and (v) to wash eyes with water as frequently as possible. He asked the Hotel Manager to given milk to all. Milk works as an antidote in such situations because casein and other constituents of milk work as adsorbents for the toxic substances and minimize their residual effects on the body systems, particularly their passage into the blood stream.

They struggled throughout the night and suffered a lot in spite of the above precautions. It was at about 4.0 A.M. that the intensity of the gas started decreasing. By 5.0 A.M., it appeared to be nearly normal when he called his client at Indore and informed him about the ordeal at Bhopal. He told him that he would be leaving for Indore by the first available vehicle. He requested him to locate a good physician and an eye surgeon at the medical college at Indore for my medical check-up and treatment.

He checked out of the hotel at about 6.30 A.M. and walked down to the nearby taxi-cum-bus stand. He was pleasantly surprised to find the situation at the bus stand nearly normal. There were many more passengers who must be stranded at Bhopal like him. He boarded a Luxury bus for Indore and reached there by 11.00 A.M. At Indore he checked into a hotel and learnt by news from the All India Radio that a lot of people had died in Bhopal that night due to the gas tragedy. It was also reported that most deaths occurred on the roads. These were mostly the poor people, who tried to run away on foot and collapsed on the roads due to excessive inhalation of the toxic gas. Those who remained in-doors, including the plant personnel at the site of the gas leakage, survived, though many may have taken ill or suffered from gas exposure and died during later years due to lack of proper diagnosis or treatment.

His client at Indore had contacted an eye surgeon at the Medical College, Dr. Nahta. He was under his treatment for a few days and returned to Kanpur feeling nearly normal.

Negative Compensation for Claim

He was among the six hundred and fifty thousand persons who filed their claims for compensation. Documentation and Medical Examination occurred at Bhopal more than once. A bronchial attack on his lungs and on-set of cataract in both the eyes were noticed as after-effects of the exposure to MIC. Another half a dozen visits to Bhopal took place for the judicial proceedings. The claim was settled during 1997 with a payment of Rs. 35,000/- (about 800 US dollars). It virtually meant a negative compensation since much more money had been spent by him during this period on medication and frequent travels to Bhopal for documentation and judicial proceedings.

Concluding Remarks

Like several other travellers, his presence at Bhopal at the time of the gas tragedy was merely accidental. He escaped major suffering due to prior knowledge of toxic chemicals and on account of simple precautions as described earlier in the text. A much larger section of the local population was badly affected. As per confirmed reports about three thousand persons died (mostly on the roads) on that fateful night. Several thousand suffered from moderate to serious illness - most of it persistent and irreversible owing to exposure to the toxic gas and died in later years due to lack of proper treatment. Over twenty thousand persons are reported to have died till date. Pregnant women have had miscarriages and given births to deformed babies. Thousands lost their eyesight. The aged and the children continue to suffer. As for the compensation: payments of Rs. one to two hundred thousand (2500-5000 US dollars) to the families of the dead and Rs. 25,000 to 35,000 (600-800 US dollars) to him and others, after 10-15 year's of claim proceedings are very meagre sums.

Prevention is better than cure. Stringent inbuilt safety norms in plant design, location of hazardous plants away from the habitation, vigilant plant operations, frequent mock drills to continually test the safety systems for its proper functioning and operators' preparedness are needed to move towards zero accident rate in industrial practice. It is a great challenge to the plant engineers and planners but surely worth the effort.

22

TSUNAMI RISK IN INDIA AND ITS ASSESSMENT

V. Rajkumar*, Aftab Ahmad* and G.C. Mohanta*

ABSTRACT

With its vast territory, large population and unique geo-climatic conditions, in the last few decades India has experienced many extreme hazardous events that have turned into disasters. High human casualties and economic losses from the 26 December, 2004 Indian ocean tsunami have resulted in heightened awareness not only in India but also on global scale, of the potential extraordinary destructiveness of tsunamis, and of the vital need to better understand and manage the risks that they pose. Generally a hazard and risk analysis encompasses many complex issues, methodologies and practices. In this paper an overview of these concepts is provided. Since the recent tsunami have triggered serious deliberations from many quarters on the urgent need for versatile tsunami warning and communication system, an attempt has been made to address issues like how should we gear up to handle such events in future? What are the shortcomings in our existing set up? And what should be our approach towards setting up a tsunami warning system in the Indian ocean?

Key words: Hazard, Risk assessment, Mitigation, DART.

Introduction

The great earthquake of 26 December, 2004 of magnitude 9.0 in Richter scale that originated 200 km off the west coast of Sumatra was perhaps nature's wake-up call. A wake-up call to tell us that nature will continue its own acts, and we need to prepare ourselves to face the inevitable. This time it occurred in the form of a tsunami, quite an unusual occurrence in the Indian coast. Not that it has happened in the past. History tells us of three older episodes - 1881, 1941 and 1945 - none so devastating as the 2004 tsunami. Approximately 2,260 km of the coastal area besides the Andaman & Nicobar Islands were affected. According to Government reports 10,881 people in India lost their lives and 5,7924 persons were reported missing with 6,913 injured. The overall damages are estimated to be $574.5 million and losses to be $448.3 million. The largest proportions of the damages were concentrated in fisheries, housing and infrastructure.

---

*Scientist, Directorate of Safety and Environmental Engineering, Defence R & D Laboratory, Hyderabad-58.

Tsunami Characteristics

A tsunami is a series of waves with a long wavelength and period (time between crests). Time between crests of the wave can vary from a few minutes to over an hour. Tsunamis are often incorrectly called tidal waves; they have no relation to the daily ocean tides. Tsunami (soo-NAH-mee) is a Japanese word meaning harbour wave. Tsunamis can occur at any time of day or night. Tsunamis are generated by any large, impulsive displacement of the sea bed level. Earthquakes generate tsunamis by vertical movement of the sea floor. If the sea floor movement is horizontal, a tsunami is not generated. Earthquakes of M >6.5 in Richter scale are critical for tsunami generation. Tsunamis are also triggered by landslides into or under the water surface, and can be generated by volcanic activity and meteorite impacts. Tsunamis range in size from centimetres to over 30 m height. Most tsunamis are less than 3 m in height. In deep water (greater than 200 m), tsunamis are rarely over 1m high and will not be noticed by ships due to their long period (time between crests). As tsunamis propagate into shallow water, the wave height can increase by over 10 times. Tsunami heights can vary greatly along a coast. The waves are amplified by certain shoreline and bathymetric (sea floor) features.

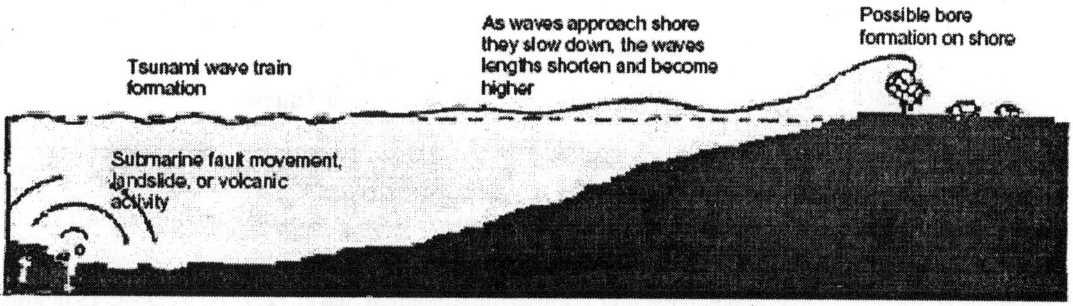

Fig. 1 : Tsunami wave trainformation

A large tsunami can flood land up to more than 1.5 km from the coast. The force of some tsunamis is enormous. Large rocks weighing several tons along with boats and other debris can be moved inland hundreds of feet by tsunami wave. Homes and other buildings are destroyed. All this material and water move with great force and can kill or injure people. Normally, a tsunami appears as a rapidly advancing or receding tide. In some cases a bore (wall of water) or series of breaking waves may form.

Sometimes a tsunami causes the water near the shore to recede, exposing the ocean floor, and then the wave crest comes with a high speed. Tsunamis can travel up rivers and streams that lead to the sea. Wind-generated waves usually have periods (time between crests) of 5 to 20 seconds. Tsunami periods are usually between 5 minutes and an hour. Wind-generated waves break as they shoal and lose energy offshore. Tsunamis act more like a flooding wave. A 6 m tsunami is a 6 m rise in sea level.

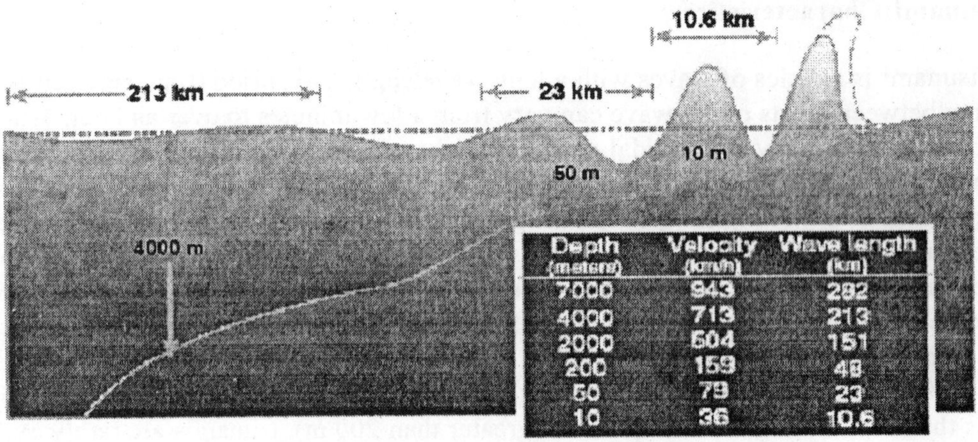

Fig. 2 : Tsunami Velocities

List of Tsunami that Affected India

Date	*Remarks*
326 B.C.	Alexander the Great
Between 1st April and 9th May, 1008	Tsunami on the Iranian coast from a local earthquake
27th August, 1883	Karatoa 1.5 m Tsunami at Madras, 06 AM at Nagapattinam, 0.2 m at Arden
1884	Earthquake in the western part of the Bay of Bengal Tsunamis at Port Blair, Doublet (mouth of Hooghly River)
26th June, 1941	8.1 quake in Richter scale in the Andaman Sea at 12.9° N, 92.5° E Tsunamis on the east coast of India with amplitudes from 0.75 to 1.25 m. Some damage from East Coast was reported.
1945	Mekran Earthquake (Magnitude 8.1 in Richter scale). 12 to 15 m wave height in Ormara in Pasi (Mekran coast). Considerable damage in Mekran coast. In Gulf of Cambay of Gujarat wave heights of 15 meter was estimated. Damage report from Gujarat coast was not available. The estimated height of waves at Mumbai was about 2 metres, boats were taken away from their moorings and causalty occurred.
27th November, 1945	8.25 quake 70 km south of Karachi at 24.5° N, 63.0° E Tsunami amplitude at Kutch was 11.0 to 11.5m
26th December, 2004	Earthquake of magnitude 9.1 in Richter scale of north Sumatra coast generated devastated Tsunami waves affecting several countries in South East Asia. In India Andaman & Nicobar Island, Tamil Nadu, Pondichery, Andhra Pradesh, Kerala and Lakshadweep have been affected: about 9700 people lose their lives and about 6000 more reported missing. (Till end January 2005)

Tsunamis in India

Facts indicate that the coastal region of Gujarat is vulnerable to Tsunamis from great earthquakes in Mekran coast. Earthquake of magnitude 7 or more in Richter scale may be dangerous. It may be noted that all earthquake do not generate Tsunami. Research is still being undertaken in this field. For the Indian region, two potential sources have been identified, namely, Mekran coast and Andaman to Sumatra region.

Tsunami risk

It will be assessed by a deterministic approach according to the following:
Tsunami Risk = Tsunami Hazard. Exposure. Vulnerability.

(a) For the Tsunami Hazard Assessment:
- Preparation of database from historical and archival information such as newspapers, archives, anecdotal information, literature survey of relevant Indian Tsunamis, with the emphasis clearly on the December 26, 2004 event.
- Analyses of these data:
  - To define the scenario of Tsunamis from various earthquake sources.
  - To prepare the Tsunami hazard map.

(b) For the Exposure:
- List all habitations below 15 m contour level and locate on a map.
- List and locate all vital installations below 15 m contour level (Ports, Harbours, Schools, Hospitals, Power Plants, Bridges, etc.).

(c) For the Vulnerability Assessment:
- Based on the earthquake vulnerability assessment, define the vulnerability of various exposed elements on the coastal, island and reef environments and in the Ports and Harbours.
- Prepare vulnerability charts and matrices.

(d) For the Risk Assessment:
- Integrate these hazard and exposure data with vulnerability assessments to obtain the risk assessment.

The following parameters will need to be defined:

- Tsunami source region,
- Mode of generation,
- Potential wave heights,
- Maximum Run-up (maximum height of the water onshore observed/inferred above the mean sea level. Usually measured at the horizontal inundation limit),
- Tsunami intensity $I = 0.5 \log 2H$ (Pelinovsky, 1996), with H = average maximum run-up height >3 m, $I_{max} = 2.5$

Tsunami Hazard Map

The Tsunami hazard map may be empirically defined using a deterministic approach, based upon potential maximum wave heights for the scenario of tsunamis. The definition of the tsunami hazard zones, as preliminary estimates, is given in the Table. For the terrestrial environment the hazard may be presented as inundation levels, in terms of run-up heights at specified land contours. For the marine environment ("ON WATER") Harbour, Bay and Reefs - hazard may be given in terms of potential maximum wave heights.

Tsunami Hazard Zones Definition (Preliminary)

Characteristic	*Tsunami Hazard Zone*		
	High	*Medium*	*Low*
On Land - Inundation Level - Maximum (m Contour)	5	3	1
Run-up Height - Average (m)	>3	1-3	0-1
Tsunami Intensity (I)	>2	1-2	0
Likelihood of Tsunami	Yes	Yes	Possible
Damage Observed in Earlier Tsunami	Severe	Minor	None
Coast Adjacent to Tsunami Genie Source	Yes	Yes	No
On Water - Wave Heights (m)	>2	1-2	<1
Reef Damage	Severe	Minor	None

Tsunami Vulnerability Assessment

The exposure inventory with vulnerability to tsunami impact for both the built and natural environments will need to be developed for shores and harbours. Potential damage is related to the hydrological controls of wave action (surging), flooding and debris deposition, and consequent geotechnical controls to damage by liquefaction, cracking and slumping. These results in structural damage to buildings, water damage to contents, flooding damage to infrastructure (roads, bridges, water supply, sewerage, wharves, sea-walls), damage to navigational aids and reef damage. There is the potential for "seiching" in the shallow harbour areas where, alternately (from the tsunami waves), water is drained from the harbour and then flooded to depths greater than high tide levels. This has the potential for threat to human life (death and injury) from people collecting fish from the harbour seafloor. In the Harbour, waves are a threat to shipping (sinking, striking wharves) and fishermen (drowning). The vulnerability assessment is expressed as details of elements of the built, natural and human environments vulnerable to potential tsunami-related damage. These need to be considered in terms of the Tsunami Hazard Zones for the terrestrial environments around the shores and the marine environments.

Tsunami Risk Assessment

By integrating the hazard and vulnerability assessments, the tsunami risk assessment is to be developed in terms of zonation and inundation maps and associated affects.

Practical Applications

The key factors to reduce potential losses due to tsunami are AWARENESS and PREPAREDNESS. The practical applications of this tsunami risk assessment, in both quantitative and qualitative terms, for implementation into mitigation strategies for the terrestrial and marine environments include:

1. Building Codes	(Potential damage due to wave action and flooding)
2. GIS Mapping	
3. Land-use Planning	(Taking note of wave action & flooding)
4. Disaster Planning	(In identified hazard zones)
5. Emergency Management	
6. Emergency Personnel Training	(Necessary aspects relevant to marine situations)
7. Rescue and Response (marine situations related to shipping)	(Cargo, tourist, inter-islands fishing community, recreational boating)
8. Insurance Needs	
9. Community Education	
10. Simulated Tsunami Exercises	

Tsunami Risk Mitigation

Is the existing Tsunami risk acceptable or tolerable?

Yes => Nothing needs to be done
No => Risk should be reduced

We know that Tsunami hazard cant be changed. To reduce the risk we should mitigate the consequences.

Challenges in Application of Risk Management Theory to Tsunamis

Tsunami hazard changes with time - Tsunami hazard is mostly due to movements along the subduction zone. Lower seismic activity expected in coming decades because of the major earthquakes that occurred.

Different groups of potentially affected population have different exposure to tsunami danger - people who lived in the exposure areas permanently, tourists who only live in the exposed area one or two weeks and locals who don't live in the exposed areas but work there during the tourist season.

The real risk and the perceived risk for the tsunami are likely to be quite different. Since the perceived risk is very high, the potentially affected population expects that tsunami risk mitigation measures be done, even if one can't document the immediate need for such measures or justify them through a cost benefit analysis.

Present Status of Disaster Preparedness

After visiting the tsunami-affected areas in India, the multi-national mission team has the following observations:

Lack of:

- Awareness at all levels about disasters and disaster management in general, tsunami in particular,
- Preparedness at all levels about disasters and disaster management in general, tsunami in particular,
- Early warning system for tsunami,
- Implementation of norms and regulations [including Coastal Zone Regulation (CRZ)] norms,
- Building codes and bye-laws,
- Hazard, vulnerability and risk assessment for disaster management,
- Appropriate database for disaster mitigation,
- Holistic approach towards disaster mitigation and management,
- Sufficient plantation along the coast, and
- Proper mechanism to identify the beneficiaries.

The Department of Ocean Development in Cooperation with Department of Space, Science and Technology is evolving a plan of tsunami warning system in the Bay of Bengal and in the Arabian Sea. The data from observing points to Warning Centre(s) will be sent through satellite links. Specific systems called Deep Ocean Assessment and Reporting of Tsunamis (DART) using Bottom Pressure Recorder, acoustic modem, acoustic release system, battery pack bolted to platform and float action and recovery aids will be deployed.

International Status of Tsunami Warning and Communication System

Present techniques of Tsunami prediction are severely limited. The only way to determine, with certainty, if an earthquake is accompanies by a Tsunami, is to note the occurrence and epicenter of the earthquake and then detect the arrival of the Tsunami at a network of tide stations. While it is possible to predict when a Tsunami will arrive at coastal locations, it is not yet possible to predict the wave height, number of waves, duration of hazard, or the forces to be expected from such waves at specific locations.

Tsunami Warning Centres

As part of an international cooperative effort to save lives and protect property, the National Oceanic and Atmospheric Administration's (NOAA), National Weather Service operates two Tsunami warning centres. The Alaska Tsunami Warning Centre (ATWC) in Palmer, Alaska, serves as the regional Tsunami Warning Centre for Alaska, British Columbia, Washington, Oregon, and California. The Pacific Tsunami Warning Centre in Ewa Beach, Hawaii, serves as the regional Tsunami Warning Centre for Hawaii and as a national/

international warning centre for Tsunamis that pose a Pacific-wide threat. This international warning effort becomes a formal arrangement in 1965 when PTWC assumed the international warning responsibilities of the Pacific Tsunami Warning System (PTWS). The PTWS is composed of 26 international Member States that are organized as the International Coordination Group for the Tsunami Warning System in the Pacific.

Deep-Ocean Assessment and Reporting of Tsunamis System (DART II)

Recently developed by USA, these have been deployed in Open Ocean in small number since five years. Figure shows DART II system and related telecommunications nodes. It consists of two physical components: a tsunameter on the ocean floor and a surface buoy with satellite telecommunications capability. The DART II systems have bi-directional communication links and are thus able to send and receive data from the Tsunami Warning Centrr and others *via* the Internet. Uses unique pressure recorders that sit on the ocean bottom. These recorders are used to detect slight changes in the overlying water pressure. The DART system is capable of detecting a tsunami as small as a centimeter high above the sea level. DART bottom package mooring consists of a Bottom Pressure Recorder, an acoustic modem, acoustic release unit and battery pack bolted to a platform, to which a disposable anchor, flotation, and recovery aids are attached. Moorings are designed to free-fall to the bottom and are deployable for 24 months at depths of 6000 m; recovery is initiated by triggering the acoustic release to separate from the anchor, at which point the flotation brings the unit to the surface. These systems have measured tsunamis characterized by amplitudes less than 1 cm in the deep ocean, using a quartz crystal pressure transducer that is sensitive to changes corresponding to less than a millimeter of equivalent sea level change in the tsunami frequency band.

Tsunami Watch and Warning Dissemination

The objective of the PTWS is to detect, locate and determine the magnitude of potentially Tsunamigenic earthquake occurring in the Pacific Basin or its immediate margins. Earthquake information is provided by seismic stations operated by PTWC, ATWC, the U.S. Geological

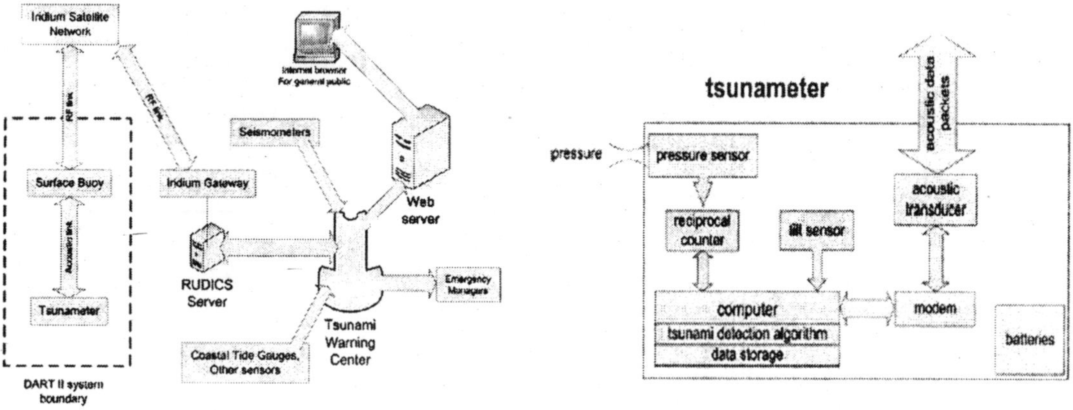

DART System

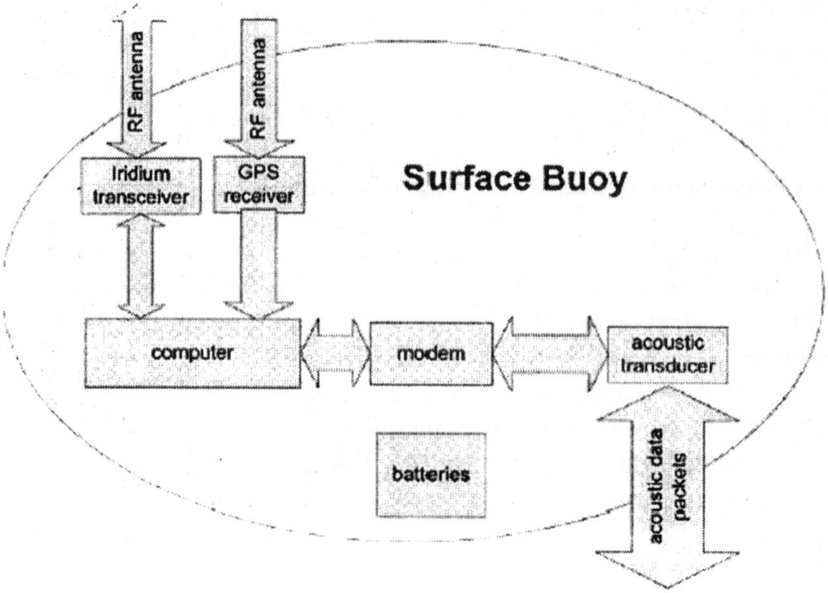

Warning Path

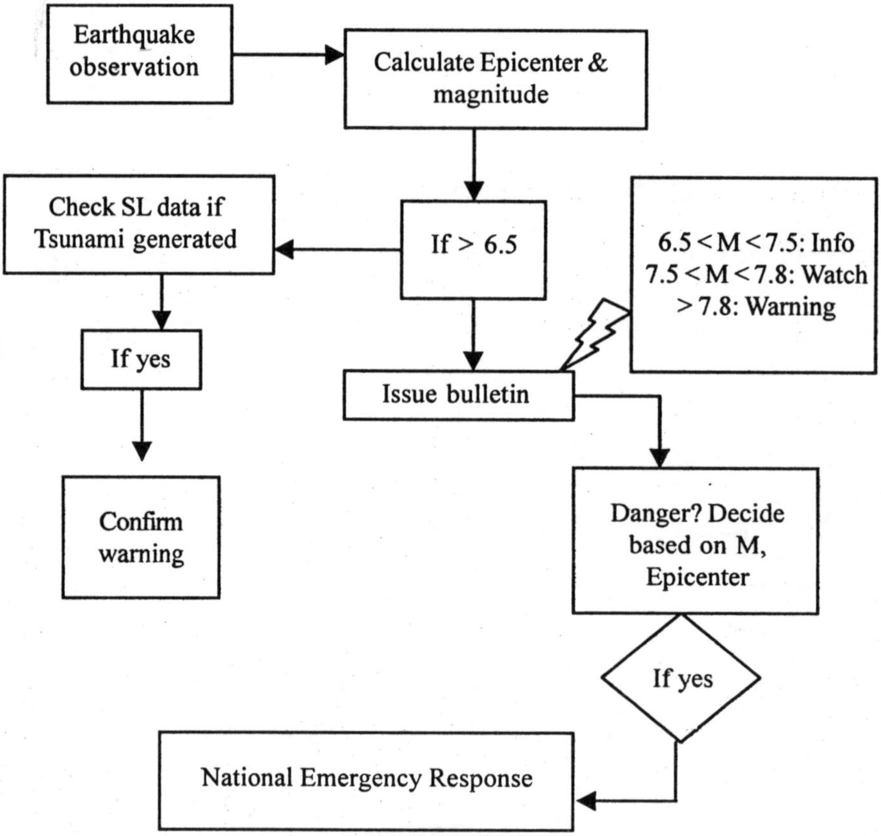

Survey's National Earthquake Information Centre and international sources. If the location and magnitude of an earthquake meet the known criteria for generation of a Tsunami, a Tsunami warning is issued to warn of an imminent Tsunami hazard. The warning includes predicted Tsunami arrival times at selected coastal communities within the geographic area defined by the maximum distance the Tsunami could travel in a few hours. A Tsunami watch with additional predicted Tsunami arrival times is issued for a geographic area defined by the distance the Tsunami could travel in a subsequent time period. If a significant Tsunami is detected by sea-level monitoring instrumentation, the Tsunami warning is extended to the entire Pacific Basin. Seal level (or tidal) information is provided by NOAA's National Ocean Service, PTWC, ATWC, university monitoring networks and other participating nations of the PTWS. The International Tsunami Information Centre, part of the Inter-governmental Oceanographic Commission, monitors and evaluates the performance and effectiveness of the Pacific Tsunami Warning System. This effort encourages the most effective data collection, data analysis, Tsunami impact assessment and warning dissemination to all TWS participants.

Conclusion

Thus, the Tsunami tragedy has exposed lack of preparedness in dealing with natural calamities. The Tsunami of December 26, 2004 has thus left in its trail of destruction, among other things one ponderable poser - "how prepared really we are?" in every sense of the term in dealing with such tragedies. There's no point in spending all the money on a fancy monitoring and a fancy analysis system unless we can make sure the infrastructure for the broadcast system is there. Our Country needed "Emergency response infrastructure".

REFERENCES

Preliminary report by the multi-national mission to tsunami affected areas of India - Asian disaster reduction center, Kobe, Japan. April 8-13, 2005.

Probabilistic tsunami risk management framework, safety policy and applications, www.sthjournal.org

Tsunami risk reduction measures, International Dissemination Seminar, 9 March, 2006, Bangkok.

Country paper on India for International Workshop on strengthening the resilience of Local communities in coastal areas to water related natural disasters, Copenhagen 16-18, Nov. 2005.

Towards a tsunami warning system in the Indian ocean - Current science, Vol. 89, No. 2, 25 July, 2005.

www.en.wikipedia.org

www.pmel.noaa.gov/

www.ndbc.noaa.gov/

www.i4donline.net

www. mha.nic.in

www.ndmindia.nic.in

SAFETY IN ELECTROSTATIC DISCHARGE SENSITIVE AREAS

N. Vijay,* R. Rukmoji,* Aftab Ahmad* and G.C. Mohanta*

ABSTRACT

Accumulation of static charges leading to an electrostatic discharge (ESD) in Electrostatic Discharge Sensitive areas may cause explosion in rocket development centres. This paper reviews the present state of knowledge in this field based on information available from literature, codes of practice and guidelines. In a short introduction, from charge generation to ignition of Electro Explosive Devices is outlined. Electro Explosive Devices are electrically initiated detonators used to fire an explosive charge or to operate a mechanical device. These explosive devices are subjected to assembly, handling, shipping and final installation that may expose them to an Electrostatic Discharge (ESD). Generation of Electrostatic discharges is explained with Human Body Model (HBM), Machine Model and Charged Device Model (CDM). Hazards of static electricity is controlled by preventing the generation of static charge, dissipate in the developed charge and neutralizing the developed charge for a charge free zone. This paper is intended to shed some light on the sources of ESD and to provide guidelines on the prevention and control of ESD.

Key Words: Electrostatic Discharge, Electro Explosive Device, Minimum Ignition Energy, Electrostatic Discharge Control.

Introduction

The phenomenon of static electricity and its effects was known by man since the time of the ancient Greeks, but did not receive much serious attention until the 17th and 18th centuries. Just before and during the industrial revolution (steam engine times) static electricity was identified, tested and measured. With mechanization came high-speed machines and belts generating large amounts of static electricity. Static sparks were blamed for fires in paper and cotton mills, explosive storage, explosions in mines and munitions factories. In 1979, the EOS/ESD Association was formed to explore static charge issues and to provide education on the same.

*Directorate of Safety and Environmental Engineering, Defence Research and Development Laboratory, Kanchanbagh (PO), Hyderabad - 500 058.

Even though static electricity was known to the electrical industry for over several years but only recent has increased in significance with the advent of sensitive Electro Explosive Devices (EED), which are used to ignite the propellant. The electrostatic charges are generated by friction, separation and induction. The generated charge will be dissipated harmlessly by providing the electrical conductive path to the system. If the rate of charge generation is greater than the dissipation, static electric charges will build up and very high voltage can be produced quite rapidly which may lead to electrostatic discharge (ESD).

Sudden discharge of static electricity does not result in any harm to the human body, it can damage the Electro Explosive Device (EED), which is sensitive to electrostatic discharge (ESD). It is possible for Electro Explosive Device (EED) to get damaged by ESD that is imperceptible to the human body. Human being gets electrostatically charged while walking over an insulating floor surface. The body's capacitance can be charged to several kilovolts. A discharge occurs when contact is made to an electronic unit or system.

Basics of Static Electricity

Charge

Atoms have protons, electrons and neutrons. Proton has a positive charge, electron a negative charge and neutron no charge. If an atom has the same number of electrons and protons, the atom has no net charge. This is because the positive and negative charges balance each other. If an atom gains an electron, it gains negative charge. If an atom loses an electron, it becomes positively charged (Figure 1). We can summarize by saying that positive and negative charges are due to a lack or overabundance of electrons orbiting the nucleus of an atom.

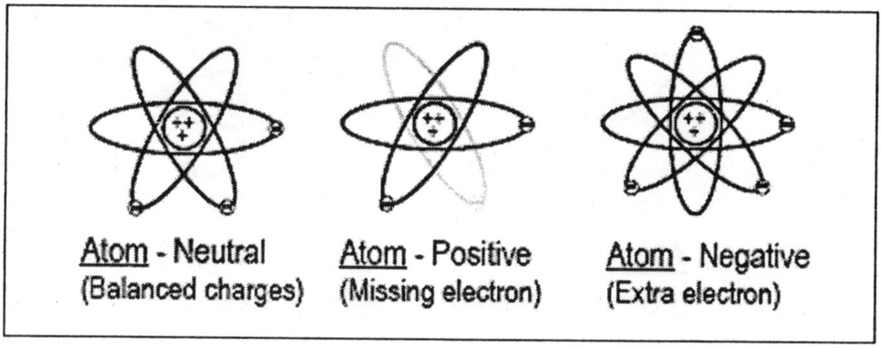

Fig. 1: Charged

Fields

Charges on an object can affect other charges at a distance. We call this force a field. Let us visualize a field as a group of lines reaching out in all directions looking for a charge that is opposite to grasp. We know that like charges repel each other and opposite charges attract each other (Figure 2). This is the result of the electric field acting on an object. All charged objects have a field around them.

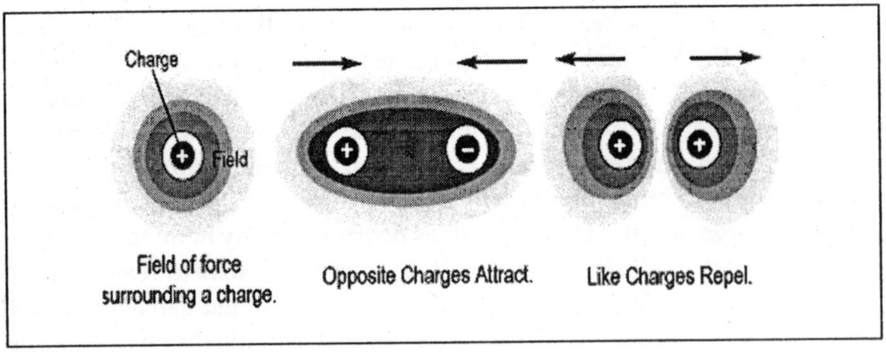

Fig. 2 : Fields

Example: Combing hair with a plastic comb. Both the hair and the comb become charged. It is possible to move the hair by bringing the comb close to the hair.

Triboelectrification

Most static electricity is generated by Tribocharging. It occurs when two materials contact each other and are then separated. Charges (electrons) are exchanged by the materials, leaving one material with a positive charge and the other with a negative charge (Figure 3). Since an object has many billions of electrons, charge on an object grow to significant amount. This is the most common way static charge is accumulated.

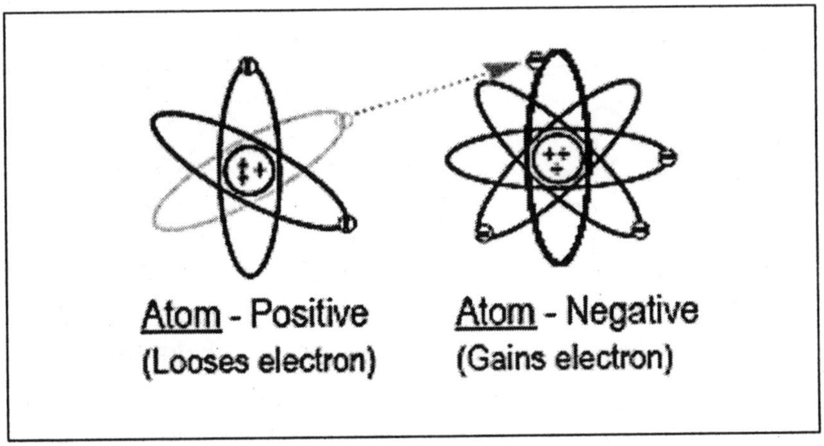

Fig. 3: Tribocharging - Charge Transfer

Example: Walking is one of the biggest source of tribocharging. Shoe soles contact and then separate from the floor or carpet effectively leaving both person and floor charged. Conveyer belts and other moving machinery are also sources of tribocharging.

Induction

Induction is the process by which a charge's field establishes a charge in a nearby conductive object without physical contact. When a conductor cuts across a field at a right angle, a current is generated in the conductor (Figure 4). Induction is the process by which generator turn mechanical motion into electricity.

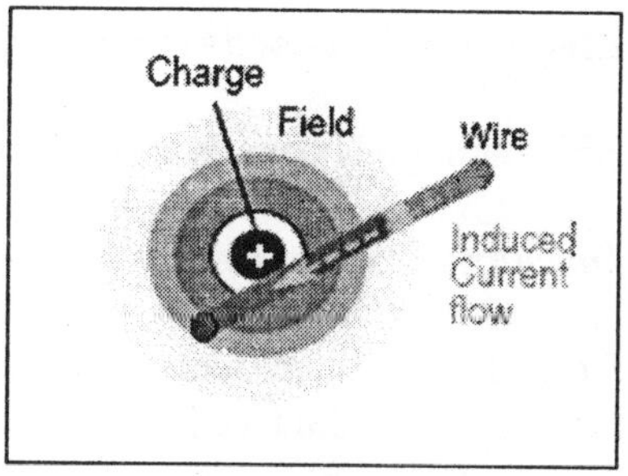

Fig. 4 : Induction

Conduction

Conduction is the transfer of charge through direct contact. Conduction occurs when a charged object directly contacts an object with a different charge.

Polarization

Polarization occurs when the charges on an object are redistributed from a mixed state to a segregated state, where all positive charges are in one area and all negative charges are in a different area. The object must be a conductor and must be ungrounded.

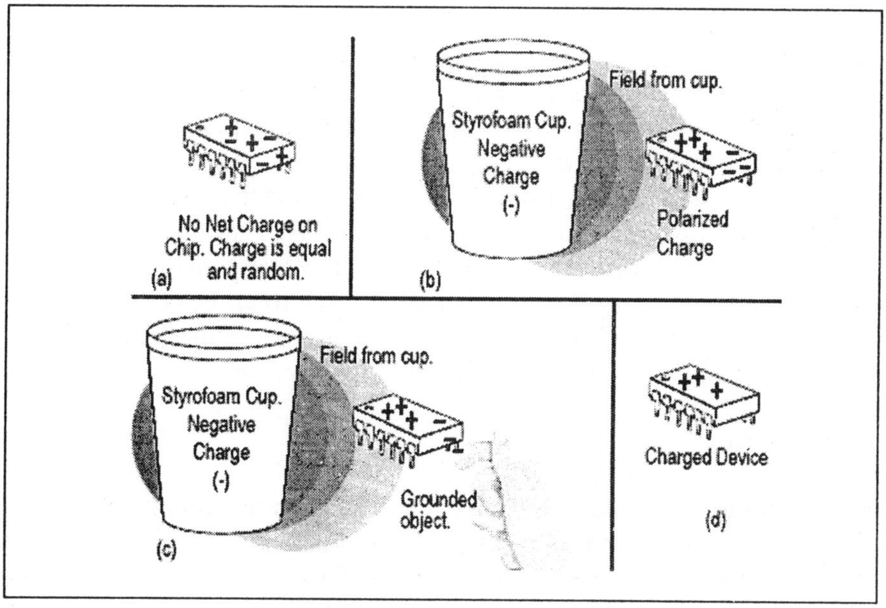

Fig. 5 : Polarization

Example: This process has several steps (Figure 5). First, an ungrounded, conductive material (a), (an IC for example) is moved into the field of a charged object (Styrofoam cup) (b). This polarizes the charges on the IC. While still in the field, the IC contacts ground (a person with a wriststrap) or an object with different potential (c). The polarized charge transfers to ground. The IC is left with an imbalance of charge (d).

Electrostatic Discharge Events

ESD damage is usually caused by one of the following events:

Discharge to the Device

An ESD event can occur when any charged conductive mass discharges electrical energy to another conductive mass with the discharge occurring in the pico or nano second range. The most common cause of electro static damage in semi-conductors is the direct transfer of electrostatic charge from a human body or other charged conductive mass to an electrostatic discharge sensitive (ESDS) device.

Discharge from the Device

The transfer of charge from an ESDS device is also an ESD event. The trend towards automated assembly would seem to solve the problems of HBM ESD events. However, it has been shown that components may be more sensitive to damage when assembled by automated equipment.

Field Induced Discharges

A very rare event that can directly or indirectly damage devices is termed Field Induction. As noted earlier, whenever any object becomes electrostatically charged, there is an electrostatic field associated with that charge. If an ESDS device is placed in that electrostatic field, a charge may be induced on the device. If the device is then momentarily grounded while within the electrostatic field, a transfer of charge from the device occurs.

One of the key elements in a successful static control programme is the identification of those items (components, assemblies and finished products) that are sensitive to ESD and the level of their sensitivity. The severity of damage to an ESDS device by an ESD event is determined by the device's ability to dissipate the energy of the discharge or withstand the current levels involved. This is known as device "ESD sensitivity" or "ESD susceptibility".

Human Body Model

One of the most common causes of electrostatic damage is the direct transfer of electrostatic charge through a significant series resistor from the human body or from a charged material to the electrostatic discharge sensitive (ESDS) device. When one walks across a floor, an electrostatic charge accumulates on the body. Simple contact of a finger to the leads of an ESDS device or assembly allows the body to discharge, possibly causing damage to the device. The model used to simulate this event is the Human Body Model (HBM).

Machine Model

A discharge similar to the HBM event also can occur from a charged conductive object, such as a metallic tool or fixture. Originating in Japan as the result of trying to create a worst-case HBM event, the model is known as the Machine Model. This ESD model consists of a 200 pF capacitor discharged directly into a component with no series resistor.

Charged Device Model Testing

The transfer of charge from an ESDS device is also an ESD event. A device may become charged, for example, from sliding down the feeder in an automated assembler. If it then contacts the insertion head or another conductive surface, a rapid discharge may occur from the device to the metal object. This event is known as the Charged Device Model (CDM) event.

Ignition of EED

Electro explosive devices are electrically initiated detonators to fire an explosive charge or to operate a mechanical device used in the rocket development process. Human beings are charged by movement or by handling objects which can build up a static charge and transferred to the person, and then discharges to the device by touching it. The average capacitance of the human being is 200pF and he can generate more than 7.5kV while walking on the vinyl floor at 55 per cent RH.The Energy of the charged capacitor is given by $W=1/2CV^2=0.005J$ ($W=1/2 \times 200 \times 10^{-12} \times 7500 \times 7500=0.005$ joules). The minimum ignition energy required to initiate the EED is 0.001 J or below. The minimum ignition energy required initiating the substance (mixed with air) which is used in rocket development industries are given below:

Table 1 : Minimum Ignition Energy (MIE)

Substance	*MIE (mJ)*
Acetylene	0.017
Acetone	1.15
Hydrogen	0.11
Hydrogen Sulphide	0.068
Toluene	0.24

The generated energy is more than enough to ignite the substance, which is used in the industry. Hence, it is required to take ESD control measures to prevent the ESD in Electro-static Discharge Sensitive areas.

ESD Control

Basic Principles of Static Control

The six basic principles in the development and implementation of effective ESD control programmes are given below:

Design in immunity by designing products and assemblies to be as immune as reasonable from the effects of ESD.

Define the level of control needed in the environment.

Identify and define the electrostatic protected areas (EPA), the areas in which sensitive parts are handled.

Eliminate and reduce generation by reducing and eliminating static charge generating processes, keeping processes and materials at the same electrostatic potential, and by providing appropriate ground paths to reduce charge generation and accumulation.

Dissipate and neutralize by grounding, ionization, and the use of conductive and dissipative static control materials.

Protect products from ESD with proper grounding or shunting and the use of static control packaging and materials handling products.

At the facility level static control efforts concentrate on the last five principles. In this column we will concentrate on the primary materials and procedures that eliminate and reduce generation, dissipate and neutralize charges, or protect sensitive products from ESD.

Electrostatic discharge is controlled by following methods:

1. Humidity Control

The control of electrostatic discharge can easily be implemented by employing basic control practices and principles in conjunction with the proper control products. The most significant environmental factor in ESD Control is the relative humidity (RH).

Activity@70°F	*Static Voltages*	
	20% RH	80% RH
Walking across vinyl floor	12kV	250V
Walking across synthetic carpet	35kV	1.5kV
Arising from foam cushion	18kV	1.5kV
Picking up polythene bag	20kV	600V

Humid air helps to dissipate electrostatic charges by keeping surfaces moist, therefore, increasing surface conductivity. Substantial electrostatic voltage level can accumulate with a decrease in relative humidity. However, it is also evident from the Table that significant electrostatic voltages can still be generated with relative humidity as high as 90 per cent. Relative humidity between 40 per cent and 60 per cent in ESD protective areas is desirable as long as it does not result in corrosion. Where high relative humidity levels cannot be maintained, ionized air can be used to dissipate electrostatic charges.

2. Grounding

Effective ESD grounds are of critical importance in any operation, and ESD grounding should be clearly defined and regularly evaluated. A primary means of protecting of ESD susceptible (ESDS) items is to provide a ground path to bring ESD protective materials and personnel to the same electrical potential. All conductors in the environment, including personnel, must be bonded or electrically connected and attached to a known ground or contrived ground, creating an equi-potential balance between all items and personnel. Electrostatic protection can be maintained at a potential above a "zero" voltage ground reference as long as all items in the system are at the same potential. It is important to note that non-conductors in an Electrostatic Protected Area (EPA) cannot lose their electrostatic charge by attachment to ground

ESD Association Standard ANSI EOS/ESD 6.1-Grounding recommends a two-step procedure for grounding ESD protective equipment.

The first step is to ground all components of the work area (worksurfaces, people, equipment, etc.) to the same electrical ground point called the "common point ground." This common point ground is defined as a "system or method for connecting two or more grounding conductors to the same electrical potential."

This ESD common point ground should be properly identified. ESD Association Standard EOS/ESD S8.1-1993 recommends the use of the symbol to identify the common point ground.

Fig. 6 : ESD Common Point Ground Symbol

The second step is to connect the common point ground to the equipment ground. This is the preferred ground connection because all electrical equipment at the workstation is already connected to this ground. Connecting the ESD control materials or equipment to the equipment ground brings all components of the workstation to the same electrical potential. If a soldering iron used to repair an ESDS item were connected to the electrical ground and the surface containing the ESDS item were connected to an auxiliary ground, a difference in electrical potential could exist between the iron and the ESDS item. This difference in potential could cause damage to the item. Any auxiliary grounds (water pipe, building frame, ground stake) present and used at the workstation must be bonded to the equipment ground to minimize differences in potential between the two grounds.

Controlling Static on Personnel and Moving Equipment

In many facilities, people are one of the prime generators of static electricity. The simple act of walking around or repairing a board can generate several thousand volts on the human body. If not properly controlled, this static charge can easily discharge into a static sensitive device, a human body model (HBM) discharge. Even in highly automated assembly and test processes, people still handle static sensitive devices in the warehouse, in repair, in the lab, in transport. For this reason, static control programmes place considerable emphasis on controlling personnel generated electrostatic discharge. Similarly, the movement of carts and other wheeled equipment through the facility also can generate static charges that can transfer to the products being transported on this equipment.

Wrist Straps

Typically, wrist straps are the primary means of controlling static charge on personnel. When properly worn and connected to ground, a wrist strap keeps the person wearing it near ground potential. Because the person and other grounded objects in the work area are at or near the same potential, there can be no hazardous discharge between them. In addition, static charges are safely dissipated from the person to ground and do not accumulate. Wrist straps have two major components, the cuff that goes around the person's wrist and the ground cord that connects the cuff to the common point ground. Most wrist straps have a current limiting resistor molded into the ground cord head on the end that connects to the cuff. The resistor most commonly used is a one megohm, 1/4 watt with a working voltage rating of 250 volts. Wrist straps should be tested on a regular basis. Daily testing or continuous monitoring is recommended.

Floors, Floor Mats, Floor Finishes

A second method of controlling electrostatic charge on personnel is with the use of ESD protective floors in conjunction with ESD control footwear or foot straps. This combination of floor materials and footwear provides a ground path for the dissipation of electrostatic charge, thus reducing the charge accumulation on personnel and other objects to safe levels. In addition to dissipating charge, some floor materials (and floor finishes) also reduce turboelectric charging. The use of floor materials is especially appropriate in those areas where increased personnel mobility is necessary. In addition, floor materials can minimize charge accumulation on chairs, carts, lift trucks and other objects that move across the floor. However, those items require dissipative or conductive casters or wheels to make electrical contact with the floor.

Shoes, Grounders, Casters

Used in combination with ESD protective floor materials, static control shoes, grounders, casters and wheels provide the necessary electrical contact between the person or object and the floor material. Insulative footwear, casters, or wheels prevent static charges from flowing from the body to the floor to ground.

Clothing

Clothing is a consideration in some ESD protective areas, especially in clean rooms and very dry environments. Clothing materials can generate electrostatic charges that may discharge into sensitive components or they may create electrostatic fields that may induce charges on the human body. Because clothing usually is electrically insulated or isolated from the body, charges on clothing fabrics are not necessarily dissipated to the skin and then to ground. Grounded static control garments are intended to minimize the effects of electrostatic fields or charges that may be present on a person's clothing.

Workstations and Worksurfaces

An ESD protective workstation refers to the work area that is constructed and equipped with materials and equipment to limit damage to ESD sensitive items. It may be a stand-alone station in a stockroom, warehouse, or assembly area, or in a field location such as a computer bay in commercial aircraft. A workstation also may be located in a controlled area such as a clean room. The key ESD control elements comprising most workstations are a static dissipative worksurface, a means of grounding personnel (usually a wrist strap), a common grounding connection, and appropriate signage and labelling. A typical workstation is shown in Figure 7. The workstation provides a means for connecting all worksurfaces, fixtures, handling equipment and grounding devices to a common point ground. In addition, there may be provision for connecting additional personal grounding devices, equipment, and accessories such as constant ground monitors and ionizers.

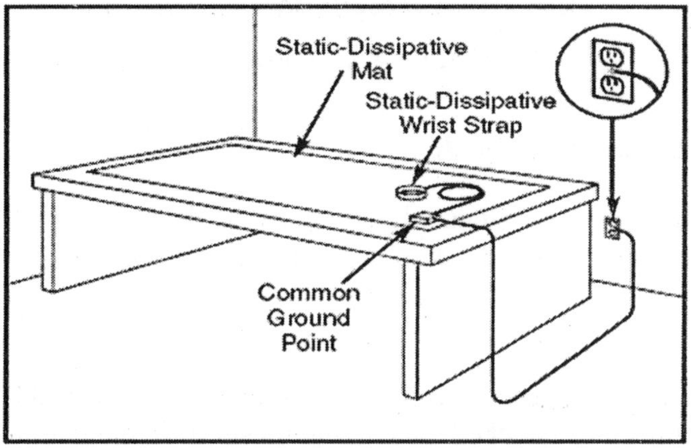

Fig. 7: ESD Workstation.

Static protective worksurfaces with a resistance to ground of 10^6 to 10^9 ohms provide a surface that is at the same electrical potential as other ESD protective items in the workstation. They also provide an electrical path to ground for the controlled dissipation of any static potential on materials that contact the surface. The worksurface also helps define a specific work area in which ESD sensitive devices may be safely handled. The worksurface is connected to the common point ground.

3. Neutralization of Charge

The terminology used to describe the effect ionization will have non-conductors. An example of a non-conductor would be a foam coffee cup. It can accumulate several thousand volts, and because the non-conductor cannot be grounded, it must be neutralized through the introduction of ionized air.

Fig. 8 : Air Ionizer

4. Shielding for Electrostatic Fields

The correct packaging used to safeguard static sensitive devices during transportation and storage must possess at least one layer of near metallic conductivity.

Conclusion

Electro explosive devices are electrically initiated detonators used to ignite an explosive charge or to operate a mechanical device in the rocket development inductries, which is sensitive to electrostatic discharge areas. While handling ESD sensitive devices, personnel grounding systems must be designed to limit body voltages to less than 100 volts. The ESD protective equipment should be checked as per JEDEC Standard No. 625A. The ESD hazard can be controlled by above-mentioned safety measures. However, safe products alone do not assure a risk-free work in hazardous areas. It is also necessary that these products are only handled by workers who are specially trained for this purpose.

REFERENCES

Electrostatic Discharge Control Handbook for Protection of Electrical and Electronic Parts, Assemblies and Equipment (excluding electrically initiated explosive devices), MIL-HDBK-263B, Appendix I, Section 40.1.17, 1994.

ESD Control Measures - ESD Control Handbook.

JESD 625 A- Requirement for handling Electro Static Discharge Sensitive Devices, Electronic Industries Association, December 1999.

Babrauskak, V., *Ignition Handbook*, Fire Science Publishers, Issaquah, WA, 2003.

FIRE SAFETY NORMS AND STANDARDS FOR A DEFENCE R & D ESTABLISHMENT ENGAGED IN EXPLOSIVE RELATED ACTIVITIES

K. Ashoka Vijayan*, Aftab Ahmad** and G.C. Mohanta**

ABSTRACT

The fire disasters involving explosives often give little chance for escape and cause damage that is extensive and irrepairable. The risk involved in this type of fire is always very high which can be minimized by reducing the Severity of Hazard or Probability of Occurrence or both. The severity, in many cases, cannot be reduced much due to the inherent property of the explosives involved but the probability of occurrence can be reduced by following the applicable fire safety norms and standards. This paper gives an overview of the fire safety norms and standards for a facility engaged in development, processing, inspection, storage, testing, handling and transportation of explosives or assemblies containing explosives in a Defence R&D establishment. In this paper we tried to compile the salient features of various norms and standards, as per STEC (Storage and Transportation of Explosives Committee) regulations and Indian Standards (IS), applicable for a Defence R&D establishment.

The STEC regulations stipulate the norms for the entire spectrum of storage, quantity distance, regulation on fighting fires and provision of fire protection facilities, transportation of military explosives by Rail, Road and Air, regulation for provision of electrical installations for areas containing military explosives, etc. The Indian Standard is applicable for the selection, installation and maintenance of automatic fire detection and alarm system, first-aid fire extinguishers, heat and smoke detectors, fire grading and classification, details of construction, exposure hazard, provision and maintenance of water supplies and fire fighting, etc.

Key Words: Fire Safety, Fire norms & standards.

*Scientist 'B' Directorate of Safety and Environmental Engineering, Defence Research and Development Laboratory Hyderabad 058

**Scientist 'F', Directorate of Safety and Environmental Engineering, Defence Research and Development Laboratory, Hyderabad 058

Introduction

The frequency of fire accidents, loss patterns and extinction techniques vary vastly. Fires have a momentum of their own, but controlling their frequency and occurrence is yet to get a good deal of developmental attention in a Defence R & D establishment. The protection of people and property from fire is the responsibility of an organisation. The fire prevention and protection guidelines/standards for an establishment under Ministry of Defence vary from other organisations and civil laws. There are certain guidelines framed by STEC for follow up in Defence explosive establishments and certain National standards applicable to all. These guidelines/standards can be broadly classified into two groups.

(i) STEC guidelines regulating Storage, Processing, Transportation, Handling, Electrical Installation, fire fighting, etc.
(ii) Indian Standards regulating the Fire detection systems, Fire extinguishers, Fire grading, Construction details, etc.

The first group comprises of a set of guidelines provided by STEC. These guidelines regulate the Storage quantity distance for military explosives, regulation regarding the handling of explosives, transportation of military explosives by Road, Rail & Service aircraft, Fire fighting in explosive establishments and Provision of fire protection facilities to government explosive buildings.

The second group comprises of a set of standards provided by Bureau of Indian Standards. These standards regulate the Selection, Installation and Maintenance of automatic fire detection & alarm system, first-aid fire extinguishers, heat and smoke detectors, fire grading & classification, details of construction, exposure hazard, provision and maintenance of water supplies and fire fighting.

STEC Regulation

These regulations are applicable for explosive facilities under Ordnance Factory Board, DGQA, DRDO establishments and the three services.

Storage

The STEC pamphlet No. 1 gives the Storage quantity distance regulations for military explosives and ammunitions. This regulation is based on the international UN system of classification of explosives. According to this system, explosives are divided into thirteen compatibility groups and six hazard divisions depending on their characteristics and expected behaviour when suitably initiated.[1]

An overview of the STEC regulation No. 1 is given below:

(a) UN international system of classification,
(b) Storage compatibility,
(c) Test procedures for classification of Military Explosives,

(d) Effects of explosion at various levels of protection,
(e) Principle of Quantity distance,
(f) Determination of quantity distance,
(g) Storage quantity distances for various hazard divisions.

Handling

The STEC pamphlet No. 4 gives the management and administrative guidance for the promotion of safe and efficient working operations in explosive areas. These guidelines describe a list of useful considerations with particular emphasis on "Dos' and Don'ts" to reduce/minimize the chances of mishaps/accidents.[2]

An overview of the STEC regulation No. 4 is given below:

(a) General Safety requirements (w.r.to siting of explosive buildings, responsibility of stakeholders, personnel safety, utilities, limit boards etc.),
(b) Arrangement of ammunition and explosives in a building or stack (storage, stacking, ventilation, temperature, authorization etc.),
(c) Handling of ammunition and explosives,
(d) Maintenance of ammunition and explosives,
(e) Disposal of ammunition and explosives.

Transportation

The STEC pamphlet No. 9, 10 & 11 gives the regulation for the conveyance of military explosives by Rail, Road and Service aircraft respectively. These regulations have been framed keeping in view the international practices and requirements of the user organisation discussed and approved by the transport panel of STEC from time to time.[3,4,5]

An overview of the STEC regulation No. 9, 10 & 11 are given below:

(a) General requirements of all vehicles carrying explosives,
(b) Special requirements,
(c) Types of vehicles to be used,
(d) Mixing of groups, quantity restrictions and types of vehicles,
(e) Security and administrative arrangements,
(f) Safety precautions,
(g) Conveyance of explosives for disposal,
(h) Packing,
(i) Relaxations,
(j) Fire symbols for transport,
(k) Instructions to drivers,
(l) Instruction regarding loading/unloading and conveyance of explosives,
(m) Instructions on fire actions.

Electrical Installation

The STEC pamphlet No. 7 prescribes the requirements for electrical installations like power supply/distribution, lighting, heating, lightning and electrostatic protection, electrical and electronic apparatus and air-conditioning in building or areas containing or likely to contain military explosives/ammunitions.

These regulations do not apply to administrative building, residential or other personal accommodation and workshop not containing explosives within an enclosed explosive area.[6]

An overview of the STEC regulation no. 07 is given below:

(a) Categories of explosive buildings,
(b) The supply of electricity, its control and using systems,
(c) Electrical equipments,
(d) Lightning protection, earthing and static electricity,
(e) Periodic inspection and testing of categories of installation,
(f) STEC specification for totally enclosed lighting fittings,
(g) List of explosives and explosive stores requiring anti-static precautions.

Fire Fighting

The STEC pamphlet No. 6 prescribes guidelines for fighting fires in government explosive establishments based on the international practices and recent developments in the field of fire fighting. It shall be noted that a fire can be fought as long as the fire does not involve explosives.[7]

An overview of the STEC regulation No. 6 is given below:

(a) Responsibilities, planning and fire fighting measures,
(b) Fire division symbols,
(c) Fire classification of explosives,
(d) Fighting fires in above ground sites,
(e) Fighting fires in multi-storeyed building,
(f) Fighting fires in underground sites,
(g) Fire fighting measures involving explosives with radiological hazard.

Fire Protection Facilities

The STEC pamphlet No. 15 prescribes guidelines for provision of fire protection measures viz., first-aid fire appliances, sources of water supply and their layout, protection to electrical installations and air-conditioned buildings utilized for processing, handling and storage of explosives. These fire protection measures are essential to minimize the chances of fire and its hazard to personnel, plant and property in an explosive facility.[8]

An overview of STEC pamphlet No. 15 is given below:

(a) Fixed installation system,
(b) First-aid fire appliances including fire point, maintenance, testing & training,
(c) Sources of water supply,
(d) Protection to electrical installation,
(e) Manual call points and warning system.

Indian Standards (IS)

The Indian Standard codes were formulated by Bureau of Indian Standards to promote harmonious development of the activities of standardization, marking and quality certification of goods and attending to connected matters in the country. These standards are applicable for civil and other establishments throughout India.

Water Supplies for Fire Fighting

The Indian Standard IS 9668 (Provision and maintenance of water supplies for fire fighting-code of practice) deals with the requirement of water for the purpose of fire fighting and its maintenance for its supply to hydrants and sprinkler system so as to cover various fire risk areas. The requirements in this code have been kept to minimum possible level in view of the shortage of water in some areas.[9]

This standard covers the following aspects:

(a) Source of water supply,
(b) Water supply requirements (for industries, process units etc.),
(c) Static water tanks,
(d) Inspection, checks and maintenance.

Fire Grading and Classification

The Indian Standard IS 1641 covers general principles of fire grading and classification in respect to fire safety aspects. This standard speaks about the following aspects[10]:

(a) Fire load,
(b) Classification of buildings based on occupancy,
(c) Fire zone (Demarcation, number & designation, etc.).

Automatic Fire Detection and Alarm System

The Indian Standard IS 2189 prescribes the Code of practice for Selection, Installation and Maintenance of Automatic fire detection and Alarm system so as to detect fire at the earliest practicable moment and to give an alarm so that appropriate action can be taken. This standard deals about the following aspects[11]:

(a) General requirements,
(b) Selection of Automatic fire detector,
(c) Siting of fire detectors (including spacing requirements),
(d) Panels and Control and Indicating equipment,
(e) Power supply,
(f) Cables and their installation and circuits,
(g) Control centre,
(h) Inspection, testing and maintenance.

Fire and Smoke Detectors

The Indian Standards IS 2175 and IS 11360 prescribe the specification for heat and smoke sensitive detectors for use in automatic fire alarm system respectively. These standards deal about the following aspects.[12,13]

(a) Types and grades,
(b) General requirements,
(c) Performance test and criteria for conformity (viz., Test for time of response, Directional dependence, vibration test, corrosion test, shock test, supply voltage variation test),
(d) Marking,
(e) Data and instrumentation.

Construction

The Indian Standard IS 1642 prescribes the Code of practice for Fire safety of buildings w.r.to details of construction. The provisions given in this standard are those which are necessary at the time of construction of building new or addition or alteration for adopting fire safety measures. These provisions are applicable for all types of buildings including high rise buildings. This standard deals about the following aspects.[14]

(a) Types of construction,
(b) Fire resistance of various types of walls, columns & beams, flooring & roofs, etc.,
(c) Air-conditioning,
(d) Smoke and fire venting,
(e) Service ducts,
(f) Basements,
(g) Chimneys,
(h) Staircase and lifts,
(i) Refuse area,
(j) Drainage,
(k) Electrical services,
(l) Finishes.

Exposure Hazard

The Indian Standard IS 1643 prescribes the Code of practice for fire safety of buildings w.r.to exposure hazard. This standard expresses the exposure hazard which poses a danger or risk of spread of fire through the open air in a building on fire to another building situated in the vicinity. The precaution taken by keeping proper spacing of the building to prevent spread of fire by direct contact of flames and hot gases emitted from the burning building or by radiated heat and flying brands.[15]

This standard deals about the following aspects:

(a) Maximum height,
(b) Floor area ratio,
(c) Open spaces,
(d) High rise buildings.

Conclusion

Though this compilation does not bring out the exhaustive list of fire safety norms and standards that are required to be followed in a Defence R&D establishment dealing with explosives, following the norms/standards given will definitely bring down the risk both in terms of Severity and Probability to a greater extent.

NOTES

1. STEC - 1, 'Quantity distance regulations for Military Explosives/Ammunition'.
2. STEC - 4, 'A Manual on safe working practices in Explosives area'.
3. STEC - 9, 'Rules for Conveyance of Military explosives by Rail'.
4. STEC - 10, 'Rules for Conveyance of Military Explosives and Ammunition by Road'.
5. STEC - 11, 'Regulations for Conveyance of Military Explosives by Service Aircraft'.
6. STEC - 7, 'Safety for Electrical Installations and Apparatus for buildings and areas containing Military Explosives'.
7. STEC - 6, 'Regulation on fighting fires in government explosive establishments'.
8. STEC - 15, 'Guidelines on provision of fire protection facilities to explosive buildings'.
9. IS 9668:1990, 'Provision and Maintenance of Water supplies for Fire Fighting - Code of practice'.
10. IS 1641:1988, 'Code of Practice for Fire Safety of Building (General): General principles of fire grading and classification'.
11. IS 2189:1999, 'Selection, Installation and Maintenance of Automatic fire detection and alarm system - Code of practice'.
12. IS 2175:1988, 'Specification for Heat sensitive fire detectors for use in automatic fire alarm system'.
13. IS 11360:1985, 'Specification for Smoke Detectors for use in automatic electrical fire alarm system'.
14. IS 1642:1989, 'Fire safety of buildings (General): Details of Construction - Code of practice.
15. IS 1643:1988, 'Code of practice for Fire Safety of Buildings (General): Exposure Hazard.

Section–VI

Industrial Safety

25

CASE STUDIES—SOME ACCIDENTS

G.C. Mohanta* and Aftab Ahmad**

ABSTRACT

The paper discusses some of the accidents which happen frequently in our daily life. The accidents may be due to slippery bath room, loose nut in the easy chair, keeping the gas burner open without lighting it, short circuiting of geyser, loose nut in the ceiling fan, over speeding of vehicle, not wearing helmet, poor house keeping, operating machine without machine guard, not being vigilant while operating machine, not wearing safety goggle, not wearing shoes at shop floor, moving heavy metal overhead with crane at working area, driving vehicle with absent mind, etc. All these accidents can be avoided, if we take required safety precautions.

Introduction

Safety is one of the very important aspects in our daily life. We meet with accidents as we do not follow the required safety precautions, safe work practices and safety guidelines. Some of us are reluctant to use protective equipment. It is a well known fact that many two-wheeler riders meet with head injuries during accidents as they do not wear helmets. Four-wheeler drivers meet with sever injuries as they are reluctant to wear seat belts. Almost all the accidents are preventable with little precautions on our part. Some of us feel that the accident will not happen to him, it will happen to others only, whether he takes safety precautions or not. There is a need to change this attitude if we are interested to avoid the accidents.

Some Accidents and Suggested Safety Measures

We discuss below some of the accidents, which happened due to unsafe practices and also discuss how these accidents could have been avoided.

*Director, Safety and Environmental Engineering.

**Head Safety Engineering Division, Defence Research & Development Laboratory, PO: Kanchanbagh, Hyderabad-500 058 *email* : mohantag@yahoo.com

1. Mr. Ramesh got up in the morning and went to toilet to attend nature's call. The bath room-cum-toilet was very slippery due to some green fungus grown on the floor. Mr. Ramesh fell down while walking on the bathroom floor. His left leg was broken.

Mr. Ramesh should have cleaned the bath room floor regularly so that the green fungus would not have grown on the floor.

2. Mr. Girish was sitting on an easy chair at the drawing room and was reading the Newspaper. While reading the Newspaper he was also swinging on the chair. Suddenly one nut came out and the chair collapsed and Mr. Girish's both hands got crushed.

Mr. Girish should have checked the condition of the easy chair before sitting on it and periodically he should have done the tightening of the nut, then the accident could have been avoided.

3. Mr. Rabin's wife was in the kitchen to prepare tea for Mr. Rabin. She opened the gas stove and was looking for the gas lighter for igniting the gas. Suddenly she heard the cries of their 1½ year old daughter, Pinky who had just then woken up. As Mr. and Mrs. Rabin both were not near to Pinky, she was very much panicky and started crying with full intensity. Mrs. Rabin immediately rushed to Pinky and was asking her what she wanted. Pinky stretched her hands and jumped on the lap of her mother and she wanted to go to the toilet. Mrs. Rabin took her to the toilet and helped her for attending nature's call and came back to the kitchen along with her on the lap, holding her by the left hand. Mrs. Rabin located the gas lighter and took it near to the gas stove and pressed for lighting the gas with right hand. All of a sudden the full room engulfed with fire and Mrs. Rabin and their daughter had third grade burn injuries.

Mrs. Rabin should have switched off the gas stove before going to Pinky, then the accident could have been avoided.

4. After finishing his Newspaper, Mr. Vijay went to bathroom for switching on the geyser. He returned and was sipping the morning tea prepared by his wife. He finished the morning tea and went to the bath room again for taking bath. He opened the tap for hot water, suddenly he got a severe electrical shock, and collapsed on the floor of the bath-room. There was short circuit in the Geyser and the earthing was not proper.

Mr. Vijay should have got the earthing done properly, then the accident could have been avoided.

5. Mr. Bimal got dressed up and went to the dining hall for breakfast, the ceiling fan was making severe noise and was vibrating vigorously. Mrs. Bimal brought the breakfast for him. He was about to start his breakfast, suddenly the ceiling fan fell down on his head. He became unconscious and got head injuries.

Mr. Bimal should have done the maintenance of the ceiling fan to overcome the noise and vibration of the ceiling fan, this could have avoided the accident

6. Mr. George finished his breakfast and got ready for proceeding to his work place. He went to the garage and took out his scooter. He saw his watch and found the time to be 8.30 AM. Normally he takes forty minutes to reach his work place from his residence. He was required to reach his work place by 09.00 AM, otherwise he had to apply for half day leave. That means Mr. George was ten minutes late before starting from residence. Mr. George started driving the scooter at a very high speed. One scooter was also coming from the other side with high speed. Suddenly Mr. George noticed one dog was running in

front of him. He tried to save the dog and drove his scooter towards the right side. The speeding scooter from the other side collided with him. Both the scooterists got severe head injuries.

Mr. George should not have driven his scooter at a very high speed to reach his work place quickly and he should have used the helmet, this could have avoided the accident and also the head injuries.

7. Mr. Dhananjay went to his work place and entered into his office. Lot of junk materials were dumped on the floor hither and thither in the office. He was precariously passing through those dumped materials to reach his seating place. Suddenly one cobra snake came out from the dump and bit Mr. Dhananjay. Mr. Dhananjay cried aloud for help and suddenly he collapsed due to fear of the snakebite. All the people were watching from outside and no body were prepared to enter inside the room due to the presence of the cobra. Suddenly his friend Mukesh got enough courage to enter insidc. He took Mr. Dhananjay outside and rushed him in an ambulance to Hospital.

Mr. Dhananjay should have kept his office tidy without dumping various junk materials on the floor, this could have avoided the accident.

8. Mr. Moinuddin was operating a Press Brake and his Assistant, Mr. Dilip was placing the materials underneath the Press Brake. Mr. Moinuddin pressed the switch of the Press Brake, Mr. Dilip was still holding the materials underneath the Press Brake. The fingers of Mr. Dilip got crushed.

The accident could have been avoided if there was a machine guard with the Press Brake. Also Mr. Moinuddin should have been vigilant enough before pressing the switch, otherwise he should have alone loaded the materials and operated the machine.

9. Mr. Reddy was operating a Grinding machine. He was grinding a hardened steel material. A metal chip came out from the grinding machine and fell on one of his eye. Mr. Reddy lost his eye due to the injury.

The accident could have been avoided, if Mr. Reddy could have worn a Safety Goggle while doing the grinding operation.

10. Mr. Parmesh was walking on the workshop floor. There were some metallic scraps all around the place. He did not notice the same and placed his feet on the metallic scraps. He got injured and also did not take anti-septic injection. His foot got septic and he lost his leg.

The accident could have been avoided if Mr. Parmesh was wearing the shoes supplied to him by his establishment and also if he could have taken the anti-septic injection.

11. Mr. Paritosh was working on a Milling Machine. Mr. Jagannath was moving a heavy metal from one machine to another machine by an overhead crane. The metal was being taken over the Milling Machine of Mr. Paritosh. Suddenly the metal fall on the head of Mr. Paritosh as the sling got torn. Mr. Paritosh got head injuries.

The accident could have been avoided if Mr. Paritosh could have worn a metallic helmet, also the capacity of the sling should have been properly assessed by Mr. Ravinder, In-charge of the Shop before allowing Mr. Jagannath to shift the metal and Mr. Ravinder should not have allowed Mr. Jagannath to move the heavy metal through the area where Paritosh was working.

12. Mr. Amarjit was working on the integration of electronic components. He was wearing a synthetic dress and was not wearing the cotton dress as was required. While entering into the work area, he did not discharge the statical electricity by touching the

statical electricity discharge system. As he was working on the integration of electronic components, it was found that number of very sensitive electronic items got damaged.

The incident could have been avoided if he could have discharged the statical electricity from his body and could have worn pure cotton dresses.

13. Mr. Dipak was working in the vicinity of the explosives. He was carrying a mobile Phone along with him. As he was working there, a telephone call came in his mobile phone. He was about to answer the call. Suddenly the explosives got ignited due to spark from the mobile phone. Mr. Dipak got 3rd grade burn injuries, the building in which he was working got damaged and some of his colleagues nearby also got injured.

The accident could have been avoided, if Mr. Dipak had not carried the mobile phone along with him while working near the explosives.

14. Mr. Kannan was scolded by his boss in the office on that day, as he was not able to meet the expectation of the boss. Mr. Kannan was returning home from office. While driving the scooter he was absent minded. One small boy, Nitish was crossing the road at the time, Mr. Kannan did not notice him and hit him. Nitish got seriously injured and while taking him to hospital, he died.

The accident could have been avoided, if Mr. Kannan could have driven the scooter consciously and cautiously or he should not have driven the scooter as he was mentally disturbed.

15. It was summer season, the air-conditioner of an explosive storage room was not operational to achieve the desired level of temperature, due to which the temperature shot up to such a level that the explosives stored in the room got ignited and there was explosion. It damaged the 60 cm thick concrete wall to such an extent that the identification of the storage room was difficult due to severity of the explosion and blast pressure. As the accident happened in the night and no personnel was present there at that time. There was no casualty of personnel. Due to this mishap, the unit was closed down.

If proper control of the temperature was there, the accident could have been avoided.

16. One casting of a huge quantity of propellant was made during the summer season. At the time of extraction of the propellant, a hammer blow was given by Mr. Harihar to the base plate of the mould as there was some difficulty to remove the casting from the mould. Due to this blow a spark was generated and the whole grain got ignited and exploded. The level of blast pressure and temperature was such that Mr. Dhiresh, one of the colleagues of Mr. Harihar who was standing at a distance of 10 m from the work spot, got 80 per cent burn injury and died in the hospital. His other colleagues who were engaged in the extraction activity including him, were burnt to ashes.

If proper care was taken during preparation of mould and extraction, the accident could have been avoided.

17. Mr. Omkar was engaged in the manufacture of detonators. He was having a cell phone with him. He got a call in his cell phone from his friend. The moment call came, the detonators which he was handling, got fired and eight of his colleagues including him died on the spot. The severity of the explosion was such that the body parts of one of his colleague Mr.Venkatesh could not be traced.

This accident demonstrated that, if cell phone was not used at the process facility, the accident could have been avoided.

18. It was in the month of April, a carton of double base cast propellant was being transferred from assembly facility to inspection facility by Mr. Naresh with the help of a battery trolley. As the trolley moved from assembly facility towards the inspection facility, the battery got ignited due to spark generated at the leads of the battery. Cartons of the propellant grains were immediately removed by Mr. Naresh and his other colleagues, from the trolley. Luckily nothing had happened to the propellants and personnel.

Spark generating material handling equipment should not be used while handling propellants/explosives.

19. During charging of air bottle, air bottle hose pipe got bursted and the blast pressure was so severe that Mr. Giridhar who was operating the system, died on the spot. On investigation it was found that the pressure gauge was not calibrated regularly and the hose pipe was also not tested for the operating pressure.

If calibrated pressure gauge and calibrated hose pipe were used, the accident could have been avoided.

20. In one of the rocket assembly facility, the earth pit of electrical protection system was not tested properly. The earth pit was having a very high resistance to earth, which was beyond permissible limit. The rocket was earthed to the earth pit and check out was being conducted on the rocket. All on a sudden, the rocket motor got fired due to leakage current. Mr. Lakshman, one of the workmen died on the spot due to severe burn injury.

If a properly calibrated earth pit was used, the accident could have been avoided.

21. In one of the establishment where hydrogen gas is being used to inflate the balloons, there was leakage of hydrogen. This was not detected. Mr. Kadam was lighting a cigarette nearby, this initiated a fire and led to serious burn injuries to his colleagues including Mr. Kadam.

The hydrogen gas should be handled with great care and hydrogen detection systems should be used to avoid the accident.

Conclusion

The above accidents happened due to the following reasons:

(i) Failure to follow safe practices,
(ii) Operating an equipment without knowing the operation and maintenance procedures,
(iii) Failure to follow mandatory Government Acts, Rules & Regulations,
(iv) Failure to use personal protective equipment,
(v) Failure to use machine guard with the machine,
(vi) Poor house-keeping,
(vii) Over confidence, and
(viii) Negligence

If we all follow the safety precautions, almost all the accidents can be avoided and we can make our home, work place and environment safe.

A NOVEL APPROACH FOR ESTIMATING COST OF RESOLVING POTENTIAL FAILURES IN A PROCESS USING PREDICTIVE RISK INDEX AND FMECA INPUTS FOR SAFETY PERFORMANCE ENHANCEMENTS

S.R. Iyer*

ABSTRACT

It is generally believed that failure is a process of slow degradation and if left unattended interrupts the continuity of production leading to loss of asset availability, that could perhaps lead to a threat to life, therefore we must try to eliminate or mitigate the effect of losses due to failures that could be an eventual hazard, where even the safe operating procedures (SOP) are no saviours in detecting disasters, but one can mitigate catastrophic failure by incorporating risk analytical capabilities.

A system of safeguards needs to be built into the system. The goal is to reduce the likelihood of being caught unprepared and to mitigate the impact of unexpected events an effort that is directed towards reducing the failure effects and also eliminating the loss in as much the same way as Six Sigma approach attempts to do so.

Cost of potential failure (COPF) is a vital parameter analogous to cost of poor quality in six sigma, that determines the approach to safeguard. This paper provides a framework for evaluating cost of potential failure, based on Predictive Risk Index and FMECA inputs, which finally dictates the rigor needed for the safeguards.

Introduction

No matter how robust the design is yet there is a chance failure. Risk management addresses these uncertainties. Risk management and compliance may be non-negotiable, but cost often dictates the need. The safeguards needed to mitigate the failure could be rigorous or may be simple depending upon the perceived threat. More rigorous the safeguard, more is the cost and *viseversa*. Cost of Potential Failures (COPF) is a risk dashboard to enable

*S.E.(E), IEOT, ONGC. *email:* iyer_sr@ongc.co.in

better strategic thinking on safety performance enhancements that is optimum that is neither too rigorous nor is too lax.

Two tools viz Predictive Index Rating (PRI) and FMECA provides a framework for COPF calculations upon which hinges the rigor required for safeguard. The synergies between PRI and FMECA must uncover the strategic application of programme to address these issues leveraging better and safe operations.

The Risk Index (RI) Concept

Senior management don't want to waste precious time chasing poltergeist, they need alarms to sound early particularly when the issue is plant safety, so that serious accident and thereby loss to human life, equipments, are avoided, therefore, management must ensure that its potential disaster are under check. This can be achieved by:

(1) Finding tangible, predictive indicators for the effectiveness of safety management, using interview and questionnaire techniques, audits and incident reporting data.
(2) Integrating the management effectiveness indicators in an operational index for site-dependent and safety dependent performance.

Such an index should reflect the current safety performance and help in predicting potential risk in the operation or in the facility can be predicted in advance, so that proactive actions can be taken in advance to avoid or reduce the occurrence of the incident.

An appropriate measure of the safety performance is crucial for effective safety management of hazardous facilities and operations. Numerous method exists for measuring safety performance such as *accident statistics, accident control charts*, and *attitude scale*. These are generally passive or subjective but not quantitative. They also reflect inadequate information. Safety climate in an industry is dynamic, depends upon the perception of the worker and management enforcement of safety regulation, work place ergonomics, hazardous material handling, etc.

Evaluating Risk Index (ERI)

An injury caused by accident, which in turn is caused by unsafe acts or conditions. Insufficient unsafe acts or conditions may give rise a near miss or learning event. It should be possible to formulate a predictive model that can reflect the current status of safety activities in a work place through continuous observations, recording and analysis of unsafe actions of workers or unsafe conditions in work places. The number (frequency) and potential severity (consequence) of unsafe events may be a good indicator for the current status of safety climate in the process plant. By continuously observing the change in safety climate through some quantification of these events it is indeed possible to forecast the occurrence of a real incident.

The unsafe factors contributing to accidents are classified and graded according to the four factors:

- *Probability of danger (PD)* - the likely hood of danger in the observed event to become real.
- *Frequency of work exposure (FE)* - the likelihood of worker exposed to the danger in the observed event.
- *Number of persons at risk (RN)* - the possible number of people affected by the danger in the observed event should the danger become real.
- *Maximum probable loss or severity (MPL)* - the maximum possible losses associated with the danger in the observed event should the danger become real.

Assigning weights in a scale of 1-15, with 1 being lower end of the continuum representing unlikely, infrequent, less number of persons at risk, and if incident does happens results in minor injury while a score of 15 at the other end of continuum represents certainty, that which happens several times a day with 50 plus persons at risk, and results in near fatality.

Scale 1-15	*Probability of danger (PD)*	*Frequency of work exposure (FE)*	*No. of persons at risk (RN)*	*Max Prob loss (MPL)*
1	Unlikely though Conceivable	Infrequent	1-2	Minor injury
2	Possible but unusual	Annually	3-7	Treatment at hospital, influence hearing
5	Even chance - could happen	Monthly	8-15	Head injury, body chemical burn, equipment damage, environment pollution
8	Probable not surprised	Weekly	16-30	Eye injury, electrical shock or causing plant shutdown
10	Likely only to be expected	Daily	31-50	Disablement
15	Certain - no doubt	Several times/day	50+	Fatality

The grading are subjective and likely to change according to the particular plant/ facility being applied. The Risk Index (RI) is the geometric average of the four factors as listed above:

$$RI = (PD \times FE \times RN \times MPL)^{1/4}$$

The use of geometric average rather than arithmetic means is due to the fact that all factors are related to each other rather than truly independent.

An Example

A technician works at a platform in monkey board area of rig mast with a broken ring fence to service a light fitting, he has a potential to fall from this 8 m platform. The grading is as under:

Probability of danger (PD) - score = 8; from safety observation it was found the platform has broken ring fence, hence practically no barrier.

Frequency of work exposure (FE) - score = 8; bi-weekly service.

Number of persons at risk (RN) - score = 1; one person works for this job.

Maximum probable loss or severity (MPL) - score = 10; fatality or disability in case of falling down from the platform.

Risk Index (RI) = $(8 \times 8 \times 1 \times 10)^{1/4} = 5.03$, this is more than safe zone RI of 3, so the installation is unsafe and calls for immediate action.

The type of factors and the grading of each factors can be adjusted according to the type of occupancy, operation, focus on risk, etc. More factors can be added and the generalization of the RI is nth root of products of the n-factors.

The observations needs to be performed in a regular interval, to gain immediate insight in the safety performance. A word of caution here - the observation of unsafe acts is not an audit. The person being observed bears no penalty, however he should be informed of the unsafe acts or condition. A record is then made of unsafe act or condition.

Operation faults that leads to only emergency stop of operation is not listed as incidents in the present case. Incidents occurred not in facility are also discarded. Compiling of grading of all the observation calculate the average risk index and compare it with incidents occurred. The annual average RI is a good indicator of safety performance.

Predictive Risk Index (PRI)

If we plot the time series of RI for years. The sequence of RI is scattered which reflects the statistical distribution of the observations. The moving average generally give a goods insight of the time series resulting in a smooth, oscillating curve from which sufficient inference can be deduced. This moving average of 15 consecutive observations of RI is defined as Predictive Risk Index (PRI).

PRI is purely a moving average of past observations, yet it trend successfully predicts the occurrence of incident. Not every peak in PRI trend leads to an accident, but a raising PRI trend does have a greater chance of occurring incident.

PRI > 3	Warning Zone
PRI > 4	Action Zone - immediate action warranted to prevent incident occurrence.
PRI < 3	Safe Zone - plant considered low risk for accident.

- The increased activities in the plant will certainly result in more unsafe acts, which means higher PRI.

- The other factor affecting PRI trend is education and training. Effective training should bring more safety awareness to workers, reduced unsafe acts thus bring down PRI. Thus PRI can be used as a measure of the effectiveness of training or education.

Inference from PRI Trends

Raising PRI	When PRI goes above warning level - It is likely to have an accident	The PRI value after the incident may be raising or falling depends on how the incident has changed the worker's awareness.
Persistent high PRI	PRI reaches a warning level but incident did not occur immediately	Not every unsafe act immediately meets the condition to incident, however persistent unsafe actions or conditions eventually lead incident unless actions are taken.
Oscillating PRI	The PRI is raising and falling	If PRI is oscillating in high level and if the incident did not raise sufficient awareness or if the action taken too late then PRI rebounds and incidents are also likely to occur.

The only mode ensuring safe operation is persistent PRI value below safe zone. To do this will require continuous and persistent action to refresh worker's memory and awareness and to reduce unsafe conditions in the facility.

Limitations of PRI

1. PRI does not focus on risk reducing measures. But it does fulfil the purpose of providing a early warning signal that gives a plant manager a very effective tool of monitoring the current safety performance in the plant.
2. PRI hinges upon a large number of unsafe operation data to maintain the statistical validity of PRI. Roughly about 200 unsafe operations/year will be minimum requirement for a reasonable inference to be drawn. For less number of observations, the definition of PRI may need to be modified accordingly.
3. The safe level of PRI varies across industry. For petro-chemical plant the safe level PRI is very low, since it has several hazards and can tolerate no major incident. For example, a large spill may give rise to a catastrophic disaster. For other facilities with different potential hazards, the safe, warning and action levels can be re-evaluated and adjusted accordingly.

Cost of Failure *vis-à-vis* Safeguards

Failure is a process of slow degradation and is a process threat. Threats originate from two sources mainly improper functional activities and often due to poor technological safeguards that enable malfeasant or maverick employees to operate beyond control.

Procedures alone can't guard against such instances. Rules implementations are not all or - nothing exercises because systems can be structured incrementally. What is important is how quickly you respond to degraded performance, that may eventually lead to failure and complete collapse of the system.

This calls for a system of risk management/governance that is agile and be able to learn and transform knowledge into codified behaviour so that inferences can be drawn and counter measures cost effectively devised for safe operation for the perceived threat of failure. As seen earlier PRI is indicative of how safe the plant is managed. In order to reduce the impact of unexpected events an effort that is directed towards reducing the failure which may eventually lead to accidents is essential. Such an action could be devising an effective training and awareness programme and also, providing safeguards in the form of safety instrumented systems, passive or active protection systems etc., this entails lot of cost. The safeguards needed to mitigate the danger/failure could be rigorous or may be simple depending upon the perceived threat. More rigorous the safeguard, more is the cost and *vise versa.* Therefore the approach should be risk based.

Next if PRI suggest unsafe operation, FMECA is carried out to digress the causes considering a host of factors such as probability of occurrence of each possible failure events, potential impact or severity of each failures, current detection in place and resolution cost of failure. FMECA essentially gives RPN that is used to calculate Weighted Average Cost of Resolution (WACR) this when multiplied by target reduction desired gives COPF and the strategy for necessary safeguards.

Failure Modes and Effects Analysis

FMEA is a way of looking into future and determining where the potential failures might be located. FMEA process is used to determine what failures are occurring, in our facility, and what their impact and frequencies are. The loss due to the failure is computed by multiplying the frequency of occurrence with its impact. Using Pareto's principle delineate vital few from trivial many - 20 per cent or less failures results in 80 per cent of the losses. This helps in evaluating Cost of Potential Failures (COPF).

While COPF does not necessarily contribute to the success of any preventive maintenance programme, it is valuable in prioritizing projects. The challenge for any estimation comes when no measurements are available at the initiation of the project. But there is an approach to calculating the cost of the existing process using a weighted risk of potential failures.

Using FMEA to Calculate COPF

COPF also is defined as the current cost of resolving existing failures in a process. This cost is composed of four factors:

- Probability of occurrence for each possible failure event
- Potential impact or severity of each failure
- Current detection provisions in place
- Resolution cost of a single failure

The COPF translates into an estimation of these four components.

Process Step	Types of Failures (Failure mode)	Failure Impact	SEV 10 is Worst	Potential Causes	OCC 10-highest	Det Pro	DET Ability 1 highest	RPN

Failure Mode and Effects Analysis (FMEA) is a tool used to identify the potential failure modes within a process and to prioritize them based on their severity, occurrence and detection provisions. The Risk Priority Number (RPN) is obtained by estimating the effort required to resolve each incident and the unit dollar cost of such an effort.

Step 1: Import all process inputs from, I/O into FEMA tool. Remove any uncontrolled factors.

Avoid any initial prioritization of inputs such as through a cause-and-effect matrix, to ensure that all possible failure modes are included in the COPF analysis. This is important, as existing costs for uncontrolled factors cannot be calculated with confidence.

Step 2: Add any potential failures that are not included in I/O.

Step 3: Perform the risk prioritization using the FEMA tool.

Record the Risk Priority Number values as a calculation of severity, occurrence and detection scores as follows:

$$\text{Risk Priority Number} = \text{Severity} \times \text{Occurrence} \times \text{Detection}$$

Step 4: Extract all failures and their RPNs from the FEMA tool. Estimate average effort and cost/hour to resolve each failure.

Using team inputs and any available estimation tools, calculate the average cost to resolve (ACR) for each potential cause of failure. The cost will be a multiple of estimated effort hours to resolve (EHR) and the average cost per effort hour (ACH). Note that the estimation in this step tends to have a 90 to 95 per cent confidence level, which is an acceptable level for isolating the COPF.

$$ACRi = EHRi \times ACHi$$

Where: ACRi = Average cost to resolve incident i
EHRi = Effort hours to resolve incident i
ACHi = Average cost per hour for incident i
i = 1 to n (n being the total number of failures)

Step 5: Calculate the average cost to resolve any failure.

Calculate the average effort cost required to resolve a random incident by using the weighted average of time to resolve the failure weighted by the risk priority of each failure.

Weighted Average Cost to Resolve (WACR) = [Sum of (RPNi × ACRi) / Sum of (RPNi)]

Step 6: Estimate COPF.

Calculate the COPF for the project by multiplying the random incident cost and the potential reduction in incidents (per year) as identified in the project charter.

COPF = WACR × Reduction in Events Due to the Project

Case Study : Repeated failure of feeder line (Estimating COPF)

A Six Sigma influenced analyst engineer team was given the task to analyze the repeated failure of a feeder line under bay "A". The team was assigned the task to reduce the number of yearly failures by 200. No data was collected in the past on the primary metric and all the team knew was that there were a large and frequent number of failures on an average once/shift of 12 hours i.e . 730 failures/year.

The team used the risk prioritization approach using FMEA to estimate COPF:

Step 1: The team used an input-output diagram to identify all potential causes of failure. Four causes were identified which were imported into the FMEA tool.

Step 2: The team then met for another brainstorming session to identify any additional causes. This resulted in the addition of another cause, bringing the total to five.

Step 3: Risk Priority Numbers were calculated for all five potential failure causes using the FMEA tool.

Step 4: Next the team reviewed each failure cause and calculated the average cost to resolve it. This was done by estimating the time required to resolve the problem and the average cost per unit of time.

Step 5: Using the above average cost per event, the weighted average cost to resolve a random event was estimated:

Weighted Average Cost to Resolve (WACR) = (RPN × ACR)/ RPN = 56700/117 = $484.60

Step 6: Finally, the project COPF was estimated by multiplying the random incident cost and the potential reduction in incidents (per year).

Target Reduction in Events Due to the Project = 200
COPF = $484.60 × 200 = $96,920

No.	Potential Causes	RPN	Effort Hours to Resolve (Hours)	Average Cost Per Hour ($)	Average Cost to Resolve ($)	RPN × ACR
1	Chain breaks-material defect	21	2	50	100	2,100
2	Chain slippages due to lubrication problems	21	8	25	200	4,200
3	Chain slippages due to mis-alignment problems	27	8	50	400	10,800
4	Log of failures and action taken not often recorded or not available in CMMS	30	30	20	600	18,000
5	Design defect	18	12	100	1200	21,600
		117				$56,700

Bottom Line

The COPF calculation is summarized as:

COPF (annualized) = [Sum of (RPNi × ACRi) / Sum of (RPNi)] × Annual Reduction in Events

This approach lends objectivity to the estimation of COPF when no measurements are available at the project initiation stage. Additionally, as FMEA offers a structured approach, this calculation method becomes easy to use. When capturing the dependence of any event's cost on its severity, occurrence and the ability to detect it, the derived COPF offers a closer estimate to the actual project benefit.

Conclusions

Central to the effectiveness of that chosen strategy is a mindset that treats risk management and compliance expenditures not just as cost, but as an investment with a potential to significantly increase production at minimal loss to the asset be it men or material. Thus while risk management and compliance may be non-negotiable, but cost often dictates the need.

- Cost of Potential Failures (COPF) is a risk dashboard to enable better strategic thinking on safety performance enhancements that is optimum that is neither too rigorous nor is too lax, necessitating senior management to better understand risk and compliance elements to equally challenge the designers of such systems.
- It makes sense to leverage such an approach to identify ways to restructure processes for optimal performance with less effort, risk and cost and thus remain safety complaint.

- Highlight "hot spots" for needing immediate attention also recognizing the need to build an adaptive, cost effective system to quickly respond to continuing regulatory changes.
- Provides a framework for evaluating cost of potential failure, based on Predictive Risk Index and FMECA inputs, which finally dictates the rigor needed for the safeguards.
- Improvements in cost flexibility, efficiency and change management (depending upon the rigor required to handle the perceived threat).
- Provide a modelling framework for safety management systems that makes explicit and transparent the objectives, means, constraints and methods for safety management.
- Developing a general guidelines on safety barriers and lines-of defense to avoid and mitigate major accidents.

REFERENCES

Oien, K., Risk Indicators as a tool for risk controls, Reliability Engg Syst Safety, 74(2).

Yang, Y.T., The study of safety predictor for safety management performance.

ONGC HSE - accident and incident report.

27

SAFETY IN HANDLING OF CRYOGENIC FLUIDS

Kadiyala Venkatachalam*

ABSTRACT

Cryogenics has multiple and diverse applications. Be it a steel industry or a space industry or a chemical industry or a food industry or a medical department cryogenics is having its major role. Different fluids may be handled in industries but handling of cryogenic fluids is a unique activity which needs lot of technological understanding of their properties. This subject is completely alien to the normal experience of most people and consequently introduces hazards of which they will almost certainly not be aware of.

These cryogenic fluids which are below 125 degrees Kelvin are to be handled with proper safety precautions else we may be entangled with the major hazards like frost bite due to cold burns, explosion due to exponential change of volumes at boiling points etc. Therefore, given the knowledge of hazards and precautions, it is not difficult to overcome the ill effects associated with handling of cryogenic fluids. Hence, this paper will highlight various hazards associated with handling of cryogenic fluids and necessary precautions for safe handling of these fluids.

Introduction

The production, distribution and utilisation of low temperature is coined as cryogenics. To that extent, it is a science of ultra low temperature. In an Air separation plant cryogenic liquids like liquid Oxygen, liquid Nitrogen, liquid Argon, etc. are produced from liquid air by fractional distillation. This liquid air will be produced from the dry air through repetitive expansion process. The products are collected at different levels of the distillation chamber according to their boiling points. These products will be transported either in the shape of liquids or in the shape of gases to the required applications viz., food processing and refrigeration, steel making, rocket propulsion fuels, space craft, life support systems, space simulation, nuclear weapon development, electronic industry in the research of superconductivity, chemical plants in the recovery of valuable feed stock from LNG, micro biology in the preservation of organs, cryogenic surgery in medicine, etc.

*AMIE (Mech.), MBA (Mktg.), M Tech (CST), Junior Manager, Visakhapatnam Steel Plant.

Both in the production and utilization of cryogenic products, lot of hazards are associated which can be broadly classified into Personnel hazards (related to physical hazards like cold burns, asphyxia, etc.), Flammability hazards (related to gases like Hydrogen, Methane, etc.), High pressure gas hazards (related to entrapped fluids and stored fluids), Material hazards (non-compatible materials used in cryogenic area especially in Oxygen service). These hazards and precautions to contain these hazards are expanded in this paper.

Hazards Involved with Cryogenic Fluids

The following are the major hazards associated with handling of cryogenic fluids:

1. Hazards on human beings (Physiological hazards).
2. Hazards involved due to the properties of cryogenic fluids.
3. Hazards involved due to materials and construction.
4. Hazards involved due to oxygen.
5. Hazards due to flammability and explosion.
6. Hazards due to entrapment and high pressure gas hazards.
7. Hazards involved in storage of cryogenic fluids.
8. Hazards involved in transportation of cryogenic fluids.
9. Hazards due to unexpected activities.
10. Hazards involved due to Environmental issues.

1. Hazards on Human Beings (Physiological Hazards)

If the human body is in contact with the cryogenic fluids (or) surface cooled with cryogenic fluids, severe cold burns may be inflicted which may result in frost byte and amputation of effected areas.

2. Hazards Involved due to the Properties of Cryogenic luids

One should have understanding regarding some of the properties of cryogenic fluids in comparison to those of other fluids in improving the safety.

(a) *Density of gas.*
 (i) Hydrogen is more explosive because of its lighter density and mixibility with air to form different explosive mixtures.
 (ii) Argons more density may cause blanketing if it accumulates in low lying areas and trenches.

(b) *Boiling point*
 It is due to the low boiling points of Nitrogen than Oxygen, a mixture primarily of Oxygen and Nitrogen will clearly condense if exposed to liquid Nitrogen temperatures. The use of inert liquid Nitrogen can thus lead to creation of non-inert atmosphere which supports combustion.

(c) *Volumetric ratio of gas to liquid*
The Volumetric Ratio of gas at room temperature to liquid at the boiling point lies between 450 and 850 for most of cryogenic fluids with an exception to Neon with a value of 1415. This ratio indicates the pressure in bars that would be generated by the vaporisation of the liquid confined in a closed vessel at 1 bar and is a reminder of the importance of providing a relief device in any section where liquid can be positively trapped.

3. Hazards Involved due to Materials and Construction

Construction materials for non-cryogenic services usually are chosen on the basis of tensile strength and fatigue strength etc. In case of cryogenics the designer must consider ductility of the material otherwise the cryogenic fluids will make the materials brittle and fragile. Normally used materials for cryogenic purposes are stainless steel and non-ferrous metals with some exceptions.

4. Hazards Involved due to Oxygen

The normal concentration of Oxygen in air is 21 per cent by volume. If this is raised by four percentage points to 25 per cent, there is a significant increase in the burning rate of nearby cloth, textiles, wood, hair and so on. Degreasing is the other important issue in the case of vessels containing Oxygen.

5. Hazards due to Flammability and Explosion

If the presence of all the three limbs of a fire triangle i.e. igniter, fuel and Oxygen occur, there will be a fire and if it is in the presence of explosive mixture of gases like Hydrogen and air (4-75 mol%) or Hydrogen & Oxygen (4-95 mol%) or Methane and air (5-15 mol%) etc., explosion may also occur.

6. Hazards due to Entrapment and High Pressure Has Hazards

The stored energy concept of gases which are highly compressed is an important hazard to be addressed with. In cryogenics such high pressures are obtained by gas compression during liquefaction or refrigeration, by the pumping of liquids to high pressure followed by evaporation, and by confinement of cryogenic liquids with subsequent evaporation. If this confined gas is suddenly released through a rupture of a break in a line, a significant thrust may be experienced.

7. Hazards Involved in Storage of Cryogenic Fluids

The relevant hazards associated with storage vessels are hazards like asphyxia due to lack of Oxygen in confined areas, high pressure hazards due to failure of insulation of storage tanks.

8. Hazards Involved in Transportation of Cryogenic Fluids

There are two important aspects due to which hazards may occur which are as follows:

(a) *Type of construction* : When the tank is filled with liquid cryogen, due to huge temperature gradient the inner vessel contracts and hence the connecting pipe line and supports may break if suitable flexibility is not given.

(b) *Type of insulation* : The inner vessel is covered with insulation which is held in position by outer vessel. In case of perlite (hydrated silicate pre submitted to an expansion by thermal treatment) insulated tanks, the perlite shall be suitably compacted to avoid setting at an early stage. Care shall be taken to avoid any pockets are voids in the perlite. If it fails the vessel will be subjected to high pressure due to evaporation.

9. Hazards due to Unexpected Activities

There are different hazards under this heading. They are as follows:

(a) *Leakage of hydraulic oils* : It is dangerous to employ Hydraulic actuation systems in Oxygen systems or where Oxygen formation due to condensation of atmospheric air takes place. It is due to the leakage of hydraulic oils into the system from hydraulic actuators. Here Pneumatic actuator systems are preferable.

(b) *Cold transmission* : Cryogenic storage vessels or pipelines shall not be placed directly on floor. Even though insulation is there, cold will take its path to migrate into the ground. This hazard can be overcome by constructing storage vessels or pipelines containing cryogenic fluids on stilts.

(c) *Improper direction of venting from safety valves* : Normally cryogenic vessels often have mild steel outer vessels. If the discharge from safety vents are allowed to impinge on such outer vessels there is a chance that the outer vessel becomes fragile and crack.

(d) *Improper direction of installation* : The long extended stem valves of cryogenic service, if they are not fixed vertically or near to vertical, the cryogenic liquid will flow till the gland of the valve and hazards may occur. So verticality shall be maintained to avoid such hazards.

10. Hazards Involved due to Environmental Issues :

Pre-cooling of feed air before entering into distillation column of any Air separation plant is mainly by means of refrigerants and leakage of these refrigerants (either CFCs or HCFCs) into the atmosphere may cause depletion of Ozone layer due to which the unfiltered Ultra-voilet rays may cause severe damages to the beings on earth.

Precautions to be taken with Cryogenic Fluids

For elimination of hazards precautions are required to be taken right from the design stage. It means proactive design requirements like correct placement of safety valves in cryogenic circuits, proper mounting and insulation of cryogenic vessels, proper direction and instrumentation of valves will lead to a safe operation of cryogenic plant.

Following are the different precautions that are to be followed while handling of different cryogenic fluids, so that hazards will be at their distance.

1. Precautions for Physiological hazards.
2. Precautions for Material and Construction hazards.
3. Precautions for Flammability and Explosion hazards.
4. Precautions for High pressure gas hazards.
5. Precautions in Storage of cryogenic fluids.
6. Precautions in Transportation.
7. First-aid for Cryogenic Exposures.

1. Precautions for Physiological Hazards

(i) Awareness Training programmes

All employees in the handling of cryogenic fluids must be adequately trained. In this connection, the training should be different for operators, drivers who handle cryogenic fluids. It is also required to explain the case studies of previous incidents or accidents related to cryogenic handling. The training course shall contain following subjects:

- Properties of materials at low temperatures.
- Cryogenic fluid hazards and proper precautions.
- Principle and control of safety equipment.
- Personal Protective Equipment (PPE) in handling of cryogenics.
- Case studies of previous accidents.
- Emergency procedure and first-aid.

(ii) Awareness of different ill effects on persons: Cold burns, Asphyxia, etc.

Cold burns : These are resulted when skin is in contact with cryo fluids or the uninsulated containers of the cryo fluids that results in frostbite inturn leads to amputation of limbs.

Precautions to be taken :

- Do not over fill containers.
- Never make direct skin contact with cryo fluids or its uninsulated containers.
- Wear suitable PPEs like full face shield, impenetrable apron, gloves, shoes, etc.
- Transfer or pour cryogens slowly to minimize boiling and splashing.
- Use a phase separator or special filling funnel when transferring cryogen.
- Don't inhale cold vapours which can cause damage to lungs or may trigger asthma attack in susceptible individuals.

Asphyxia : One of the most significant risks of cryogenic liquids is death by asphyxiation where a spill or leakage depletes the atmospheric Oxygen. If the Oxygen concentration falls below 18 per cent adverse effects will occur that may result in loss of mental alertness and performance combined with distortion of judgment. Oxygen less than 10 per cent will cause immediate death.

Precautions to be taken :

- Never enter into cryogenic vessels without checking of percentage of Oxygen.
- When the feeling of breathlessness is sensed person shall immediately quit the premises.
- If it is required to work in an environment where more spillage of cryogen is there, persons should work with self-contained breathing apparatus.

(iii) Awareness of insulation hazards

Normally use insulation material in cryogenic field are perlite powder or rock wool. Both are lightly irritant and itching material.

Precautions to be taken to work in a box insulated with perlite and Glass wool:

- Scaffolding around the work area is required.
- All the persons have to be equipped with security harness linked to a stable point strong enough to carry the worker.
- Persons shall be supervised permanently by other workers from a place out of the dangerous zone.
- Every worker shall wear glasses, gloves and dust protecting breathing mask.

2. Precautions for Material and Construction Hazards

This is an important precaution to know what all the different materials that can be used with cryogenics. Construction materials for cryogenic service usually are chosen on the basis of tensile strength, fatigue life, corrosion resistance, etc. Normally cryo materials made of stainless steel or non-ferrous materials like copper, monel metal, brass, aluminium, etc. or non-metals like PTFE (Teflon, fluon), Viton, Kcl-F, Neoprene, Bura N, Polyethelene, Nylon, Natural Rubber, etc. If the cryo fluid is liquid oxygen, even the oxygen compatibility also need to be taken care of. Some materials used for this purpose are like glass fenall refractory, Quartz which resist oxidation and ignition under all practical conditions of temperatures and pressures.

3. Precautions for Flammability and Explosion Hazards

- When flammable gases are used, potential ignition sources must be carefully controlled.
- Oxygen's presence will increase the flammability of ordinary combustibles. Keep all organic materials and flammable substances away from contact with Oxygen.
- Extreme cold surfaces can condense Oxygen from atmosphere. Beware of the situation.

- Liquefied inert gases can condense Oxygen from the atmosphere, that may caüse entrapment of Oxygen in unsuspected areas.
- Explosive gases like Hydrogen, Methane, Acetylene should be kept free from other two limbs of fire triangle.
- Work areas, rooms, laboratories, etc. should be suitably monitored to automatically warn personnel when dangerous condition is developing.
- Oxygen compatible lubricants shall be used like FOMBLIN Y04/25 to avoid any fire/explosion.

4. *Precautions for High Pressure Gas Hazards*

- The large expansion ratio from liquid to gas causes a build up of high pressure due to evaporation of the liquid. Therefore, entrapment of fluids shall be identified and required relief valves shall be utilized.
- Inspect at regular intervals for leakage, frosting and dirt accumulation.

5. *Precautions in Storage of Cryogenic Fluids*

- Periodic inspection of insulation shall be done to avoid fatal failure of cryogenic tanks.
- Cryogenic storage vessels shall be placed on stilts to arrest cold migration.
- The direction of safety relief valves should not be on to the outer vessels to not to have embrittlement problems of outer vessel which normally made of mild steel.
- Enough flexibility shall be there in the construction of connecting pipeline and supports to avoid breakage due to temperature gradient.
- Large storage tanks are usually provided with a remotely operated internal valve which can be shutoff in the event of leakage caused by damage to the external pipe work. Leakage can also prevented or reduced by directing water on to the leak in such a way as to form a sealing ice plug of ice blanket that will hold back the liquid.

6. *Precautions in Transportation*

- The drivers shall be given appropriate training regarding hazards involved with cryogenic liquids, MSDS of the handling liquid, loading /unloading procedures, symbols of cryogenic liquids being transported and emergency handling procedures including first aid.
- Prior planning is to be made to transfer the liquid in a truck or in a tanker to take care of the stability ratio.
- Over filling of the tanker shall not be there to eliminate the overflow problems which may lead to embrittlement of chassis and outer tank of the truck/tanker.
- The tanker or truck needs duel pressure relief system and bock and bleed valves in its construction.
- Periodic inspection of insulation shall be done to avoid fatal failure of cryogenic tanks of the truks/tankers. It is better to use composite insulated tankers which

have low weight when compared to perlite insulated tankers and also they can sustain the liquid for some duration even if the vacuum fails.

- All the hand operated valves and gauges of the tank shall be located in a closed cabinet at the rear of the tank. The cabinet shall be vented to atmosphere. All the vent and drain line shall be taken out of the cabinet at the top or towards the ground.

7. *First aid for Cryogenic Exposures*

Following are the different first-aid practices or some of the do's and don'ts that are to be dealt in case of exposure to cryogenic fluids :

Lungs : If there is any respiratory distress for the injured patient due to exposure to cold gas, obtain medical attention immediately.

Eyes : If there is a direct contact of cryogenic fluid with eyes do not apply dry heat or rub the eyes only soak them in lukewarm water for some time and take the medical assistance.

Skin :

- Obtain medical attention and remove any clothing that may constrict the blood circulation to the burn.
- Thaw slowly in lukewarm water between temperatures of 42 to 45 degrees centigrade.
- Do not use dry heat.
- Cover burn with a large sterile dressing.
- If there is extensive frozen area or deeply frozen, take the casualty to nearby hospital.
- Do not give alcohol or allow smoking.
- Do not remove sticking clothing until completely thawed.

General Safety Guidelines for Cryogenic Fluids

- If spillage occurs, immediately quit the area and return after conformation with gas measuring device that the dangerous gases are at their threshold limits.
- At least six exchanges per hour ventilation shall be there in the room.
- If there is an experience of symptoms like dizziness, light head ache or confusion, immediately seek plenty of fresh air or provide rescue breathing or CPR until paramedical assistance arrives.
- If any person or persons become unconscious in a confined area of cryogenic application or cryogenic liquid storage they shall only be retrieved by personnel using proper PPE such as self-contained breathing apparatus.
- In the event of contact with cryogenic fluids follow the first-aid procedure described above.

In addition to the above, logical sequence of operations, proper maintenance of plants will add extra flavour in containing the unexpected consequences.

Conclusion

Cryogenic products have the potential of a wild lion. But a skillful ring master who has understanding in the technology and safety aspects of cryogenics can tame and make it to perform as per his direction. It is required to sustain the acquired skill by continuous and repetitive actions.

Cryogenic products and processes now-a-days have a wider application and it is, therefore, became important to inform on dangers which may be encountered. It should perhaps also be mentioned that even cryogenic experts have some times failed to appreciate some of the more insidious dangers which may arise and this has led to injuries and fatal accidents also that could be avoided with comprehensive training, previous case studies and with proper statutes.

However it is clear that the best designed facility or training or statutes are no better than the attention that is paid towards safety in day to day activity.

REFERENCES

Cryogenic air separation - A training guide for engineers and mangers of IIT Kharagpur.

Perry's Chemical Engineering Handbook.

MANAGEMENT OF GASEOUS EMISSIONS AND AIR QUALITY

Ravindra S. Mali*

ABSTRACT

There are five concentric layers within the atmosphere, which can be differentiated on the basis of temperature. These include the troposphere, the stratosphere, the mesosphere, the heterosphere and the exosphere. The lowest layer of atmosphere in which man along with other living organisms live is called TOPOSPHERE. The gaseous mixture of troposphere is called AIR.

Air pollution is aggravated because of four developments: increasing traffic, growing cities, rapid economic development and industrialization. The Industrial Revolution in Europe in the 19th century saw the beginning of air pollution as we know it today, which has gradually become a global problem.

Severe air pollution affects human health and causes many fatal diseases in them. For e.g. there occurs lung diseases in workers exposed to occupational hazards, such as Black lung disease among coal miners who inhaled mine dust for many years; or Asbestosis among pipe fitters and insulation workers, exposed to airborne asbestos fibers. A variety of air pollutants have been found to cause many human diseases such as emphysema, chronic Bronchitis, Pollen Allergies, Lung Cancer.

Air pollution also affects weather, climate and atmospheric processes. Many gaseous pollutants and fine aerosols reach the upper atmosphere, where they have basic effects on the penetration and absorption of sunlight. The Green house Effect, Peeling of Ozone Umbrella, Global Warming, etc. are all the effects of Air Pollution.

The protection of Environment has assumed great significance in recent years. The Stockholm Conference on Human Environment held in 1972, served as a catalyst to focus the attention of mankind to the deteriorating quality of the environment. Over the years man has assumed powers to transform the environment to meet his requirements.

In India, air pollution control legislation envisages the formation of Air Pollution Boards at the Central and State Level "with powers to issue and revoke licenses to polluting industries, enforce emission standards and frame rules and regulations for the control of air pollution". The Board will have power to prohibit certain trades and manufacturing processes in notified areas and prescribes emission standards in scheduled premises. The legislation is also understood to ban the burning of garbage and other waste products in urban areas as well as the fouling up of air by burning smoking fuels for domestic purposes.

*Assistant Officer (Safety), Ispat Industries Ltd., Dolvi - Pen, Raigad Maharashtra-402 107, India.

Introduction

I will go out for a breath of fresh air' is an often-heard phrase. But how many of us realize that this has become irrelevant in today's world.

The moment you step out of the house and are on the road you can actually see the air getting polluted; a cloud of smoke from the exhaust of a bus, car, or a scooter; smoke billowing from a factory chimney, fly ash generated by thermal power plants, and speeding cars causing dust to rise from the roads. Natural phenomena such as the eruption of a volcano and even someone smoking a cigarette can also cause air pollution.

Air pollution is aggravated because of four developments: increasing traffic, growing cities, rapid economic development and industrialization. The Industrial Revolution in Europe in the 19th century saw the beginning of air pollution as we know it today, which has gradually become a global problem.

Man facing one of the horrible ecological crises - the problem of pollution of his environment, which sometimes in past was pure, virgin, undisturbed, uncontaminated and basically quite hospitable for him.

Details

Atmosphere

The multi-layered gaseous envelop surrounding the planet earth is called atmosphere. It is an ocean of air, which blends into outer space some 1000 KM or so above the Earth's surface. The atmosphere is a reservoir of several elements essential to life and it serves many functions, including the filtering of radiant energy from the sun, insulation from heat loss at earth's surface, and stabilization of weather and climate owing to the heat capacity of the air.

There are five concentric layers within the atmosphere, which can be differentiated on the basis of temperature. These include the troposphere, the stratosphere, the mesosphere, the heterosphere and the exosphere.

The lowest layer of atmosphere in which man along with other living organisms live is called TOPOSPHERE. The gaseous mixture of troposphere is called AIR. Air is a mixture of gases consisting Nitrogen (78.01 %), Oxygen (20.95 %) Argon (0.93 %), Carbon Dioxide (0.03 %) and other gases like Neon, Helium, Methane, Krypton, Hydrogen, Nitrous Oxide, Xenon, Ozone, etc. Air is utilized by most of the organisms in respiration to liberate chemical energy from food during oxidation.

When due to some natural processes or human activities the amount of solid waste or concentration of gases other than Oxygen increases in the air which normally has constant percentage of different gases in it the air is said to be polluted and this phenomenon is referred to as Air or Atmospheric Pollution.

One of the formal definitions of Air Pollution is as follows - 'The presence in the atmosphere of one or more contaminants in such quality and for such duration as is injurious, or tends to be injurious, to human health or welfare, animal or plant life.'

Air pollution has been defined by WHO (World Health Organization) as the presence of materials in the air which are harmful to men and environment. Air stays nowhere for a long time. Because air is freely moving pollutants in the air spread over a wide areas soon.

Modernization and progress have led to air getting more and more polluted over the years. Industries, vehicles, increase in the population, and urbanization are some of the major factors responsible for air pollution. The following industries are among those that emit a great deal of pollutants into the air: thermal power plants, cement, steel, refineries, petro-chemicals and mines.

Air pollution results from a variety of causes, not all of which are within human control. Dust storms in desert areas and smoke from forest fires and grass fires contribute to chemical and particulate pollution of the air. The source of pollution may be in one country but the impact of pollution may be felt elsewhere. The discovery of pesticides in Antarctica, where they have never been used, suggests the extent to which aerial transport can carry pollutants from one place to another. Probably the most important natural source of air pollution is volcanic activity, which at times pours great amounts of ash and toxic fumes into the atmosphere. The eruptions of such volcanoes as Krakatoa in Indonesia, Mt. St. Helens in Washington, USA and Katmai in Alaska, USA, have been related to measurable climatic changes.

The rapid and tremendous industrial growth, expansion of industries is looked upon as a symbol of country's progress. Larger the number of industries the greater is the progress of the nation. But one can't be blind to the fact that with the growth of industries the dangers of pollution also grow. Industrial growth is indeed necessary for the progress of the nation. But it should not be at the expense of its own people. The health of workmen and their family members and also of local public should be given as much importance as is now given to industrial growth. Air pollution, water pollution, noise pollution, land pollution and the aesthetic pollution are all the gifts of urbanization and industrialization. Smoke nuisance is a grave health hazard in cities like Culcutta, Kanpur, Delhi, Ahmedabad, Nagpur and Mumbai. Chemical industries pollute air by discharge of number of pollutants gases like Carbon-dioxide, Carbon monoxide, hydrogen sulfide, ammonia, fluorine, chlorine, oxides of Nitrogen, Sulphur, etc.

The first case of severe Air Pollution in modern time were in the Meuse Valley of Belgium in 1930; a Killing Smog in Donora, Pennsylvania along the Monongahela River in 1948, in which hundreds of people died; deadlier smog in London in 1952 in which 4000 to 5000 people died from respiratory failure.

Kinds of Air Pollution

1. Industrial pollutants released from industrial units and power houses, are the main sources of air pollution. They are mainly Sulphur dioxide, carbon monoxide, carbon dioxide, hydrogen, sulfides, chlorine, nitrous oxide, arsenic, ozone, ash and endless number of metal particles and gases.
2. Domestic pollutants from fossil fuels burnt by men.
3. Automobile exhausts.
4. Radiations.

Major Air Pollutants and Their Sources

Carbon monoxide (CO) is a colourless, odourless gas that is produced by the incomplete burning of carbon-based fuels including petrol, diesel and wood. It is also produced from the combustion of natural and synthetic products such as cigarettes. It lowers the amount of oxygen that enters our blood. It can slow our reflexes and make us confused and sleepy.

Carbon dioxide (CO_2) is the principle Greenhouse gas emitted as a result of human activities such as the burning of coal, oil and natural gases.

Chlorofluorocarbons (CFC) are gases that are released mainly from air-conditioning systems and refrigeration. When released into the air, CFCs rise to the stratosphere, where they come in contact with few other gases, which leads to a reduction of the ozone layer that protects the earth from the harmful ultraviolet rays of the sun.

Lead is present in petrol, diesel, lead batteries, paints, hair dye products, etc. Lead affects children in particular. It can cause nervous system damage and digestive problems and, in some cases, cause cancer.

Ozone occurs naturally in the upper layers of the atmosphere. This important gas shields the earth from the harmful ultraviolet rays of the sun. However, at the ground level, it is a pollutant with highly toxic effects. Vehicles and industries are the major source of ground-level ozone emissions. Ozone makes our eyes itch, burn and water. It lowers our resistance to colds and pneumonia.

Nitrogen oxide (NO_X) causes smog and acid rain. It is produced from burning fuels including petrol, diesel, and coal. Nitrogen oxides can make children susceptible to respiratory diseases in winters.

Suspended particulate matter (SPM) consists of solids in the air in the form of smoke, dust, and vapour that can remain suspended for extended periods and is also the main source of haze which reduces visibility. The finer of these particles, when breathed in can lodge in our lungs and cause lung damage and respiratory problems.

Sulphur dioxide (SO_2) is a gas produced from burning coal, mainly in thermal power plants. Some industrial processes, such as production of paper and smelting of metals, produce sulphur dioxide. It is a major contributor to smog and acid rain. Sulphur dioxide can lead to lung diseases.

Methods of Detection and Measurement of Air Pollution

Air pollution is usually measured by sampling of air by High Volume Air Samplers/Respirable Air Samplers/Portable Air Samplers. Air borne dust is collected on Glass Micro Fibre Filter Paper (GF/A) and is analyzed by Gravimetric method. Gaseous pollutants are absorbed in different absorbing solutions and these are analyzed by titrimetric/colourimetric methods. The concentration of some gaseous pollutants is also measured by dragger tubes, digital meters.

Effects of Air Pollution

Severe air pollution affects human health and causes many fatal diseases in them. For e.g. there occurs lung disease in workers exposed to occupational hazards, such as Black lung disease among coal miners who inhaled mine dust for many years; or Asbestosis among pipe fitters and insulation workers, exposed to airborne asbestos fibers. A variety of air pollutants have been found to cause many human diseases such as emphysema, chronic Bronchitis, Pollen Allergies, Lung Cancer.

In many areas, air pollution has dramatic injury to both agricultural crops and natural plants communities. There has been injury to agricultural livestocks, particularly from airborne fluoride and arsenic pollution. Excessive fluorine compounds, which have contaminated forage by fall-out, have sometimes caused cattle to develop Fluorosis, an abnormal calcification of bones which leads to lameness. Air pollution also takes its toll of buildings and other man made objects. When moisture accumulates in polluted air, the oxides of Sulphur, carbon and nitrogen form weak Sulphuric, carbonic and nitric acid, which are corrosive to metal, stone, paint, rubber, textiles and even some plastics.

Air pollution also affects weather, climate and atmospheric processes. Many gaseous pollutants and fine aerosols reach the upper atmosphere, where they have basic effects on the penetration and absorption of sunlight. The Green house Effect, Peeling of Ozone Umbrella, Global Warming, etc. are all the effects of Air Pollution.

Major Air Pollutants and their Associated Health Hazards

S.No.	*Name of the Pollutant*	*Health Impacts*
1	Respirable Particulate Matter (RSPM)	Respiratory illness, including chronic bronchitis and asthma; heart diseases.
2	Sulphur Di-oxide (SO_2)	Heart diseases; respiratory problems including pulmonary emphysema, cancer, eye burning, headache, etc.
3	Nitrogen Di-oxide (NO_2)	Lung irritation, viral infection, airway resistance, chest tightness, etc.
4	SPM	Pneumoconiosis, restrictive lung diseases, asthma, cancer, etc.
5	Benzene	It causes immunotoxicity, carcinogenicity, asthma, anemia, unconsciousness, etc.
6	Ozone	Impaired lung function, chest pains, coughing, irritation of eyes, nose, etc.
7	Carbon Monoxide (CO)	CO poisoning cause cherry lips, unconsciousness, death by asphyxiation, etc.
8	Lead	It causes decreased hemoglobin synthesis, anemia, damage the nervous and renal (kidney) systems, etc.

The protection of Environment has assumed great significance in recent years. The Stockholm Conference on Human Environment held in 1972, served as a catalyst to focus the attention of mankind to the deteriorating quality of the environment. The quality of the environment has a direct bearing on the environment. Over the years man has assumed powers to transform the environment to meet his requirements. The growing awareness for projecting of environment emphasized the need for treating the wastes before disposal in to environment. For effective implementation of protective measures, environmental laws were enacted the world over.

Control of Air Pollution

Most kinds of air pollutions can be controlled by modern technology, but the costs ultimately be borne by the public in the form of higher prices for manufactured goods, higher taxes, reduced profit margins in industry, and more restrictions on individual activities such as burning leaves and trash and use of automobiles. The benefits involve not only improved environmental quality, but improved health, improved agriculture and plant growth, and reduced deterioration of material goods.

Various devices such as the Positive Crankcase Ventilation Valve and Catalytic Converter have been developed to reduce exhaust emissions by automobiles, but these are not always fully maintained by the public. Likewise particulate pollution from industry and power generation can be controlled by Electrostatic Precipitators, which are capable of dramatically reducing smoke and dust. Gaseous pollutants of industry and power stations can be removed by chemical means, i.e., differential solubility of gases in water. A fine spray of water in a device known as a "Scrubber" can effectively separate many gases such as ammonia and Sulphur dioxide. Other gases may be removed by filtration or absorption through activated carbon, and still others by chemical conversion to inert or innocuous materials.

Legal Control of Air Pollution

In India, air pollution control legislation envisages the formation of Air Pollution Boards at the Central and State Level "with powers to issue and revoke licenses to polluting industries, enforce emission standards and frame rules and regulations for the control of air pollution". The Board will have power to prohibit certain trades and manufacturing processes in notified areas and prescribes emission standards in scheduled premises. The legislation is also understood to ban the burning of garbage and other waste products in urban areas as well as the fouling up of air by burning smoking fuels for domestic purposes. Bombay Smoke Nuisance Act has been enforced only in case of smoke emanating from the chimneys of industrial units. Air (Prevention and Control of Pollution) Act, 1981 was made effective from May 1981.

Powers of State Government under Air Act, 1981

The State Governments have powers to declare air pollution control areas, to give instructions for ensuring standards for emission from automobiles, restriction on operation of certain industrial plants or their operation in certain areas. It is not permitted to allow emission of certain air pollutants in excess of the standards laid down by the state boards for certain industries. The entrepreneurs should seek advice of the State Government authorities on the various steps to be taken to confirm to be required standards of pollution control in the initial stage of project planning. It is one of the conditions of conversion of a letter of intent into an industrial license that environmental clearance to the satisfaction of the Government is obtained by the entrepreneurs.

National Air Quality Monitoring Programme (NAMP)

Central Pollution Control Board (CPCB) has executed a nation-wide programme of ambient air quality monitoring known as National Air Quality Monitoring Programme (NAMP). The objectives of the NAMP are to determine status and trends of ambient air quality; to ascertain whether the prescribed ambient air quality standards are violated; to Identify Non-attainment Cities; to obtain the knowledge and understanding necessary for developing preventive and corrective measures and to understand the natural cleansing process undergoing in the environment through pollution dilution, dispersion, wind based movement, dry deposition, precipitation and chemical transformation of pollutants generated.

Under NAMP, four air pollutants viz., Sulphur Dioxide (SO_2), Oxides of Nitrogen as NO_2 and Suspended Particulate Matter (SPM) and Respirable Suspended Particulate Matter (RSPM/PM_{10}), have been identified for regular monitoring at all the locations. The monitoring of meteorological parameters such as wind speed and direction, relative humidity and temperature is also integrated with the monitoring of air quality.

The monitoring of pollutants is carried out for 24 hours (4 - Hourly sampling for gaseous pollutants and 8-Hourly sampling for particulate matter) with a frequency of twice a week, to have 104 observations in a year. The monitoring is being carried out with the help of Central Pollution Control Board; State Pollution Control Boards; Pollution Control Committees; National Environmental Engineering Research Institute (NEERI), Nagpur. CPCB co-ordinates with these agencies to ensure the uniformity, consistency of air quality data and provides technical and financial support to them for operating the monitoring station. NAMP is being operated through various monitoring agencies, large number of personnel and equipment are involved in the sampling, chemical analysis, data reporting, etc. It increases the probability of variation and personnel biases reflecting in the data, hence, it is pertinent to mention that these data be treated as indicative rather than absolute.

Based on Annual Mean Concentration ($\mu g/m^3$ of ambient air) of SO_2, NO_2 and SPM and the Notified Ambient Air Quality Standards, the Ambient Air Quality Status is described in terms of Low (L), Moderate (M), High (H) and Critical (C) for Industrial (I), Residential and mixed use (R) areas of Cities/Towns in different States/UTs.

Conclusion

In past air was pure, virgin, undisturbed, uncontaminated and basically quite hospitable for man. Now a days it is getting deteriorating due to increasing traffic, growing cities, rapid economic development, and industrialization. It has become a global problem and as an effect man is facing various health ailments. Air pollution affects weather, climate and atmospheric processes. Many gaseous pollutants and fine aerosols reach the upper

National Ambient Air Quality Standards (NAQS)

Pollutants	*Time-weighted average*	*Concentration in Ambient Air*			*Method of measurement*
		Industrial Areas	*Residential, Rural & other Areas*	*Sensitive Areas*	
Sulphur Dioxide (SO_2)	Annual Average*	80 µg/m³	60 µg/m³	15 µg/m³	- Improved West and Geake Method
	24 hours**	120 µg/m³	80 µg/m³	30 µg/m³	- Ultraviolet Fluorescence
Oxides of Nitrogen as (NO_X)	Annual Average*	80 µg/m³	60 µg/m³	15 µg/m³	- Jacob & Hochheiser Modified (Na-Arsenite) Method
	24 hours**	120 µg/m³	80 µg/m³	30 µg/m³	- Gas Phase Chemiluminescence
Suspended Particulate Matter (SPM)	Annual Average*	360 µg/m³	140 µg/m³	70 µg/m³	- High Volume Sampling, (Average flow rate not less than 1.1 m³/minute).
	24 hours**	500 µg/m³	200 µg/m³	100 µg/m³	
Respirable Particulate Matter (RPM) (size less than 10 microns)	Annual Average*	120 µg/m³	60 µg/m³	50 µg/m³	- Respirable particulate matter sampler
	24 hours**	150 µg/m³	100 µg/m³	75 µg/m³	
Lead (Pb)	Annual Average*	1.0 µg/m³	0.75 µg/m³	0.50 µg/m³	- ASS Method after sampling using EPM 2000 or equivalent Filter paper
	24 hours**	1.5 µg/m³	1.00 µg/m³	0.75 µg/m³	.
Ammonial	Annual Average*	0.1 mg/ m³	0.1 mg/ m³	0.1 mg/m³	.
	24 hours**	0.4 mg/ m³	0.4 mg/m³	0.4 mg/m³	.
Carbon Monoxide (CO)	8 hours**	5.0 mg/m³	2.0 mg/m³	1.0 mg/ m³	- Non Dispersive Infra Red (NDIR)
	1 hour	10.0 mg/m³	4.0 mg/m³	2.0 mg/m³	- Spectroscopy
*	Annual Arithmetic mean of minimum 104 measurements in a year taken twice a week 24 hourly at uniform interval.				
**	24 hourly/8 hourly values should be met 98% of the time in a year. However, 2% of the time, it may exceed but not on two consecutive days.				

Ambient Air Quality Standards in Respect of Noise

Area Code	*Category of Area*	*Limits in dB (A) LEQ*	
		Day Time	*Night Times*
(A)	Industrial area	75	70
(B)	Commercial area	65	55
(C)	Residential area	55	45

Note :

1. Day time is reckoned in between 6.00 AM and 9.00 PM.
2. Night time is reckoned in between 9.00 PM and 6.00 AM.
3. Silence zone is defined as areas up to 100 meters around such premises as hospitals, educational institutions and courts. The Silence zones are to be declared by the Competent Authority.

   Use of vehicular horns, loudspeakers and bursting of crackers shall be banned in these zones.
4. Mixed categories of areas should be declared as one of the four above-mentioned categories by the Competent Authority and the corresponding standards shall apply.

atmosphere, where they have basic effects on the penetration and absorption of sunlight. The Green house Effect, Peeling of Ozone Umbrella, Global Warming, etc. are all the effects of Air Pollution.

The emissions from various sources can be effectively controlled by adopting proper pollution control devices at source of pollutant generation it self and thus we can prevent air pollution by adoption of latest clean air pollution technologies and complying national and international air pollution control norms. To have a status check on emission level, set up of emission/air quality monitoring system is required. Monitoring data helps us to take timely corrective measures to control pollutant emissions in to air.

It is the need of the day to have a control on our developmental activities and to protect our environment for our future generation. It is right of the every citizen to get wholesome, fresh and uncontaminated air to breath.

REFERENCES

Environmental Biology (Principles of Ecology), by P.S. Verma and V.K. Agarwal, Edition 1996 (Reprint) pp. 111 to 121 and 495 to 504. (S. Chand & Company Ltd., Ramnagar, New Delhi - 110 055.

Text Book of Environment and Industrial Safety by National Institute of Labour Education and Mangement, Chennai, pp. 9 & 14.

Website - http://dpcc.delhigovt.nic.in/airstd.htm, http://www.cpcb.nic.in/air.htm.

29

OSH &E AND SUSTAINABLE ECONOMIC DEVELOPMENT
OSH &E Aspects - Measurements and Indicators

G. Muruganandan*

ABSTRACT

With the rapid growth in industrial manufacturing, the occupational safety and health of the employees & others and Environmental protection to preserve the nature plays vital role in our Nation. To survive the business in the Global market and satisfy the stakeholders, OSH&E management system helps the Organization to win the race. Maintaining this system is very much challenging and it is not one time investment. Understanding the concepts and monitoring the system are essential part to perform the OSH&E. This paper describes the out line of Safety, Health and Environment management system, how to select the SHE performance indicator and how to measure the performance indicator. Hope this will useful to SHE Managers, line functional mangers and process owners.

Introduction

Even then Industrial growth is accountable, present national accident data shows 15 per cent reduction in lost time cases. This indicates our national effort to promote SHE through various councils and forums like Safety and Quality Forum. In line with SQF objective, the theme of the paper is to promote Safety, Health &Environment (SHE) Management system in a systematic approach. To fulfill the expectation from the readers, this paper designed in such a way, first described the concept of SHE Management system and then the determination of key performance indicators, measurements for effective implementation of SHE management, Barriers for the SHE Management, the steps to over come the barriers and future development on SHE success.

*Presently working as Dy. Manager SHE in a multi-national organisation. *E-mail*: g.muruganandan@yahoo.co.in

Concept of SHE Management

It is an integrated management system which covers occupational safety health of the employees, labours and nearby community and the environment surrounding us. There are five common stages which are systematically explained the system. Any de-link in the stages might cause severe damage to the system.

SHE Management System Pictorial View

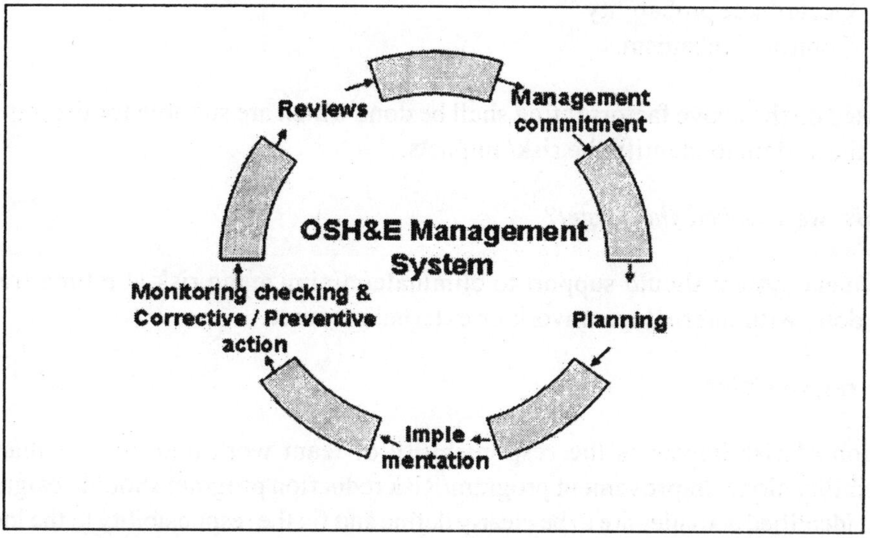

1. Management Commitment
2. Systematic Planning
3. Implementation
4. Monitoring & Measurements
5. Reviews.

Management Commitment

Management commitment on SHE is an axle for the management system functioning. Management commitment towards SHE aspects should reflect in the policy. To show the commitment of the organization, top management should declare the policy to the stake-holders. Provision of resources, review of continual improvement in management system are the key roles of the management commitment.

Systematic Planning

Planning is a continuous process which evaluates the SHE risk/environmental aspects and impacts. This process enable us to find out with 3Ws.

'where are we ?'

When are we reached the target to eliminate or minimize the risk/impacts?
Who is responsible?

Where are we?

To start with simple assessment can be adopted to find out the risk and impacts. The minimum requirement for the assessment should contains

(a) Severity
(b) Occurrence probability
(c) Control Mechanism.

Based on the above factors rating shall be done which are suitable for the requirements and aid the system to identify the risk/ impacts.

When are we reached the target?

Management system should support to eliminate/minimize the risk at a time frame. This may be done with internal team work or external resource.

Who is responsible?

Reduction of risk/impact is the responsibility of team work and not the management responsibility alone. Improvement program/Risk reduction program should design in such a way that identified activities are to be clearly define and fix the responsibility to the individuals.

Implementation

Structure and responsibility are the first part of the implementation step. It should clearly define the responsibility from the top management to the line function. Training and competency development is the part of implementation to upgrade the knowledge of individuals to promote SHE Management. Transparent and clear procedures are the mandatory to implement any management system. Emergency /Contingency plan is necessary to act in case of any eventuality.

Monitoring and Measurement

To check the system performance, monitoring and measurement acts key role in the management system. Performance indictors are necessary to monitor and measure the requirements. This chapter will be discussed in details in this paper.

Reviews

The reviews should be carried out under the chairmanship of top management who is responsible for committed Policy. The review should focus on system improvements, corrective and preventive measures.

Determination of Performance Indicators

It is derived from management commitment, planning process and implementation lessons. Performance indicators should relevant to the facility operation and should reflect the SHE performance.

The performance indicator can be categorized in three ways:

Committed Performance Indicators

It is the performance indicator which is committed to obey the legal and other requirements. This indicators are mandatory and reporting is required to the statutory body. This indicator may be performed better, if we keep the internal limits well below the statutory limits. Eg. As per the statutory limits, stack dust emission should be maintained below 150Mgm/M3. Our objective is at no time dust limit should not exceed the statutory limit. Check the present operating dust level. If the level becomes 75Mgm/M3, it is more advisable to fix the performance indicator level of 100Mgm/M3.At any point if the values exceed the internal performance indicators level, immediate corrective and preventive action to be taken to bring the system sustainable.

Positive Performance Indicators

It indicates positive performance/innovative ideas which are directly/indirectly benefit to the SHE Management system. It must be emphasized that an important factor in the success of this positive approach to measuring safety performance will be the ability of an organization to go beyond an exclusive focus on indicators of employee's behaviour, to encompass indicators which address the total work place environment. Positive performance indicators can be used to measure relevant OHS systems, processes, and compliance with OHS practices in work place. Example of positive performance indicators include the number of safety audits conducted; the percentage of sub-standard conditions identified and corrected as a result of the audit; and the percentage of workers receiving SHE training.

Implementation Performance Indicators

This indicator is determined from the lessons of implementation. This may be called negative indicators. The first is to place the negative indicators such as accident rate or incident rate, in the context of positive programs of change and improvement at the work place. The most relevant category for measuring SHE performance is the Work force Contribution and it is here the organizations can supplement negative indicators with programs to eliminate work place hazards and improve safety procedures and awareness, and can devise additional measures of work force cooperation and compliance with these programs and procedures.

The ultimate target of this indicator is to achieve zero accident level. Once we achieved the zero accident level we should aim for zero incident level as an Implementation Performance indicator. Each and every first-aid cases are to measured in the following ways to identify the exact reason and to take preventive measures which prevent recurrence.

To find out the cause and eliminate the hazard is an unique exercise. It is suggested to plot graphs in the following headings on regular basis:

(i) Nature of Injury (Minor or Major): Plot No. of Incident/Accident *Vs*. Nature of Injury.

(ii) Cause of the Injury (Unsafe act/Unsafe condition): Plot disc chart in terms of percentage of unsafe acts and unsafe conditions.

(iii) Injury occurred in which part: For this human anatomy chart can be used to clearly visible to all.
Attached the human anatomy chart.

(iv) Location of the Injury: Plot various locations (Plant areawise) *Vs*. No of injury in the locations.

(v) Time of the Injury: (a) Plot time of the injury Vs. No of injury. (b) Plot No. of Injury *Vs*. Office hours (0900 - 1700) and Non-office hours.

(vi) Status of the Injured: No. of Injury *Vs*. Employees and contractors and can be combined whether the injured are male or female.

By consolidating all the information, we can exactly identify the point where we focus our concentration to eliminate the potential hazard.

Injury Analysis Data ...
No. of Injuries - 2005/2006

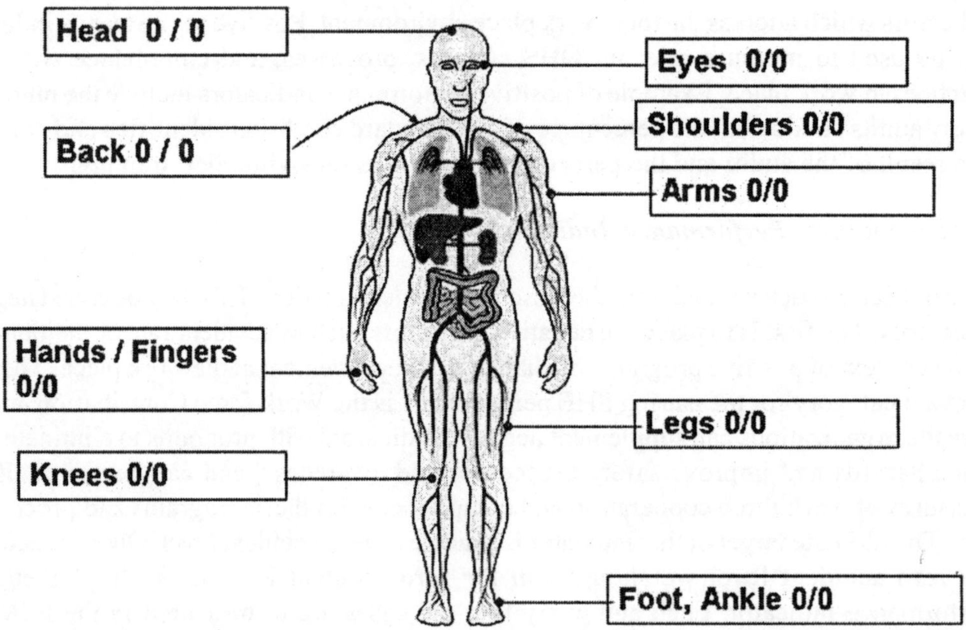

Measurements

'You can't manage what you can't measure'- Drucker

'If you don't know where you are going, chances are you will end up somewhere else'-Yogi Berra

Measurement is a key step in any management process and forms the basis of continual improvement. If measurement is not carried out properly, the effectiveness of the management system is undermined and there is no reliable information to inform managers how well the health, safety and environment risks are controlled.

The guidance on measuring health, safety and environmental performance is organized under these main headings.

1. Why measure?
2. What to measure?
3. When to measure?
4. Who should measure?
5. How to measure?

Why to Measure?

Measurements are essential for providing information assuring questions arising from performance indicators, decision-making and addressing different information needs.

The primary purpose of measuring SHE performance is to provide information on the progress and current status of the strategies, processes and activities used by an organization to control risks to safety, health and environment.

Measurement information sustains the operation and development of the SHE Management system, and so the control of risk, by

(i) Providing information on how the system operates in practice.
(ii) Identify the area where the remedial action is required.
(iii) Providing the basis for continual improvements.
(iv) Providing feedback and motivation.

What to Measure?

Measurement should reflect the performance indicators status. However it should cover the following criteria:

1. Measuring the hazard burden.
2. Measuring the health and safety management system.
3. Measuring failure-reactive monitoring.
4. Measuring the SHE culture.
5. Planning and implementation.

When to Measure?

Measuring SHE is a going activity. It is to be consider the following criteria:

1. Suitable intervals to ensure that specific planned milestone are achieved.
2. Where intervals for monitoring are prescribed by legislation?
3. Where there is evidence that there is non-compliance/compliance?
4. The relative frequency and time at which a particular activity takes place.
5. The potential for change from the state to another over-time.

Who should Measure Performance?

Organizations need to decide how to allocate responsibilities for both active and reactive monitoring of performance at different levels in the management chain. The management should be given responsibility for monitoring the achievement of plans and objectives and compliance with standards for which they and their subordinates are responsible for direct implementation of standards should monitor compliance in detail and be competent to do so.

How to Measure the Performance?

The foundation of effective performance measurement is an effective planning system which produces specifications and performance standards for the management arrangements and risk control systems. These provide yardsticks for the measurements process.

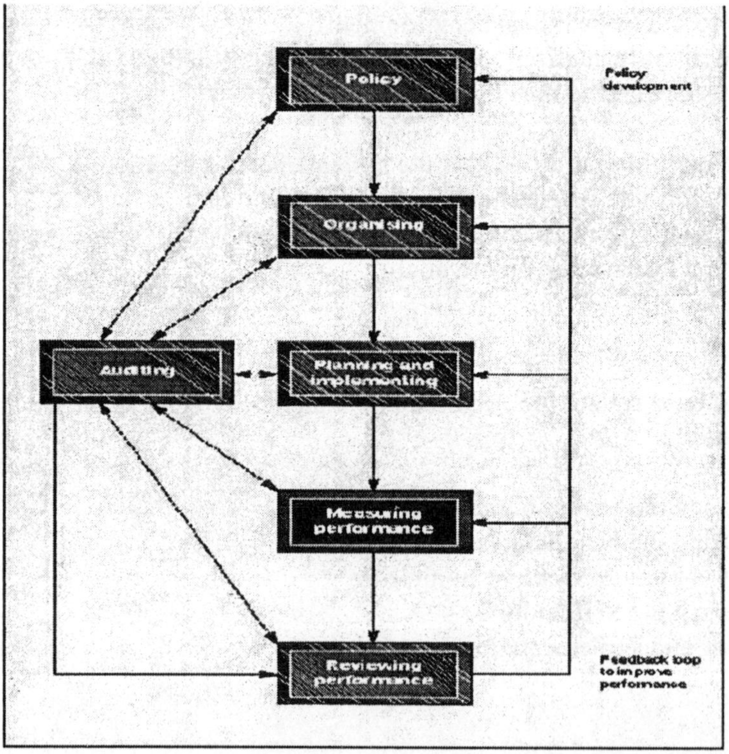

The measurement process can gather information through:

1. Direct observation of conditions and of people's behaviour;
2. Talking to people to elicit facts and their experiences as well as gauging their views and opinions; and
3. Examining written reports, documents and records.

Attached the Performance measurement within the SHE Management System.

Barriers for OHS&EM

The tabular column given below describes briefly about the factors contributing effective management system and barriers of each contribution

Factors Contributing to Effective OHSMS	Barriers to Effective OHSMS
A. Type of System	
Customised to organisation's needs	Off-the-shelf system imposed without modification
Developed with support and involvement of all organisation stakeholders	Imposed by senior management without consultation
Safe place/Innovative system	Safe person/Traditional system
B. Internal Organisational Factors	
(i) Management Commitment	
Strong senior management involvement	Delegation of OHS responsibility to line & OHS management positions
OHSMS introduced to improve OHS	Introduced & supported for non-OHS reasons
Provision of adequate resources	Inadequate resources
OHS integral to management performance appraisals	Limited accountability mechanisms
Leading by example	Words unsupported by practice
(ii) Integration into Management Systems	
All organisational functions incorporate OHS	OHSMS activities marginalised
(iii)Employee Involvement	
All employees encouraged and capable of participation	OHS restricted to 'technical' experts Inadequate training of employees in OHS & in consultation
Independent representation of employees encouraged and supported	Selective employee involvement at management's discretion
(iv) Workforce Characteristics	
Stable workforce	High labour turnover, extensive casual and part-time workforce Reliance upon and exclusion of labour hire employees from OHSMS
C. Nature of Organisation	
Larger organisation familiar with systems and with adequate resources	Small business, with limited resources and unfamiliar with systems concept
Stable workplace	Labour hire company with employees working between multiple client sites Disorganisation of work associated with presence of labour hire employees and contractors
D. Contractor Relations	
Principal contractor works with subcontractor to develop compatible OHSMS	Principal contractor simply requires subcontractor to have OHSMS Principal contractor simply imposes their OHSMS on subcontractor Sub-contractor's OHSMS inconsistent with principal's OHSMS
E. Audits and Audit Tools	
Appropriately used audits can verify and validate OHSMS and facilitate continuous improvement	Inappropriately used audits encourage 'paper systems' and an instrumentalist approach to OHSMS
Adequate audit tools are tailored to organisational needs and reflect key OHSMS success factors	Inadequate audit tools support mediocre OHSMS
Audit processes are robust and auditors are technically competent	Quality-style audit processes and inadequate auditor skills limit audit comprehensiveness
Audits are integrated within a comprehensive approach to measurement	Use of audits as the primary measurement tool

Barriers to Success

To establish the business in global market, management commitment should be dedicated to sustainability and social responsibility.

Well defined SHE Policy must be framed and to be reviewed periodically. To over come the above barriers all the points are to be specifically addressed in management reviews. Second barrier to success is training and motivation. It should be covered to all the levels including labours. Since the level of understanding is low to most of the labours, we should patiently encourage them to develop our expected level. Third barrier to success is the Audit tools. The audit tool should frame in such a manner to identify the positive points and scope for improvements. Audit should not be done to find the false alone.

Future Development on SHE Success

To strengthen the SHE Management system, it needs to promote

— Establishment for effective implementation
— Guidelines on establishing 'Best Practices'
— Promoting SHE hazard management.

The objective of the SHE Management system should focus improvement by the way of Safe work culture, systematize practices, sustainable development in environment and innovative management concept.

Conclusion

Most of the organized industrial sectors in India implemented the integrated Safety, Health and Environment Management system. Now the system implemented managements feel the benefit in terms of risk reduction, environmental protection and cost saving. The benefits are reflected in the annual reports which satisfy all the stake holders.

This paper briefly explained the process of SHE Management system, how to establish the performance indicators and measurements to enhance/activate the performance indicators. We expect 'Best SHE Practices' in India in near future.

REFERENCES

Occupational Health and Safety Management System - A review of their effectiveness in securing healthy and safe work places by Clare Gallagher, Elsa Under hill, Malcom Rimmer.

A guide to measuring health and safety performance - Health and Safety Executive, December 2001.

Positive Performance indicators for OHS - Beyond lost time injuries - Part-I Issues.

Positive Performance indicators for OHS Summary paper - Verna Blewertt.

Positive role for OHS Performance Measurement - Dr. Roy Green, Director Employment Studies Centre, University of New Castle.

DGFASLI Web site - Statewise fatal and non-fatal injuries in Factories.

Opportunities/Strategies and tactics for going beyond time injuries - Stewart Sweeney, Elton Mayo School of Management and University of South Australia.

INDUSTRIAL HYGIENE: INDIAN *VERSUS* GLOBAL PERSPECTIVE

Swati Jadav*

Introduction

Globally, the graph for the Need of Industrial Health and Safety has always progressed and improved. The Safe Working Environment as well as its Attitude, not only leads towards increased *Productivity*, but also provides an Industry with measurable and quantifiable *Profitability*.

Today, the knowledge as well as the requirement of Industrial Health and Safety is growing very fast. "Industrial Hygiene" is an upcoming field, which is being practiced successfully across the Globe past century, provides *Concrete* path and creates *Firm* Platform for the "to the mark" achievement in the Safety and Health, both.

Industrial hygiene is the science of anticipating, recognizing, evaluating, and controlling workplace conditions that may cause workers' injury or illness. Industrial hygienists use Workplace Exposure Assessment and Monitoring along with the specialized Analytical Methods (not the bulk analysis methodologies) to detect the extent of worker exposure and employ engineering, work practice controls, training, awareness, process changes as well as other technical and administrative methods to control potential health hazards existing and further anticipated in the industries.

There has been an awareness of Industrial Hygiene, past centuries across the Globe, may it be the direct recognition as Industrial Hygiene or through Employees' Health and Safety Aspect. The workplace environment and its relation to the employees' health was recognized as early as the fourth century BC when Hippocrates noted lead toxicity in the mining industry. In the first century AD, Pliny the Elder, a Roman scholar, devised a facemask made from an animal bladder to protect workers from exposure to dust and lead fumes.

*Division Head, Industrial Hygiene Services, Baroda.

Benefits of Industrial Hygiene

Occupational illness costs are very much difficult to estimate and thus there are many reasons for industrial hygiene to take a backseat to safety-related issues in general. Industrial Hygiene exposures often are transparent and chronic, which makes them more difficult to recognize and report. In addition, occupational illnesses also are difficult to trace back to a specific source.

An Industrial Hygiene Workplace Exposure Assessment Programme can help the industries to:

- Prevent work related illnesses thereby reducing the lost workdays and workers' compensation costs;
- Increase the awareness, willingness and interest in the Safety, Health and Industrial Hygiene Aspects within the employees;
- Improve the working standards within the work premises; and
- Increase the productivity.

Basically, if seen, Industrial Hygiene is not just the Air, Noise or Heat Stress Monitoring within the workplace. It goes much more far, then these specified and specific parameters. It also includes following and much more:

- *Effective Hazard Communication* - where effectiveness plays an important role especially while communicating the hazardous situations, works, exposures in a good, acceptable language and thus, creating the Positive Attitude of the employees towards Safety, Health and Industrial Hygiene.
  Effective Hazard Communication - Integrity of Information Communication, as such a very simple word which is used and practiced in day-to-day life. Communication, enhances and destroys the relations, brings profits as well as loss to business, cures as well as creates many problems between people, and much more. Industrial Communication though may be a part of regular communication, but has a specific and very important hold from the top line employees to the last line employees. Industrial Communication has its own importance as it incorporates multi-emotional techniques as well as specialties.
  When Industrial Communication is further converged on it's specific sub-category, i.e. Hazard Communication - the relevance, importance and effectiveness comes into limelight. Hazard Communication is as such combination of two big fields in its own, i.e. Hazards (Health, Safety Aspects) and Communication.
  Current scenario in any industrial setup for the hazard communication is either class-room training or notice boards or material safety data sheets or face-to-face meeting. No doubt, the current traditional methodology, is not wrong, but with the changing world what becomes more important is "The Effectiveness and the Integrity" of the Hazard Communication.
  The main components of the Effective Hazard Communication includes: (1) Target Audience (2) The Speaker (3) The Methodology (4) The Content and Context and

(5) The Reason for the Communication. The Professional Analysis of these components determines the Effectiveness of Hazard Communication.

Visual Aids for Hazard Communication is very powerful communication media and is often overlooked. Charts, slides, videos or films provide an immediate and clear message. Electronic means of communication are increasingly becoming more relevant, now-a-days. It becomes more relevant when the SHE video films are produced/made specifically for the particular company. The SHE Training Programmes should be specifically designed departmentwise including photographs and original case studies. Material Safety Data Sheets (MSDS) is a vital part of Chemical Hazard Communication till last level of employee. It becomes more and more necessary to have an Effective, Small, Complete, Approachable MSDS within the workplace. Further, its an Art and Science to present MSDS in Pictorial Format or one page local language Format.

Thus, if the Hazard Communication, when designed, conducted and evaluated based on specific requirements of the Industry, then the Integrity and Importance of the Information which is intended to be transferred remains intact. This becomes more powerful and to-the-target approach for conducting an effective hazard communication. *Clear communication is not easy, but also not impossible*!. The method, context, structure, language, knowledge and an understanding of the needs of the recipients to whom the information is being transmitted are vital in understanding the importance of Effective Hazard Communication in any organization.

- *Real Time Ergonomics* - where the ergonomics is no more just "Back Pain". Ergonomics is considered and hailed beyond Back Pain, in synonymous terms like Productivity, Profitability, Positive Human Behavior Change, Primary Insight towards doing things in correct ways and much more...
- *Industrial Training and Education* - where training is no more "One : All", i.e. synonymous to boring lectures, classroom attendance, return of the college life. No, Training and Education is enlightenment of the employees, through practical sessions, active and willing involvement of both the trainers and the participants and much more ahead is through the practical tailor-made training videos.

Industrial Hygiene - Walk Towards Productivity and Profitability

Linking Industrial Hygiene to Productivity and Profitability is not at all wrong as "An healthy and safe workplace and employee will definitely give optimum output". Though Safety and Industrial Hygiene are more or less mistaken as one and the same, their lies a very thin but significant differentiation between the both. Industrial Hygiene Exposure Assessments not only reduces the exposure levels and provides a comfortable working environment to the employee it also creates Baseline Data for any industrial setup as well as provides an indepth insight regarding the unseen and hidden losses, too.

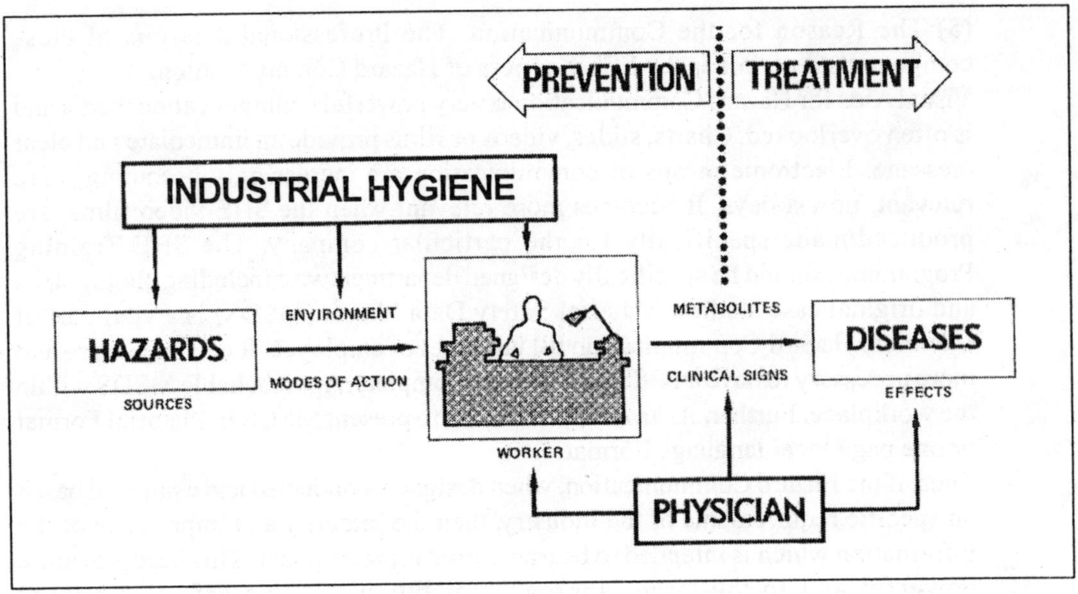

The Employee - Nucleus of the Industrial Growth

Employee, which is considered as the nucleus of the industrial growth, may he/she representing top management or the last line staff, contributes more or less equally for the growth and progress of any industry. If we look back and have a thought, all the major accidents, industrial deaths, occupational impaired health caused to the employees, could have been able to restricted or rather avoided. This avoidance or restrictions could only have been possible with timely awareness and regular watch on the exposures and specific exposures causing impaired health of the employee.

Present Scenario of Industrial Hygiene in Indian Industries

Past decade, the awareness of Industrial Hygiene in India, have been on its top move. Many industries have now been thinking in terms of Industrial Hygiene apart from the Safety Aspect. And those industries have concretely seen the benefits, too. Till past few years, Indian Industries have been hiring International Industrial Hygienists or the Corporate Offices of the respective industries, have been providing their Corporate Industrial Hygienists to their Indian and other Asian Offices. But now, the entire, scenario have changed. These valuable services are available locally to the Indian Market, itself, at the Indian Prices, affordable to Indian Industries. It would not be wrong, if we say, that locally the service providers are providing the services, equivalent to the International Standards and Requirements.

Employer Liability and Base Line Database

Industrial Hygiene Workplace Exposure Assessment Baseline Data have much more uses than thought of. This Data when used along with the Regular Medical Surveillance Data, correlation between the onset or existing of any occupational diseases could be derived very easily and in advance. Further, this Baseline Data will provide industry with an concrete initial platform for the exposure scenario within the working complex. It also helps industries to recognize, identify, know, evaluate numerically abnormal conditions prevailing within the workplace area. Regular Workplace Exposure Assessment will provide the organization a graph regarding the working conditions, engineering controls effectiveness as well as health status of the employees.

Future Requirements for Growth of Industrial Hygiene in India

- Review of the Occupational Safety and Health Legislation.
- Improvement in enforcement of Occupational Safety and Health Legislation.
- Nation-wide awareness and promotional activities on Industrial Hygiene.
- To accelerate the process of providing Industrial Hygiene Services in organized sectors, government may initiate local level organizations with industrialists, medical professionals, and researchers and trade unions as partners.
- The public-private partnerships are very much important and integral part of the success of this goal.
- Provide recognition or license to the private consulting sectors. Accreditation to the private consultants will enhance the outreach and willingness of the Industries for Industrial Hygiene related services as well as enforcement of the extensive and planned Industrial Hygiene Programmes.

31

APPROACH TO BEHAVIOURAL SAFETY

Somesh Sarkar*

ABSTRACT

Behavioural safety is one of the important tools which can be used for improving the safety culture of the organization. This will help to supervisors/managers to achieve best results in terms of productivity and quality improvement, reduction in absenteeism, follow up of safety guidelines. The entire work culture is improved by the way of imparting a behavioural safety culture. If behavioural problems are ignored or inappropriately handled, there will be adverse effects on entire system. In order to combat this situation behavioural safety is considered to be a very important tool which will help in maintaining good safety culture and over all improvement.

Accidents are caused by a sequence of events that includes five different stages - Strategic, Technical, Operational, Behavioural and Defensive.

As per the study conducted by H.W. Heinrich about 80 per cent of accidents are caused by unsafe acts and conditions that is to say most of the accidents happen due to unsafe behaviours of persons. As such it is essential to control unsafe behaviours to reduce the rate of accidents. To practice a behavioural safety it is essential to work in close coordination with employees including contract workers and address the safety, health and environmental aspects in a proper way.

Safety efforts and performance of the organization can be measured by Safety Assessment. Based on the findings of safety assessment action plan to improve and maintain the highest safety status can be prepared. Adoption of behavioural safety observation process helps to create safe work culture.

Introduction

A critical challenge to the manager's productivity effort lies in the area of uncooperative subordinate behaviour. The few employees who refuse to cooperate, who come to work late, who argue over the assignments, who fail to follow the direction and who are chronic rule violators, provide constant barrier to productivity. Some employees have family difficulties; others may suffer from alcoholism, drug dependency or a variety of physical or psychological ailments. All these personal difficulties have the potential to interfere with the workers'

*Functional Head (Fire, Safety & Environment), Ispat IIndustries Ltd., Dolvi - Pen, Raigad-Maharashtra-402 107, India.

abilities to satisfactorily perform their jobs. Such behavioural problems if ignored or inappropriately handled by the shop managers, they may result in various organizational problems such as loss of productivity; increase in absenteeism; deterioration of quality of product or services; ignorance of safety guidelines; disobeying of company policies, procedures, rules; and ultimately affecting the entire work culture and there by leading to increased incidents which may cause damage to assets, injury to persons or it may even lead to loss of lives.

Details

Accident Causation Chain: Accidents are caused by a sequence of events that encompasses five discrete stages.

Strategic - Technical - Operational - Behavioural - Defensive

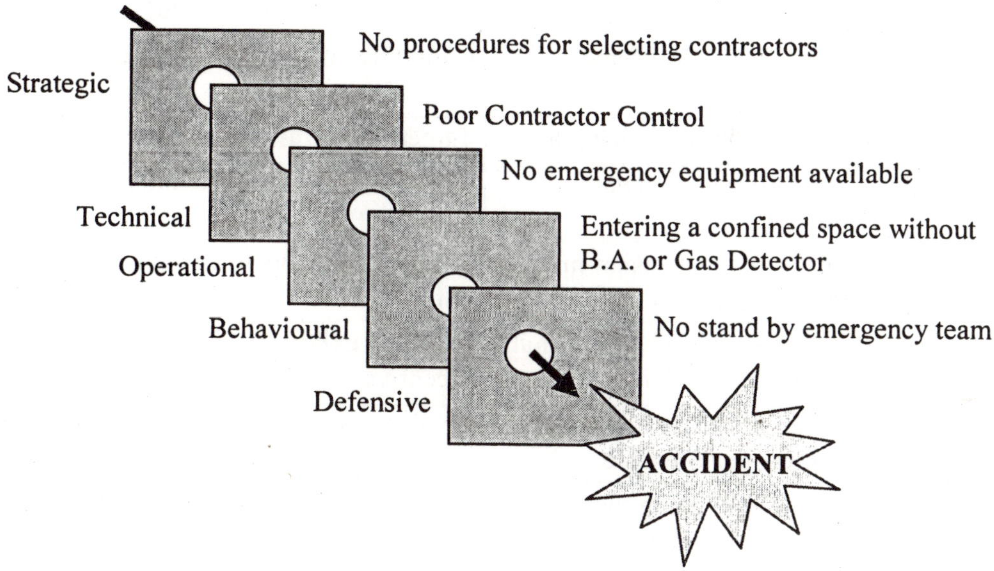

Behaviour and the Accident Causation Chain

To avoid accidents the first step is to Stop the unsafe behaviours and then examine the organizations management systems that are causing that behaviours.

Unsafe behaviours can be stopped by analyzing unsafe behaviours; pinpointing desired safe behaviours, measuring safe behaviours on daily basis; giving feed back to peoples, supervisor recognition for having No accidents/injuries.

Consequences and Behaviour

Consequences always follow behaviour. Consequence either strengthens behaviour or weakens behaviour.

The main factors affecting consequences are Timing, Consistency, and Perceived Value.

Consequences reinforce behaviour in different ways:

- Positive consequences reinforce and increase the desired behaviour.
- Alleviating consequences reinforce and increase the desired behaviour to a certain point.
- Punishment decreases the undesired behaviour.
- No consequence for a behaviour tends to extinguish behaviour.

Difference Between Behavioural Safety and Traditional Safety Process

Behavioural Safety differs from traditional safety in following respects -

Sl.No.	*Behavioural Safety*	*Traditional Safety*
1	Involves significant workforce participation.	Generally Top Down directives.
2	Targets specific unsafe behaviours.	Targets every aspect of safety.
3	Is based on observational data collection.	Are reactive to accident and injury rates.
4	Involves data-driven decision-making processes.	Sole reliance on line-management for enforcement.
5	Involves a systematic, observational, improvement intervention.	Involves exhortations to be 'Safe' and incentives for injury free days.
6	Involves regular focused feedback about on-going performance.	Involves punishment for non-compliance.
7	Requires visible on-going support from all management levels.	Requires visible on-going support from all management levels.

Understand Current Safety Efforts

To understand current safety efforts it is required to conduct a Safety Assessment. It serves the followings -

Provides an accurate understanding of current safety efforts; Helps induce commitment to the improvement process; Helps the implementation plan to build on existing efforts; Identify High Risk Areas; Identify Training needs.

Method of Conducting a Safety Assessment

1. Review Safety Data (Statistics and Actual Accident Reports)

Activity	*Observation*	*Action*
Review safety reports that summarize incident data	a. The rate of recordable injuries b. Areas with high injury rates	Compare with industry average. Interview people in high risk areas.
Review individual accident / incident reports	a. Tasks and equipment involved in injuries. b. Management systems involved in injuries	Prepare questions about high risk tasks / areas. Prepare questions about management system failures. Begin to identify tasks to include in observation process.
Collect data on accident, compensation and property damage costs	Calculation of specific and average costs per incident	Estimate cost savings that may result from reduced accident rates.

2. Conducting Interviews

Conduct interviews of senior managers, Front-line management and Employees to access actual facts.
To conduct interviews develop a set of questionnaire and related standards.

Behavioural Safety Readiness Survey: It can be done as follows -

	Motivation	*Ability*
Individual	Am I happy to behave safely?	Do I know how to behave safely?
Team	How a team does responds if person behaves safely?	Will others provide the help, authority, information and resources I need to behave safely?
Organisation	What rewards are available for good safety performance?	Do our structures, systems or our environment, facilitate or block us from behaving safely?

3. ***Review of Safety Meetings*** - Develop set of questionnaire -

Are the meetings well run?
Do they actually discuss safety issues?
Do they develop remedial actions?

4. ***Observe Weekly Safety Inspections*** - Do these focus on conditions or behaviour or both?

5. ***Observe Safety Practices in Work Areas*** - Develop Questionnaire -

Are they safe/unsafe?
How do people react to the observations?
How do the observers react to safe/unsafe behaviours?

6. ***Analyse Safety Culture in Focus Groups***

Organisational Behavioural Pattern

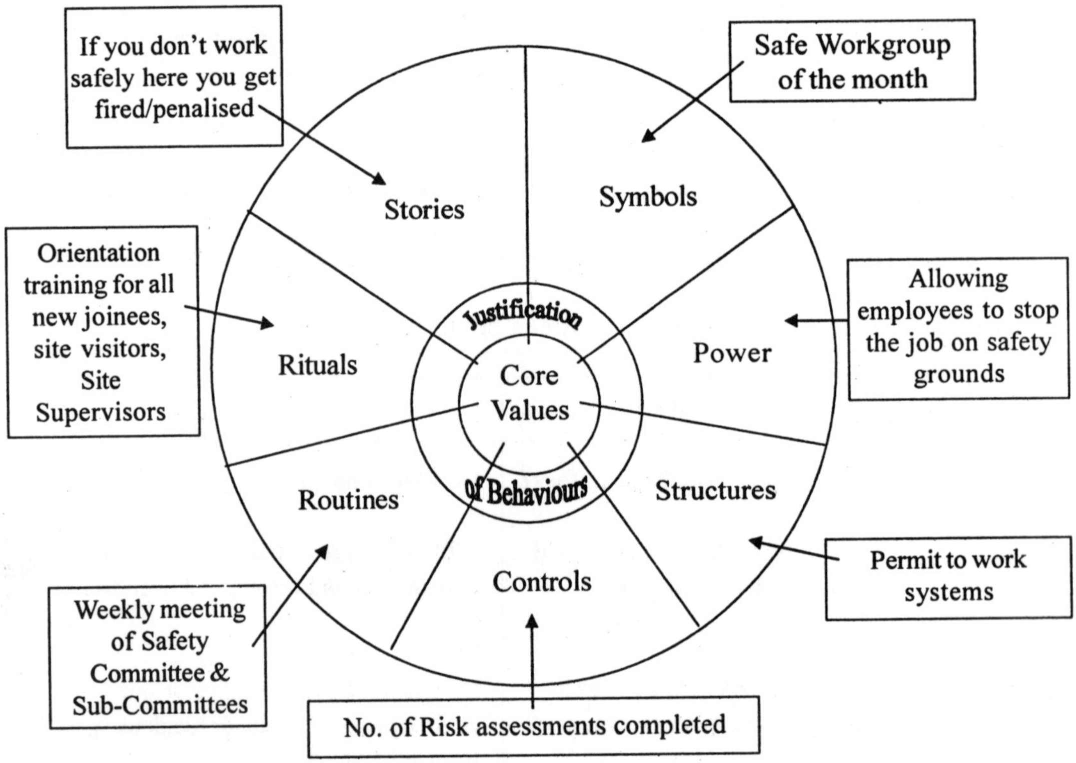

7. Core Underlying Assumptions about Safety

Negative	*Positive*
Cost too much	Good for business.
Safety is a bolt-on extra	Safety is the number one priority.
Required by law	Legal compliance is the absolute minimum standard.
Too much effort for too little return	Safety as an integral part of the management system.

8. *Collect and Analyse Information about Current Processes* - in respect to -

- How well they are working and where they are not
- Recommendations in general, and specific to behavioural safety

9. Develop Final Report by Providing Implementation Guidelines -

- Pinpointing unsafe behaviours
- Creating the safety observation process
- Feedback and employee involvement
- Safety awards
- Supplemental programs

Creating Behavioural Safety Observation Process

A behavioural safety observation process involves significant workforce participation.

To Create a Behavioural Safety Observation Process -

—Address Scope of the project

- Which Business/Departments will be involved?
- Who will be involved?

Management/Employees/Contractors

- Who will run project?

Employee led Project Team? / Employee led steering committee?

- What resources are required?

Fully/well equipped office, Observers, Remedial Action Resources, Time.

It is important to get Management agreement on these issues.

—Form Project Teams

- Employee led steering committees -
  It includes 5 - 12 peoples (Part time). Out of total members at least 70 per cent should be employees and each person has different roles (Checklist developers, ambassadors, observers, data entry/computation, etc.).
  Advantage of employee led steering committees is it gives site wide representation but it leads to slow decision-making.
- Employee led project team -
  It includes full time project co-coordinator from Employees. There can be separate co-coordinator from each department and there will be Project Champion who could be a Sr. Manager or so.

Advantages of Employee led project team are -

- Only two people can run the project
- It Minimizes resources
- It Speeds up decision-making

And main disadvantages are it induces -

- Huge work load for one co-coordinator
- Project could fail if co-coordinator remains absent.

Observational Approaches

Workgroup (Team)

Develop checklist to cover activities of entire workgroup. Monitor whole workgroup everyday at work for 15 - 20 minutes. Provide verbal feedback at point of observation.

Self-management: Employees develop their own checklist, monitor themselves, and provide their own feedback.

Pinpoint Safe Practices

Scrutinize Previous Accident Records on the basis of -

Location of Accident
Types of Injury
Place on Body

Examine Standard Operating Procedures, Examine risk assessments and Brainstorm with personnel.

Draft and revise observation Checklists

- Only include Safe practices on the checklists
- Categorize behaviours (e.g. Housekeeping, PPE, Forklift Driving)

Do NOT Provide any means to record peoples names

Train Observers

Train observers on following -

- How to observe
- How to use checklist
- How to calculate per cent safe Score
- How to give verbal feedback
- Practical Onsite Field Observation
- Feedback about checklist/Observation Process

The purpose of training observers is to -

- Fine tune checklist
- Allows observers to practice their observation skills
- Ensure inter - observer reliability (strike for > 95 %)
- Check mechanism for picking up/dropping off checklists

Trained observers have to practice for a week until all are comfortable with the task

During this observation verify that checklist distribution system works properly and ensure feedback charts are available and are in place.

At the end of the practice period observers have to use next four weeks data to establish a baseline. This provides picture of how safe everyone is working.

At the end of baseline period set safety improvement targets.

Target setting with workgroups (Teams)

Target setting with workgroup takes place after a workgroup's observer has established a baseline to find out the current levels of Safety Performance (30 - 45 Minutes) and targets are set for a fixed period of time (4 - 6 months).

Target setting meetings includes - The purpose of the meeting, How the observation checklists were developed, How the per cent safe score is calculated, Informing the workgroup of their per cent safe baseline score, Highlighting any improvements that could be made, Setting a challenging but achievable target and Thanking everybody for their time and effort.

Conclusion

Behavioural Safety is an effective tool to prevent accidents by controlling unsafe acts and unsafe conditions and there by maintaining highest safety standards. On the contrary if behavioural safety problems are not properly observed by the shop manager they may result in various organizational problems which affects the production; quality of product; increase in absenteeism; ignorance of safety guidelines; disobeying of company policies, procedures and rules; which intern affects work culture.

To practice behavioural safety it is essential to work in close coordination with employees and contract workers by selecting the right coordinator and addressing the safety, health and environmental aspects at work.

Behavioural safety influences employee safety behaviour, accident rates and remedial actions. Hence it is required to stop the unsafe behaviours first and then examine the organizations management systems which cause such unsafe behaviour. The primary role of the senior management is essential in shaping the employee behaviour and shaping lower management behaviour which has got a direct impact on employee behaviour.

REFERENCE

International Business Conferences (IBC, Inc.) workshop on "Behavioural Safety", by Prof. Dominic Cooper (Indiana University, Bloomington, USA), Mumbai, November 2005.

IMPACT OF IMPLEMENTATION OF "OCCUPATIONAL HEALTH AND SAFETY MANAGEMENT SYSTEM (OHSAS:18001)" IN INTEGRATED STEEL PLANTS

Sateesh Kumar Atluri*

ABSTRACT

With increased awareness of Occupational Health and Safety in the country, Organisations have started attaching importance for achieving high Occupational Health and Safety (OHS) performance just as they do for their performance in other aspects of business. Improvement in Occupational Health and Safety performance are possible with adaptation of a structured system approach like **"Occupational Health and Safety Management System (OHSAS:18001)"**. It provides guidelines on structural approach in determination of Risk Levels associated with Hazards in each activity. It emphasizes on Pro-Active Approach for improvement in safe work environment. OHS Management not only improves the confidence of the workers in the plant but also builds the image of the company in India and Abroad. Being the product produced under the safety net it gives confidence to the overseas customers also. Steel industry being highly hazardous, effects of implementation of OHSAS:18001 and results achieved are dwelled in this paper.

Introduction

The economy of any nation depends on strong base of Iron and Steel industry. Countries having a strong potentiality for Iron and Steel production have played a prominent role in the advancement of civilization in the world. Consumption of the steel is one of the index of the economic development of the country. Steel is versatile and indispensable item. Steel making process in integrated steel plants involves conversion of raw materials into finished products at one place under single administrative control. Integrated steel plants are capital intensive and labour intensive.

Amongst all the manufacturing industries Steel Industry is the most hazardous one. The steel making process involves handling of huge quantities of raw materials, hot metal,

*AMIE (Mech.), MBA(Mktg.), Junior Manager (Safety), Safety Engineering Department, Visakhapatnam Steel Plant.

liquid steel, finished products, etc., which involves many hazards. The gases evolved in the process of steel making are also to be handled safely, otherwise they may create hazards to the personnel working in the plant and also to the people residing in the nearby surroundings. It is because of all these ill effects, there are chances of life threat and health hazards to the employees working in the industry.

Objectives of the Paper

- To understand the hazards of an integrated Steel Plant
- To know about concept of OHSAS 18001
- To observe the safety and occupational health practices before implementation of OHSMS
- To observe the safety and occupational health practices after implementation of OHSMS
- To analyse the impact and results of implementation of OHSMS.

Hazards in an Integrated Steel Plant

In spite of considering safety aspects of the equipments in the design stage itself in modern steel plants with the state of art of technology, during process of steel making, many hazards will be encountered. The following are some of the identified hazards .

- Hazards due to spillage of Hot Metal and Liquid Steel
- Hazards associated with leakage of by-product gases like Coke Oven gas, Blast Furnace Gas, LD Gas etc.
- Heat Hazards
- Hazards due to Working at Heights
- Fire and Explosion Hazards
- Material Handling Hazards
- Electrical Hazards
- Chemical Hazards
- Burns due to hot metal/hot objects
- Slip and Fall of material on persons
- Slip and Fall of persons
- Health hazard due to exposure of Dust Hazards
- Health hazard due to exposure of Noise.

For managing these hazards "occupational health and safety management system" becomes key function of the top management. Steel Plants manages the above safety and health hazards with the help of Safety Engineering Department and Occupational Health Centres by proper control measures to reduce/eliminate hazards for maintaining the safe and healthy environment to its workforce. Though, elimination of Unsafe Conditions/Unsafe Practices, Meeting the Legal requirements are being complied by Safety Engineering Department, there is need for system support to move the things systematically and qualitatively with responsibility by the respective managers. Then, Occupational Health and

Safety Management System (OHSMS) is as per Occupational Health and Safety Assessment Series (OHSAS-18001) come into picture which has an international recognition.

Concepts of Occupational Health and Safety Management System (OHSAS:18001)

The Occupational Health and Safety Management System - Specification as per Occupational Health and Safety Assessment Series 18001:1999, have been developed by British Standards Institute in response to customers demand for recognisable Occupational Health and Safety Standard against which their management systems can be assessed and certified. This Occupational Health and Safety Assessment Series (OHSAS) specification gives requirements for an Occupational Health and Safety (OH&S) Management System, to enable an organisation to control its Occupational Health and Safety Risks and improve its performance.

Important Clauses of OHSAS : 18001

1.0 Scope
2.0 Reference Publications
3.0 Terms & Definitions
4.0 OH & S Management System Elements
4.1 General Requirement
4.2 OH & S Policy
4.3 Planning
4.3.1 Planning for hazard identification, risk assessment and risk control
4.3.2 Legal and other requirements
4.3.3 Objectives
4.3.4 OH & S Management programme(s)
4.4 Implementation & operation
4.4.1 Structure and responsibilities
4.4.2 Training, awareness and competence
4.4.3 Consultation & communication
4.4.4 Documentation
4.4.5 Document and data control
4.4.6 Operational Control
4.4.7 Emergency preparedness and response
4.5 Checking and corrective action
4.5.1 Performance measurement and monitoring
4.5.2 Accidents, incidents, non-conformances and corrective and preventive action
4.5.3 Records and records management
4.5.4 Audit
4.6 Management Review

Impact of Implementation of OHSAS in Integrated Steel Plants

For better understanding of this topic, we will now study the case of Visakhapatnam Steel Plant (VSP) which happens to be the First Integrated Steel Plant in India in getting OSH AS:18001 certification in January 2002. This is a voluntary effort of the Management to implement OHSAS:18001 for improving the Occupational Health and Safety Standards. Implementation of OHSAS:18001 involves lot of documentation, monitoring of the controls, record and record management, besides Identification of Hazards, Risk Assessment and providing necessary control measures.

Visakhapatnam steel plant is the most modern integrated steel plant with annual liquid steel capacity of 3 MT located on the coast of Bay of Bengal, 16 km to the South-West of Visakhapatnam, Andhra Pradesh. The total area of plant and township is 9219 hectares with regular and contract manpower of around 20,000.

The following are some of the special features of Visakhapatnam steel plant:

1. 7m tall coke oven batteries with coke dry quenching.
2. 2 Nos. of biggest Blast Furnaces with 3200m^3 use full volume with bell less top charging.
3. 100 per cent slag granulation at BF cast house itself.
3. Suppressed LD gas recovery system.
4. 100 per cent Continuous Casting System.
5. On line heat treated products by means of Tempcore and Stelmore Cooling processes in Light and Medium Merchant Mill and Wire Rod Mill respectively.
6. Extensive waste heat recovery through Back Pressure Turbine Station and Gas Expansion Turbine Station.
7. Comprehensive pollution control measures.

Various cross-sections of employees from all departments participated in the preparation of OHSMS Documents, Procedures, implementation and maintenance of the same. It has been observed that OHSAS:18001 implementation has brought significant change in the safety culture and over all standards of Occupational Health and Safety. All activities of Visakhapatnam Steel Plant are identified, listed out, rationalised and Hazards involved in each activity are identified. The Risk Assessment Process is carried out for each Hazard. Proper control measures are listed out for every hazard and responsibility of monitoring of controls is fixed and is being done at defined intervals by designated personnel.

VSP before Implementation of OHSMS

In VSP Safety Engineering department was established as a nodal agency to take care of personnel safety, operational safety and other legal requirements. To bring safety awareness among the regular employees as well as contractor workers. Safety awareness programmes and safety training programmes are being conducted by safety engineering department. For reduction or elimination of unsafe conditions, safety inspections are carried out by zonal safety officers. The inspection reports are submitted to the concerned HODs from time to time for the liquidation of the same.

If any reportable accidents occur, all the relevant statutory formats are submitted with in the stipulated time to the concerned authorities. Accidents are investigated and remedial measures are suggested. These remedial measures are implemented by the concerned departments. Internal safety audits are conducted for major departments once in six months by a team consisting of Zonal Safety Officer, concerned departmental officers from operation, Mechanical & Electrical. Audit findings are submitted to the concerned HOD for taking corrective actions. A copy of Audit report is also given to higher management.

Personal Protective Equipment like safety helmets, safety shoes, fire retardant coats, face shields, dust masks, ear plugs, ear muffs, etc. are procured and issued to employees according to the requirements. Safety Engineering Department liaisons with the Factories Department and comply with all the legal requirements as per the statute. One central safety committee and 25 departmental safety committees are constituted, to discuss the safety related problems and to suggest remedial measures. To monitor the health conditions of all employees. The Occupational Health and Research centre was established. It carries out periodical medical examination of the employees and maintains the health records.

VSP after Implementation of OHSMS

To plug the gaps in safety management systems, VSP being the initiator, adopted OHSAS prior to any other steel major. Within a short span, with voluntary involvement of every cross-section of employees and guidance of M/s. BVQI, VSP achieved the herculean task of getting OHSAS-18001 certification in January, 2002. To its credit most of the lacunas in previous system like a weak link of follow up activities, lack of involvement of different personnel, etc. are fulfilled by well defined and documented procedures and Hazard Identification and Risk Assessments (HIRAs), defined responsibilities to the specified individuals etc.

Thus, the implementation of OHSAS brought the following major changes in the system to work towards achieving the fundamental goal of any organisation to provide safe and healthy work environment to its employees.

Activities of each department are identified and rationalised. Around 2122 Nos. of Hazard Identification and Risk Assessments were carried out and risk level is estimated. As all the Hazards of the activities and control measures are documented and available, the persons performing that activity are aware of the hazards and risk control measures. According to the risk level the controls are monitored by concerned persons and recorded.

Objectives for each department are set and management porogrammes made to achieve them. Each department prepared procedures for carrying out the jobs safely. Proactive measures like finding out deficiencies through safety inspections by Zonal Safety Officers along with the shop representative and liquidation of the same by the concerned are carried out systematically as per the documented procedure. Check lists are prepared for inspection of different equipments like conveyor, cranes, lifts, locomotives, transfer cars, shop-floors, contractual works, etc.

All the incidents and near misses are also being recorded now. Every accident and incident are investigated for the root causes and remedial measures are implemented.

Whenever any accident occurs in an activity, HIRA of that activity is reviewed and if required additional control measures are incorporated. A monthly report on remedial measures of Incidents and Accidents is prepared and widely circulated to all HODs for implementation of the remedial measures if similar situations are prevailing in their shops also. Accidents mentioned in the monthly report are discussed in the departmental safety meetings to go to the grassroots level of the employees. The status of implementation is reviewed periodically by the Zonal Safety Officer.

High Quality Personal Protective Equipment (PPE) are procured and are issued to the shop personnel as per requirement. Customer complaints regarding PPEs are recorded and attended. Material Safety Data Sheets (MSDS) were prepared for all chemicals used in the plant.

On site Emergency plan is prepared and implemented. Departmental persons are trained to fight against the Emergencies. Emergency preparedness is tested by conducting mock drills for fire and other emergencies at departmental level and at plant level. Mock-drills are also conducted for Electric shock, Snake Bite, Fall from height, etc. Deficiencies noticed during the mock drills are noted and corrected in the forth coming mock-drills.

Occupational Health & Safety Management System is audited once in three months by Qualified Internal Auditors and once in six months by Eternal Auditors (M/s. BVQI). The non-conformities raised are liquidated to improve the system. The status of the OHSMS is reviewed at Departmental level by HODs once in a month and at Plant level by Chief Executive and Chief Management Representative once in two months.

Impact/Benefits Accrued Through OHSAS-18001

After Implementation of OHSAS-18001 there is a visible improvement in the safety awareness among the shop-floor employees. Involvement of the departmental persons in improving and implementing safety measures have considerably increased. As Hazard Identification and Risk Assessment (HIRA) sheets were prepared for all the activities and control measures are monitored, the hazards associated while performing such jobs have considerably reduced. As all incidents are also noted, investigated and remedial measures are implemented as a whole, this has helped in reducing the occurrence of accidents.

By the implementation of systematic documented procedures the following spectacular results are achieved:

- OHSAS has increased the face value of the organisation and brand value of products in domestic and international market.
- Safety function has been understood and recognized as a staff function. Better co-ordination established between safety personnel and departmental personnel.
- Now shop personnel have accepted and recognized that safety of their work place and their workmen is also one of the prime functions as important as their production function.
- Departments are taking challenging, measurable safety objectives and management programmes and fulfilling them every year.
- OHSMS laid the clear delegation of responsibility. All the activities of shop floor are owned by the department itself.

- Implementation of OHSAS has given good indication to the employees that company is concerned about their health and safe work environment.
- Incidents and near misses are now captured and preventive actions are implemented. This is clearly helping in reduction of serious accidents.
- Implementation of remedial measures of Incidents/Accidents is being done globally. This means even though accident happened in one department, if such situations are applicable to other department the remedial measures are implemented so that such incident/accident will not occur. The review/revision of HIRAs helped in controlling the recurrence of similar accidents.
- Information sought from the other steel plants regarding accidents/incidents and suitable remedial measures are implemented in the applicable areas for preventing such type of accidents in our plant.
- It is because of extensive awareness training programmes, given to various categories of employees, there had been a significant change in their out look and attitude towards safety and occupational health.
- A legal manual consisting of all relevant acts were available with concerned persons which helps them in complying the statues in time and making them to understand the implications.
- Frequent audits of OHSAS are helping the department in continual improvement from the OHS angle.
- An OHS policy expressing the concern and commitment signed by Chief Executive is distributed to the employees and interested parties.
- All the process built-in-safety systems were kept in order and if it is required to be by-passed, a systematic documented procedure is followed with proper authorization. This made the system more practical.
- VSP is now geared up to meet any eventualities by periodic mock drills for fire, electric shock, gas poisoning, snake bite, rescuing person from height, etc.
- Work environment surveys like noise, heat, etc. are carried out to measure the present levels. Corrective actions were taken to bring them to the permissible levels by applying engineering controls. Where engineering controls are not feasible persons are provided with the required personnel protective equipment to reduce the intensity of hazard.
- MSDS are prepared for 105 hazardous chemicals and displayed/made available to the users, so that they are well aware of the hazards and precautions to be taken incase of emergency.
- All the statutory requirements are brought into the system. Because of this, the requirements are periodically reviewed by the designated person and requirements are complied, without any slipout.
- Non-conformances/Observations pointed out during internal/external OHSMS audits are implemented in all departments wherever such situations prevail. This is resulting in improving the safe working environment.
- "Zero Fatal Accident" for both regular & contractual employees
  - for a period of 22 months from June 2001 to April 2003
  - for a period of 19 months from Oct. 2003 to May 2005
- "Zero Fatal Accident for Regular Employees" in 2005.

- " Zero Accident" achieved :

Sl. No.	Year	No. of Zero Accident Departments
01	2005	18
02	2004	19
03	2003	15
04	2002	14

- Accident Free Million Man-Hours Achieved:

Sl. No.	Year	1 Million Accident Free Man hours	2 Million Accident Free Man hours	3 Million Accident Free Man hours	4 Million Accident Free Man hours
01	2005	07 times	04 times	—	01 time
02	2004	08 times	—	01 time	—
03	2003	10 times	02 times	01 time	—
04	2002	10 times	—	—	—

- Frequency Rate of Accidents has come down from 2.16 in the year 2002 to 1.32 in the year 2005.
- Incident Rate of Accidents has come down from 6.6 in the year 2002 to 3.17 in the year 2005.
- Reportable Accidents in 2005 are reduced by 23 per cent when compared to 2004.
- VSP received appreciation award from A.P. Government and N.S.C, AP Chapter in recognition of the efforts made by VSP collective for achieving high standards in Occupational Health and Safety.
- 'SAIL Chairman's Silver Plaque' for No Fatal accident in the year 2002.
- 'Green Tech Silver Safety Award' in steel sector 2002-03.
- 'Ispat Suraksha Puraskar' for No Fatal Accident in 2004.
- Leadership and Excellence Award in SHE from CII -2004.

Conclusion

As the size of the company grows, the difficulty in providing a safe environment to every individual worker is also growing. Truly the efforts of a department like Safety, some cross section of employees like Unions, Top management or few individuals cannot a provide a complete safe environment to all the employees. It is possible to provide a complete safe environment to all employees and contract workers and other connected people in and around a work place, only by implementing a system but not by any other means. When this system is comprehensive & effective and results of implementation are positive any organisation will accept and adopt the same.

Hence, after the critical study of the above case, it is clearly visible that the Implementation of "Occupational Health and Safety Management System" in integrated Steel Plants is a wise move towards a fair expectation of establishing a standard safety system and reduction of accidents. Therefore, this time-tested system which is meticulously developed, implemented and maintained can be adopted in all other Steel Plants.

REFERENCES

OHSAS-18001 Specification.

Orientation and Training guide for Management Trainees of Visakhapatnam Steel Plant.

33

TERRORISM AND ITS IMPACT ON THE SOCIETY

Lt. Gen. B.S. Dhaliwal*

The world today is a witness to unabated increase in terrorism and related use of bomb attacks which is not likely to change in the foreseeable future, since terrorism is slowly becoming all pervasive. Future conflicts will not be fought by a set of rules but unfortunately will be aimed at the masses. This is therefore a clear indication of the emergence of a new dimension of terrorism as lately witnessed in USA, UK, Iraq and India. This is making it all the more necessary for the security forces to update their overall knowledge of terror tactics and be a step ahead of the anti-national elements (ANEs) while countering them. Hence, there is a need for all of us to contribute implicitly and whole-heartedly towards this growing concern. Spreading terror by attacking the innocent public through bomb blasts, Improvised Explosive Device (IED) blasts or by using Nuclear Biological Chemical agents or conventional explosives.

The usage of bombs/IEDs is as old as the history of warfare itself and is in fact a modern name for booby traps and the likes. The use of IEDs by ANEs with tacit support from vested interests is a global phenomenon. It has spun a worldwide web and is steadily growing both in lethality and sophistication. Security forces, civil populace and sensitive installations are being targeted alike. The availability of munitions in the form of commercially made/home made explosives as the main charge and easy availability of sophisticated technology for triggering devices have made IEDs a potent and destructive tool in the hands of ANEs.

Taking any bomb/IED blast amongst the civil populace as a test case. The post-blast analysis systematically unfolds the facts, which indicate the links between various ANEs involvement of techno-savvy youths and other experts in explosive handling interlaced with the alleged involvement of other support cadres. The reason for highlighting this aspect is to stress upon the alleged links between all these categories of people involved in the spread

*AVSM, VSM, Engineer-in-Chief

of a reign of terror. If one has to quarantine such groups and neutralize their activities, there is a requirement of even greater coordination between various agencies which include not only those manned by the security forces but also with NGOs and the media, so as to act simultaneously to defeat the perpetrators of such a heinous crimes against the society.

Our security forces have been engaged in a low intensity conflicts for over 15 years and have gained a lot of experience. However, due to a variety of reasons beyond ones control, we have not been able to arrest the spread of terror. It has rather multiplied in a geometric progression in its spread and lethality. Countries like UK, USA, Israel, Spain, Indonesia, parts of Africa and India have been combating terror for quite some time now. In order to take a quantum jump in this direction, we need to look at the methods being employed by UK, USA and Israel critically and take a cue from them as regards intelligence gathering and sharing, their concepts, organizations, equipment philosophy (to include civil defence organizations) and post-blast analysis. These need to be translated to suit Indian conditions.

Focusing on to India, if we have to seriously improve our records in the field of counter IED operations, it is high time an integrated approach is taken in sharing of actionable intelligence on a real time basis, employing all available resources for IED handling and analysis; and most importantly speedy action. Unless this menace is struck down with a heavy hand, ingress of terror to destroy the basic fabric of our civilized society will be a foregone conclusion. The best option is not to let the terrorist succeed in carrying out blasts. This can be achieved if there is a lateral sharing of info between various agencies at appropriate levels. For example, the action taken by Delhi Police to involve the coolies, taxi drivers and shopkeepers for obtaining information is a very practical method. Some awareness programmes need to be run, the media needs to be coopted and requisite infrastructure created to involve the civil populace in stemming the tide of terror attacks. We thus need to appreciate the need of the time and restructure the existing system of security management by examining the strengths and weaknesses of various agencies and integrating all available resources. The employment of security forces should not get restricted due to tedious procedures and narrow outlook because of their current modus operandi in watertight compartments. The macro aim of combating terrorism at the national and international level should not be lost sight of.

As regards IED handling equipment is concerned, we are slowly reaching a level of self-sufficiency. With the technical expertise and guidance of Public Sector Undertakings and College of Military Engineering (CME), Pune, a Jammer-cum-Initiator vehicle has already been developed which is presently undergoing field trials. Research and Design (R&D) (Engineers), Pune has also come out with a remotely operated vehicle for which user assisted technical trial has already been completed. Once indigenized, its cost will almost come down by one-third. We need to understand that the war on terror is very dynamic and has a major component which is reactionary. The ANEs are taking advantage of the easily available advanced technology to avoid detection by the equipment being used by Security Forces. In fact, it is here that the challenge lies for R & D and all the firms manufacturing marketing counter IED equipments. They need to correctly analyse the ground requirements and give us technically advanced equipment. On our part, we must interact, advise and provide them the relevant inputs. At present there is a void in the area of miniaturization of IED equipments which can be remotely employed in restricted spaces of aircrafts or trains. We are also looking for more sensitive and effective hand held equipments for X-ray scan and vapour detection. The need to out wit the ANEs mind is crucial in order to make a difference.

Most Indians feel that the action taken against perpetrators of terror has to be quick and severe and they should not be spared at any cost. But, in order to nab them, apart from good intelligence network, we need to have swift post-blast analysis. We should not forget that there is a human mind behind all the terrorist acts which brings in variation in type of explosives, or initiation mechanism and mode of placing. In view of the limited number of forensic laboratories, more so in the present context, when the terror has already spread to almost all parts of the country, establishment of field analysis centres, can really help reducing the OODA loop. Training hubs like CME and NSG should also have facilities for analyzing post-blast samples and we should work towards establishment of such a facility.

Today we have reached the threshold of tolerance. Loss of innocent lives in hundreds and thousands will reach uncontrollable limits unless a deliberate step is taken to fight a coordinated battle by employing all available resources. Constant and timely up-gradation of equipment is a must. Simultaneously, the man behind the machine has to be imparted the right kind of training by bringing in variety and ingenuity so that he is confident to operate in any type of situation.

It is time for all institutions to join hands so that we can jointly contribute in a significant way to counter IEDs, likely to be encountered in the future.

ACHIEVING SAFETY AND OCCUPATIONAL HEALTH THROUGH EFFECTIVE CONTRACT CONDITIONS - EXPERIENCES OF DELHI METRO RAILWAY PROJECT

L. Baskaran*

ABSTRACT

Delhi Metro Rail Corporation engaged in construction of Mass Rapid Transit System started its construction activity on 1st October 1998. Realising the importance to maintain highest safety standards DMRC engaged international safety experts to guide the contractors to adopt safe work procedures. Even though all main contractors adopted DMRC safety guidelines, some of the sub- and sub-sub-contractors could not be better controlled which resulted in many fatalities. At the end of Phase-I in 2005-06 after constructing 65 km DMRC has started to construct another 85 km in Phase-II before 2010. This uphill task has made DMRC to critically analyse all fatalities of Phase-I and bring out more stringent, accountable contract conditions on Safety, Health and Environment. This paper highlights the salient observations of the analysis of fatalities of Phase-I construction accidents and Phase-II contract conditions on SHE, which will help, many organisations to adopt.

Delhi Metro Need and Master Plan

Delhi became the capital of India in 1912. In those days, it was a clean, beautiful city where everyone loved to live. Over the years, the city has undergone a sea change. Made initially to cater to a population of 70,000; the total urban population of Delhi is now around 14 million. As cities grow in size, the number of motor vehicles and consequently the number of vehicular trips on road systems go up, leading to severe congestion on the roads. This necessitated a pragmatic policy shift to discourage private modes and encourage public transport once the level of traffic along any travel corridor in one direction exceeds 20,000 persons per hour. To ensure that the metropolis' growing need of mass transport is looked

*DGM/Safety, Delhi Metro Rail Corporation, NBCC Place, Pragathi Vihar, New Delhi-110 003
E-Mial : lbaskaran@dmrc.org

after and also to make provisions for the future, a comprehensive study was completed in 1990. The study brought out the need for a rail-based transit system, which is not only capital intensive but also has long gestation periods. The Revised Master Plan for Delhi Metro has recommended a Metro Network of 8 lines and 244 kms to be implemented in four phases. The Government gave clearance for taking up the first phase of the Metro System covering three lines spanning 65.10 kms with an estimated completion cost of Rs. 10,571 crores (US $ 2.1 Bn). The Phase-I is expected to carry about 1.5 million commuters eventually.

Genesis of DMRC

Delhi Metro Rail Corporation was registered in may 1995 under the Companies Act, 1956. It has equal equity participation of Government of India and the Delhi State Government. DMRC, not falling within the category of a Public Sector Undertaking, is vested with greater autonomy and powers to execute this gigantic project involving many technical complexities, under difficult urban environment and within a very limited time frame.

The Journey thus far

Construction of Delhi Metro Project began on 1st October 1998, marking the physical commencement of the project. Since then, Delhi Metro has become a long way and has crossed various landmarks in completing its Phase-I covering three lines.

Line No.	*Total Length (in kms)*	*Underground (in kms)*	*Elevated (in kms)*	*At - Grade (in kms)*	*No. of stations*
Line 1 - Shahdara - Rithala	22.0	0.0	17.50	4.5	18
Line 2 - Vishwavidyalaya - Central Secretariat	11.0	11.0	0.0	0.0	10
Line 3 - Indraprastha - Barakamba Road - Dwarka	32.1	2.17	29.93	0.0	30
Total	65.10	13.17	47.43	4.5	58

The alignment of Mass Rapid Rail Transport System (MRTS) passes through the arterial roads and densely populated urban areas. Most of the viaduct work for elevated corridors were to be carried out within a barricaded area of width between 8 to 8.5 m only as a minimum of 2 lanes are to be left in each way for the existing road traffic. The entire tunnelling work for underground corridors was to be carried below the thickly populated Old Delhi areas. Century old structures, which were present above the influence area of the alignment, were to be protected. Construction methods of the underground stations depend to a large extent on the geological profile of the area. Two types of state-of-the-art Tunnel Boring Machines have been used for boring tunnels after conducting geological studies of the earth. These are the Rock TBMs for boring through Quartzite rock sections encountered at places like Chavri Bazar, Central Secretariat and Old Secretariat and EPBM (Earth Pressure Balance Machines) for boring through softer soil. All stations except Chawri

Construction Methodology

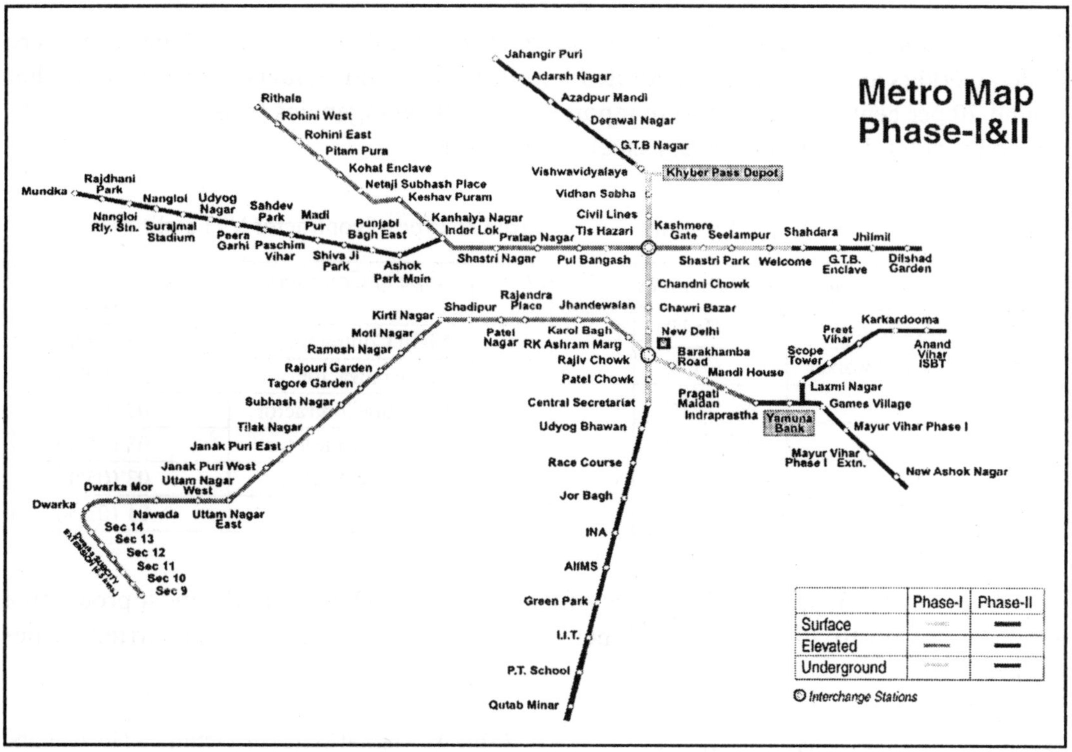

Bazar were constructed with this method. It simply implies 'covering' open the ground along the length of the station to the required depth, construction of the underground station and 'covering' it back to bury below the ground. Since the Chavri Bazaar station is located in a heavily built up area, there was no space availability on ground for 'cutting' open the ground along the length of the station. So, the station was constructed by underground mining using the New Austrian Tunnelling Method. Two vertical shafts were constructed in the available small spaces, which were then connected by underground in the available small spaces, which were then connected by underground mining and excavation.

DMRC engaged national and international safety experts to effectively monitor the safe construction practices adopted. Since 1998 till 2005, 66km of MRTS corridors has been constructed and put to operation. This gigantic task involved more than 250 million man-hours of construction. Many national and international contractors were working with DMRC in Phase-I. Even though all main contractors adopted DMRC safety guidelines, some of the sub and sub-sub-contractors could not be better controlled which resulted in many fatalities. At the end of Phase-I an analysis of all the 55 fatalities were carried out in order to understand the cause for those accidents and to incorporate prompt remedial measures in the conditions of contract for Phase-II.

Analysis of Phase-I Fatal Accidents

Table-1 shows that 57 per cent of the fatalities were unskilled workers, 16 per cent were skilled workers and 9 per cent constituted for electricians and welders. Table-2 shows that around 70 per cent of fatalities were reported from all sub-agencies (sub-contractors, sub-sub-contractors, labour contracts, casual labourers etc.)

Table 1: Occupation Vs No. of Fatalities

Sl No	*Occupation*	*No of Fatalities*
1.	Skilled worker	09 (16%)
2.	Unskilled worker	31 (57%)
3.	Electrician	03 (05%)
4.	Welder	02 (04%)
5.	Driver	03 (05%)
6.	Others	07 (13%)

Table 2: Type of contractor Vs Fatalities

Sl. No.	*Type of Contractor*	*No of Fatal Accidents*
1	Main Contractor	13 (24%)
2	Sub-Contractor	32 (59%)
3	Sub-sub-Contractor	03 (05%)
4	Labour Contractor	03 (05%)
5	Adjacent Workers	03 (05%)
6	Visitors	01 (02%)

As per Table-3, around 43 per cent of the persons died belong to the most productive age group of up to 25 years and 33 per cent of total fatalities were unmarried as per Table 4.

Table 3 : Age of Victim Vs No. of Fatalities

Sl. No.	*Age of Victim (in Years)*	*No of Fatalities*
1.	Up to 25	24 (43%)
2.	25 – 30	08 (15%)
3.	30 – 40	17 (31%)
4.	40 – 50	05 (09%)
5.	More than 50	01 (02%)

Table 4 : Marital Status of Victim Vs No. of Fatal Accidents

Sl. No.	*Marital Status of Victim*	*No of Fatal Accidents*
1	Married	37 (67%)
2	Unmarried	18 (33%)

Table 5 shows the cause of fatal accidents. The analysis of cause of accidents reveals that around 36 per cent of fatalities were due to either fall from height or fall of materials, 25 per cent of fatalities were due to hit of moving vehicles and 9 per cent of fatalities due to electrocution.

Table 5: Causes of Accident Vs No. of Fatalities

Sl. No.	*Causes of accident*	*No of Fatalities*
1.	Asphyxiations	01 (02%)
2.	Caught in between / pressed /thrown out	06 (11%)
3.	Collapse of earth work	02 (04%)
4.	Collapse of structures	04 (07%)
5.	Electrocution	06 (09%)
6.	Fall from height	10 (18%)
7.	Fall of material	10 (18%)
8.	Fire / burns	01 (02%)
9.	Hit and run over by vehicle	14 (25%)
10.	Ill health (Heart attack)	01 (02%)

Around 43 per cent of the fatal accidents occurred during 0600 hrs to 1400 hrs and 24 per cent of the fatal accidents occurred between 0000hrs to 0600.hrs as per Table 6 and around 25 per cent of the fatal accidents were occurred on Saturday as per Table 7.

Table 6: Time Vs No. of Fatalities

Sl. No.	*Time of Accident (in hrs)*	*No of Fatalities*
1	0000 – 0600	13 (24%)
2	0600 – 1400	24 (43%)
3	1400 – 1900	12 (22%)
4	1900 – 0000	06 (11%)

Table 7: Day Vs No. of Fatalities

Sl. No.	*Day of Accident*	*No of Fatalities*
1	Sunday	02 (04%)
2	Monday	10 (18%)
3	Tuesday	05 (09%)
4	Wednesday	10 (18%)
5	Thursday	06 (11%)
6	Friday	08 (15%)
7	Saturday	14 (25%)

Table 8, shows that around 32 per cent of the fatal accidents occurred between 6th to 10th of any month. According to Table 9, in 38 per cent of fatal accidents the persons were found spot dead and around 31 per cent died within 5 hours after the occurrence of accident.

Table 8: Date of Accident Vs No. of Fatal accidents

Sl. No.	*Date of Accident*	*No of Fatal accidents*
1	1 – 5	05 (09%)
2	6 – 10	17 (32%)
3	11 – 15	10 (18%)
4	16 – 20	09 (16%)
5	21 – 25	05 (09%)
6	26 – 31	09 (16%)

Table 9: Lead-time Available Vs No of Fatalities

Sl. No.	*Lead-time available before death*	*No of Fatalities*
1	Spot dead	21 (38%)
2	Less than 5 hrs	17 (31%)
3	5 – 24 hrs	10 (18%)
4	More than 24 hrs	07 (13%)

Table 10 reveals that 15 per cent of fatal accidents occurred during the month of December and no fatal accidents were observed during the month of May.

Table 10: Month of Year Vs No of Fatal accidents

Sl. No.	*Month of Year*	*No of Fatal accidents*
1	January	02 (04%)
2	February	04 (07%)
3	March	07 (13%)
4	April	06 (11%)
5	May	00
6	June	05 (09%)
7	July	05 (09%)
8	August	05 (09%)
9	September	06 (11%)
10	October	04 (07%)
11	November	03 (05%)
12	December	08 (15%)

Phase-I Learning and Remedial Measures for Phase-II

The main observations and remedial measures to be incorporated in phase-II contracts based on the causes of fatalities occurred in Phase-I, are as follows:

Sl No.	*Observation in Phase-I*	*Phase-II : Reason / Remedy Proposed*
1.	57 per cent of persons died were unskilled workers. Only 24 pe cent of fatalities occurred with main contractors and 69 pe cent of fatalities belonged to sub-contractors, sub-sub-contractors and labour contractors.	(i) The main contractors were directly bound by DMRC safety conditions. In turn the main contractor did not ensure the same degree of importance to safety by all sub-agencies. In order to avoid these situations it has been made mandatory to the main contractor to provide the required safety manpower to all sub-contract works by himself accepting direct responsibility. (ii) Minimum educational qualification and experience prescribed based on contract value for safety organisation. (iii) Daily Safety Oath and Induction training made mandatory to all.
2. (a)	36 per cent of fatalities occurred due to either fall from height of fall of materials.	Working at Height continues to be a critical safety issue. Hence international guidelines (Work at Height Regulations 2005, UK and OSHA standards) have been exclusively included in the contract conditions on safety appropriately.

Contd. ...

Sl No.	*Observation in Phase-I*	*Phase-II : Reason / Remedy Proposed*
(b)	25 per cent of fatalities occurred due to hit and run over by vehicles (including Hydras)	Training on Defensive Driving for all vehicle drivers had been made mandatory. This training for duration of 8 hours is provided along with field test at Delhi Government and Maruti, Institute of Driver Training & Research, Wazirabad Road, Adjoining Loni Road Flyover, Delhi-94. This step will help reduce accidents due to unsafe driving. This training is mandatory for all vehicles used by contractors.
(c)	9 per cent of fatalities occurred due to electrocutions	(i) Many electrocutions occurred due to sub-standard DGs of sub-contractors. Hence a contract condition is made to supply power from a central source by the main contractor to the sub-contracts. This will reduce noise also apart from ensuring better safety. (ii) IP44 electrical fixtures made compulsory even for any small temporary jobs.
3.	43 per cent of persons died were in the most productive age group of upto 25 yrs and 15 per cent in the age group of 25-30.	(i) Daily Safety Oath shall help to make the youngsters more responsible. (ii) Poster campaigns are also planned to make youngsters more responsible by contractors.
4.	Almost 33 per cent of victims were unmarried	(iii) Counselling by industrial psychiatrists are also be planned to create awareness to youngsters on their social responsibility.
5.	35 per cent accidents occurred in the night time between 1900-0600 hrs	(i) Minimum lighting level for different locations at site has been prescribed. (ii) Portable handheld digital lux-meter made mandatory to be provided to safety department by contractors, to ensure required lighting. (iii) Monthly lighting safety audit made mandatory
6.	25 per cent (maximum) occurred on Saturday.	The effect of weekly wage day (Saturday) shall be monitored by contractors.
7.	15 per cent of fatality (maximum in any month) occurred in December.	Effect of cold weather shall be monitored by the contractors, if any.
8.	38 per cent of persons spot dead after an accident. 31 per cent of persons died in less than 5 hours from the time of occurrence of accident.	(i) It is pertinent to note that 31 per cent of fatalities occurred within 5 hrs. after the incidence took place. Probably had there been best medicare facility provided many would have been saved. Hence as per BOCWA and DBOCR, Ambulance room, occupational health center, hospital tie-ups made compulsory (ii) In case if the contractor fails to provide the above the same will be provided by DMRC by evolving a common scheme to all contractors through external agency at the cost of the contractor.

Salient Parameters of the Conditions of Contract on she for Phase-II

These conditions were framed after a through study of existing contract conditions of organizations like: NTPC, BHEL, SAIL, GAIL and a few international firms. There are 58 clauses included in Version 1.2 of the Conditions of Contract on Safety, Health and Environment document, which is to be issued as a part of any tender document for Phase-II works. The salient parameters in each clause are summarized below:

Abbreviations used in this document:

BOCWA	-	The Building and Other Construction Workers (Regulation of Employment and Conditions of Service) Act, 1996
BOCWR	-	The Building and Other Construction Workers (Regulation of Employment and Conditions of Service) Central Rules, 1998
DBOCWR	-	The Delhi Building and Other Construction Workers (Regulation of Employment and Conditions of Service) Rules, 2002

Clause No.	*Clause Title*	*Salient Parameters*
Part-She Managemet		
1.	General	Application and purpose of the document explained. The meaning of usage of 'shall, should and may' have also been specifically explained.
2.	SHE targets and goals	Every contract shall aim zero total recordable injuries and least disturbance to the environment and road traffic.
3.	Compliance	(i) Normally contractors do not attach more importance to safety items given in the contract document and due to oversight either tend to ignore it or does not read and understand it. To make the contractor binding to read all the provisions thoroughly, a specific MOU is introduced, which is to be executed before award of the contract. (ii) Contractor shall develop thorough understanding about BOCW Act, 1996, Central Rules 1998, Delhi Government Rules 2002, Building and Other Construction Workers' Welfare Cess Act, 1996 and Central Rules, 1998 and Delhi Building Construction Workers' Welfare Board Rules, not only to satisfy the Inspectors' perspective but the use of legislation as the strong tool for effective SHE management at construction worksites. In order to familiarise the Act and Rules quickly the related sections and rules were tabulated and given in the contract condition itself as a ready reckoner. The copy of the same is given in ANNEXE NO.: 1 at the end of the paper. (iii) The contractor shall ensure that all his employees/workmen are covered under 'Workmen Compensation Act'. (iv) Every contract shall aim to achieve ISO 14000 and OHSAS 18000

Contd....

Clause No.	*Clause Title*	*Salient Parameters*
Part-She Managemet		
4.	Contractor SHE policy and plan	(i) SHE policy and plan as per Section 39 of BOCWA*. (ii) Within 4 weeks of the notification of acceptance of the tender, the Contractor shall submit a detailed and comprehensive Contract specific SHE Plan for approval. (iii) Minimum Contents of SHE plan are detailed out. (iv) Penalty for late submissions, non-distribution to all supervisors/Managers and non-updating prescribed.
5.	Designer's role	Designer shall enlist all SHE risks in the drawing itself.
6.	Contractor SHE organisation	(i) Minimum qualification, minimum experience and number of posts in different cadres required for the contractor' SHE organisation are provided. (Refer the general instructions : DMRC/SHE/GI/001/ MPR/281105 and DMRC/SHE/GI/002/QE/ 281105) (ii) In order to effectively interact with the Employer and the statutory departments enforcing the labour welfare legislations, every contractor shall employ a full time "Labour Welfare Officer" duly qualified and experienced. (iii) Including the works executed by sub, sub-sub and petty contractors, the main contractor shall provide safety personnel for effective monitoring. (Clause 4.4) (iv) If the contractor fails to provide safety manpower the Employer will provide the same at the cost of contractor and any administrative expenses involved in the process like manpower consultant charges will be deducted from contractor bills. (v) Every contractor shall provide minimum facilities like computer and projector, camera, handheld lux meter, sound level meter, loud speaker for conduction safety oath and tool-box talks, for Safety organisation as per DMRC/SHE/GI/003/AVE/ 28112005). (vi) Penalty for non-compliance of above.
7.	Contractor SHE committee	(i) To be constituted within 14 days of award of contract and noted to the Employer. (ii) SHE committee meeting to be conducted once in every month and minimum periodicity in between any two meetings shall be 21 days. (iii) Penalty for not attending the meeting by any member as Rs.5000/- (iv) Minutes of meetings to be sent within 2 days to all concerned including DMRC.
8.	ID card and first day at work SHE, orientation training	(i) Format for ID card of size 85 × 55 mm to be issued for all personnel shall be provided as per DMRC/SHE/ GI/005/IDC/ 281105. (ii) Induction training for all newly joined employees. (iii) Personal SHE handbook to be issued for all employees by the contractor.

Contd....

Clause No.	*Clause Title*	*Salient Parameters*
Part-She Managemet		
9.	SHE training	(i) Daily Safety Oath by all employees to be taken during start of the work/day. (ii) Toolbox talk for all high risk workmen every time (iii) Training to all employees as per the matrix provided (iv) Training to drivers (including crane and hydra operators) on defensive driving at Delhi Government and Maruti Institute for Driver Training and Research, Delhi made mandatory. (v) Skill development training for work at height, crane safety, welding safety and electrical safety for all workmen/foremen. (vi) Once in six months refresher training to all. (vii) If the contractor fails to impart training the same will be done through accredited agencies at the cost of contractor.
10.	SHE inspection	(i) Detailed guidelines given for 4 types of inspections: planned general, routine, specific and other inspections. (ii) Involvement of competent persons as per statutory provision for specific inspection of lifting appliances and gears once in 6 months.
11.	SHE audit	(i) Monthly Audit Rating Score (MARS) to be conducted once in every month as per the audit format covering 20 major items provided by DMRC. (ii) Monthly electrical safety audit to be conducted jointly by SHE (Electrical) Engineer and DMRC's representative (iii) External SHE audits to be conducted once in 3 months by engaging international audit organisations with the approval of Employer.
12.	SHE communication	(i) Important days to be observed for creating safety awareness throughout the year have been prescribed. (Ref: DMRC/SHE/GI/008/DAY/281105) (ii) Requirements of posters and signage to be displayed as per DMRC/SHE/GI/009/PS/281105)
13.	SHE submittals to Employer	(i) Daily reporting of total no. of workmen within 2 hours of start of shift. (ii) Monthly SHE report. (iii) SHE committee meeting minutes. (iv) SHE inspection reports. (v) SHE audit reports. a. Monthly audit rating score (MARS) report. b. External SHE audit. c. Electrical safety audit. (vi) Air and noise quality monitoring report.

Contd...

Clause No.	*Clause Title*	*Salient Parameters*
Part-She Managemet		
14.	Reporting of accidents to Employer and Government organization	(i) All accidents and dangerous occurrences shall be immediately be informed verbally to the Employer and as per the format within 24 hours to the same (ii) Reporting to the Govt. organisations as per Rule 210 of BOCWR (iii) Heavy penalty for either delay in reporting or suppression of accidents.
15	Emergency preparedness plan	(i) Procedures to be drafted and practiced incase of fire, collapse of lifting appliance and transport equipment, collapse of building structure, gas/dangerous substance leak, drowning of workers, landslides, bomb/terrorist attack. (ii) Periodical mock-drill is made mandatory. (iii) Arrangements for emergency medical treatment and evacuation of the victim. (iv) Contractors' tie-up with hospitals and fire stations in the neighbourhood for attending casualties.
16.	Experts/Agencies for SHE services	Service of SHE experts/agencies for the purpose of training, audit and other SHE services as per Rule 297 of DBOCWR provided for easy reference of the contractors vide DMRC/SHE/GI/010/AE/ 281105
PART-II : SAFETY		
17.	Housekeeping	(i) Cleanliness is next to Godliness. (ii) General housekeeping to be carried out at all times and the same shall be ensured by the housekeeping team of the contractor throughout the site including offices, store rooms, toilets etc. (iii) Barriers and barricades to be provided to prevent the surrounding area from excavated soil, debris etc that may cause inconvenience to and endanger the public. (iv) Maintenance of worksites including barricades by the contactor in good condition with aesthetic appearance (v) Penalty for bentonite splashing over the road (vi) If the contractor fails to maintain good housekeeping the same will be done through external agency at the cost of the contractor.
18.	Working at height	All conditions regarding work at height complying to Work at Height Regulations, 2005, UK have been redrafted to suit our requirements and provided.
19.	Overhead protection	Protection against falling objects as per Rule 41 of BOCWR stating the minimum requirements which shall be followed for (i) Overhead protection along the periphery of the building/ structure. (ii) Guarding of inadvertent hazardous areas.

Contd....

Clause No.	*Clause Title*	*Salient Parameters*
Part-She Managemet		
20.	Slipping, tripping, cutting, drowing and falling hazards	Compliance as per Rule 42 of BOCWR stating the following: (i) Environmental Condition where work to be undertaken (ii) Fall protection equipments such as safety nets where fall is possible in accordance with national / international standards
21.	Lifting appliance and gears	Safety requirements for lifting operations which includes: (i) Safety test certificates for crane, hooks, shackles, pulley/ chain blocks, ropes and slings etc. (ii) As stipulated in Rule 57 of DBOCW Rules, every lifting appliances and gears like cranes, hydras etc, if so constructed that the safe working load may be varied by raising or lowering of the jib or otherwise shall be attached with an automatic safe load indicator (ASLI) approved by Bureau of Indian standards/International certifying bodies which gives a warning to the operator and arrests further movements of the lifting parts. (iii) Other requirements such as laminated photocopies of fitness certificates, competency certificates to be kept with the operator. (iv) Once in 6 months all lifting appliances shall be tested and certified by competent person.
22.	Launching operation	(i) Method statement to be prepared by the contractor to ensure safety during the operation of launching girders. (ii) Operations shall also comply to work at height regulations. (iii) Test certificate for all lifting appliance which are to be used. during launching operation. (iv) Lighting to be provided during work at dark.
23.	Const. machinery	Safe worthiness statements of all equipments made mandatory.
24.	Machine and general area guarding	All motors, cogwheels, chains and friction gearing, flywheels, shafting, dangerous and moving parts of machinery shall be securely fenced or legged
25.	Manual lifting and carrying of excess weight	The maximum weight to be carried by a adult (male - 55kg and female - 30kg) at a time during the construction process complying to Rule 38 of BOCWR
26.	Site electricity	(i) SHE (Electrical Engineer) is made mandatory as per the general instruction DMRC/SHE/GI/001/MPR/ 281105 (ii) Power assessment shall include the requirement of sub-contractor also. (iii) System for control and distribution of electricity from a main AC supply of 50Hz for typical appliances (iv) Electrical protection devices such as GFCIs, RCCBs made mandatory (v) Different cables for different use complying to BS 6007, BS 6346, BS 6500, BS 6708 and BS 7375 (vi) Plugs, sockets and couplers corresponding to IP44 in accordance with BS EN 60529 which is of splash proof design (vii) Inspection and maintenance of electrical appliances

Contd...

Clause No.	*Clause Title*	*Salient Parameters*
Part-She Managemet		
27.	Lighting	Guidelines for selecting luminaries as per the requirements of the work being performed. Minimum illumination level is dealt at clause 44.
28.	Hand tools and power tools	Guidelines for Guarding, earthing, training, PPEs to be provided during the execution of the work with the help of hand tools/ power tools by the contractor to his employees including his sub-contractors.
29.	Welding and cutting	(i) Every welding/cutting set has to be certified by the contractor SHE Manager. (ii) Safety requirements during welding and cutting appliances such as metal cap for valve protection, flashback arrestors, non-return valves, pressure gauges (iii) Electrical requirements such as voltmeters and ammeters to be as a part of the system (iv) Requirements such as fire extinguishers at close proximity to act upon emergency (v) Other electrical requirements such as installations complying to IS: 5571: 1997 and NFPA 70 for operating of gas cylinders at hazardous areas.
30.	Dangerous and harmful environment	Confined space entry only after certification by competent person.
31.	Fire prevention, protection and fighting system	(i) Adequate amount of water at ample pressure to be stored for fire fighting always as per national standards. (ii) Fire fighting training to employees to operate fire extinguishers and to extinguish fire. (iii) Other requirements such as fire extinguishers to be placed in all lifting appliances' driver cabin as per Rule 63 (a) (vii) of DBOCWR.
32.	Corrosive substances	Guidelines for use and storage of corrosive substances, acids, alkalis and other solvents as per Rule 44 of BOCWR.
33.	Demolition	Planning to be executed before demolition for barrication, waste removal, adjacent structure protection and also protection to the workers and the public.
34	Excavation and tunnelling	(i) Proper shoring to be provided when the depth of the excavation exceed 1.5m by adequate piling and bracing operation against banks or side walls to protect workers. (ii) Storage of excavated materials in the site beyond a distance of 0.65m.. (iii) Appointment of responsible person for safe operation for tunnelling work as per Rule 121 and 125 of BOCWR. (iv) Reliable means of communication to be provided during tunnelling as per Rule 136 of BOCWR. (v) Allowable temperature not to exceed 290 inside the tunnelling area as per Rule 165 of BOCWR. (vi) Warning signs and barrications to be installed at conspicuous areas to illustrate the presence of work.

Contd...

Clause No.	*Clause Title*	*Salient Parameters*
Part-She Managemet		
35.	Work permit system	(i) The Contractor shall develop a Work Permit system, which is a formal written system used to control certain types of work that are potentially hazardous. (ii) Work to be started only after safe procedures have been defined and provided a clear record that all foreseeable hazards have been considered. (iii) Permits to Work are usually required in high-risk areas like confined spaces, close proximity to electric live lines, hot work, excavation, heavy moving machinery, radioactive isotopes, electrical appliances.
36.	Traffic management	(i) All construction workers and traffic marshals shall be provided high visibility waistcoats during the work for protection against speeding vehicular traffic (ii) Legal permission to be obtained by the contractor from the concerned govt, officials for traffic management where the work interferes with the public traffic which includes traffic diversion and selection of alternative routes for transport of equipment wherever necessary (iii) Regulatory signs, warning signs, delineators, traffic cones and cylinders, drums and barricades to be provided to streamline the traffic flow (iv) Arrangements of two away vehicle and cleaning of roads which may be inconvenient to the public when left unattended.
37.	Work adjacent to live railways	Requirements of railways to be followed mandatory.
38.	Batching plant and casting yard layout	(i) The batching plant to be maintained in such a way that the dust being emitted is under the permissible level (ii) Layout to be well maintained and the area to be segregated properly for batching plant and casting yard (iii) Barrications to be provided and made as a compulsory PPE zone.
39.	Personal protective equipments (PPEs)	(i) List of PPEs to be provided to workmen during work to protect against physical and other health hazards. (ii) All PPEs complying to BIS Standards/ International standards (iii) High visibility waistcoats for all workmen (including traffic marshals) engaged in the construction work complying to BS EN 471:1994 (iv) Colour coding of helmets (including visitor's helmet) to be followed throughout the contract for uniformity (v) Maintenance of 10% spare of PPEs to act upon emergency (vi) A penalty of Rs.200/- for non-usage of PPE
40.	Visitors to site	No visitors are allowed without the permission of Employer

Contd...

Clause No.	*Clause Title*	*Salient Parameters*
Part-She Managemet		
PART-III : OCCUPATIONALHEALTHANDWELFARE		
41.	Physical fitness of workmen	All employees need to undergo medical examination and a record of the same shall be maintained.
42.	Medical facilities	(i) Medical facilities need to be provided for all workers including vehicle drivers. (ii) The site shall have a occupational health centre and the services and facilities shall be as per Schedule X of BOCWR. (iii) Ambulance van shall be provided at sites. First aid boxes to be provided at site for every 100 workers and it shall contain the articles as mentioned in Schedule III of BOCWR. (iv) The contractor shall adopt Employer's policy on "HIV/AIDS prevention and control for workmen engaged by contractors" as per the policy (Ref: Appendix No.: 4) (v) Suitable measures shall be made to avoid mosquito breeding at site and also at labour accommodation areas (vi) No employees shall work under the influence of alcohol / drugs which may invite penalty.
43.	Noise	(i) Noise monitoring and control plan (NMCP) shall be made by the contractor and identify area/appliance of noise levels for effective control. (ii) Vibration shall also be taken for consideration to avoid damage to adjacent structures which includes historical/ heritage sites.
44.	Ventilation and illumination Experts/Agencies for SHE services	(i) Fresh air supply shall not be less than 6m3/min for each building worker employed underground. (ii) Oxygen level shall not be less than 19.5% in the working environment. (iii) Minimum illumination at worksite shall be as per the general instruction DMRC/SHE/GI/011/ILL/281105. (iv) Monthly illumination monitoring shall be conducted using hand held digital Lux meter and the shall be reported to the Employer before 7th of each month.
45.	Radiation	(i) All instruments and apparatus shall comply with the Govt. regulatory requirements and subsidiary legislation. (ii) Warning notices shall be displayed at areas of work involving radioactive substances.
46.	Welfare measures for workers	(i) One latrine shall be provided for every 20 workers upto 100 and additional 1no. for every additional 50 workers. (ii) One urinals shall be provided for every 20 workers upto 100 and additional 1 no. for every additional 100 workers. (iii) Separate toilet facilities for women if engaged. (iv) Where the workers' strength exceeds 250, canteen shall be provided and shall run in no loss no gain basis.

Contd....

Clause No.	Clause Title	Salient Parameters
Part-She Managemet		
		(v) Wholesome drinking water of 5 litres/day/worker shall be provided by the contractor. Quality of the drinking water provided for the workers shall be as per public health requirements. (vi) Accommodation facilities shall be provided for all workers.
PART-IV : ENVIRONMENTAL MANAGEMENT		
47.	Air quality	(i) Dust emission, monitoring and control to be made by the contractor to safeguard the environment (ii) All vehicles shall confirm to emission standards to minimise pollution
48.	Water quality	Proper drainage system to be maintained.
49.	Archaeological and historical preservation	All archaeological and historical preservations shall not be disturbed during the execution of the work and consultation with the Archaeological Survey of India (ASI) shall be made by the contractor.
50.	Landscape and greenery	(i) The contractor shall maintain ecological balance by preventing deforestation and defacing of natural landscape. (ii) Where destruction, scarring, damage or defacing may occur as a result of operations relating to permanent or temporary works, the same shall be repaired, replanted or otherwise corrected at Contractor's expense.
51.	Felling of trees	(i) The contractor shall identify the number and type trees that are required to be felled as a result of construction of works and facilities related to Delhi Metro Project and inform the Employer. (ii) The Employer shall arrange permission from the forest department for trees to be felled or transplanted.
52.	Fly ash	(i) The Employer may require the contractor to use fly ash as a percentage substitution of cement, in concrete for certain structures and works. (ii) In all such uses of Flyash, the contractor shall maintain a detailed record of usage of Flyash.
53.	Waste	The contractor is required to develop, institute and maintain a Waste Management Programme (WMP) during the construction of the project for his works
54.	Hazardous waste management	If encountered or generated as a result of Contractor's activity, then waste classified as hazardous under the "Hazardous Wastes (Management & Handling) Rules, 1989, amendments 2000, 2003" shall be disposed of in a manner in compliance with the procedure given in the rules under the aforesaid act.
55.	Energy management	The contractor shall use and maintain equipment so as to conserve energy and shall be able to produce demonstrable evidence of the same upon Employer's request.

Contd....

Clause No.	*Clause Title*	*Salient Parameters*
Part-She Managemet		
PART-V : PENALTY AND AWARDS		
56.	Charges to be recovered from contractor for unsafe act or condition	(i) Any reportable accident (fatality /major injury) results in loss of life and/or property damage. These accidents not only result in loss of life but also damage the reputation of DMRC. (ii) Most of the accidents are avoidable and caused due to contractors' negligence. Hence DMRC shall recover the cost of damages from the contractors for every reportable incident (fatality /major injury). (iii) Penalty shall be imposed only as a last resort. (iv) Detailed penalty amount for individual unsafe acts/conditions are provided in the table at clause 56.3 (v) Minimum penalty of Rs.200/- for non-usage of PPE. (vi) Rs. 5,00,000 for first fatality and Rs.10,00,000 for subsequent fatalities.
57.	Stoppage of work	If any work carried out is in such a way that it may cause accidents and endanger the safety of the persons and/or property/ equipments, the contractor shall be informed to stop the work unless suitable measures are taken.
58.	Awards	DMRC engages the 'safe work' practices at all construction sites and in order to encourage contractor who adopt safety in their work culture appropriate awards to be presented.

Conclusion

In the absence of precisely enforceable contract safety conditions for Employers, it becomes very difficult to enforce safety regulations during construction by Contractors. An attempt has been made by DMRC to streamline the process and a comprehensive document has been prepared and put into practical implementation in Phase-II. According to Liberty Mutual Research Institute for Safety, USA, for every $1 invested in safety, there is between a $3 and $6 savings. In line to it DMRC not only aims to achieve Zero fatality in Phase-II, but also expects substantial financial return. In addition these contract conditions are expected to keep the safety image of DMRC high above in the days to come. This document can also serve as a reference for many organisations and also to bring out a national guideline on safety at construction sites, which is long pending to the country.

ANNEXURE—I

DMRC Safety, Welfare and Occupational Health requirements as per Building and Other Construction Workers (Regulation of Employment and Conditions of Service) Act 1996 and Rules, 1998 and Delhi Building and Other Construction Workers (Regulation of Employment and Conditions of Service) Rules, 2002.

Sl. No.	*Items*	*Relevant Section/Rules in BOCWA and BOCWR and DBOCWR*
1.	Registration of establishment	S – 7, R – 23 to 27
2.	Display of registration certification at workplace	R – 26 (5)
3.	Hours of work	S – 28, R – 234 to 237
4.	Register of overtime	S – 28; S – 29 R – 241(1) Form XXII
5.	Weekly rest and payment at rest	R – 235
6.	Night shift	R – 236
7.	Maintenance of workers registers and records	S – 30, R – 238
8.	Notice of commencement and completion	S – 46, R – 239
9.	Register of persons employed as building workers	R – 240
10.	Muster roll and wages register	R – 241(1) (a); Form XVI and XVII
11.	Payment of wages	R – 248
12.	Display of notice of wages regarding	R – 249
13.	Register of damage or loss	R – 241(1)(a); Form XIX, XX, XXI
14.	Issue of wages book	R – 241(2)(a); Form XXIII
15.	Service certificate for each workers	R – 241(2)(b); Form XXIV
16.	Display an abstract of BOCWA and BOCWR	R – 241(5)
17.	Annual return	R – 242; Form XXV
18.	Drinking water	S – 32
19.	Latrines and Urinals	S – 33, R - 243
20.	Accommodation	S – 34
21.	Creches	S – 35
22.	First-aid boxes	S – 36 R – 231 and Schedule III
23.	Canteens	S – 37, R – 244
24.	Food stuff and other items served in the canteens	R – 245
25.	Supply of tea and snacks in work place	R – 246
26.	Food charges on no loss no profit basis	R - 247
27.	Delhi BOCW welfare Board Rules	R – 250 to 296
28.	Safety committee	S – 38, R – 208
29.	Safety officer	S – 38, R – 209 and Schedule VII
30.	Reporting of accidents and dangerous occurrences	S – 39, R – 210
31.	Procedure for inquiry in to the causes of accidents	R – 211
32.	Responsibility of employer	S – 44, R – 5
33.	Responsibility of Architects, Project Engineer and Designers	R – 6
34.	Responsibility of workmen	R – 8
35.	Responsibility for payment of wages and compensation	S – 45
36.	Penalties and Procedures	S – 47; S – 55

Contd .....

37.	Excessive noise, vibration etc.	R - 34
38.	Fire Protection	R - 35
39.	Emergency action plan	R - 36
40.	Fencing of motors	R - 37
41.	Lifting of carrying of excessive weight	R - 38
42.	Health, Safety and Environmental Policy	R - 39
43.	Dangerous and Harmful Environment	R - 40
44.	Overhead protection	R - 41
45.	Slipping, Tripping, Cutting, Drowning and Falling Hazards	R - 42
46.	Dust, Gases, Fumes, etc	R - 43
47.	Corrosive substance	R - 49
48.	Eye Protection	R - 45
49.	Head Protection and other protection apparel	R - 46; R - 54
50.	Electrical Hazards	R - 47
51.	Vehicular traffic	R - 48
52.	Stability of structure	R - 49
53.	Illumination	R - 50; R - 124
54.	Stacking of materials	R - 51
55.	Disposal of debris	R - 52
56.	Numbering and marking of floors	R - 53
57.	Lifting appliances and gears	C - VII; R - 55 to 81
58.	Runways and Ramps	C - VIII; R - 82 to 85
59.	Working on or adjacent to water	C - IX; R - 86 & 87
60.	Transport and earthmoving equipments	C - X; R - 88 to 95
61.	Concrete work	C - XI; R - 96 to 107
62.	Demolition	C - XII; R - 108 to 118
63.	Excavation and Tunnelling works	C - XIII; R - 119 to 168
64.	Ventilation	R - 153
65.	Construction, repair and maintenance of step roof	C - XIV; R - 169 to 171
66.	Ladders and Step ladders	C - XV; R - 172 to 174
67.	Catch platform and hoardings, chutes, safety belts and nets	C - XVI; R - 175 to 180
68.	Structural frame and formworks	C - XVII; R - 181 to 185
69.	Stacking and unstacking	C - XVIII; R - 186 & 187
70.	Scaffold	C - XIX; R - 188 to 205
71.	Cofferdams and Caissons	C - XX; R - 206 to 211
72.	Explosives	C - XXI; R - 212 & 213
73.	Piling	C - XXII; R - 214 to 222
74.	Medical Examination for building and other construction worker, Crane operator an Transport vehicle drivers	R - 81; R - 223(a)(iii) and Schedule XII

Contd .....

75.	Medical examination for occupational health hazards	R - 233(a)(iv)
76.	Charging of workers for Medical Examination	R - 223(b)
77.	Occupational health centres and Medical officers	R - 225 and Schedule X & XI
78.	Ambulance van & room	R - 226 & 227 and Schedule IV & V
79.	Stretchers	R - 228
80.	Occupational health service for building workers	R - 229
81.	Medical examination for occupational health hazards	R - 223(a)(iv)
82.	Emergency care services and emergency treatment	R - 232
83.	Panel of experts and agencies	Central Rule 250 Delhi Rule 297
84.	Power of inspectors	Central rule 251 Delhi rule 298

REPORT AND RECOMMENDATIONS

G.S. Yadava*

The Safety Convention 2006 has been organized by Safety and Quality Forum in partnership with Quality Council of India, Export Inspection Council of India, Bureau of Indian Standards, National Safety Council of India and Vellore Institute of Technology. The Convention attracted over 300 participants from over 100 organizations, covering leading public sector, private sector, government agencies and NGOs.

The Convention was organized with the theme "Occupational Safety, Health and Environment and Sustainable Economic Development".

The Safety Convention was inaugurated by Hon'ble Shri R.V. Shahi, Secretary, Ministry of Power, Government of India. The Chief Guest emphasized on the importance of safety in all aspects of life and industry. He said that safety in any organization is not a responsibility of only those who are in-charge of safety, but it is the responsibility of every individual in the organization.

Dr. (Prof.) S.C. Naik, President, The Institution of Engineers (India) also spoke in the Inaugural Function. He appreciated the efforts of Shri Pradeep Chaturvedi, Chairman, Safety & Quality Forum in bringing up this Forum to a great height in past three years. He also appreciated large number of activities carried out by this Forum throughout the country.

Shri G. Viswanathan, Chancellor, Vellore Institute of Technology, Vellore also addressed the delegates and informed them about the setting up of Centre for Disaster Management and Mitigation. He wished that deliberations in the present Convention will be useful to all concerned.

Shri Pradeep Chaturvedi, Chairman, SQF welcomed the Chief Guest and explained the technical programme of the Convention.

During the Inaugural Function, following companies involved in the Safety Innovation were awarded prestigious Safety Innovation Award 2006:

*Chairman, Technical Committee

1. VST Industries Ltd., Hyderbad
2. GAIL
3. HPCL, Mumbai
4. ONGC, Ahmedabad, Asset
5. ONGC, Ankleshwar, Asset
6. Indian Oil Corporation Ltd.
7. Mfar Constructions Pvt. Ltd.
8. Ballarpur Paper Industries
9. Grasim Industries (Staple Fibre Division)
10. Gujarat Alkalies & Chemical Ltd., Bharuch
11. Gujarat Alkalies & Chemical Ltd., Vadodara
12. Powergrid Corporation of India Ltd.
13. NTPC Power Plant, Korba
14. NTPC Power Plant, Ramagundam
15. NTPC Power Plant, Kahalgaon
16. NTPC Power Plant, Narora
17. Heavy Water Plant, Kota
18. Heavy Water Plant, Tuticorin
19. Karnataka State Road Transport Corporation, Bangalore
20. Defence Research & Development Laboratory (DRDL), Hyderabad
21. Chittaranjan Locomotive Works, Indian Railways, Chittaranjan
22. Cordite Factory, Aruvankadu
23. Mineral Exploration Corporation Ltd.
24. Steel Authority of India
25. Visakhapatnam Steel Plant, Visakhapatnam
26. ISPAT Industries Ltd.
27. Jindal Stainless Ltd., Hissar
28. Jindal Stainless Ltd., (Hot Rolling), Hissar
29. Hindalco Industries Ltd.
30. Motor Industries Co. Ltd., Bangalore
31. Moser Baer India Ltd.

The commendation certificates were presented to those companies who could not qualify for the Safety Award.

Two eminent personalities, Dr. P.S. Rana, Chairman and Managing Director, HUDCO and Shri G.Viswanathan, Chancellor, Vellore Institute of Technology were also falicitated in the Inaugural function for their significant contribution in the area of Safety.

There was also an Overview Session which was chaired by Shri B.N. Nawalawala, Member, UPSC and Shri O.P. Goel, Past President, IEI.

In this Session there were presentations from four eminent speakers, Dr. P.S. Rana, Chairman and Managing Director, HUDCO; Prof. A. Arya, Seismic Adviser to Government of India, Dr. R.K. Bhandari, Chairman, Centre for Disaster Management and Mitigation, Vellore Institute of Technology; and Lt. Gen. (Retd.) J.S. Ahluwalia, Vice President, IOD. Topics like Safe Building after Tsunami; Lessons from Natural Disasters in India; Safe living in Earthquake Prone Areas; and Occupational Safety, Health & Environment and Development were discussed.

During the Convention following Plenary Sessions were Organized

Environment and Occupational Safety and Health; Food Safety; Safety in Construction Sector, Safety in Energy Sector; Disaster Management and Safety; Industrial Safety, Occupational Health and Safety Certification.

Three case studies sessions were also organized where companies who have won Safety Innovation Award shared their innovative practices for the benefit of all other delegates. The sessions were chaired by Brig. S.V.S. Chowdhary, Past Chairman, IEI-DSC, Lt. Gen. S.K. Jain, past Chairman, IEI-DSC, Dr. R.K. Dave, Council Member, Shri H.S. Bhasin, Executive Director, Heavy Water Board, Kota and Shri J. Mohapatra, General Manager, NTPC.

The session on Environment, Occupational Safety and Health was chaired by Shri K.C. Gupta, Director General, National Safety Council of India. The session attracted a number of papers on the following topics:

- Safety in Aviation Sector
- Terrorism and its impact on society
- Legal Framework for Occupational Safety & Health in India
- Insurance Solutions for Occupational Safety & Health in the Wake of New Risks
- HR in Safety
- Occupational Health & Safety and Related Standards
- Occupational Safety, Health, and Environment Management in Mineral Exploration Projects
- Case Studies—Some Accidents

The Session on Food Safety and was chaired by Mrs. Shashi Sareen, Director, Export Inspection Council of India and following papers were presented:

- Food Safety and the Common Man
- Food Safety & Industry Perspective
- Integrated Food Law & its Implementation
- Uptake of Benomyl Fungicide from Post Harvest Treatment and its Persistence in Modified Atmosphere stored Banana Fruits
- Food Safety, A Planning Commission Viewpoint
- Food Safety in the Services Sector

On the second day of the Convention the session on "Safety in Construction Sector" was chaired by Shri S. Ghosh, President, Consulting Engineers Association of India. Following papers were presented in this session:

- Safety in construction Session Worksites — SAIL Experience
- Constraints and Solutions in Enforcing Safety in Construction Works
- Safety Aspects in Planning & Construction
- Safety during Construction of Transmission Line
- Safety in Electrical Installation
- Safety in Construction
- National Disasters in India

The Session on Energy Sector was chaired by Shri Lehmbar Singh, Executive Director-ONGC — Ahmedabad and Shri V.K. Dutt, Chief Electrical Engineers, Northern Railways. Following papers were presented:

- Health Hazards in Exploratory/Development Mining
- Role of Electrical Safety on Indian Railways
- Occupational Health Monitoring in Indian Oil Corporation Ltd. : An Experience at Gujarat Refinery
- Holistic Approach to Process Safety
- Development of Safety Culture in Nuclear Power
- Improving Occupational Health & Safety Aspects

The Session on Disaster Management and Safety chaired by Shri M. Gopalakrishna, Secretary General, International Commission on Irrigation and Drainage and co-chaired by Shri P.K. Chatterjee, Former Chief Fire Officer, ONGC. Following papers were presented:

- Failure of Engineered Structurs During Earthquake in Urban Gujarat—A Hazard Analysis Study
- Bhopal Disaster—A Personal Experience
- Tsunami Risk in India and its Assessment
- Safety in Electrostatic Discharge Sensitive Areas
- Fire Safety Norms and Standards for a Defence R&D Establishment Engaged in Explosive Related Activities.

The Session on Safety was chaired by Shri Pradeep Chaturvedi, Chairman, SQF and the following papers were presented in this session:

- Safety with Cryogenic Fluids
- Management of Gaseous Emissions and Air Quality
- OSH & SE and Sustainable Economic Development
- Industrial Hygiene Services
- Approach to Behavioural Safety
- Impact of Implementation of Occupational Health & Safety Management System in Integrated Steel Plants

The last Session on "OHS Certification" was chaired by Shri S.K. Chaudhuri, Deputy Director General, BIS. Following topics were covered:

- Safety Standards Certification for Safety and Sharing of Safety Management System Experience.
- Capacity Building Measures for Implementation of IS 18001 at the National Level

Safety and Quality Forum

Shri N.N. Gautam, former Adviser, Coal, Government of India made a presentation on Safety in Coal Mines, narrating recent accident at Dhanbad.

RECOMMENDATIONS

1. The Government should take serious note of safety concerns in its development perspectives and planning so that the best techno-economic and legal regime is established to ensure 9-10 per cent GDP growth rate. Appropriate safety policy measures can make India's products globally competitive.
2. Awareness should be created and systems developed so that the common man starts to live confidently in this world ridden with terrorism. New and innovative methods and strategies will have to be evolved by the Government at State, national and local levels.
3. The threat of natural in one form or the other disasters has adversely affected most parts of the country. It is not sufficient to take only rescue, relief and rehabilitation measures but to focus on preparedness in all areas of industrial and manmade disasters. In this regard, it is necessary to evolve and disseminate the principles and strategies through professional institutions of practicing engineers and upgrading programmes from time to time.
4. Coal is the mainstay of India's energy sources. It has been observed that mine safety has not been given due consideration. In view of our infrastructure requirement, mine safety should be given top priority.
5. Curriculum in engineering colleges, professional institutions and schools should include information on natural and manmade hazards and disasters.
6. Basic norms and codes should be evolved to make structures and systems resistant to natural hazards. The buildings and structures should be earthquake and cyclone protected. The existing codes and standards should be strictly followed and adhered to and strict penalties should be imposed against the offenders.
7. Food Safety is a matter of deep concern for the common man and the farmers. All measures should be evolved to ensure food safety and security.